DYNASTY: THE ASTROLOGY OↃ

The ancient science of astrology, founded on the correlation between celestial movements and terrestrial events, recognizes the universe as an indivisible whole in which all parts are interconnected. Mirroring this perception of the unity of life, modern physics has revealed the web of relationship underlying everything in existence. Despite the inevitable backlash as old paradigms expire, we are now entering an age where scientific explanations and models of the cosmos are in accord with basic astrological principles and beliefs. In such a climate, astrology is poised to emerge again as a serious study offering a greater understanding of our true nature. Arkana's *Contemporary Astrology Series* offers, in readable books written by experts, the insight and practical wisdom the world is now ready to receive from the newest vanguard of astrological thought.

Erin Sullivan was born in Canada, and is an astrologer, counsellor and lecturer of international repute. She has been awarded three distinctions for her work by the Fraternity for Canadian Astrologers, and is a founder-member of the AFAN network in the United States, forming the Media-Watch Committee. Her work takes her to Europe, Australia, America and regularly to South Africa, where she is the co-director of the Southern Cross Academy of Astrology in Johannesburg. She is a tutor for the Centre for Psychological Astrology in London, and has been the series editor for Arkana's *Contemporary Astrology Series* since 1990. Her other books include *Saturn in Transit: Boundaries of Mind, Body and Soul*, the breakthrough book *Retrograde Planets: Traversing the Inner Landscape*, both of which are published in Arkana's *Contemporary Astrology Series*, and *Venus and Jupiter: Bridging the Ideal and the Real* (CPA Press, 1996), as well as the chapter entitled 'Hermes: Trickster, Teacher, Theos' in *Planets: The Astrological Tools*. Her professionally produced series of teaching videos, *Astrology, Mythology and the Psyche*, is available in all formats around the world and is exceptional. She lives in London during summer and autumn, and has a winter home in Scottsdale, Arizona, where she also practises psychoanalytic astrology, teaches a core of students, and writes.

Other books in Arkana's *Contemporary Astrology Series*:

Chiron and the Healing Journey: An Astrological and Psychological Perspective by Melanie Reinhart

The Gods of Change: Pain, Crisis and the Transits of Uranus, Neptune and Pluto by Howard Sasportas

The Karmic Journey: The Birthchart, Karma and Reincarnation by Judy Hall

A Handbook of Medical Astrology by Jane Ridder-Patrick

Saturn: A New Look at an Old Devil by Liz Greene

Saturn in Transit: Boundaries of Mind, Body and Soul by Erin Sullivan

*Working with Astrology: The Psychology of Midpoints, Harmonics and Astro*Carto*Graphy* by Michael Harding and Charles Harvey

Hymns to the Ancient Gods by Michael Harding

Retrograde Planets: Traversing the Inner Landscape by Erin Sullivan

The Moment of Astrology by Geoffrey Cornelius

forthcoming:

*The Psychology of Astro*Carto*Graphy* by Jim Lewis with Kenneth Irving

CONTEMPORARY ASTROLOGY
Series Editor: Erin Sullivan

DYNASTY

The Astrology of Family Dynamics

ERIN SULLIVAN

To Jenny,
Enjoy — and
the family well
grow larger!

Erin Sullivan

ARKANA
PENGUIN BOOKS

FAS Open Day 5 Oct 96

ARKANA

Published by the Penguin Group
Penguin Books Ltd, 27 Wrights Lane, London w8 5 tz, England
Penguin Books USA Inc., 375 Hudson Street, New York, New York 10014, USA
Penguin Books Australia Ltd, Ringwood, Victoria, Australia
Penguin Books Canada Ltd, 10 Alcorn Avenue, Toronto, Ontario, Canada m4v 3b2
Penguin Books (NZ) Ltd, 182–190 Wairau Road, Auckland 10, New Zealand

Penguin Books Ltd, Registered Offices: Harmondsworth, Middlesex, England

First published 1996
1 3 5 7 9 10 8 6 4 2

Set in 9.5/12 pt Monotype Garamond
Typeset by RefineCatch Limited, Bungay, Suffolk
Printed in England by Clays Ltd, St Ives plc

Contents

Acknowledgements

The cover of this book implicitly illustrates that origins and roots cannot be amputated or divorced by conscious will – by one's self or by another. Our roots and ancestral heritage cannot be dissolved by will or human mandate. There is that which seems, and that which is, and the illusions of both are as real as we might imagine. Because of this I acknowledge my ancestors, my parents and my family of origin. Just as there is no real beginning or end of a cycle, there is no beginning or end of a family or an individual. However much we are made of others, there is a spark of originality, of something unknown and new, which lies in the soul of each of us. This is the Promethean fire of truth-seeking and survival, of renewal and continuance. Thanks to my family, my Promethean side is very, very well developed!

The two Geminis, my brother Robbie Lamoureux and his father – my stepfather – Bob Lamoureux, are a very important part of my own unconventional family experience, and have spread the genes out a bit. Especially my stepfather, who was an objective, compassionate eye.

Many of my astrological friends have at various times fed me with their family stories and allowed themselves the freedom to talk about their planetary family dynamics and listen to some of my own, but especially I want to mention a few whose stories have been shared in conversation and confidence and who in some way, indirectly, gave me the confidence that what I was seeing was working: Melanie Reinhart, Lindsay Radermacher, Jim Lewis, Brian Clark and Anne Black. Many, many of my clients have affirmed the phenomenon of dynastic lineage through the planets and those are too numerous and confidential to list, but thank you each and every one.

Most importantly, I thank my daughters, Spirit and Yesca, for being the next step forward into a new world, one which I can inhabit for only part of their time; now, for twenty-seven years, I have shared life with two of the most remarkable combinations of historic family dynamics! Both are prisms of their origins, but absolutely unique unto themselves; both are finding ways of being that have no exemplar. They too are Promethean *creatrices*! And to the next in line, my as yet unknown grandchild who was announced as I proofed these pages. Thanks, Yesca, for being first in continuing the family line! And to Ralf for the new blood.

Thanks to Carmen Reynal for helping midwife the manuscript; to the late Jim Lewis for sharing ideas and family stories; to Nigel Barlow for encouragement and support for the book through its development and final draft.

On the practical side of things: thanks to Robert Curry and Barry Street at the Astrology Shop in Covent Garden for supplying me with chart-service and for the astrological contribution to the cover-art; to Bernadette Brady for her understanding of the 'heat of the moment' of the writer's seizure and for faxing, writing and sending me the *JigSaw* graphics I have used for 'Toby' and for the Kennedy family case-example in the appendix; and to Philip Ginn for the 'big picture' diagrams. In the publishing department, thanks go to Lily Richards for finding me the astounding family tree for the cover; to the Penguin art department and Andrew Barker for coping with last-minute diagrams and graphs; and to Annie Lee for her copy-editing. And, as always, to Barbara Levy, my literary agent, who has also helped with the process by indulging some very elaborate ideas which took place throughout the development of the book!

And, last but not least, to the individuals whose stories appear in *Dynasty*. These people have my deepest respect; they are all courageous in their own ways and they are amazing individuals, each and every one. There are five stories in this book – all of which are more remarkable than I can even begin to portray; they shared these stories with me, and worked with me to bring myself and thus you, the reader, a deeper understanding of how mysterious is the web in which we find ourselves at centre! They are all exemplars of individuals who have needed to go back into their family matrix to wrest from it a measure of their own essence, and who understand this process to be just that – an ongoing, evolutionary drama which lies in infinity.

Introduction

Devotion 17

No man is an Iland, intire of itselfe;
every man is a peece of the continent, a part of the maine;
if a Clod bee washed away by the Sea, Europe is the lesse
as well as if a Promontorie were,
as well as if a Mannor of they friends, or of thine owne were;
Any Mans death diminishes me,
because I am involved in Mankinde;
And therefore never send to know for whom the bell tolls;
It tolls for thee.   (John Donne)

In these days there seems a strange longing to understand our origins in new ways. Family values, family structure and the maintenance of the family has become increasingly topical in the minds of the collective on a global scale. There is a powerful need to discover how to keep families intact during times of sweeping change. People talk of going back to old values, creating new structures and finding new ways of coping with social chaos but still retaining the sustaining aspects of families. Families are indeed changing in some ways, but we are still bred from the same sources and are contained in the archetypal family structure even though the social aspect and the apparent function of the family has and will likely continue to alter drastically. But, since there is nothing new under the sun, only old things uncovered, recovered and re-discovered, there is very little that can be said about individuals and families that has not already been considered. Except in the astrological framework.

Very difficult, this business of families. The power of the individual lies in his or her attachments to others, which is a paradox. We can only be unique by comparison, free by realizing our entrapment, individual in relation to the collective. There is an inherent difficulty in families that is an amplified magnification of the same aspect of difficulty in the analysis of an individual. That difficulty seems rather like trying to fix the fan-belt in a car while the motor is still running. How can one come to an absolute, final opinion about a fluid entity made up of as many moving components that a person, let alone that a 'family' has? The answer is it cannot be done.

Astrology comes closest to replicating the dynamics of individuals and their families. The solar system itself operates much in the same way as a family does. Within the solar system itself we can isolate various bodies, such as the Sun and the Moon, or Saturn and so forth, and find cycles and patterns within their own individual behaviour. We can pair them up and see large cycles, phases etc., *but we cannot find a repetitive pattern in the solar system as an entire entity* and thus it cannot be contained in any rigid model – physical, mythological or psychological. The astronomical-astrological system is in perpetual motion, re-configuring and re-constellating on a constant, fluid basis. It is the exemplar of hyman dynamic action and is in itself a family of individual, powerful bodies inextricably tied in together, creating a self-supporting life-system – an organic whole made up of unique and indi-vidualistic parts.

In this way, the individual is both enhanced and annihilated by his or her participation in a family. It is evident that we need families, for it strikes me that a person without a family at all is in a more damaged and desperate state than one who has had to deal with even the most venomous of nests. Families are the testing ground for all our experience in life. They are with us everywhere, both inside and out. To be able to extend ourselves out, beyond the confines of the immediate nuclear family, is a must. We are in a new leap in the global population constellation. At this writing Pluto has just entered Sagittarius and Uranus has just entered Aquarius. With this sig-nature to leave its imprint for several generations to come, the late 1990s and the first decade of the 2000s are the years in which we become acutely aware of the shift in perspective needed for families to survive.

This means change – and change means a period of chaos. And chaos is the genesis of all things. The 'global family' means that as individuals we are now truly dependent on each other as well as each of us as individuals having a measure of power in the collective force. There is always, and likely always will be, a longing for some archetypal soft place, wherein we are loved and nurtured and all is peaceful in the kingdom. The kingdom now happens to be very large, very round and very much a metalogue. We are in-capable of thinking something without it actually arising in the world –

the amazing thing about this is that we are also going to know about it at about the same time.

The future family seems highly unpredictable at this stage, but we can speak in themes, motifs, tones and symbols. And since the family system has been changing all around the world – fairly consistently – there is a theme for the future of them. If we speak of family breakdown, for example, we see it, but we only see it within the *Zeitgeist*. In the majority of the post-war Western world change was wrought by volition, desire and conscious effort because of the vast array of possibilities available in a reasonably stable, comfortable society. In other less materially, socially or politically fortunate cultures it has come through loss of civil rights, breakdown in religious order, via forced invasion by enemies, and so forth. But it has happened in all cultures around the world.

The 'family' as we have known it in our lifetime has become as shattered as it can. There is a re-combination of elements about. Families will re-form in accord with the new times and respond to the demands of individuals within them. People will become more creative in their groupings and inter-relations. They will incorporate more people into their family groups, rather like the extended families of old. In the Athenian οικως, for example, the family was based on a system of individual members which moved out, lat-erally and hierarchically, from the blood-ties of the immediate relations, into the community. This might be just where we are headed again in another form – much more connected to the world through the mind and ideas. Finding ourselves insecure within the smothering nuclear family, we begin to incorporate others who are 'family', rather than 'our family'. Like the womb in the hours before birth, the family which once was a protective container becomes a perilous prison.

Still and all, philosophy and metaphysics aside, we are made up of our families and shall continue to create our own families based upon that same archetype. The more we become comfortable with that fact, the less we will be chafing at the bit. I have found that by looking at the astrology of fam-ilies and the astrology of the concerned individual in the family, each person feels restored and affirmed by the fact that there is some precedent and val-idation for their feelings and being. They all, myself included, find that it is a better thing to know whence they came than to assume that we are all alone with no predecessor to claim.

I hope that some of the ideas in this book will stimulate greater compas-sion first towards yourself, then towards your own family, past, present and possibly future, and then out to your clients and their family concerns. The main focus of the book is on themes, nuances, hints, suggestions, lineage, nets and webs – all the subtle connections between family charts. I have done this because that is what all patterns do – they usually hint and imply. Not all family-systems scream 'Sun/Pluto'! Or 'Moon/Venus'. For those that do, then this book will also be of great interest, because the interpretation and delineative sections can be taken whole!

To my mind, the most interesting section of *Dynasty* is the third section, the life stories. These stories evolved in a fabulous way – and in the course of the writing the people in the stories continued to grow and change. Really, once begun, their story will never end – and I was in the difficult position of having to make static, at some point, a kinetic organism! Right up to the last moment of editing, there was life, change, newness, evolution, individuation and continuance. It is in this section that you will find astrology alive and well, working with the fluidity of the heavens and seeing how not only individuals but also their familiars are in harmony with the cosmos. There is something magical about it, but it is also very logical – metaphysics is simply the 'large overall nature of things', and certainly much of what happens in families falls into this category.

To my pleasure, but not to my surprise, I found that the moment I began to work on the stories, the process of growth and discovery for each of the protagonists and their families quickened. Events and changes began to evolve rapidly – as if, by attention, they were nurtured to achieve greater momentum in their own sphere. There is the phenomenon of watching, feeding and promoting that delivers liberation to facets of oneself that recline sleeping. The mystery of it lies in the fact that by focusing through the eyes of one person, the perspective of the entire family begins to alter. They need not even know this is happening for it to occur spontaneously. I was acutely aware that this would transpire, and thus was very careful about whom I asked to take part in my work. I knew that it would blow open whole avenues of unexplored material and would loosen things stuck or sleeping in hidden or secret places in the psyche – that is part of what the astrologer is about.

The best side of all of this looking and seeing is that it really works – by knowing what unresolved complexes lie in the centre of the family, they *can* be expiated and the chances of healing them in successive generations is very good. It is true that the unresolved problems and complexes of the parents and the previous generations are manifest in the children in various ways, but it is equally true that working on these problems or bringing them to consciousness, and thus to light, does lessen the burden – in that area – for the next generation.

Oxford, January 1996

PART I

The Big Picture:
The Organic Family

I.

The Individual and
the Collective

THE FAMILY OF HUMANITY

DYNASTIC LINEAGE: THE BIG PICTURE

We might look back over aeons and recognize our own personal self-development – just as we emerge from the womb, into our infancy, through our developmental years, past adolescence, into our twenties, the Saturn-return, the thirties, the mid-life transition, to maturity in the fifties and second Saturn-return phase and on into dotage, so does the collective culture emerge and develop. If we see this as a cycle, and not as a linear experience, then the relationship between the individual and the collective becomes quite intimate. Just as a culture evolves, so does an individual: from embryo – total psychic participation with the environment – to birth through the initial stages of individuation, into full ego, or awareness of self, and the subsequent developmental periods, the process is remarkably parallel to how we appear to have evolved as a collective world-humanity.

We like to believe that the archaic mind was holistic, in that it perceived no split between nature and culture. There existed no differentiation between the individual and his environment, no split between man and god, no vast chasm between thought and feeling or the sacred and profane. This kind of consciousness is called mythopoeic and can best be described as a state of mind in which one participates wholly in the environment without conscious awareness of the separation from others or from the natural environment. These archaic peoples, so-called primitives, appear to have been peaceable, relating to their environment as they would to their own inner selves. Their known rituals involved what the French mythographer Lévy-Bruhl termed *participation mystique*. That is, their consciousness was at one with the external world and their psychic relationship with nature wholly participatory – they did not subordinate nature in the way in which we now do, but took from nature what was needed for survival and apparently had a respect for animals, trees, the elemental forces and various celestial phenomena which is keenly lacking today.

We know little about these most archaic humans – palaeontology shows us bony structures, the skeletons of our ancestors, some of their relics and tools, but not much about their culture. We truly *know* nothing. Just as we *know* nothing about our intra-uterine experience. We speculate and have ideas, but no real knowledge of prehistorical humanity. It is the same with consciousness before birth. In the womb we existed in a realm beyond temporal and spatial differentiation, suspended in a warm, nurturing, eternal space. The rustic lifestyle of the archaic man was clearly fraught with survival-danger and primal terror, but he likely did not have neurosis or anxiety complexes. Just as archaic civilization did, the incubating embryo has danger during its development and psychologically it appears that this psychic knowledge of threat-in-the-womb affects the development of consciousness in the maturing person. Just as archaic man knew of his environmental threats, so does the gestating infant, and though those threats are pre-conscious, they are highly effective in the psychological developmental process.

Infants, once born, *do* have survival concerns just as infant cultures have survival issues – but they do not have conscious worries about their relationship with their environment. Those problems arise much later in development – in parallel with the emergence of the individual ego and, in the case of cultural development, the collective ego. Babies are not neurotic, but the seeds for such a condition are embedded in this infantile ground. Serious threats to an infant's development will register in both the psyche and the viscera, setting the tone for its future growth, body and soul. Likewise, serious threats to the process of culture arrest, or even retard to extinction, entire cultural collectives. At worst, a culture can die out like the Inca did, but at best a culture flexes, mutates and adapts creatively to its external conditions and inner impulses. These potentials are also ours, as individuals.

As the ego of a child emerges from its psychic-womb, it begins to separate out its own identity from that of its mother and recognize itself as distinct and different from others. The baby is still wholly dependent, but clearly recognizes itself in relationship to others, and gradually begins to experiment with that relationship as the ego grows stronger and more impelling – and as its physical prowess increases. Cultures break out of the insular mode and begin to transgress the boundaries of different cultures, becoming assimilated, antagonistic, or allied . . . so do we with *our* 'others'.

Ultimately, this breach between subjective self and objective other – which we call perspective – is good and necessary; however, it can become so vast a rent in consciousness as virtually to destroy an individual's connection to his or her deepest, inner Self, and divorce him or her from the sacred and divine aspect of life. Certainly we have seen this chasm in cultural development grow increasingly vast – the ancient Greeks worried about it, fretted and developed a philosophy based upon the separation of the sacred and the profane. Hesiod, the sixth-century BC Greek agrarian-poet, felt that cutting trees, making canoes and plying the waters was unnatural and would result in all sorts of abominations against natural law. If only he had known – or maybe he *did* in diachronous time – just how far his descendants would impose themselves upon nature's reserves.

As our global culture has developed, so have we as individuals: our own small frames of reference – our families – have undergone radical rearranging in just the last century, and particularly in the last thirty years, and are now rapidly fragmenting into unique formations. All these changes have rendered a social chaos, which truly is the genesis of all things. The long-term result will likely re-form collective groups into new cultural, philosophical and familial arrangements. The movement of the planets in a generational fashion describes how this is so and how we, as individuals, operate within that big picture.

The last 2,500 years have shown a remarkable evolutionary leap – technically, intellectually, physically and socially.[1] The quickening of consciousness results now in a time in which a re-connection with natural law is urgent. The movement towards the epoch which will be ruled by the sign Aquarius, and away from the 2,100-year period of Pisces, marks a turning point from one way of viewing the world collectively towards a new, idealistic yet practical view. These epochal shifts are relative to our development as individuals within the collective ethos. As individuals we cannot move beyond the parenthetical boundaries of the epochal vision – even the rare Atman is a product of the time.

The Piscean age (ruled by Neptune and being the epoch from *c.* 1 BC to AD 2060) seems to have acted as a collective womb in which the compartmentalized concepts of the body-mind-soul of humanity have gestated to the point of giving birth to themselves as a single entity. The global family – – *unus mundus* – is in the last stages of incubation, indeed, it is in the birth canal. The fast-approaching Aquarian epoch (ruled by Uranus and also around 2,100 years long) will demand a relationship between the individual and the collective which is more mutually interdependent. This is in direct contrast to the Piscean Christian imagery wherein someone else died for our sins, or wherein a monotheistic male god is the one responsible for all earthly and mortal action, and a cultural ethos in which the collective is responsible for the individual. This has ultimately resulted in a great fracturing of societies, and an alienation of individual persons not only from their culture, but from their families, and, more dangerously, from their own sense of self and divinity. It seems that major transitional periods are fraught with uncertainty, wherein unity is nowhere, and global disintegration threatens. Parallel to the collective disintegration lies the loss of identity of individuals.

The shift between the two epochs in which we find ourselves in the millennial period is one marked by a proliferation of new and experimental ideas. We are, and will be for decades to come, between the old epoch of Pisces moving in transition towards the coming epoch of Aquarius. In brief the two ages bring this imagery to mind:

o *Piscean Age* – individuals make up the collective, and the collective itself is responsible for the individual.
o *Aquarian Age* – the collective itself *is* an organic entity and each individual within it is responsible for the whole of the collective.

Naturally, this great leap will not in itself be complete until the era is almost done – in about 2,000 years time! It is a journey of heroic proportions, to be undertaken one-by-one in the name of all. One must not hold one's breath, however, and must continue to work within the existing systems to push them out beyond the boundaries of convention. This requires listening to a deep inner Self which has greater intelligence and longer memory than our intellectual mind.

As Joseph Campbell wrote: 'The modern hero, the modern individual who dares to heed the call and seek the mansion of that presence with whom it is our whole destiny to be atoned, cannot, indeed must not, wait for his community to cast off its slough of pride, fear, rationalized avarice, and sanctified misunderstanding . . . *It is not society that is to guide and save the creative hero, but precisely the reverse.*'[2] Indeed, we have arrived at the time where the individual is responsible for the collective.

We might look at the big picture in this way (see Figure 1):

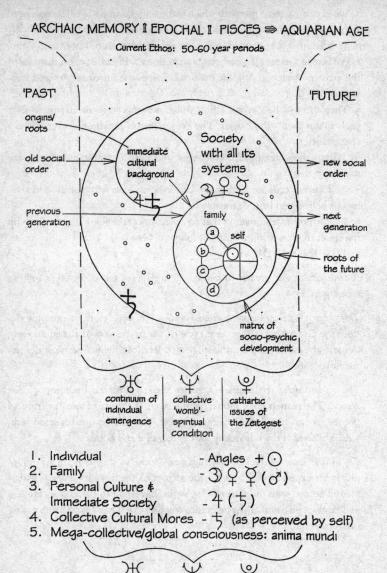

Figure 1

1. We have an archaic memory which is the underpinning of all human need for connection to one another – this is time-out-of-mind.

2. In turn, this is contained within an epochal signature (the Ages: Virgo, Leo, Cancer, Gemini, Taurus, Aries and our own Pisces Age, on through to the arriving Aquarian Age, etc.) which oversees the major images and symbols of the time.

3. Then there is the 'current ethos' which is at this stage about fifty to sixty years in duration – the *Zeitgeist*. The *Zeitgeist* moves rapidly, however, and is a shape-shifter.

4. Within those temporal motifs exist the various ethnic cultures in the world.

5. And the cultures are further sub-divided into sects with social orders, religious beliefs and historical context.

6. We further differentiate in that structure into families. Families make up the small clusters, within which, at long last, lies:

7. THE INDIVIDUAL.

Astrologically, and greatly simplified, we might see this depicted as follows (see Figure 2):

The zodiac: circle of heaven, *anima mundi* – the world soul. It not only defines the Great Year (26,000-year cycle of the precession of the equinoxes), but also the earth-year, and the single day. In the individual sense, it defines the horoscope.

The planets: archetypal human agencies seen against the backdrop of the zodiac. The planets are a global picture, seen in the same heavens from all points on earth at different times of day. The planets are rendered individual by *locus* in the horoscope, by degree, sign and house.

The houses: *oikos* – Greek for 'family' and 'house' – they contain and mundify inner experiences. These are the sectors of the heavens as they are divided in accord with the time of day, again in relation to the zodiac. Houses and families give immediate relevance to outer life. They are one step out of one's own self.

The Development of the Individual in the Horoscope

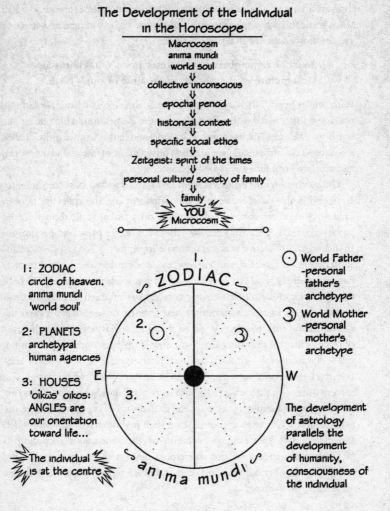

Macrocosm
anima mundi
world soul
⇓
collective unconscious
⇓
epochal period
⇓
historical context
⇓
specific social ethos
⇓
Zeitgeist: spirit of the times
⇓
personal culture/ society of family
⇓
family
YOU
Microcosm

1: ZODIAC
circle of heaven.
anima mundi
'world soul'

2: PLANETS
archetypal
human agencies

3: HOUSES
'oikōs' oikos:
ANGLES are
our orientation
toward life...

The individual
is at the centre

ZODIAC

anima mundi

⊙ World Father
-personal
father's
archetype

☽ World Mother
-personal
mother's
archetype

The development
of astrology
parallels the
development
of humanity,
consciousness of
the individual

Figure 2

Summary

Transits are just that – moving planets. The planets do not screech to a halt when someone is born; however, we do fix the planets in time and space to create a horoscope for that person.

**It must be remembered at all times that a natal horoscope
is a picture of the transits at the time of one's birth.**

With this in mind, it becomes apparent that a person is a living, breathing, walking transit, and thus is an emblem of the *Zeitgeist* into which he or she was born. We are all of us moments in time, and in this way we individualize a collective circumstance – we are the constellation of the mundane world, and thus are born into a very large family.

The incubation of a human is short and fast in ratio to its succeeding life-span, and if this parallel between the individual and the collective is even vaguely close, there is hope for humanity on a global scale, though in the 1990s – the turn of the millennium – there has been a prevailing pessimism. If, indeed, the collective is *not* to detonate itself, then a very rapid individuation process is required, and *will occur on a consciousness level*. Critical mass is fast approaching, and the generational impetus which might largely be a deeply unconscious motivation for survival has mutated already, and will continue to do so rapidly towards a new level of relationship between the individual and the collective. Without this shift, survival would not be possible. It seems that the only place to go now is 'up' and 'out', which is 'mind' and 'consciousness' – towards greater understanding of, and greater relationship between, the sacred and the profane, the mortal and immortal. The current obsession with knowledge and facts which has been in profound ascendancy since the mid-1500s will need to make room for the unknown, the magical, and give way to wisdom, or we shall find ourselves fast outmoded and extinct as a species. The evolution of the generations according to planetary array speaks of this movement beyond the Cartesian split between nature and culture, art and science, human and divine, towards a new unified vision of being.

In the section which follows, we see how movement and acceleration might occur through the most recent generations into future ones – keeping in mind that each individual is going to 'translate' his and her own outer-planetary configuration though the more personal planets and in other more mysterious, fated and metaphysical ways.

EVOLUTION AND REVOLUTION: ROUND AND ROUND WE GROW

Today's Planetary Configuration is Tomorrow's Leading Generation (see Figure 3)

In the course of Western development, the essentially positive process of emancipating the ego and consciousness from the tyranny of the unconscious has become negative. It has gone far beyond the division of conscious and unconscious into two systems and has brought about a schism between them; and, just as differentiation and specialization have degenerated into overspecialization, so this development has gone beyond the formation of individual personality and given rise to an atomized individualism.   (Erich Neumann, *History of Consciousness*)

GENERATIONAL CONFIGURATIONS OF PLUTO AND NEPTUNE: PURPOSE AND VISION

Pluto in Leo sextile Neptune in Libra

We are fast arriving at a time in society where the concept and relationship of families is charged with *Angst* because no coherent picture exists of what, in fact, 'a family' is. Families are becoming as individual and unique in structure and content as individuals! Family-consciousness and consciousness of families is shifting forms rapidly, and, as we have seen, the collective urge plays a tremendous parallel role, as it always has. Many of us born in the post-Second-World-War period are still in the thrall of the ideal Western family: mummy, daddy, little girl and little boy – 'us four and no more'. The American artist Norman Rockwell depicted this fantasy-family brilliantly in his illustrations, complete with gambolling family dog and cat napping by the fireside. It was so adorable it hurt to look at. The horror of this image is that not only does it now emerge as being patently untrue, but many of the largest group-generation to hit the planet (born between 1941 and 1958) are still clinging to the mummy–daddy picture and are reluctant to let go of that interior image, though shattered and saddened by its lack of reality. These people are all born with Pluto in Leo, the sign of the child, and will take their childhood to the grave. They (myself included in this generational imprint) may never leave off blaming mummy and daddy for everything

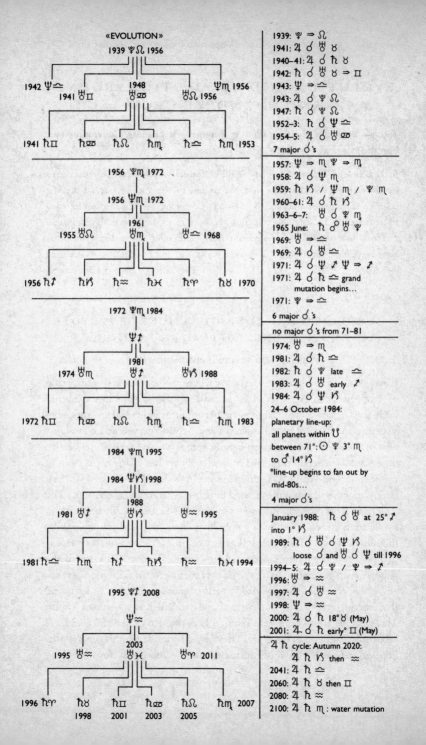

physical and psychological. The Pluto in Leo generation identifies with the child archetype, which ultimately needs a parental context within which to operate functionally.

Most of the Pluto in Leo generation have parents with Neptune in Leo – their (the parents') dream of their children was dashed by the storming passage of Pluto over their Neptunes and heralded the death of the fantasy-child. The vast majority of the Pluto in Leo people did not want the burden of carrying the fantasy-flame of their parents and, especially in the North American and European-origin cultures, they set about dashing the hopes, dreams, fantasies and generosity-to-the-extreme of their parents. Though other cultures (Asian, Oriental, indigenous, etc.) did not express this *en masse* as dramatically and immediately in the 1960s, their collective unconscious contained it, and over the last thirty years they too have had the same catharsis resulting in the slow rumble of mass rebellion (or inevitable loss of culture) and have been just as destructive of their cultural histories as the noisy, colourful front-runners of the Western cultural revolution in the sixties.

Also, the Pluto in Leo children had parents whose own Pluto was in Cancer – the sign of the family. To be specific – the indicator of the 'nuclear (isolated) family'. This Cancerian generation of Plutos were destined to have their children deny the traditional roles and make every attempt to decimate the image of the family which was lodged in the collective Western psyche – this disintegration has seeped into almost all cultures, now, globally. Essentially, the Pluto in Leo generation was born to destroy the king, the *tyrannos* – leader – of the times. However, the dictator that arose with the sighting of Pluto on 21 January 1930 was a penultimate archetype of the demon embodied, and his tyranny was of such large scale that all individuals born after the 1940s have the image of the tyrant-king embedded deeply in their psyches and live in conscious or unconscious terror of their individuality being abducted by inappropriate authority. Pluto in Leo symbolizes the rise of the individual to its highest level, to its most grandiose imagination of itself as all-powerful. There is a deep fear embedded in the Pluto in Leo generation of losing its individuality to the masses; an innate terror of being absorbed by the collective psyche, yet, being coupled with Neptune in Libra, the paradox lies in the general desire to fuse and merge with another and lose itself in dream-like fantasy of perfection, idealism and harmonious relations.

That the Pluto in Leo generation have Neptune in Libra even more

Figure 3

powerfully attests to their dream that the ideal relationship could exist between the sacred and the profane – the divine and the human. The idealism and values of this generation have been both exalted and denigrating – all the 'radical' thinkers of the Pluto in Leo generation often conveniently forget that the other half of them have contributed to the loss of soul and defiling of Gaia, the very thing that the more 'conscious' individuals have been in despair about since the advent of change in the sixties. However, we have now seen the enemy and they are us! The Neptune in Libra generation (Pluto in Leo) have projected their divinity on to human relationships and have suffered a crash in ideals and loss of innocence in the area of 'profane' (that is, plain old ordinary) relationships, while still clinging to the concept of 'divine' relationships – which do not necessarily happen on earth between mortals. Hence the phenomenal rise in 'gurus', cult and spiritual leaders, the concept of soul-mates, twin-flames, and so on, which have in paradox resulted in many disappointments and disillusions in the area of both personal and collective relationships.

The shadow lies in Leo, where by our very mortality we are not gods, thus fall short of the mark, yet in attempting to be gods commit the sin of hubris. This is part of a deeply unconscious collective awareness that the shadow of the age, that is, Leo as polar opposite of Aquarius, is god-like, and the past Age of Leo, the Golden Age, underlies the coming 'New Age'. If the gods walked the earth back then, they are straining to return today. This collective impulse is manifest in individuals in ways both sacred and profane. Pluto in Leo/Neptune in Libra feels the resurgence of the gods and can mistake that for an individual godliness.

Owing to the process of mass aggregation, the original group continues to exist only in the form of the family; but here, too, we can already discern a disintegrative tendency which increasingly restricts the effectiveness of the family group and assigns it a place only in childhood, or rather, only in infancy. The existence of the family, however, is of paramount importance for the preconscious and transpersonal psychology of the child.   (Erich Neumann, *History of Consciousness*)

For example, the Neptune in Libra/Pluto in Leo vision is one of global unity, an ultimate fusion of cultures along with the power of the individual in relationship to the collective. The axis for the individual-collective image *is* Leo-Aquarius; with the quickening advent of the Aquarian Age (astronomically *c.* 2060), there is a collective anxiety afoot which heralds massive change. As the first wave on the shores, the Pluto in Leo people inherently felt their work was cut out for them – to assert individuality (Leo) over the collective (Aquarius) and hopefully to (Neptune in Libra) institute a system in which the individual is responsible for the collective. In some ways this is still a rebellion against *auctoritas sine superioritas* – authority without superiority – because it is still one against the many. Massive ego inflation has occurred with this generational impulse – not only have there been multitudes of false gurus and deluded (lacking in playfulness) leaders, but also the generational stamp includes genuine resourcefulness and inventive genius.

On the darker side, the playfulness of Leo (*ludo* – I play) is corrupted by the de-luded – un-playful – aspect of the visionary side: the deadly serious mien of New Ageism, a millenarian phenomenon which purports itself to be the advent of various types of messiah. Also, the longing to remain in childhood, to play at life, has resulted in the paradox of the child-*senex* – remaining youthful in the ageing process. These people are deadly serious about playing. An industry of leisure has arisen, one which has stripped the shores and beauty spots of nature in favour of adult playgrounds. Go anywhere in the civilized world where there is a beach, a mountain lake or a natural phenomenon and you will find hordes of tourists queuing up at arcades and clubs, booking into monolithic blocks of flats stretching for miles, playing in the sun – and, like children, wholly unconscious of their impact on nature and the environment.

All this affects our relations within the context of families. The greater family, the family of humanity, is deeply influenced by the 'my toy' attitude of the supreme child, the collective which is most currently in vogue or power. Changes evolve over time, and the movement of Pluto and Neptune in sextile for still many generations to come (they begin to move out of orb of sextile around AD 2040) will show marked attitudinal changes both within small collectives (the genetic family) and the global collective – the family of humanity. The collusion of Power-Pluto and Vision-Neptune will move towards new forms, mutate into new shapes and contain new archetypal images for all. The Pluto/Neptune sextile has been and will be the subtext of the new era as it emerges over the next centuries.

We are still reeling under the impact of Pluto's sighting in 1930, but waves of its influence will continue to hit the shores of our consciousness in ever-increasing further-implicating events and patterns for many decades. Though we might find the idea of evolutionary mutation a bit far-fetched, we are already experiencing it now and will see it quicken in the 2000s. Fortunately, the planets move on as do we, and each successive generation has its work cut out for it by the previous one, as does each current generation set the task for the coming one. The fact that Pluto spends a leisurely thirty-two years transiting the backdrop of the sign Taurus and a hasty twelve in Scorpio might suggest that its 245-year orbit can sustain only a short so-journ in its own sign – certainly, any longer in Scorpio, and little of life would be remaining!

In the generational sequence, Pluto symbolizes the collective purpose and Neptune the vision. What follows is an evolution of purpose and vision from the late 1950s through to the millennium. Families are set in the con-text of the *Zeitgeist* – but more momentous is their placement in the heavens. These comprehensive groupings talk about long-range shifts in collective values and perspectives which are vastly more descriptive of the global tone.

Pluto in Virgo sextile Neptune in Scorpio

The Pluto in Virgo generation (1956–71) has Neptune in Scorpio. Its dreams were darkened while Pluto transited Scorpio between 1982 and 1995. The eccentric orbit of Pluto has some fated aspect to certain group-ings of planets, signs and people – the Pluto in Cancer people with Neptune in Leo (1915–30) experienced their Pluto transit over Neptune during the 1940s and mid-1950s and found their dreams to be powerful and grand, building dynasties and creating monuments to independence and the power of the individual, but as we have read, their dreams were not sufficient to support their children's needs for drama and revolution. This is not the tone for what Pluto in Virgo/Neptune in Scorpio people will experience. Pluto transiting Neptune is akin to having the anaesthetic shut off. There is no escape from *Weltschmertz* – world pain. The scales do not drop slowly from the eyes, they are ripped away and the stark truth of one's own personal self-delusion and the entire collective fantasy is revealed.

Generally, the people with Pluto in Virgo have not and do not find their nuclear families to be a nest of neuroses – even if they *are* such, the level of concern over parental influence is not as strongly focused as with the Pluto in Leo people. For them, individual families are unrecognizable by the old definition, and though many of the Pluto in Virgo people have emerged from exceptionally unconventional families (that is, the old norm is broken), some even from horribly dysfunctional families, they are largely disinclined to censure the parents themselves, but are more inclined to lay blame on a more collective level, on a more existential, cosmic level. They are a more accepting group – they understand inherently that there is a fate to things, a time of life and a job to do.

When I was studying classics in the mid-1980s, my Greek mythology professor told me that he suffered a great embarrassment when he was telling the Oedipus myth to his young students (generally all Pluto in Virgos – or o° Libra – except for the odd 'mature student' like myself) – the one where the boy kills his father so he can sleep with his mother, the source of the now famous Freudian complex. He interpreted the myth in the contemporaneous psychological fashion, one which he admitted applied to him on an archetypal level (he too has Pluto in Leo). He then posed to the students the question whether or not they felt this mythic triangulation in their own relationship between themselves and their parents. He was met with a collective blank stare. The children of the fifties/sixties did not know what he was going on about! They likely found him odd and possibly deranged to be 'confessing' to Oedipal feelings – *they did not resonate to the story in a personal, psychological way*. He and I had a good laugh about this, but it set me to thinking and realizing that we must, as a generation, stop imposing our models on our children, and burdening them with the guilt (sins) of our own pasts.

Though it is part of the survival instinct to indoctrinate our youth with our own perspective and beliefs, it is impossible to infuse totally our own generational values into succeeding generations, just as we cannot bring our contemporary bias to the study of cave-drawings. *As we do not know what archaic man thought, we cannot know what the future people will feel*. However, with the planetary pictures in mind, we can arrive at some intelligent suppositions about what might be evolving in the archetypal mind.

Pluto in Virgo/Neptune in Scorpio bring new purpose and vision to the world, based on deep cleansing. Not only the old values of family relationships but also the new values emerging in global relationships sit heavily on the shoulders of the Pluto in Virgo generation. To speak frivolously, the function of Virgo is to clean up after the party (previous sign Leo), in order to create a new diplomatic equilibrium (Libra, next sign) within relationships, both personal and collective. With Pluto in Virgo their innate legacy is one which charges them to purify and articulate more precisely the fabulous vision of the past generation – but to do it within the scope and limitations of reality. The reality-frame for Pluto in Virgo/Neptune in Scorpio is stark and clear. The functional practicality of Virgo in dealing purposefully with tools and materials at hand is tremendous, while the existentialism of the

Scorpionic Neptune is an asset in coping with the death of old ways – part of the vision of Neptune in Scorpio actually includes endings. Their relationship to family dynamics is quite unique – their perspective on the hapless limitations of their parents is fair and benign at best, or cold, unsympathetic and distant at worst. They recognize how human we all are, and that in the end, death is the great equalizer.

It appears that the purpose of the Pluto in Virgo generation is to heal many wounds, and their awareness of their own parents' guilt and *Angst* will work wonders for their future expectations of family groups. The Pluto in Virgo people will very likely be the healers of their family complexes and the nurses of the psyches of their Pluto in Leo parents' battered egos! In plain language, the Pluto in Virgo generation do not have the leisure, resources, time or inclination to spend a great deal of their energy whingeing about their parents! They are impatient to get on with it, and feel burdened by their parents trying to work out their own complexes through their children (i.e. them!). The leitmotif of Virgo is compassion (literally, 'suffering with') and their generational impetus is to throw off their parents' suffering and move beyond it towards a future fraught with uncertainty and potential chaos. The underlying unconscious theme in Virgo is the descent into collectivity and primal chaos (polarity: Pisces) which annihilates individual order, hence, ego-loss in favour of soulfulness. Essentially they are here to resurrect what the Pluto in Leo generation have crucified.

The vision (Neptune) is Scorpionic – both fatalistic and realistic. The generational psyche faces the death of the old bravely, seeking solace in both spiritual and practical matters. Through work, diligence, humanitarianism, awareness of the terminus of the old way of life – a way not long passed – they are the nascent foundations of a new type of family dynamic – a dynamic which has been forced to include the concept of a global family. It appears that the global family, though idealistically envisioned by the Pluto in Leo generation, really only began to emerge with the arrival of the Pluto in Virgo generation. The efforts to decentralize the nuclear family concerns during the years of their maturing, which opened up into the perspective of relationships of 'families' to include larger more culturally and internationally centred values, will still take several generations to become stabilized into a new status quo, and firmly established.

It is this generation that took the vision of the previous generation of Pluto in Leo/Neptune in Libra to the edge of the information superhighway, to the global network, and perfected technology to move the world towards a seamless, organic whole – *unus mundus*. Though admirable in its technology, there is a paradox within the vision of Neptune in Scorpio. Scorpio is a reclusive sign, singular and morose. It is water, so it is deeply feeling and needs the emotional contact with others, but is often repelled by prolonged intimacy and tries to kill the thing upon which it grows dependent. The global network which this generation has brought to maturity has two sides. On the one hand, theoretically, everyone is in connection with everyone else. But they are only so if they are alone in their room at their computer.

The awareness of psychic entropy, the gradual decline of energy, is strong in the Virgo/Scorpio combination. Nihilism cannot sustain itself in groups, but can only find solace in the quiet isolation of aloneness. Generally their expectations of happiness are not high – they do not recall the Golden Age as did their immediate predecessors. But this is the reactionary aspect to their legacy from dramatic, flamboyant, demanding parents. Parents who have not yet overcome their anger at *their* parents, parents who, at the age of fifty-plus, are still crying about their own dysfunctional families! Many of the Pluto in Leos are so self-absorbed about their pasts that they have unwittingly perpetrated their own destiny in creating absent families – distant children who want nothing of them but their freedom. It seems that a great number of Pluto in Leos chose to have children in their thirties, creating the phenomenon called 'The Baby Boomer's Baby Boom', of which Pluto in Virgo and Neptune in Scorpio are the result.

Pluto in Libra sextile Neptune in Sagittarius

There is a shift, yet again, with the next group, who were born between 1971 and 1984. Pluto in Libra and Neptune in Sagittarius people come in with an overwhelming desire for freedom and new futuristic vision. It is significant to note that *there were relatively few births in that decade (seventies) in relation to the number of potential parents* (the Pluto in Leo/Neptune in Libra people). It is fascinating to note that in parallel to this decline in birth-rate, *there were no major conjunctions* between planets from Jupiter out to Pluto from 1971 to 1981 (see Figure 3, page 12), whereas in the previous generational periods, there were:

       o Seven major conjunctions between 1939 and 1955.
       o Six major conjunctions between 1957 and 1971.

There were none from 1971 to 1981, and there were:

o Four from 1974 to 1984.

o Six from 1984 to 1997.

And then, all the planets from Saturn outwards will fully change signs by 1998. The 1970s were a dormant, incubating period, unremarkable on the outside, but deeply fruitful on a gestating level. Everything went underground. The children of the 1970s are a potential 'lost generation', one which seemingly fell through the cracks.

Even though so small in numbers, real objectivity enters the picture with the Pluto in Libra/Neptune in Sagittarius group. They embody a great move towards liberation from the confines of old mores and dictates of all the previous generations. This is coupled with a strong commitment to relationship and ideals which can be met more realistically – a reaction to the 'love the one you're with' parents. These are the majority of children born to the Pluto in Leo/Neptune in Libra group – and they too will disillusion their parents, but in a very different fashion. Pluto is in the sign of their parents' Neptune, and just as the Pluto in Leo group dashed the fantasies of their parents, so it seems that history will repeat itself, yet again in a new way. This group arrived on the planet as the Neptune in Libra people were becoming uncomfortably aware that their fairy-tale attitude towards relationships was not working terribly well, and perhaps re-thinking or re-feeling the whole picture would be a good idea. As with all generational issues, those complexes which remain unresolved in the parents are passed on to the children to be further processed, and hopefully broken and re-integrated in new forms.

The fantasy of the ideal relationship, one which does not require work but can be jettisoned when it lacks idealistic perfection, is the shadow of Neptune in Libra. Neptune in Libra sought to recapture in adulthood the primary relationship found only in the womb, where two hearts beat as one. However, the subsequent people with Pluto in Libra were born with the inherent awareness that harmony, balance and fair play are *not* automatically inserted into relating, and that it requires civilization and work, mutual philosophy and beliefs to keep a relationship or a group or a family together. The collective ethos of this generational motif is one which contains the possibility that because individuals are *not* perfect or identical, relationships between these imperfect, dissimilar beings are bound to be fraught with imperfections and contrasts. This sound philosophy can result in very fruitful new types of families and relationships.

The combination they produce – Pluto in Libra and Neptune in Sagittarius – is essentially an objective perspective arrived at by thinking, rather than feeling. Naturally, individuals in this collective image are of various types and are distinctly individual and have deep, emotional feeling natures, but their generational imprimatur, stamp, or archetype is one of emotional detachment with strong collective social values, rather than of individual supremacy or personal gain. Their family patterns will likely be based more on tribal or even global, humanitarian values – they are the real fulcrum between the past and the future, the connection to the global family.

Neptune in Sagittarius has a strong inclination towards idealizing the global family, possibly to the detriment of the deeper, feeling tone. They would be far more inclined to abandon family systems altogether as we know them, and mark the true separation from the pre-Second World War values so badly mangled in the sixties. The high-mindedness of Sagittarius can become pathologically impartial and unbiased, treating all things as the gods of myth treated mortals. Like puppet-masters pulling the strings of their puppets, their attitude can be disdainful of emotion and human individual need. This prevailing wind would certainly shift the tide of family consciousness if it took that tack *en masse*. The vision (Neptune) of One World, One Family (Sagittarius) will need to undergo the test of Pluto's full transit of Sagittarius from 1995 to 2008, and, hopefully, people will still be reading this book to see if things have, indeed, changed much at all! We will likely be experiencing the marriage of heaven and hell – the deepest, inmost self connecting to the highest, most cosmic mind.

Pluto in Scorpio/Neptune in Capricorn

When Pluto entered Scorpio in 1983–4 for twelve years, Neptune also began its fourteen-year transit of Capricorn, and they trotted along in sextile together for around thirteen years – but towards the end of their reign in those signs, a major conjunction of planets took place on 11 January 1994 – seven planets in Capricorn with an eclipsing moon conjunct Mars retrograde in opposition to the Capricorn stellium. The entire transit of Pluto in Scorpio is a period now seen as one which signalled the death of the past age, the disintegration of a flagging system; the loss of cultural integrity; the pandemic AIDS virus; the muting of boundaries, borders and cultural distinction; and the final death-knell of the old ways. But we are not clocks, it would seem. The heavens may impel, but humans delay. It takes about (or once took, shall we say) sixty years for a new idea to enter the mainstream fully – approximately two generational maturation cycles. The process of assimilation is necessarily slow and thorough. It must first move through the one and *then* the many.

There are times in history when the significance and power of the individual is greater than at other times. The astounding developments in the sensitive areas of science have been prolific – individuals in the race against time, ideas in the collective brain are continuing to be funnelled through human minds at a most incredible rate; information having accumulated over decades, centuries, millennia has been and is being collated and is producing some very sane open-ended deductions – a revolution in evolution is on the doorstep.

How, then, in the light of such fantastic happenings and such truthful transits, can we possibly adhere to hypocrisy? Evidently, with great ease. However, if that is so, how long can this be supported? Probably not for long. If anything, what does this portend for families in the decades to come? With hindsight as our lens, let us turn our scope on the future of families and, using pure astrological symbolism, moving beyond psychology, let us see what the planetary family has in store for its human representatives – a form of astropomorphism, we might say.

The AIDS virus seems a chilling messenger – that the immune system, once so reliable in humans and animals, can actually break down completely is a horrific biological metaphor for the loss of immunity to invasive forces that our very earth has sustained. In effect, if the pollution rate isn't balanced by a radical correction, Gaia, herself, may turn HIV-positive. This is the reality that the Pluto in Scorpio and Neptune in Capricorn people are born into, and will carry imprinted in their collective consciousness. It is no wonder that a scorn is felt for sentiment and nostalgia, both rather wasteful emotions, though both Scorpio and Capricorn are known for their sensitivity to deep and historical issues. With imminent threat of global disintegration, these people want to place their values in areas other than small, secretive, insular, nuclear family conclaves.

Pluto in Scorpio and Neptune in Capricorn (conjunct Uranus for many of those years) gives birth to a generation of wise or jaded people, whose souls have come in with the knowledge of the ages. Nothing shocks them, nothing amazes – only the future is open to them, as the past is closed. The models of the past have been shattered beyond redemption, *nothing* works as it 'used to in the old days', systems are limping along, hoping for reconstitution. And it will be this generation who will, indeed, repair and redo, resurrect and reclaim, regenerate and renovate. Able to work with the minimum of resources and capable of accepting the few viable routes left from which to carve a future path, these people are the hope of the long future. By the images that are presented in this configuration, we will see a total restructuring of politics, money, resources and relationships. The combination of Scorpio and Capricorn is not a terribly cheerful image, and considering the mundane events of the time in which this transit occurred, we would be fools to consider that the product of those times might be a light-hearted, happy-go-lucky bunch of *puers* and *puellas*. On the absolute contrary, they contain a very serious, terribly realistic *senex*-consciousness.

Theirs will be the job of re-visioning power, social order, a new status quo and a dissolving trust in 'history' as a great teacher! The disenchantment of the way things are will lead to a new way of creating a system and world order.

Their approach to relationship is filled with pragmatism and awareness of the power of love to transform all rigid states. Their allegiance to their groups will be undying, everlasting and profoundly tribal. They instinctually know their tribe and tend to cluster around and within it, nourishing and protecting their own. Though other tribes are acknowledged, they will generally stick faithfully close to home but create working systems which will 'handshake' with other tribes, but they will not integrate. This is not a signature of 'one world, one people'. It would appear that the deep, systemic shocks which occurred to the collective psyche between 1983 and 1995 have locked a generation of people into defence and protection mode, which will result in a complete review of the concept of loyalty. It is not that they don't think globally – as I have already pointed out, this concept is now fully assimilated and integrated into the psychic whole – but that they know inherently that each of them as individuals is made up of and make up little collectives, which in turn comprise the whole. They are aware of the cellular make-up of all things. And they see themselves as an essential cell in an organic whole. This is the fruit of the Gaia Theory in human form. This is individualism at its most intense and focused – awareness of individuality, but acknowledging its relationship within its tribe.

In 1984 there was a *true* planetary line-up – a harmonic convergence – as opposed to all the fraudulent 'harmonic convergences' advertised at odd times during the eighties and nineties in New Age magazines. Between 24 and 26 October 1984, *all the planets, Sun and Moon, were between 3° Scorpio and*

14° Capricorn. A 71° orb! All the planets starting with Sun and Pluto at 3° Scorpio and ending with Mars at 14° Capricorn! The bunching formed a stellium contained within a quintile – an aspect which talks of seeding deep knowledge. This was the turning point towards the future – this was the last 'harmonic convergence' and the harmonic it struck was the fifth.[3]

This fifth-harmonic group of individuals have a Mandelbrot for a brain. (Remember, we are walking transits.) In a sense they are all psychic manifestations of the Pythagorean philosophy. Tied into the Golden Section, they embody all knowledge ever passed before and to come after. It is a mystical, yet terribly practical – the number of Man – configuration. They *think* differently from any other generation before or since them. This could be said of all of us, but this is a unique, turning-point generation – it marks the death of the past and the conception of the future. They live in a world in which anything might happen. Nothing can happen which will be shocking or amazing unless, of course, it is in their lifetime that the unified theory is proved or the visitation from other intelligence takes place at last. This characteristic, the uncertainty principle inherent in the consciousness of the collective group, will result in a backlash, a conservationist and traditionalist-minded group of people.

The major configuration which marked the passing of this generational period was the Uranus/Neptune conjunction. This aspect, occurring only once every 171 years, created an atmosphere of total chaos both in the collective and in individual people's lives. Between the years of 1991 and 1995, Uranus weaved its way towards, through and beyond the orb of Neptune. That Uranus is the planet of individualism and individuation, and Neptune the planet symbolizing the ultimate loss of individual identity in the zone of the group-consciousness and the collective, speaks of a massive identity crisis on a global scale. A loss of group identity was balanced by the extremist organizations rising to declare supremacy. Whole countries lost their identity. Individuals lost their concept of a personal future and a coherent purpose in life. Dreams were no longer sufficient stuff to live on. Capricorn is a harsh realist, and with Neptune dissolving realities right and left for fourteen years, then challenged by Uranus crying out for distinction among the confusion, all systems teetered and many collapsed. People born under these configurations will have tremendous tolerance, but little in the way of anaesthetics to prevent them from seeing through pretence. Hence their family structures will be likely to be based on a vision of stability, coherence, loyalty, inheritance and continuity. This is a reaction to the independent nihilism of the previous group – they will want assurance of their continuation and will likely re-form the nuclear family archetype.

Neptune is like a great sleeping-pill, and Uranus an alarm-clock . . . all the while wanting to descend into the arms of Morpheus, the bell is going off! Those who were born with Pluto in Scorpio sextile the Uranus/Neptune conjunction will find solace in chaos, uniqueness in sameness, will want security and will create it in ways which seem unfathomable to their parents. The underlying uncertainty of Neptune will for ever change the criterion for convention, standards, status quo and authority. And the passage of Uranus through the Neptune-zone in 1994–5 shattered the dream of a spiritual leadership. However, it did begin to reinstate the power of the individual, which seemed at a loss. Families were shattered by a wave of sexual allegations in this era, a real *Crucible* period of time. Children born carrying this stamp will have a vision of a highly moral culture with strong laws for conventional behaviour.

Pluto in Sagittarius sextile Neptune in Aquarius

Pluto and Neptune moved into these signs in the 1995–6 period and will stay there together until around 2009–11, weaving in and out of perfect orb of the sextile with each other. The planet Uranus, like the previous configuration, will be in Aquarius for part of this time, as well, until 2003 or so. The conflict generated by ideas has been a historical fact – and most wars have been based on ideology, not territorialism as is commonly thought. More people have killed other people for what they thought or believed than for what they owned or governed. Here we have a group of ideological warriors, ones who organize their groups around philosophy, religious views, cultural fluidity, international attitudes and global-unity beliefs.

People born in this grouping will come into their maturity – Saturn return – roughly between 2025 and 2040. It is in these years that the Pluto-Neptune sextile will truly be over. After almost a century of being in the sextile formation, Pluto will begin to lag behind and its movement will begin the slowing process as it heads towards Pisces through Taurus, on through its most apparent elongated point in its orbit. Pluto in Sagittarius/Neptune in Aquarius people will step over the threshold into the new world. With this in mind – being that we are more made up of our futures than our pasts – the seed of the new world lies in the psyche of this group of people.

This aspect does, finally, speak of 'one-world, one-people' – in this time, the seeds of such a potential take root, lending the people born during this time strong ideologies and a global-thinking attitude. How this occurs is not terribly clear, but there are some inherent horrors in Pluto in Sagittarius which must be addressed. Sagittarius has to do with formalized and legislated ideologies; it also has to do with the shadow of internationality – xenophobia. Zeus was the god of 'guests' and 'strangers', but he was ruthless with any who transgressed the laws of the guest–host relationship. One of those laws was this: in the liminal zone of transition, or travel, or unrootedness, one must never own an ego; to have the hubris to declare individuality or independence from the 'gods' who guide (i.e. political heads) is a breach of mortal law. This configuration of Pluto in Sagittarius/Neptune in Aquarius could lead to a highly moral culture which abhors interracial or interreligious contact or even travel among foreign nations! The potential for extremist reactions and dictatorial cultures is very, very strong.

Family dynamics are not deeply, psychologically enmeshing – this is an Air/Fire combination which leaves a lot of room for growth, change, movement and space. Families will be very important to them, but relationships within the family will need to be based on values, beliefs, ideas, relevance and participation in the larger collective – the culture, religion and, further, the world itself. These people will speak out against false values that their parental generation might subscribe to and will override them, creating new laws and new boundaries within which to execute laws. They are a reaction to the previous conservative group and will break away from the fears of loneliness and establish families which are cross-cultural and international. There is a strong adherence to philosophy, law, dogma and various cultural ties which supersede family bonding. A phase of cultural loyalty is very much a part of this group, which does not hold the old 'family values' in any esteem at all.

Theirs will not be a loud revolution, but one that takes place covertly and intellectually. Outrage will be marked by thinking, teaching and creating, not bombing, invading or oppressing by force. There is a kind of cold objectivity and high idealism (not romanticism) to this generational stamp, a lack of feeling-tone or emotion. Fire and air are largely rational and thinking-based.

The technology developed during this time is a double-edged sword which will cut society at large in two. As previously mentioned, there is a paradox inherent in the technological family dynamic. On the one hand, computer technology will connect individuals to individuals on a global network, but on the other hand, it will serve to further alienate human beings from each other in an emotionally interactive way. Also, the technology will connect those who have with those who have, and will further separate those in the know from those who have neither the resources nor the abilities to take part in the cultural revolution which will be a direct result from on-line and internet cultures. So the split between individuals and 'cultures' will be even more vast.

Obviously, each person will react in his or her own way to the ethos of their time; however, as a stamp or an archetype, we are looking at a rapid movement out and away from the main themes of the Piscean age, even as early as the millennium. People of this generational stamp will come of age during a time when the era of brotherhood and love (Pisces) will already be a thing of the past, and the age of technology and information will be just beginning to reach its ascendancy.

NOTES

1. Rick Tarnas, *The Passion of the Western Mind*, Harmony Books, New York, 1991. This is the most succinct, recent and accessible book on the movement of ideas and intellectual thought in the Piscean age. Tarnas is an astrologer as well as a philosopher at the California Institute of Integral Studies. He is also author of *Prometheus – The Awakener*.

2. Joseph Campbell, *The Hero with a Thousand Faces*, Princeton University Press, 1973, page 391.

3. For other references to the astrology around fifth-harmonics see Michael Harding and Charles Harvey, *Working with Astrology*, Contemporary Astrology Series, Arkana, 1990, Chapter 12; Erin Sullivan, *Retrograde Planets: Traversing the Inner Landscape*, Contemporary Astrology Series, Arkana, 1993, Chapter 5, pages 88 ff., 'Venus Retrograde'.

2.

The Nuclear Family
as a System

'I believe we get sick in twos and threes, not alone as individuals. You follow me?'
(Dr Harry Hyman in *Broken Glass* by Arthur Miller)

'All together now – "We are all individuals".'

(Monty Python, *The Meaning of Life*)

WHAT IS A FAMILY SYSTEM?

Having looked at the 'Big Picture' and the cosmic or world family, let's now concentrate on a small system within that large system – our nuclear family. One useful concept of families is the family as an organic whole, an entity in itself. In this way the family is an interactive and interdependent structure of individuals each of whom revolves around a mysterious common hub: a myth, a story, an individual, a cultural tie or some other central focus. This immediately implies that it is an organization in which individual behaviour and expression is simultaneously influenced by and influences all other.

If a family itself is a living entity, then each of its members and their individual natures can be looked at as purposeful 'cells' of the organic whole. The immediate family – either your family of origin, or your family of creation – is a small collective, wherein each member of this collective simultaneously enhances the group and also is defined by it. The family grows, shrinks, moves and shifts in accord with its people, but also there is a mysterious holding force that keeps it together and thus makes the family recognizable as a certain 'type' – something that does not appear to change much over many generations. The family is largely defined by the people it comprises, and the people in the family are also influenced by the family as a psychic and physical power.

Therein lies the fascinating aspect of the family as an entity . . . it both enhances and annihilates the individual. The family not only creates the individual but also swallows it, while at the same time individual members each both create and also destroy the family's integrity as they grow and develop their own unique characters. A wonderful paradox, if we can contemplate it in its entirety and use the objectivity gained by this view. Then we might understand more fully the complexities *and* the difficulties inherent in developing as an individual, maintaining one's *own* boundaries, all the while living within the boundary of the family itself!

There has been a polemic about families, a psychological and ideological attack in recent years, as if the family – that is, the nuclear family – is simply a nest of neurosis in which all members are restricted and horribly undermined. Frankly, an individual without a family is bound to become far more neurotic, even more likely insane and psychopathic, than one with a family! From there, we accept the basic fact that families endure, no matter how they are experimented with, and thus, we work with what we have. All people have problems, no person is perfect, and thus families remain problematic and imperfect. This is the *no mens rea* clause.

However, it seems that most problems arise in families when certain expectations are not met. Some of these expectations are deeply unconscious and stem from generations past. Some expectations lie in the archetypal realm, wherein there are ideals, perfect 'forms' of behaviour and so forth. However, usually the greatest difficulty arises when two people are saying the same thing only in different ways. How many times have arguments resolved themselves after both people realized, ultimately, that each was saying or wanting virtually the identical thing, however expressing it in ways unfamiliar or unacceptable to the other? Too often this arises in a family context and creates no end of misunderstanding and pain. Within the astrological picture, there is the possibility of reducing misconceptions and enhancing the comprehension of one's family and thus fostering greater sympathy and harmony.

Fear of change threatens everyone. If we could come to understand that change and variety are the creative sources of building a stronger, more resilient family, then the stress associated with movement, variation, diversity, and even contrast or divergence would be greatly diminished. Even within our friendships, we can become alarmed when we note fundamental changes in their appearance, actions or endeavours. When friends divorce, move away or drastically change their status in some way, we are threatened because it means we have to change too. This is an even more powerful issue in a family situation.

The maintenance of a family motif is dependent on myriad factors; however, there is a technical term for the mysterious regulating principle which comes into play when change is imminent in any interlocking system: homeostasis. Homeostasis is the 'stay-the-same' factor; it is a characteristic deeply embedded within the system of the family itself, and it lends coherence, consistency and stability to an active, mobile entity.

Astrologically there can be Mars/Pluto homeostasis where violence is the holding pattern; or, as in the Kennedy family, seen in the Appendix (page 376), a Saturn/Pluto harmonic rigid in the structure lending power and control – and sequences of death and tragedy; or a Moon/Neptune stasis where love, dreams, religion, drugs or dependency are the norm; or a Sun/Uranus homeostasis type in which everyone is always running amok. It is a matter of finding out both by observation and understanding how the family feels and works, and looking at myriad horoscopes of them, finding patterns. More on pattern-finding will be threaded throughout the book.

The function of homeostasis in any system is to sustain balance and maintain a constant state of affairs – to keep things as they always have been. Only a certain amount of change is allowed which does not threaten the integrity and recognizable shape of the group. Homeostasis acts as a self-regulating device so that when a major shift occurs we try to regain stability and return to the known way of being. This is a most important thing to be considered when contemplating the value of change within the family dynamic. Any form of change is traumatic – marriage, major moves, births, deaths, redundancies, transitional age-periods in life – for example, the 'terrible twos', first leaving home for school, adolescence, the age of thirty, mid-life, grandparenthood, etc. These types of change happen to all people and are clearly recognized, therefore social and familial formalities endorse particular ways of coping with these kinds of changes.

More significantly, there are *unwritten* changes, inner rites of passage, that have no precedent, and it is these which are often swept under the carpet and ignored or disguised, or worse, lied about. Homeostasis is maintained in both the unconscious and the conscious mind. Conscious holding-patterns manifest thus: a child rebels, runs away from home, or steals, lies, or offends the overt family motif in some way, threatening its composure. The family seizes up: 'No one has ever done this [thing] before!' People react openly. An iron grip is put upon the offender and no amount of discussion permits change – no one learns anything, no one grows from the experience, all systems shut down and calcify. The potential for exploration and adjustment is lost, and the incident or symptom becomes a simple matter of crime and punishment. A more creative way to deal with such a *frisson* in the family is to consider the possibility that there is something in the system itself that needed change or shock to bring the whole family about, to view life differently, and that the perpetrator is making a statement that needs to be heard and incorporated as part of the dynamic of the whole.

The simplistic view of homeostasis is very superficial – the more powerful levels lie deeply under the surface in the group unconscious. In this case it is even more difficult to locate. The homeostatic principle isn't apparent at all, until something seriously pathological or extreme occurs, such as an emotional breakdown, acting-out, major crime or divorce – when symptoms of dis-ease appear in one or more of the people in the family. The first thing to consider is that no one is to blame or at fault. The next thing to consider is that something very wrong has happened somewhere within the system itself, in the dynamic of the family. No single individual is at the core but the entire fabric of the family is rent or weakened and therefore needs to find a way to re-weave itself and regulate its pattern. Unfortunately, often the most common way of coping with a severe tear in the family is by alienating the broken person, isolating him or her, and not considering what that person (or event) means within the context of the larger whole – the family itself. When a deeper, more compassionate and non-judgemental look is taken, it is often found that the hurt or broken person in the family is acting out the weak link for everyone else, and with the aid of the whole, the link is reconnected and strengthened, thus.

A creative way of dealing with an extreme trauma is family therapy, where the whole of the family is able to see objectively its healthy and unhealthy parts, where, in the safety of the therapeutic environment, and in the company of an 'outsider', the family can get to know itself and accept all its aspects – both bad and good. This can break the homeostasis and allow the 'parts', i.e. the individuals, to change, thus change the way the family works and re-establish a new centre. The main problem with psychological models and psychology itself is that, by and large, it treats the immediate situation, generally without considering the profound possibility that there are generational issues that arise in nuclear families. In the final chapter of this book, 'The Procession of the Ancestors' (page 343), there is a story of multi-levelled, intra-dimensional family/cultural/ancestral healing which is not at all an uncommon experience. I have several exemplars of such complex family webs.

A friend of mine, searching for origins of his family's 'curse', worked ardently and intelligently with all levels of processing this curse – the analytical, the psychological, the astrological and the personal – not to mention propitiation of various ancient gods. All his efforts led to some very interesting ends. There was a strong thread of Mars/Pluto and Pisces/Neptune that ran *consistently* through the family for at least five generations – on both maternal and paternal lines, and extended across the families through nephews and so forth. His paternal line seemed particularly fraught with male suppression disguised as imperialistic behaviour. He was convinced that there was some Sophoclean sin or dynastic pollution in the past that, once expiated, would ease his own driven soul, and clear the family of its anger. He has Mars in Pisces in the eighth house. The Mars theme is very strong, and in doing a thorough genealogy he found that his ancestors were slave-owners in the southern states.

Prior to his having discovered this, his own life had been dedicated wholly to the oppressed, the underdog and the catabolic elements of society, and though he, himself, was tremendously, tangibly successful in his own industry, never could he accept the accolades due him, and he was rabid about oppression of every kind. Having uncovered the 'family secret', the miasma in the family based on the sin of slavery, he felt he understood what the contemporaneous problems were in the family. Now, we could say that Mars in Pisces is fearful of being imprisoned, enslaved, abused, taken advantage of and so forth. This is true because there is a softness and an empathic quality to that signature, but the other side of it is working with those victimized people. Through his own ancestral work, he finally came to the current family and has made great strides towards healing rifts that had run down through the family into current time – as one might suspect with all the Mars/Pluto and Neptunian signatures.

Profound events such as illness, death, affairs, rebellion and various trauma have been at the base of much personal healing and the ending of many feuds in families. Sharp corrections in rigid patterns in families have resulted in the transformation of all the members into more understanding, more whole, more complete individuals, who become not only liberated themselves, but also, in turn, more supportive of the family as a whole. The strength of any system depends on the individual power of its components, and conversely, the weakness of the system is reflected in the symptom of the targeted person. The ideal end result is a strong but flexible homeostasis, one which is refreshed and renewed by crisis and less likely to break under any new crisis.

Modern psychology has developed a viewpoint centred around a scientific model called General Systems Theory – a fairly inhuman sounding caption for a group of people intimately bound by blood, viscera, feelings and destiny! However, it is an interesting and very fruitful atmosphere in which to observe family dynamics in a modular fashion. It is well worth looking at it and making use of it, because it can lead out to some more profound layers in the family soul. Here is how it works: 'In General Systems Theory, there exists the system, the system's environment (supra-system) and the system's components (sub-systems); and the theory is concerned with the description and exploration of the relationship between this hierarchy of interrelated systems.'[1]

Pretty cold stuff; however, keeping in mind that we are trying to create some sense of order out of what often appears to be a haphazard and random pattern, let us explore this framework more fully. In fact, if we refer back to Figure 1, page 7, we see this concept of 'system', 'supra-system' and 'sub-system' outlined well in the astrological model – we have the age, the times, the culture, the major planetary configurations as the 'supra-system' in great detail, and we have the natal horoscope as the individual, each of which make up small 'sub-systems' within the container of the family 'system'.

The nuclear family system has come from somewhere; it has a long ancestral line of origin, thus astrology can cope with that aspect. By adopting a genealogical viewpoint, we come closer to getting to the bottom of issues that exist in families which are not always clear in the nuclear system alone. That view is far too entrenched in mother, father, daughter and son. Not only must we expand our frame of reference to include grandmother, grandfather, uncle and aunt, but also the ancestral league whose spirit rests in the individual. And also, as we read in Chapter 1, there are cultural and epochal contexts within which our personal experiences are felt and enacted. With careful attention to a problem in a family or with an individual, we might look for contributing factors which lie outside the immediate sphere of environment or experience. That is, beyond the realm of psyche, and into the realm of soul.

Arthur Miller, in his 1995 play *Broken Glass*,[2] brilliantly dramatizes the deep unconscious and soul connections we have not only with our immediate family, but also within the collective and our ancestral lineage going back to the origins of culture. Miller demonstrates that an individual is not only enduring her own personal ordeal, but also is a repository for her ancestral lineage – as well as an empathic for the current collective experience. The play is a dramatic yet very simple portrayal of the vigour with which intra-dimensional activity takes place in the soul of a single human being.

The heroine, Sylvia Gellburg, becomes mysteriously paralysed in her legs, and the doctors can find no physiological cause. She is a beautiful, intelligent woman, married some twenty years to Philip, the head of a Gentile-owned mortgage company. The suppressed elements in their deeply unhappy marriage erupt concurrently with the oppression of the Jews in Germany. Hitler's Germany begins to show serious signs of collective psychopathology. The dramatic setting is Brooklyn, in the last days of November 1938.

As the play unfolds, we become aware of a chilling relationship between Sylvia's illness and the state of affairs both within her marriage and in the collective. These circumstances are slowly unveiled as the couple begin to explore the dynamics of their relationship in the hands of Dr Harry Hyman. Dr Hyman is a physician who believes that Sylvia's paralysis is hysterical and a direct result of something deeply repressed in her unconscious. He becomes the minion of her psyche, as he gently probes into the condition of the couple's marriage and very slowly uncovers a sad truth – they have not 'had relations' for twenty years! Philip does not admit to this, in fact, the first lie in the play is his response to the doctor's query about their intimate married life, '. . . maybe twice, three times a week.' The having of 'relations' is significant as the immediate, marital, 'cause' of Sylvia's deep unhappiness, but it is the connection Hyman makes between her symptoms and the horror which is beginning to develop in Germany which is more intriguing.

He asks Philip when her symptoms began, and Philip replies, 'I tell you, looking back I wonder if something happened when they started putting all the pictures in the paper. About these Nazi carryings-on. I noticed she started . . . staring at them . . . in a very peculiar way. And . . . I don't know. It made her angry or something.' Philip does not sympathize with this at all; in fact he has denied his Jewishness to the point of being proud of being the only Jew in his company, and 'the only Jew ever to set foot on the deck' of his boss's yacht, and of the fact that their son was at West Point and was going to make a career in the army – a rare thing for a Jew to desire or to do, as Philip says: 'I wanted people to see that a Jew doesn't have to be a lawyer or a doctor or a businessman.' In fact, there is a conspiracy in the entire extended family to suppress knowledge of the events in Germany, and all try to get Sylvia to stop reading the papers! Philip becomes angry with her and insists that her paralysis is the direct result of a neurotic reading of the horrors in a country thousands of miles away, which 'has nothing to do with us'. Sylvia responds, 'But it's in the paper – they're smashing up the Jewish stores . . . should I not read the paper? The streets are covered in broken glass!'

There is so much pain between Sylvia and her husband that it simply cannot be acknowledged; she cannot bring herself to speak of her longing for love or her anger at Philip for being a hypocrite. In turn, Philip cannot acknowledge anything at all. His sexual impotence began when he realized that she wanted more than just him, when she wanted to go back to work after their son was born twenty years ago. Philip became inadequate in his own eyes, and thus diminished in hers. Theirs was a doomed marriage, one which would live, on the surface, but rot and corrupt from within. The outrage Sylvia could express *openly* was for the racial abomination which was being perpetrated upon her culture, but she could *not* express the rage she felt for 'wasting her life' – rather her legs wasted on behalf of her.

But, in degrees, through the agency of the doctor, their mutual sickness is exposed. Sylvia has always been elegant and controlled and contained, while Philip has always considered himself to be strong and successful. At one point, her sister realizes with a shock that Sylvia has been rather happier since her paralysis, as if she has been released from a prison – in fact she has traded the psychological paralysis for the physical one. It is so often easier to demonstrate our anger, frustration or depression through a physical symptom, for then it is taken seriously by others and we may be more readily accepted and 'cured'. She also transfers her frustration and pain across the Atlantic into Germany – she is conscious of the collective agony more than of her own personal pain, and totally unconscious of the collusion between the two.

Dr Hyman wants to know why Sylvia is cut off from herself (her lower half dead), and in the end she is only freed when her husband himself becomes ill – he has a heart attack – and, through his broken heart, becomes self-realized, admits to her his fears of being Jewish, of the Germans, of his boss, of her own generous powers, and then collapses unconscious in the bed. And Sylvia rises from her wheelchair to go towards him. Freed.

So, as Dr Hyman says, people not only 'get sick in twos and threes', they get sick in the millions, as well. He is mystified and gripped by Sylvia's illness – he begins to suspect that she is connected to something very deep in the culture: 'I get the feeling that she *knows* something, something that . . . It's like she's connected to some . . . some wire that goes half around the world, some truth that other people are blind to.'

Now Sylvia's hysteria was deeply rooted in three places – in her deeper self and personal unconscious, in her ancestral realm, and also in the social-collective unconscious. Her body became the battleground for her husband's denial of his origins and his weakness, their communal lack of intimacy, the marriage as a lie – as well as her mainline to her ancestral heritage and the collective sickness which would lead to the extermination of millions of Jews in eastern Europe.

Arthur Miller's play dramatizes the fact that we cannot view anything in our environment without a context of some sort. The context in which an individual develops is the family, and the development of the family is in the context of the culture, and the development of the culture is in the context of the *Zeitgeist*, and the *Zeitgeist* is cradled in the epoch and the epoch is located within a vast universal and planetary rhythm that we call the Great Year or Cosmic Time. Thus we have the hierarchy (see Figure 2, page 9):

1. The Individual
2. The Family
3. The Culture
4. The *Zeitgeist*
5. The Epoch
6. Cosmic Time

A scientific model like GST (General Systems Theory) has rigidities which individuals, families *and* astrology lack, so we will not find perfect absolutes; however, it is the closest psychological model I have seen to assist us in laying order to something about which there appears to be only a random pattern at best and total anarchy at worst. To follow on from GST: 'The character of the system transcends the sum of its components and their attributes and belongs to a higher order of abstraction.'[3] One way of putting this – using the play *Broken Glass* as an example – would be to say that 'the system' is Sylvia and Philip Gellman. Its character is complicated and has many aspects to it, but fundamentally it comprises a marriage built on a series of lies and small misdemeanours. Now, the 'components' – each of them individually – have been living each in their *own* lie and each of them has created a careful container for their isolation from each other. As time and fate would have it, the repressed anger, hurt and fear erupted in tandem with a collective psychopathology. This resulted in a crack in their small system – Sylvia's symptoms were the manifestation of the collective illness. The '*sum* of their components' could be seen as the fraudulent portrayal of each of their deep inner needs, their individual truths being subordinated by a socio-cultural standard. Finally, the 'higher order of abstraction' is being played out in Hitler's Germany.

Astrologically, for example, it would be valid, but limited, to say that a man had Mars in Scorpio without any further elaboration. However, by saying that Mars in Scorpio was in square to Saturn – that then places Mars in a *locus* more specific, as well as adding another dimension to him. And, further, if we knew that the person's father had natal Mars in Taurus opposite Saturn in Scorpio, and that his *own* son had Mars in Capricorn, we would be in a much better place by having found a greater context for the single 'Mars is in Scorpio'. So we need to see a planet not only in a place but also placed in a larger context! We would be seeing a system composed of Mars, Saturn, Scorpio and Capricorn.

So, if we are seeing Mars in Scorpio as a significant *individual* trait, we would want to examine it within a greater context in the man's own chart and, furthermore, in the context of the family charts – as a *collective* trait. Mars in Scorpio is significant for the man in question, but the fact that it is involved with a family pattern of Saturnian Mars is even more revealing and helpful in understanding how his own Mars in Scorpio square Saturn works. We then have a place for Mars in Scorpio both in the individual's psyche and within the collective psyche of the family. The man inherited *his* hard angle Mars/Saturn relationship from his father, and has passed it on to *his son* in a variation on a theme – Mars in Capricorn. As if the youngest member of the paternal line has absorbed the Mars/Saturn square of his father and the Mars/Saturn opposition of his grandfather, putting the planet Mars in the sign of Saturn.

Family systems therapy finds the same flaw in GST that the astrologer might, as it states that it is fine as a model of inanimate things; however, it does not take into account growth, change and creativity which occur in social/people-orientated systems. The above example shows how complex planets and sign and angle combinations can become when woven into thematic patterns. There was a Mars/Saturn hard angle pattern with a Scorpio/Capricorn sign flavour – all of which does add up to a very hard-working, rather self-denying, harshly critical sense of drive and self-direction. The male patterns in the family might well have come out of very difficult origins where the men were not encouraged, in fact, were denied access to play, fun, passion or healthy time-wasting. The Mars in Capricorn youngest of the three generations will likely find his chore somewhat easier if only because his own Mars was unencumbered by Saturn at all and had also become integrated into the expression of the sign Capricorn . . . hard-working, with result-oriented drive, hence potentially quite a successful young man.

We will find that there are many such relatives in astrology – that is, things relative to other things – therefore, it is a highly volatile situation, making *both* the focus of the family *and* its regulating force a variable point, all depending upon the context within which it is operating at a given time.

WHAT HOLDS THE FAMILY SYSTEM TOGETHER?

Astrology is dynamic, and thus always in motion, just like people. Families are even more complex and dramatically in motion, so the family has to be seen as a moving system. How on earth can this rolling, listing, mobile unit hold together with so many variables in it called people? There are two main functions which hold anything together:

1. A centre, and
2. A circumference.

As astrologers, we have a good symbol for this image: the symbol of the Sun, which is a circle with a dot in the centre. The horoscope itself is an ex-cellent symbol of a system, with the earth at its centre and the zodiac wheel as its circumference, and the luminaries and planets arrayed around it. A family as a system has a centre and a circumference as well. The centre – if we think of it as the 'thing that holds' – in systems theory is called the 'homeostatic principle', literally, 'standing firm in the same way'. The cir-cumference would be the boundary of the family. *So it is held together by its homeostasis and it is contained by its boundary*. Fairly simple. Now, however, how does this work? Family systems as a theoretical technique works, but it works even better with the visuals and the images of astrology and planet-ary patterns and horoscopes.

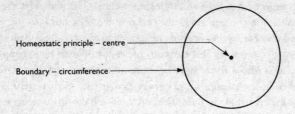

Homeostatic principle – centre

Boundary – circumference

A vital means of determining a system's identity is its boundary, along with its rules, its patterns of behaviour and its homeostatic (stay-the-same) principle. When we talk about ourselves or discuss another individual we always tend to describe within some kind of context, boundary or defining characteristic. We like to know where we, and others, 'begin' and 'end'. So the persona and the ego of the individual are part of his or her definition and the same goes for a group and, in this particular instance, the family. We need to define, first and foremost, the boundaries of the family system, then its interior focus and, finally, the principle which holds it together.

This homeostatic principle in family dynamics is powerful. An example of how it might work would be thus: a family has been struck by crisis just as everything seemed to be working out really well for all of them. However, everything had reached a time of major shift, where everyone in the family had to experience quantum changes. The three children were virtually out of the house, in college, travelling, and on their own but for visits. The husband had happily retired and was pursuing his primary interests in painting and exploring the world, and the wife was able to concentrate fully on her career, which was promising. Everything seemed perfect. But the husband had a heart attack, and suddenly, nothing had changed. The old homeostatic principle kicked into action: a major shift in the family dynamic was *just* about to become a new norm, when the heart attack occurred, and at first everything was thrown into chaos and then right back into an old pattern, but with a vast difference. The children became insecure and spent more time wandering in and out of the home, the wife was not able to get on happily with her own life, and the husband was unable to pursue his pastimes as he had just begun to do.

The situation appeared very much as it had been before the changes were established, but it was devolved from before. It was a backslide, no one was moving forward. Everyone was forced back into old positions, but with anxiety and anger underlying it all. After about seven or eight months, the husband healed, the children slowly began to move back out into the world again, and the wife felt better about reclaiming her new, independent status. It took a lot of work for this family to break out of their tight, happy nuclear situation into a freer, more open, more expansive system. Someone almost died in the attempt for necessary change, and in that event lay the potential for everything to collapse in on itself and devolve, leaving no options for growth *or* for everything to change drastically, allowing a greater circumference (boundary) for the family to exist within.

However, this is a happy story in that the conscious efforts on the part of each of the members created a new form of homeostasis, one based on a looser structure to their family system. So the family had to expand its boundaries and alter its central focus. Something deep and primal was afraid to change, and thus an 'event' was required by the deeper self of the collective psyche. The focus was and remains love and caring, but that love and caring no longer required such daily physical closeness and interdependence. The type of love and caring needed to change, and the parameters of the entire family had to alter to accommodate that necessary shift. It is not at all unusual for a crisis to precipitate a change which is positive in its outcome. Ideally, we could all anticipate such necessary changes, and say, 'Oh, this family is growing beyond the confines of its boundary and thus we all must now move on.' However, this is not the most common scenario; usually we need events, indicators and impetus to make it through a large transition, even one as apparently normal as growing up, changing status and moving on in the course of a natural life-span. This is the mystery of the family. (See Chapter 11, page 195.)

When we are examining horoscopes for family themes we need to remember that a theme is precisely that – an expression of a core tone in myriad ways. We have astrological themes and our shorthand allows us to use richly expressive terms such as Plutonian, Uranian, Martian and so on. In the family system we might find those themes becoming more elaborate, such as Sun/Saturn, Moon/Pluto, Moon/Venus, etc. The possibility of expression of a theme is as great as there are individuals to experience and relate that essential tone or theme.

US FOUR AND NO MORE

A family is a container. It holds within it all its individual members and it is within that frame that we have all developed our natures to the best of our abilities. That a family cannot *possibly* hold within it all the requirements of each individual's needs is a given, which is why families undergo change – just like people do. That this has been turned into a pathology is a great contributing factor to the spectacular breakdown of the family system in these times. The growth of the 'individual' has been so rapid, so important and so terribly indiscriminate that the blind seeking of 'self' and individuality has shattered the homeostasis of the collective's idea of 'the family'.

The family structure has been so radically altered in the last forty years that it can no longer be described as 'us four and no more' – mother, father, daughter, son. Naturally all these relationships still exist, but in so many varieties of ways and in such unique individual configurations that we have had to redefine the family as an entity. Generally we still think of our mums, dads, brothers, sisters, grandparents, etc. as our 'family', but just how are those people configured together compared to the Norman Rockwell vision of the post-war family? Not around the hearth-fire, that is evident. Combining the times, the culture, the global situation, and the social system, the family has literally been decimated and now is restructuring itself based on new, if shaky, values.

When an entire philosophy or system of belief loses its capacity to stand the same, then a form of anarchy has been loosed. In the words of W. B. Yeats:

> Turning and turning in the widening gyre
> The falcon cannot hear the falconer;
> Things fall apart; the centre cannot hold;
> Mere anarchy is loosed upon the world . . .[4]

In the 1950s the nuclear family reached its glamorous apex, and became so authoritative and influential a framework and focal point that it polarized in the extreme. The result of that intense polarization was its inward collapse and resultant 'flip' into its opposite extreme! Jung called this natural phenomenon 'enatiodromia' – when psychic energy becomes imbalanced and excessive, it literally becomes its opposite form. From the 1960s and the aspects in the heavens at the time – marked especially by the Uranus-Pluto conjunction opposed by Saturn – the cult of the family flipped to become the cult of the individual. The degree to which this has become a pathology in itself is portrayed by the alienation and general *Angst* of the now totally independent, non-tribal or family-oriented individual in a disintegrating so-ciety – society being the larger mirror of the family itself (the 'supra-structure').

The Pluto in Leo generation was the turning point (1940–54), and their collective demand for individual ascendancy was so urgent that it turned its back *en masse* on the old values of tradition – we are to feel that repercussion for many a decade still. The extremity of the rebellion against being a member of anything except a member of one, ironically, has brought one bonus to us as astrologers – it has brought natal astrology into its highest form. For millennia natal astrology has languished in the ancient and often conflicting and strangely inaccurate rules for horoscope interpretation, but in recent decades it has become very close to a fine art. None of the ancient interpretations on natal horoscopes work very well when we examine them in the context of a modern person – but maybe in another 1,000 years our smug interpretative success will be as laughable to future astrologers as Manilius, Dorotheus or Ptolemy's is to us today![1] However, that is another consideration.

Families can no longer be stereotyped by gender, either. The advent of freedom of sexuality and the increasing freedom of men and women to become who they really feel they are has produced a unique situation: that of the gay family. There are many people who form untraditional families based on same-sex parents and perfectly 'normal' children. Gay men and women *do* have children, they do raise those children with their same-sex partners and the children I have met whose parents loved them enough to be honest have become admirable young people. One of my gay male friends, whose wife, whom he married twenty-six years ago, is a lesbian, has a son by her. The boy lived with his mother and father – who had their own lives but lived together – for the first three or four years of his life, then the parents lived apart, sharing time, responsibility and love for their son. The boy is now a man, married; he loves both parents and has no more and no fewer problems than any other person I have met. Oh, there *was* a time when he was an adolescent that he asked his father not to wear his earring when he went to see the teachers at his school on parents' day, but then, what adolescent is not paralysed with embarrassment at even having parents at all?

So we can have many varieties of configurations in our families: we can have mum and her girlfriend, dad and his male lover, we can have mum and dad, we can have dad and his second wife, we can have just one parent and a series of parental figures through friends or extended families – anything goes, it all works and it is all families. Keeping in mind the multitude of possibilities as well as the mobility and fluidity of family structures, let's look at some definitions within family-based relationships.

WHAT IS THE PURPOSE OF A FAMILY?

First the young, like vines, climb up the dull supports of their elders who feel their fingers on them, soft and tender; then the old climb down the lovely supporting bodies of the young into their proper deaths.[6]

(Lawrence Durrell, *The Alexandria Quartet*)

We have looked at the energy that holds a family group in place – its mysterious central focus, the homeostatic principle, and the container in which it is safe and defined, its boundaries – but what are the main functions of a family?

The role of a family as a system should serve two primary functions:

1. To protect the young (and the individuals in it) from the outside world, and

2. To prepare the young (and the individuals in it) for the outside world.

Because information and communication are vital to the life of any organic whole, whether that be a person or a group, it is significant how people use communication to relate. An important part of communicating is defining the subject and the content which a person or a group feels is important to them. Because of that, a boundary system is unconsciously established in a family group which defines the kind of information or ideas which are received or generated by the family. The information boundary allows ideas, experiences, influences and energy to flow into the family group as a collective unit. The boundary also is the definition of the inner life of the family, and how much, or often, or necessary it is for the family to extend itself out into the community at large. Therefore, the boundaries have to do with how much transference of information is allowed to exit and enter the family at any time. Boundaries within the family itself also determine how open the communication lines are between the individuals within the family, as well as between the family and the community at large.

Therefore, boundaries really exist to allow just exactly what can and cannot be said or done without transgressing tacit or explicit rules of the people involved in the particular system. If this seems complicated, just think about your own life and how it interfaces with the lives of those around you.

The point of connection between two people is the interface of their being – the interface is where much of the open, explicit communication takes place, in the form of talking and so on. This interface is magical. The astrological interface between two (or more) people forms the composite horoscope, which shows the planetary and horoscopic midpoint of two people's energies and how they combine to form a 'third entity' between two people. Although the source of this talking-communication clearly originates in a deeper or higher place within the individuals involved, it must never be devalued because of its form – explicit communication is always loaded with deeper implications and has all the potential to be restructured to create better, more open channels between the deeper or higher place, and the surface of relating. We might not be able readily to access our unconscious intent, but we can create better awareness of what we consciously do, and thus make communication more straightforward, saying what we *really* mean. Hence the difficulties in maintaining a constant flow of receptivity and communication-links between individuals – and think of how complex this becomes when there is the multiple interface between you and all your family members!

So the interface *is terribly* important because though it appears firm temporally, it is in fact very porous and protean. We all know that mixed messages can be sent on the surface, while seething or hidden emotions are lurking under the veneer of social artifice. Conversely, we also carry on amusing forms of surface or 'interface' communication when we all know what is really being said. The intimacy levels of some relationships do not require tiresome, long-winded verbal rationalizations! So superficial communication can also be an indication of the depth of intimacy between people in families. The communion between people who are intimately bound, emotionally or viscerally, can be magical and tricksterish in its effects.

The way a family communicates itself to the community at large, and how much or little it allows the collective community to reach into it to influence it, are indications about the boundaries of the family. In other words, how much or how little feedback from the community is allowed to enter the family itself shows us what kind of boundaries exist around it.

For example, there were two types suggested by W. Jordan: 'open' and 'closed' – respectively, the centrifugal family and the integrative family,[7] while Salvadore Minuchin termed them respectively the disengaged and the enmeshed family.[8] These two broad family types were further calibrated to say, basically, that the more extreme ends of the types were distinctly pathological and the mid-range of the extremes fairly normal. If, for example, we put the extremes of either at 1 and 10, then both ends of the scale would be dysfunctional but 5 would be functional. As we shall see, the relativity of the entire concept of systems is vitally important, and astrological imagery further develops our understanding of the type of constant we have within the relative homeostasis that exists within the family and in each of the individuals in that family.

In other words, the concepts of closed-ness and openness can be seen as *relative* in the context of family and other social systems, and one can imagine a continuum moving from the relatively open family system, engaged in a high degree of communication with its supra-system (the community, the extended family, etc.) and between its sub-systems (individual members and sub-groupings); to the relatively closed family system engaged in minimal interchange with *either* its supra-system or with its sub-systems.[9]

Astrologically the extreme disengaged family is highly Uranian in character, and the other extreme, the enmeshed family, is Neptunian.[10]

Within both types of families, disengaged and enmeshed, Uranian-type and Neptunian-type, are the two primary functions of families: to protect and prepare. Each family type, disengaged *and* enmeshed, has unique ways of performing these functions – none or neither of which is good or bad, better or worse. Now, protection and preparation should both be interactive and collude entirely to be truly effective. A well-protected child is a well-prepared child and vice versa. However, we still see splits: the sending of mixed messages and other complex difficulties in the network of communications which can confuse the two mutually dependent intentions of *preparation* and *protection*.

Therefore, a vital indicator to a system's adequacy and working is its boundary. As mentioned, the GST for families has identified two main boundary-types for families: a 'closed' system and an 'open' system. First, a boundary is something arbitrary which determines what gets in and what passes out of a stated place. In a family, there is a primary boundary, that which identifies and distinguishes the family from other families. Second, there is another set of boundaries that are effective within the family itself – those that exist between sets of members or between individual members. A family-system boundary does, by and large, identify how the individuals will be able to maintain or change their own innate type of boundaries as they grow and change.

I. PROTECTION

Protection is a way of reinforcing inner structures and keeping the world at bay. Protection is the anglicized version of the Latin word *protegere*, which means literally 'to cover in front'. The direct transliterated word we still have today is protégé, which ultimately suggests that children are protégés (or protégées) of their parents! A protégé is one whose welfare, training and future are promoted by an influential person. Who more influential in a young person's life than a parent! Alice Miller has made a career on the disastrous effects of 'poisonous pedagogy' in Black Forest mentality in families, and this cannot be discounted, so it is absolutely essential that parents recognize their role as teacher, protector and pedagogue to their children.[11] So protection incorporates all levels of instruction and teachings, from the tacit (body language, facial expression, inner response mechanisms) to the gross (outer explicit expressions of beliefs, educational advantages, reading materials, access to social realms beyond its own boundaries, and so on). If there are vast schisms between spoken and unspoken forms of communicating messages, then there is a great potential for creating a split in the psyche of the child.

To protect is to foster and nurture something for the future. Clearly, for a parent, this often means drawing on his or her own past experience, including deeply unconscious patterns which have been transmitted down the family line, and projecting them into the yet-to-be future and creating whole lifestyles based on this *a priori* 'knowledge'. There can be a lot of mistaken protective devices established around the self, the child and the family if this process of protection is not reassessed frequently.

Protection means giving a child inner resources with which to care for him or herself. Feelings of self-worth, uniqueness, beauty, creativity – all these are protective devices. Those feelings foster security and self-centredness in a positive way. An adult who was approved of as a child has been protected in a very positive way. He or she is less likely to manifest hard aspects in the horoscope in deadly, destructive ways, but more likely to work with them in more positive ways. Hard charts do not always a monster make! A child who has not been injected with its parents' fears or indoctrinated with their attitudes has been protected from its own parents! As an adult, he has to spend that much less time off-loading the prejudices of his parents. There is no way that a child will adopt the values of a parent *in toto*; it is *never* the case. The child might use, enjoy or employ received values because they are akin to what he or she feels right about, but ultimately it will be their own choice.

So protection has a lot to do with not invading a child or young adult and not annexing them as if they were allied forces in a war against the rest of the world! It means discovering what the developing child's weaknesses are, and trying to give them resources with which to work around and with those vulnerable spots in the psyche. Too often parents collude unconsciously with the soft spots in their children and play into them. This is inevitable to some degree, because that is the mystery of family relationships; however, the degree to which we can become conscious of this is the degree to which we can work with the fate which befalls us.

I have always thought it rather weird that neither of my children inherited my once pathological fear of dogs – indeed, one has and loves a huge black dog. When they were small, I would avoid entire streets because some innocent spaniel sat thumping its tail on the porch. Perhaps that is because dogs are really not the issue, but are rather a symptom of something much deeper. Indeed, my children have definitely inherited other, more profound aspects – both characteristically and astrologically – with which they must struggle. These deeper issues have come down the family line on both sides, to settle in them, and I am sure they will be passed on to be further refined, on and on. This causes me both wonder and pain.

If a family has experienced holocaustic events in its history, then clearly these defences will be transferred down the line even if they are no longer currently needed. This feeling is profoundly manifest in the Jewish community, where the parents never spoke of the horrors they experienced during the European Nazi regime, yet the guilt and anxiety is experienced by their children, who are literally 'second-generation holocaust victims'. We inadvertently pass on our fears and complexes to our children without even realizing it – indeed, unrealized or unresolved psychological issues in the

adult are automatically transferred into the children to cope with and resolve. This is why the most extreme and the most difficult aspects in charts
seem to be the ones we most frequently see as problems in families. This is
not because the astrologer enjoys and only focuses on the nasty bits! Unfortunately, it is quite true that it is the most awkward, the most pathological
and the most horrible that is passed on for further purging or at least, water-
ing down! For instance, if we see such things as Moon/Pluto at the IC we
can be sure that there lies an unresolved fear of being swallowed, or be-
trayed or abandoned by the one person we need the most – and we can also
be sure that this is a long, long story, one which all the family knows about,
but particularly the mother.

If we aren't capable of opening up the dark room in the psyche, we then
rob the child of his or her freedom of choice – either to act on the problem
at hand, or to stuff it back down to be carried around for a lifetime, or
passed on, yet again, into their own children. By this we perpetrate dynastic
'pollution' and hard things that might, in fact, be ready for purgation in the
current generation! It is therefore, essential that all protective action towards children be examined by the protector *for its necessity*.

A child might be over-protected by its mother or father out of the parent's *own* fear and insecurity, which contrarily leaves the child very badly
protected – he or she might rebel from the constant watching or controlling
and endanger itself through rebelling. One woman who has five planets in
Libra expressed terror of 'losing' her son – she subsequently smothered
him and virtually turned him into her surrogate lover and thus has not protected her son at all! She kept the boy in her bed at night, allowed him to
fondle her breasts whenever he wanted, even in public, did not fully toilet-
train him until he was seven years old, anticipated his every need – in short,
keeping him in the infantile state as long as she possibly could! The likelihood of this boy eventually fleeing his mother's constant ministering at
some turning-point stage in his or her life is very high. Her own worst fear
is losing him, and she might just be creating that eventuality.

Her own Moon *exactly* semi-square Saturn shows her to tend towards
melancholy and brooding, and her emotions are tinged with fear and isolation, which can translate into cold control. Having such an impoverished
Moon does not say much about being a 'good mother', indeed, speaks of a
real limit to her generosity of feeling. Rather than admit her exasperation
with the constant aspect of motherhood, this woman claims mothering to
be her sole occupation, though she is well educated! Moon/Saturn can

make mothering a lot of work, and with the Moon in Sagittarius, this sounds more like management and control than maternal love and concern for the child. It also alludes to feelings of guilt about her own need for independence. Moon/Saturn contacts seem to indicate that there are real fears of abandonment (also there are no water planetary placements in the chart, but for the Scorpio ascendant), hence her overcompensation in the 'mothering' role with undue emotional dependency-manipulation of the child.

Also, her natal Sun is *completely* without aspect, so she has no 'maleness', no solarism of her own, no real direction, and has used other people's solarism – husband, women friends, relatives – to give her what she needs materially and psychically. And, once she has benefited, she finds their weakest point and is repulsed by that and rejects them, finding some reason in their behaviour to get rid of them. The problem with *her* Sun is that it sits exactly on her son's Mercury/Saturn midpoint, illuminating his innate point of 'inhibited communication' and, indeed, he is afraid to do anything without her approval or without acknowledging her existence somehow. However, his own natal Sun in the tenth house is opposite to Saturn/Uranus in the fourth, while his Moon in the eighth is square Mars and it is likely that his adolescence (Saturn opposition while conjoining his natal Sun) will produce a wrench from his mother towards his own solar path, even if it means doing it abruptly and rebelliously. One hopes this will not be necessary, but if so, then it will be. As he grows up, he will not relish constant protection/invasion from his mother with all that male energy around his horoscope!

Parents can attempt to protect a child from something that is *not* going to happen, but has happened to the parent in the past. This creates confusion and worry in the child. For example, if a woman was sexually abused, often she will marry an abuser, or be an abuser in some way herself. This may not always be the case, but she can treat her children as if they are about to be abused, in which case the child then might marry an abuser, having been sensitized to protect herself from what the mother might feel is inevitable. In this way, the family myth survives, though it has skipped a generation. How can we purge ourselves of these deep grooves in our psyches?

Finding ways to protect are essential but, more importantly, finding out whom we are protecting is crucial! For are parents protecting themselves or their children? In days and years to come, we will need to protect the young with information because the old way of nuclear family is virtually gone. Young people are already more inclined to attract around them 'tribal' families, familiars, and extended social families. This expands the nuclear family out into the global or tribal family, and actually enhances the relationships that many children have with their parents and siblings. Protection involves teaching a child to care for him or herself and the parent needs to allow – as much as is safely possible – the child to unfold in the way he or she is inherently patterned to do.

2. PREPARATION

Preparation is getting things ready for the future, envisioning imminent needs and assembling tools, tricks, skills, devices and attitudes that will aid in the movement forward into an unknown eventuality. It is a word oriented towards the outside world, preparing for the world outside, whereas protection is more oriented to the inner world, protecting the interior, as we read above. Being prepared means anticipating possible future events, experiences, activities and so on, and getting ready for them.

The word 'prepare' comes directly to us from the Latin *praeparare*, to make ready beforehand. In this way we anticipate what our children need and set about putting things in order before they have happened. One can see the danger in this already! Very often preparation comes in the form of teachings that are outmoded, which have been passed down through the family by dynastic themes. These things that are to prepare us for the unknown future can become obsolete before they are even useful – if they ever were to be useful, that is!

If we wish truly to allow our children to 'be ready beforehand', they must need skills which are fairly intangible, indeed they need skills we do not even know about! Therefore, they must be taught to listen to a teacher who knows what the destiny of the child is – and that is not the parent, nor is it any one particular individual. The true knowledge of the future of one's self is the Self, itself. This is a hard one for parents to prepare anyone for. Children are usually reared in atmospheres which anticipate what will happen to them in the world if such-and-such is or is not done, or if so-and-so is this or that way. Parents usually anticipate the world's impact on their child based upon their own historical and dynastic experience. This may not at *all* jive with the individual destiny of the child. The individual destiny of the child will involve working through the preparations of the parents' and its own dynastic lineage for its survival, but it needs to discover its own weaknesses and vulnerabilities, skills and gifts also, in order to be much better prepared.

This means that a certain amount of preparation must be done by the child and the parents must back off and contain their anxiety in order not to transfer it into the child, who will be ill prepared indeed for his or her own path. If we are prepared to follow our mother's path, for example, we are bound to stumble and fall. However, if our mother helped us prepare for our path, we are doubly blessed. How can we be sure that we are preparing our children and not ourselves? By looking closely at the inherited aspects. Not all charts of family members are as loaded as others. Some family members do get off more lightly, they seem not to be carrying the weight of the family, but there is usually one who is doing it for everyone else.

A man who was not acknowledged by his own father will not have been taught how to relate to his own son and will pass on the theme of the absent father. He prepares his son for the same fate he had. This is a theme which can be played many ways. The 'absent father' is, on the one hand, archetypal and likely to be quite positive, for the father is not supposed to be hanging around the house all day, knitting and doing the laundry; however, the extreme of the abandoning father, the rejecting father, the 'strong-silent' father is deplorable. The role-changes and societal changes have created quite a spectrum of possibility for men these days. Men now have the option of working at home, or becoming the main parent in the home if they can or wish, or they can go out to work if that is the way for them to find their living. There are no models any more. The days of the father-master, son-apprentice ended with the sighting of Uranus (Industrial Revolution, mid-1700s), and the male-to-male rite of passage is much more subtle now and thus has raised some problems for men and their sons. The poet Robert Bly feels that our entire Western society lacks the kind of male-to-male mentoring which many of today's men have missed in their lives, and he says we must see that as a collective breakdown in protection or fostering. The mentorship between same-sex parents is paramount, but it has become increasingly difficult for men to find common ground with sons. It seems that men now must pass on a more feeling-tone relationship to their sons, and be more tangible and feel that they have contributed to their well-being.

Women have bonds that can never be broken – for better or worse! Nature has provided an innate system of a rite of passage which inextricably links a woman to her female children and back to her own mother.

Women, being of the earth, tend to take much for granted in their relationships with each other, but rather than longing for closeness with mother, the young daughter needs to separate from her mother in order to grow. She must find herself distinct from her mother because she is so like her. One young woman, whose mother's Venus was exactly conjunct her Moon, found that she needed simply not to see her mother or be around her for a while when she reached her early twenties. This was not through lack of love or because they had a bad relationship – they did not have a bad relationship and the bond was strong and deep. However, it was time for the girl to become her own person, rather than someone's daughter. This is a difficult thing to articulate at the best of times; however, in this situation, it was a mutual experience, but generated by the daughter. Her mother was in a stage in her life when it was time to be the mother of a grown-up daughter, and since she had Venus square Saturn, her daughter did her a favour by 'promoting' her to the status of being a free woman, with a daughter with whom she might share an adult relationship.

ASTROLOGICAL MODELS OF OPEN
AND CLOSED FAMILY SYSTEMS

Below we explore the broad meaning of the open-system Uranian and closed-system Neptunian family with both extremes, the sublime and the pathological. How each of these systems tends to prepare and protect their family members is also discussed.

I. THE DISENGAGED FAMILY: URANUS
– AN OPEN SYSTEM

The first indication that a family system falls into the loosely defined Uranian type is that there are *no consistent themes*. There are no strong astrological patterns which are replicated over and over and over in myriad ways. The strongest of bonds will be through choice, not fate. It can produce some of the most frightened individuals and the most brave. A family of this nature seems to be able to create new patterns all the time. Their astrological maps and pictographs show a high degree of variation. If we were to do a *JigSaw* pattern on the group in question, it would show a variety of pictures. The strongest harmonic grouping would be the Sun/Moon/Venus/Mercury ties – all 'social' and trans-Saturnian planets will figure only periodically. They are not locked into a collective fate, except the fate of having to be different all the time, and finding family outside the family. In Toby's family (page 231), we see this kind of pattern.

There is a high regard for interaction in this system; the individual reigns supreme and is given much freedom to communicate his or her ideas and share with others received knowledge from outside the family. The family is generally highly integrated into the community and performs important functions in the collective around it. There is often a great emphasis on the extended family, where the importance of elders and grandchildren is paramount, even to the smaller unit of the immediate family.

The energy of a Uranian family is largely masculine-orientated. That is, extraverted, solar and highly energized. The focus is outward-bound and socially active, finding itself more happily identified within the larger framework of the collective, the community or the world at large. They tend towards a joyful competitiveness and more brisk activities and attitudes than restful or reclining ones. This does not mean that they are all male, but it does often mean that the pivotal parent was the father and that his energy permeated the entire family system and the patrilineal line is very strong. All the women would feed into this as well, but the archetypal energy is considerably masculine in tone, highly object-focused and achievement- and goal-motivated.

People who marry into the extreme Uranian family must be prepared to be *primus inter pares* – first among equals. There always seems to be a lot of 'space', a great deal of room for behaviour differences between members of the family. Much time can pass before there is a pressing need for the group to congregate, and they tend to relate to each other on a sporadic, but exciting and intense level.

There is frequently a family affinity with groups in the supra-structure that improve, change, organize, create and revolutionize something within the community. These kinds of organizations feed the constant need for stimulation and growth upon which the Uranian family thrives. The feedback loop for them is exciting, challenging and slightly threatening to the integrity of the whole.

The Uranian family system prepares its young members for the outside world by exposing them early to independence, encouraging the baby or child to play independently, to express its needs clearly and openly, to consider itself, no matter what age, as an equal and contributive member of the family.

As the children grow, they are usually expected to deal with their playground and teacher issues on their own – the parents of the child will not always go to the school to sort out the problems, but will encourage the child to do so himself. He may receive some advice but is encouraged, and sometimes forced, to make his own way through the problems he encounters.

The children are given an inordinate amount of freedom as adolescents. Depending on the consistency of the advice and early messages, the Uranian individuation process of the adolescent can be remarkably precocious, or dangerously libertine. If no real boundaries are drawn, they can be ill prepared for the consequences; however, in the relatively healthy atmosphere of freedom, a sensible child will choose a sensible option. Even if it is somewhat against the status quo, it can still be correct for that child in that system.

When it is time to flee the nest, they are encouraged to do so, often in a way which is supported financially or materially in some manner – allowing the young adult to go his or her own way, but without necessarily throwing them to the world at large. They are quietly shown out of the house and into the world, firmly, at the earliest possible convenience, and with the expectation that they will remain out in the world and re-create the relationships around them that replicate their own family background.

Uranian protection is provided in the form of family 'bravery' myths, stories which reinforce independent and heroic activity.

1. Positive, Integrated Aspects of the Uranian Family

The boundaries of the Uranian family are vast and moveable – they have great compassion for all and sundry, without allowing intense emotional invasion to occur. Their love of humanity extends globally; however, it is never allowed truly to penetrate the intimacy of the immediate family. Should there be an emergency within the family, all doors to and from the family close firmly and they focus intensely on the crisis, keeping their pain within the confines of their circle.

The individual person in the system is allowed his or her eccentricities, indeed, these are fostered and encouraged, for the prime belief is that it all only adds to family interests. There is generally a great deal of respect for each person in the family, and only when one of them becomes completely deranged is there any recognition of a serious problem.

All members of the family are urged to explore ideas, behaviours, beliefs, etc., which enrich them as individuals and add to the vast accumulation of experiences which the family prides itself on encompassing. The family system needs constant input and challenge and interchange between themselves and the community at large in order not to turn on itself and begin to rebel within. Ideally, this interaction and encouragement from within the family results in real leadership qualities, where it is necessary to be one step removed from the emotional content of life situations, yet have the vision and the humanity to work for the collective cause.

2. Negative Disengaged Uranianism in the Family

There is such a high regard for freedom and space that a more feeling type of person, who wants more contact, touch, talk or relating, can feel abandoned, rejected and alone. The lack of empathetic response can result in alienation of individual members, and extreme reactions to this can be acted out in society in aberrant ways. Contrary to the extremes of the Neptunian, the Uranian pathology is often a radical or rebellious action which takes the form of antisocial behaviour which affects others or the community at large.

If the family does not impose any boundaries on the child then he or she will be likely to find it very difficult to mature towards a strong sense of his or her identity, seeking out insubstantial and weak connections to the world. When children of these families are 'treated as adults', they never grow up, because their childhood remains alive inside. They then appear to others as irresponsible, incapable of constancy, unreliable and 'flaky'. Their capacity to harness their talents can evade them, as they never received the kind of attention which fosters this – focused, one-to-one parental guidance.

On the other hand, if an individual in the Uranian family has not been able to find a unique way of expressing himself or herself that is as exciting, original or adventurous as the others, he or she may find dramatic ways of catching their attention – such as eating disorders, bipolar emotions, exotic rebellion and outrageous activities, hyper-antisocial behaviour, unorthodox political views which are against the family's values, and working hard at under-achieving. Some extreme pathologies are mania, obsessive-compulsive disorders, psychopathy, loathing of physical contact, claustro-phobia and cruel coldness.

The extreme Uranian family ill prepares the individual for relationships, for they feel trapped and smothered by intimacy. Too much freedom, not enough communal discipline and very little in the way of family 'opinions' is as disastrous for the adult in a relationship as is the Neptunian extreme of romance and the perfect love. If anything, the Uranian extreme leads to alienation and frantic attempts at individuality at the cost of intimacy and feeling relaxed in the company of one other. Frequently, Uranian families produce their opposites, as well, where the lonely member of the dis-engaged family longs for the fusion and boundary-less relationships of the Neptunian variety, and will create the safe place in his or her own nuclear family. The creation of opposites within the family is nature's way of bal-ancing a situation which begins to lose its equilibrium.

Thus, relationships can form peculiar patterns for graduates from Ura-nian families – there is often a dependence on someone who is very needy and from whom they must separate themselves as much and as often as possible. This appears to reinforce their 'individuality', but in fact can simply be an excuse for being incapable of engaging their feelings when others need something from them. Because the interaction in the family system was one of autonomy, and that love was dependent upon being as independent and emotionally unengaged as possible, it makes perfect sense that love means distance and unavailability.

2. THE ENMESHED FAMILY
– NEPTUNE: A CLOSED SYSTEM

The single most outstanding characteristic of a Neptunian-type family is its adherence to patterns. They are consistent – there are powerful repeat themes that run throughout the family line. Always they can be identified through sign, planet, modal, elemental or aspectual patterns. There will be an unbroken line of characteristics passed down, across and lying within small nuclear groups that are reflected in the greater, extended family as well as down the dynastic lines.

In the Appendix (page 376) I have shown the *JigSaw* computerized graphs of the Kennedy family. This is a prime example of an enmeshed family. All their patterns feed into each other. There is a very close segment in the zodiac in which all members fit – out of 360° there are about 15° in there where dominant signs of the group fall. All the elemental weights are balanced, and so are the modes. They all fit into a fifth harmonic pattern with Saturn/Pluto as being the sensitive points. They groove together, they are not distinct from each other, but feed back into each other and the family is a unit. They even attract those who will keep the 'balance'. This is a feedback loop.

There is little need for vocal interaction in this type of family . . . all is assumed, and frequently very accurately. All members are so familiar with each other's interior world that they speak in metaphor and hear in a secret code, understanding by feeling and intuition what the other or what the whole needs. Independent thinking is not considered a positive feature, unless it is towards the whole of the family's well-being.

Though there is a broadly based feminine archetype that underlies the Neptunian family, it is not reserved for women only. However, very often the mother *is* the most significant member of the parent-pair, whether that be through her dominance or her vulnerability, which keeps everyone in touch with her feelings on a constant basis. There is a considerable emotional concern for others and the subjective tone is very high. It is primarily an introverted family in that the system encourages focus on the more subjective issues of the inner life, and discourages extraverted focus on things that take members 'away' from the family matrix.

If there is a crisis they withdraw even more into their collective (these are attributes shared by both extremes, by the way, but experienced very differently), and no one might ever know that there has been a death, a divorce or a breakdown in the family structure. They suffer in silence and rarely use the suffering to create a new system, but adapt well into the existing circumstances, often allowing the sadness or crises to reinforce a sacrificial affect in the home.

The family is *so* self-reliant that it needs no input from outside, and usually finds no need to contribute in any major way to the community at large, but if there is interaction, it will be likely to be in a well-established and conformist group. Their relationship with the supra-system is usually one that is silent and without overt demonstration. Very often there is an affiliation with organizations which serve, heal, spiritualize, maintain, preserve and protect existing arrangements in the supra-structure. These organizations, in turn, protect, serve and maintain the family's inner belief – that they don't need anyone else or anything new to disrupt the peaceful stasis of

their nucleus. The feedback loop for them is nourishing, reassuring, soothing and secure, which reinforces their need for introversion and secrecy
while still allowing them to take part in extramural activities – minimal as
that may be.

1. Positive, Integrated Aspects of the Neptunian Family

The warm, safe, emotionally rich atmosphere of a relatively healthy
Neptunian family is palpable. There are virtually no secrets, no need to
hide anything – it would be virtually impossible anyway – and no desire
to be isolated or away from the matrix at all. There is a mood of deep
satisfaction, of inner harmony, and an almost smug complacency about the
group and within each individual. Rarely do they need anyone else except
possibly a spiritual or ideological focus such as a teacher or a priest-figure in
their sphere.

There is rarely a need to venture outside the immediate or extended
family for counsel or relationship, because each member has a mainline to
the others and the interactive psyche is powerful and tied in. There is something about the air of a Neptunian family which gives them an idealized,
exalted image to the outsider. Theirs is a special space, a *temenos* of love,
understanding and support. Should there be an inner crisis in the immediate
or extended family, there is rarely a need to move outside the family to find
help or support.

They all support each other unconditionally and find reasons to understand strange or alienating behaviour by any of their members. They protect
and nurture each other to the degree that a feeling of confidence and security is embedded in their psyche from an early age. This very often leads
members into helping professions or protective types of work where their
empathy and sympathy with the suffering or the victims of society can be
valued and exploited in positive ways. Because they need a tremendous
amount of feedback, working in a social system in which they play the
mediator or supplicant role is vastly superior to any leadership position in
their eyes.

Retreating from the fray has produced some of the most innovative and
creative artists and musicians – they may have appeared antisocial and alienated from the more hectic lives of others, they may even have been overly
dependent upon their family, or specifically on the mother, but somehow,
this introversion has been a channel for genius. A positive relationship with

the divine, with the harmonies of the universe, where inner contemplation coupled with discipline has resulted in inspired work, can be a result of a supportive Neptunian family system. However, because of the incestuous nature of Neptune and its protean morphology, it is a delicate balance between sanity and disengagement from reality. If the family feeds off its one productive and contributive member, the relationship needs of the 'artist' are going to suffer.

2. Negative Enmeshed Neptunianism in the Family

The lack of privacy in the Neptunian family is so complete that a more independent and adventurous person can feel smothered and claustrophobic. It is always just assumed that one feels a certain way – usually a projection of one's own feelings – and there are no boundaries between self and others. It is rather like mother saying, 'I am cold, so *you* must put on a sweater.' There is no room for individual needs, no need for anything new, and certainly if there is, it is not needed in *this* family.

There is little or no preparation for the outside world, but plenty of protection from it! Protection takes the form of cautionary tales, of dreadful stories of what happened in the past when someone ventured out beyond the garden gate, or reinforcement of stories about a mad aunt, or mysteries about family members who went away, or disengaged from the sticky environment, daring to free themselves. The members of this 'bad' family pattern are inevitably frightened of their own individuality and have no real sense of self which is independent from the nest they hatched into.

Members are ill prepared to cope with the hazards of identity. To state categorically who one is, one needs a reasonably strong ego. A fairly healthy solar attitude, which is masculine-based in its archetypal imagery, is frightening and alien. They are constantly in reference to someone else, often quoting another member of the family in whom they have placed their ultimate trust . . . this leads to adults who are always quoting a hero or a guru or some higher authority. Unlike the extreme Uranian family, there are many family 'opinions' to which the child adheres, and thus they can have difficulty in forming opinions of their own.

The constant feeling of being watched or invaded can result in self-destructive ways of escaping from the tentacles of the enmeshed situation. Usually the mode is through an escapist method – disappearing, drugs, emotional breakdown, masochism, feelings of moral or ethical decay, or simply apathy and depression. Psychological extremes are found in cases of multiple personalities, schizophrenia, autism, synaesthesia, substance abuse and extreme forms of religious mania. These pathological reactions to lack of boundaries or a constant invasion of individual limits and standards are not always biological, but always show up astrologically as family patterns which lead back generations.

If there has been no creative separation from the mother, or from the family as a matrix, then there is a constant longing repeatedly to re-create parental relationships. Unrequited love is not uncommon for individuals who have been bound by extreme Neptunian family systems – where they are never able to fulfil their fantasies of the perfect lover and as a result, have miserable affairs which end in disillusionment – for the god or goddess of their dreams has become a mere mortal. They may never have been prepared to deal with individual needs which always arise spontaneously in a relationship, and certainly they could not be protected from the reality of relationships yet to be lived!

NOTES

1. Sue Walrond-Skinner, *Family Therapy: The Treatment of Natural Systems*, Routledge & Kegan Paul, revised edition, 1976, page 12.

2. Arthur Miller, *Broken Glass*, Methuen, London, 1994.

3. ibid., page 12.

4. W. B. Yeats, 'The Second Coming', taken from the Papermac *Yeats*, Macmillan, 1982, page 210.

5. Refer to the case history of Charles, Prince of Wales, in Tamsyn Barton, *Ancient Astrology*, Routledge, London, 1994, Chapter 5.

6. Lawrence Durrell, *The Alexandria Quartet*, Faber and Faber, 1962, page 214.

7. W. Jordan, *The Social Worker in Family Situations*, Routledge & Kegan Paul, 1972.

8. S. Minuchin, *Families and Family Therapy*, Tavistock Publications, 1974.

9. Walrond-Skinner, *Family Therapy*, page 13.

10. See Chapter 9, "The Elemental Family", page 158 below, for another set of groupings.

11. *Passim* among the entire body of Alice Miller's works, which include *The Drama of The Gifted Child*, *For Your Own Good* (in which is a chapter entitled 'Poisonous Pedagogy'), *Thou Shall Not Be Aware*, etc.

3.
Family Patterns and
Family Trees

The personal stories in this book are all illustrative of working a family system – that is, lying within the natal chart of each protagonist in the story is the tale of the family. By incorporating into the stories the horoscopes of other members of the family, we are simply elaborating on the essence of the focal person by demonstrating how their natal planets, configurations or placements are expressed in a variety of ways through their family system. We can look at a natal chart and examine it for family dynamics only by eliminating all other levels and possible interpretations of each planet and assigning those planets roles as family indicators. In doing this we are applying a microscope to the organic whole and isolating the factors pertinent to the family. Rather than reducing the horoscope and its potential by doing this, we are in fact highlighting and selecting specific characters and their traits as they are enacted by one individual on behalf of many, all of whom are linked together in a mysterious bond.

Creating your astrological family tree can be simple or complex. The more complex it becomes in the astrological analysis, the deeper, more detailed and subtle family idiosyncrasies are discovered. In the story of Toby (page 231) and in the Appendix (page 376) are examples of the most detailed and complex analysis of family data, done on a computer and set into various patterns of emphasis such as harmonic, elemental, hemispheric, quadrant, sign and so on. The horoscope of family patterns need not be overly complex, although this computer program for family dynamics could keep you fascinated at your terminal for the rest of your life, if you wanted to explore the minutiae of aspects, patterns, harmonics and weights.[1]

However, this book concentrates on the more readily evident patterns, ones which are found by looking at natal charts, their progressions or directions, midpoints, composites, while focusing on planets, signs and types, and house placements. Within those parameters lies a wealth of valuable support.

UNCOVERING FAMILY PATTERNS

In astrology we have a unique system of recognizing patterns. There are many types of patterns and even more ways of those patterns manifesting. The array of possibility is infinitely variable. This is perhaps why it is virtually impossible to write a manual on the delineation of family horoscopes; however, it is quite possible to write on themes. Often we think of some specific horoscopic keys as they relate particularly to family matters: the fourth/tenth house axis; the fourth house itself; the third house for siblings, the ninth for grandparents, the Moon for the mother, Sun for the father, and so on. These *are* very much part of family issues, but they are insignificant alone in themselves, because often the conviction of natal astrology largely limits one's horoscope potential to one's own private, personal viewpoint. Indeed, one's own viewpoint is necessarily a composite of contributions from other sources, most fundamentally from one's immediate family and ancestral source as well as one's descendants.

The problem that often arises within the study of and work on individualized natal horoscopy is the loss of the individual's relationship to a larger framework. The fact is, we are not alone. At times we bemoan this and at others, we thank god! We are suffering from alienation in these modern times. During the course of the twentieth century we have moved from relatively little focus on natal astrology for the average person, to an intense preoccupation with individuals and natal horoscopes. There was a point in the development and history of astrology when the fate of the individual was dependent upon the horoscope of the king or leader. Now we have an elegant art in natal astrology. The spotlight on the individual in astrology has evolved in tandem with the collective view of psychology and its increasing tendency to assign roles and models to human behaviour. Although the age of personal psychological enlightenment has brought us to a threshold of self-understanding, it has also involved a lot of navel-gazing and self-analysis which now borders on an illness in itself. To cross the threshold of self-understanding to an extended vista requires a fresh look at the horoscope in relation to a greater picture.

The fact that there is a confusing array of schools of thought on self-improvement and psycho-spiritual theory has put a dreadful burden on each of us as individuals. I am not suggesting that we now wholly revert to ancient astrology and consult the chart of the president, prime minister or king/queen for our personal destiny and fate; however, I am suggesting that we take one step out of ourselves.

For instance, if I truly believed that I was all there was, the only thing happening relative to myself, and that my make-up was simply a hazard of Fate with no relationship or purpose with respect to others, I would indeed be doomed. So would we all. Doomed to a mysterious and seemingly very unfair situation in which 'I' alone would have to come to terms with and understand, solve and complete a life with no meaning outside my own existence. It is at this point that we might then say, 'Thank heaven for astrology and its wisdom, with its knowledge and mystery, for in it I might find a connecting link to something greater than myself!' That greater thing we are linked with is the cosmos and, more specific to astrology, the solar system. However, in a human way, we are linked with a constellation of people who are just as locked into their orbits around some central focus as the planets are around the Sun. This constellation is the family.

Usually it is at moments of crisis that a client wants to see family patterns. Normally, something has occurred which feels instinctive, but in fact has originated 'outside' of him or herself. For example, a woman might be planning a family, and might be concerned about her mothering patterns; she might have become increasingly aware of particular patterns arising within herself in tandem with the urge for a child. Another instance is when a marriage or relationship is beginning to gel and find a way of being – and that way of being appears very much like one's own parents' relationship. Or a man might find himself at a crossroads in life with respect to his career – his father might have experienced a similar crux in his life at the same age. He wants to know if it's all right to move forward, to travel beyond his own father's manor and progress beyond the father in his own life and career.

These are all typical themes which need to be addressed not only in individual but in collective ways – in other words, the complex of the family pattern is very often replicated in individuals in age-sequences that are family-based. It is common for significant turning points to be achieved at exactly the same age that one's own parent (most frequently the same-sex parent) underwent a change. For example, if your father died at the age of forty-nine, then at forty-nine you will undergo a major life-changing experience; if your mother had a late-born child, say at forty-three, after the other children were much older, it is likely that you will experience an important 'birth' at the same age she was then – there are many, many small and large patterns that we mysteriously fulfil.

Other impetuses for seeking out collective pictures of one's horoscope are more socially, externally based – that is, if one is experiencing repeated patterns in relationships within groups of people or in one-to-one relationships. If one sees that no matter how hard one tries, one is always in the leadership place, bottom rung, mothering-role, enabler or novice when it comes to work or career or personal relationships, it would serve to look at what the family pattern is and how it is one fits into that. If it is familiar, it is familial.

More often than not, we find ourselves in precisely the same place in society as we were in the family. This can be subtle or dramatic. In an extreme example, Carla was the only child of a very powerful couple, each of whom could have succeeded at anything they might have put their will to. Her father became a surgeon, supported through his education by Carla's equally capable mother. Both parents had the same Sun sign and same ascendant sign – each was Scorpio with Capricorn ascending! Carla, their daughter, was born with her natal Sun in a square to her parent's Sun-ruler *and* ascendant-ruler! That is, she has a Taurus Sun square a Saturn-Pluto (and Mars) conjunction – and she was born in May 1948 with the same Capricorn ascendant as both parents. When Carla was seven her parents divorced under extremely acrimonious circumstances and, as we might imagine from the astrology, she was literally torn between both parents, emotionally and physically. Because her Sun was in square (tense and split) to the Sun-ruler *and* chart-ruler of each parent while her ascendant (start in life, identity-in-family point) was identical to her parents, she was *both* parents inside. Essentially, Carla more readily incorporated the split between the parents as an inner dynamic because she was bound by such dynastic planetary contact.

As time progressed and the girl grew, both her parents remarried and had formed second families by the time she was twelve years old. Carla found herself on the outside looking in. Today, as an adult, she still has the feeling of being on the outside looking in, nose pressed against the window, peering in at the fantasy of the loving family of which she is not part. This is manifest in all aspects of her life – career, social, relational and emotional. It is partly very unique and creative and partly very lonely and antisocial. She fell between the cracks. Is this a pattern? Is this the way it is now and ever shall be? If not, then how do we shift the focus? If so, then how do we turn that into a creative option?

There are several ways showing how a pattern might reveal itself through astrology. In the above case, Carla and her parents have a planetary-sign theme: specifically, a Saturn/Pluto theme – Scorpio is pronounced through all three of their ascendants but the daughter concentrated and constellated the family dynamic from her Sun in Taurus in square to the powerful (Mars) Saturn/Pluto conjunction in 1948. Her essence of being, the Sun, collected the parental themes of Capricorn/Saturn and Pluto, and created in her own chart a tight complex based on this parental legacy. The planetary-sign pattern is very stark here. It is evident that the family power-issue, the struggle for survival and supremacy (Sun, Saturn and Pluto with her Mars inserted), had settled in the psyche of Carla and became the concentrate of her family lineage. For her, this is both an advantage and a supreme challenge – her ego, her Sun, has to incorporate the battles of the family and turn them into self-generated energy.

Other patterns emerge through elemental balance – we might look at several charts in the same nuclear family and notice a distinct preference towards earth, or fire, but with a definite lack of water. In Chapter 9, 'The Elemental Family' (page 158), there is a discussion on this common elemental relationship and how it is likely to manifest a 'circuit-breaker' in the middle! It never fails that at some point in time, somewhere along the line, an individual is born into a family apparently to freshen it up or disrupt complacency or even to destroy its integrity so as to push the dynamics into a dramatic shift.

In astrology in practice, we normally consult with the person in the family who is experiencing the most discomfort with their relationships, or has become acutely aware of his or her own psychology and sees the disparity between himself and others. However, there are times when a family pattern is quite benign – as I state clearly, all families are not pathological! I can, in fact, recall a large family whose planetary array was distinct in a subtle, unusual way. Many years ago, a lovely woman in her early sixties studied with me, living out her long-term interest in astrology. Her husband was a specialist doctor and a very warm, funny man. This couple were happy in their life and marriage, had five sons, and had lived in the same house (adding on to it as the family grew) for over thirty-five years. It sounded so ideal. And, believe it or not, it was! There was a remarkable similarity in appearance to all the sons and they had all chosen professions from law to medicine; all were athletic, intelligent, handsome and apparently well-adjusted young men. A couple of the sons had already married and one had children. The sons ranged in age from twenty-three to thirty-five. Why am I writing about them? They really had no problems at all aside from normal stresses and strains of being alive.

The most remarkable circumstance showed up in their horoscopes – there was very little repetition in any sign or planetary pattern – there was no stark elemental imbalance nor hidden malice. However, both parents were born with very close full Moons and each son to the last was born with new Moons in the same phase (between five and six degree orbs) – and three of them were located in the fourth houses of their charts! I have never seen anything like it, before or since, and I shall never forget the feeling of deep content and happiness I would always sense when around any of these people, singly or together. I think this is rare and could be interpreted as a family system having reached a balance of some kind. No one person could be praised for this, nor could we suggest that they were in denial – they were a happy lot and that's the way it was.

There are sad cases, of course, where a child is so damaged by its incompatibility within the family system that real harm is done to him or her in an irretrievable fashion. However, we must come to terms with an element of fate, here, and wonder what it is that causes a serpent to settle in one soul and seemingly be only insinuated through others in the family. Naturally, an astrologer will have to address this and possibly even help point out an area in which the hurt person will be able to surmount his or her trauma, thus reducing the toxicity of the situation and hopefully creating a new vision for the client in need. There are some things which simply do not go away; there are no answers to certain questions and certainly no understanding of why some things happen. We are not here to pontificate, to indict, or even to soothe, but to talk about things as they are and to point out how they might become if the viewpoint or focus is changed. At the very least a glimmering of understanding might come about if the pattern is objectively exposed and his or her plight is seen in the context of the larger picture of the family dynamic.

The fabulous burst of astrological and psychological information in the decades of 1950 through to 2000 really shows how desperate we have become to understand natural law in a clinical or Cartesian way. We might be better off throwing back to some deeply unconscious way of being, relinquishing all the knowledge, patterns, paradigms, maps, explanations, understandings, on and on, of what is basically a fated situation.

NEW PLANETARY PATTERNS, NEW MINDS, NEW FAMILIES

I am finding now, with twenty-seven years of parenting, thirty-four years of horoscopy and twenty-four years of the intensive practice of astrology and counselling, that a new generation of people, now (1996) in their thirties, are manifesting a distinctly different psyche. Naturally, they are still looking at their parents as the origins of life and shapers of attitude and potential, but they are less – *en masse* – inclined to blame their parents for anything except their own (the parents') vicissitudes! I find this quite remarkable. And refreshing. And confusing. In dealing with my peers (and, again, I shall include myself in this) I find an unrelenting desire to prosecute the parents for every flaw in their own individual nature! This has become so prominent a feature in the post-war generation that it feeds back in on itself, selling books to itself, doing workshops for itself and creating a circuit of economy that keeps an entire generation of people afloat.

Granted, we must, as parents and as children (adult or otherwise), address our family system – we need to understand why we are the way we are and how we might improve on the model offered us. This is good. And this is what astrology can offer: it can point out some absolutes – the patterns aforementioned – and bring to bear on those absolutes some philosophy and perspective to indicate just how we might individualize a collective situation, and, in turn, offer greater self-awareness to the collective. That is, in simple language, how we might take, from our astrological family pool, aspects, signs and planets that are threaded through the family and make them our own. For example, how can Carla, who had such a hard legacy from her parents – the Sun in Taurus square Mars/Saturn/Pluto – become richer from her losses? As she matures in years, she has begun to be capable of converting the raw essence of the family configurations of rage into energy, the sublimated power into overt strength and will, and to experience depression as a lull before creativity. Astrology goes beyond psychology.

This is not to demean the richness of psychological exploration and insight – without it, the generation of post-Second World War babies would be lost. But, more, it is about fate – we have been given a vast legacy of interior examination starting at the turn of the twentieth century with the advent of personal psychology, and astrology has followed suit with its focus on individualism and self-examination, but there must be more to it than navel-gazing or it will not serve the whole of humanity. As far as we have been given this opportunity to work with ourselves in exclusive quarters and luxurious circumstances, we may not have improved the collective picture by very much. Indeed, have we improved it at all by all this interior work?

Part of the problem lies in interpreting things. Even the apocryphal quip attributed to Freud, 'Sometimes a cigar is just a cigar', is not taken as seriously as it might be. If you are having a fight with your lover, you are *not* having a fight with your father (or mother), you are having a fight with your lover. Full stop.

However, we might still use our legacy of psychological knowledge and try to understand why we are fighting with our lover and will the fight improve the relationship or is it a continually devolving erosion of it? It cannot be your father's fault, but it can be your fault because you were taught (implicitly or explicitly) by your father that you must always scratch, kick and bite your way through life because it's a hard, cruel world out there, or that they are a bunch of b—s, men, and therefore you had better stick up for yourself – or whatever the distorted philosophy was. Or maybe you never had your father as much as you would like and therefore are in terror of being abandoned by your lover, and in anticipation of his inevitable (to you) abandonment, you are going to have it out with him right now!

It may be that your lover does share some of your father's planetary patterns; after all, we are attracted to what we know. Let us say his Moon in Capricorn resonates with your father's Sun in Capricorn in the same degree – and you feel that in your body; you love him because you know him like you knew your father, but you fear and hate him because he triggers old responses. Perhaps the Capricorn Sun father was the 'strong, silent' type so exalted by the cinema in the pre- and post-war society. You were never able to feel his love of you, nor was it easy to cross the boundary of father–daughter relationship to the place where each of you exist as individuals. Your father's generation would be unlikely to change that, but your own contemporary relationship with the sign Capricorn might be able to transform your picture of a family dynamic. If you have experienced the cold side of Capricorn Sun, is that your lover's fault necessarily? Is he really behaving in the same way as your father, or are you finding it difficult to sort out who is doing what to whom and how and when? Therefore, is it your father's fault? Is it your lover's fault? Is it your fault? The answer to all these questions is likely to be a resounding 'No!'

Let us say that when you were born your mother was a nervous wreck and had a serious problem in handling your baby-body with confidence and pleasure. There could have been manifold reasons – she was afraid of dropping you, she was depressed because she had a hormonal imbalance and no money, she really wanted a boy, she was too young/old, you interrupted her Ph.D., she didn't really understand her own needs very well, etc., etc. There are many reasons why women have problems around the birth of a child – not all of them indicate hating their children. Most of the problems simply indicate problems. You might have a Moon opposition to Uranus, which suggests that there was something within the experience of your mother that was unsafe, ambivalent, erratic and compartmentalized, where you might be shut out or let in without any sense of rhythm. Your mother didn't feel 'whole' or calm to you – she may well have been terribly self-absorbed and incapable of entering into the new relationship as a mother. Yes, the Moon/Uranus in your chart does describe an anxious mother, but it is still *your* horoscope. Therefore the collusion which occurs between you and your mother, between your conscious mind and your deep unconscious, has a great rift. It is very likely that the theme of Uranian Moons, Aquarius and oppositions is something that has the flavour of a family theme. It is also very likely that deeply, inherently you don't want conventional relationships, nor would you find a cloying, smothering, over-emotionally dependent relationship very healthy.

Therefore we are looking at very complicated structures which are inherently problem-solvers. When a client presents a problem, he or she will often feel that the problem is a direct result of someone else. Usually, if they are psychologically aware, they will want to find the source of that problem in the bosom of the family, or in the parental territory. What we end up with is a way of objectifying a totally subjective experience. When we lay blame, indict and confront a problem as if it were wholly resting outside ourself, we are avoiding the enriching process of becoming more of ourself. In other words, we have to realize that your mother's problem was *her* problem, however, the problem *now* is that it has become your problem according to you. To some degree, this is true, but to a larger degree, it is not. This is why.

Often, a person with a Moon/Saturn square has difficulty demonstrating or even experiencing his own feelings. This natal aspect coupled with a mother who had a deep dislike or fear of her own maternal femininity would be likely to result in the man's own deep feelings of lovelessness or unlovability, especially in relationships which require emotional trust. However, what if his mother truly *didn't* have those feelings as a dominant aspect of herself? Then, our client would *see the small part of her that did* – his Moon/Saturn emotional lens would magnify the darker Saturnian traits of the mother and, in turn, she would be harmonizing with his Moon/Saturn. This is called unconscious collusion – the phenomenon wherein a deeply unconscious aspect of one's self is 'supported' by another who, equally unconsciously, resonates with that aspect and plays into it. This is mutually receiving, and extrapolates out into all forms of nurturing relationships.

People all suffer from self-dislike at times, but if you are experiencing a prevailing feeling of self-denigration or limitation, then there is a deep concern that just might have to do with your mother's inability to transfer her feelings of love and goodwill towards you as an infant and small child and your own inability to receive those positive feelings. This would be a combination problem for both mother and child. A Moon/Saturn configuration would demonstrate that the man will experience his emotions or feelings as something that will limit him, prevent him, lock him in, hold him fast, weigh him down, depress him, and various other Saturnian moods. He is right, that is what Moon/Saturn is all about, but it is not only about his mother. A Moon/Saturn person *is* inclined to emotional seriousness, caution and even melancholy as a prevailing mood – or he or she is inclined to attracting people and circumstances that dominate the emotional tone of a relationship – but he or she is *not* inclined to have a cold mother, as much as he or his astrologer/therapist would like that to be the answer.

HOW TO FIND PATTERNS

When we look at whole families, whether that is the immediate, nuclear family in which we were born and raised, our family of origin, or our extended family including grandparents, aunts and uncles, or our created family of spouse, children and their children, we are exploring a larger collective. Finding patterns is not mechanical in the sense that rules can be established about what to look for. In presenting the material in this book, the stories of the people who have been so helpful in contributing their family issues for us to learn from, we will see several examples of various ways to seek out a family pattern.

First, start looking for themes, even weak ones which thread through generations across and down the generational lines, or circling around and within a nuclear family. Then, begin looking for the obvious connections and similarities, like planets in the same signs or aspects between planets that are shared by a couple or a few members in the family line; then you can add up elemental balances and modes, making diagrams of them (see the example in 'Rejected in the Womb' (pages 311, 313 and 314), and in that way begin to get a feel for the charts in question. Start to look for a congestion of themes which lock into one person's chart, for example a stellium in one of the water houses or at the ascendant, IC or MC/tenth house, and so forth.

What seems to happen, after having explored many family patterns in hundreds of ways, is that there seems to be a slight flow which develops into a steady stream that begins to demonstrate a very tight and repetitive pattern. Then in one person's chart it becomes critical, the pattern or the flow dams up, and a bottleneck begins to develop in the family patterning, lodging in one person – the one who is the pivotal individual in the entire constellation of the family. As I say many times in the course of the material to follow, the mystery lies in why this happens to a person; it does, however, and that person is always aware of it but often does not get validation of his or her feelings until an astrologer finds that their story is not only true but is also mapped out in the heavens.

The fact that we are made up of many people, dating back *ad infinitum*, helps us understand ourselves better. Our parents had parents, and so on. And we carry all those who went before us in our psyches, but specifically we carry certain aspects of them more strongly than others. People who are deeply fixated on the theory that the aetiology of all neurosis lies primarily in the parents, or in the matrix of the nuclear family, will be unsettled by some of the attitudes in this book – it does not lie in the realm of responsibility of one or two hapless individuals, though they may have had a good hand in our fate. The purpose of this way of viewing things is to liberate both parents and children from absolute personal responsibility for each other and to encourage more independence – paradoxically, by stressing their intra-dependence!

CREATING A FAMILY TREE

There are several things to watch for in setting up a family tree. All families are very different and some are based on patterns which others don't seem to have. Above, for example, I have mentioned several planetary-aspect patterns. This is only one type of pattern that is created. We can look at family patterns only in accord with the specific family, therefore it is dependent upon the nature of the family to display its particular patterns. This means that one has to be very open-minded in the beginning of the analysis. To look for planetary dynamics where they don't exist, or to expect there to be an elemental weight or sign dominance, could be misleading.

The secret is to find the pattern which lies within the family itself, then draw up a linking-tree with the dominant feature(s) presenting. Naturally, all the horoscopes must be set. If there are no precise times, as often there are not with some parents and most grandparents, then use the solar-figure (dawn or flat chart as it is sometimes called). In the story of Toby (page 231) there is an example of such a tree based on his family.

For this work, I would define the nuclear family as the immediate family of mother, father and siblings. In turn one might have formed his or her own nuclear family of spouse and children. The dynastic family is formed by both parental lines feeding into an individual – for example, you, your parents and of their parents, etc., as far back as you care to go. Then there is the extended family of cross-lines, which include parental siblings, their parents and their children, who would be for you uncle/aunt and nieces/nephews. Again, this can be as complete as you care to make it.

Generally, it is good to look to the nuclear family for immediately presenting problems, to the dynastic family patterns for the underlying or possibly inherited legacy of characteristics which have constellated in the presenting problems, and lastly to include the extended family for confirmation of a valid family bond or trait. Clearly the various complexes will be played out in myriad creative ways, and it will prove to be an endless foray into the mystery of the astrology of families. If one finds that he or she appears to be the 'holder of the torch', then understanding what that torch is wanting to illuminate will quicken one's approach to self-awareness. It does not, however, guarantee the resolution of conflict, but the clarity of vision will quicken the movement of a stuck, congested condition.

Family patterns usually have some strongly consistent characteristic in themselves. While it is possible that there will be a thread of, say, water dominance, with a Moon/Pluto/Scorpio signature and a majority of members with angular or fourth house planets, it is more common for families to have certain, very particular, kinds of patterns that are distinct in their presentation, like strongly elemental, or primarily to do with planet-sign similarities, or the same aspects between the same planets. Ideally, try to find what your own astrological family pattern is and what dynamics it involves. This procedure requires that you look at all the horoscopes *en masse* and try to see what similarity or sameness is present in all or the majority of them. Then, draw a tree that shows the simplistic patterns. Patterns can be drawn for the elemental weights or the modal weights. In the story 'Rejected in the Womb' (page 290), there is an example of the Cardinal, Fixed and Mutable crosses with the family members' planets all set in to show what the balance is. This can be done by creating four triangles for each of the elements, and putting all the people's planets there. Grids can be made showing all the people concerned and their signs across the zodiac.

What follows are some guidelines for several particular family patterns to watch for when analysing either a nuclear family or an extended or dynastic family line.

SIGN PATTERNS

When a predominance of a particular sign is found in a family, we are looking at a strong family myth that is represented by the symbolism of the sign. In Toby's family, for instance, the sign of Pisces was discovered to be threaded through the entire dynastic family. There is an underlying paradigm which can be extrapolated into stereotypes, underneath which lie vast territories of unlived traits and characteristics. A family can be 'frozen' by the sign, rigid in its way of being, inflexible and intractable. This will be likely to be brought out by the missing link, the invisible sign which can be a sign of the same element but very dominant, or the sign opposite the family signature sign. In the story of Toby, the entire watery family line rested in his tenth house Scorpio stellium and Moon/Neptune opposition (see pages 252–3).

Sign patterns include the same-planet-in-same-sign phenomenon. The most common shared among entire families are the Sun and Moon, but there can be a thread, say, of Mars in Capricorn or Venus in Libra, and so on.[2] Naturally, the personal planets in the same sign imply that the birthdays are within a couple of months of each other, if not the same month, and this too is not uncommon in family lines. Clearly when there are interactive relationships in nuclear families it is noticeable, but it is far more revealing if the same-sign-planet pattern is found throughout the extended family. I know of two sisters who have their Moon in the precise same degree of Virgo, and their Venuses are in the exact same degree of Scorpio. This certainly did not indicate much compatibility when they were thirteen and fifteen, and I do not know what has happened to them since; however, it is safe to say that the type of familiarity present when there is a strong inter-action like this can be extremely uncomfortable and too intimate. In siblings especially, same-planetness can be felt as an insult, an intrusion or a transgression of boundaries which establish uniqueness. The astrological similarity is often felt as too close, too intimate, too invasive. It is different when friends have planets in the same place – in that case, the similarity is familial and creates a 'safe' place, but in families the blood-tie can bring an irrational fear of loss of identity into the relationship and a struggle for separation ensues.

This is also the source of misunderstood intimacy between parents and children. When one (or more) of the children has planets which are the same as a parent's, the child may need to assert more individuality in order to become wholly him or herself. To individuate away from a parent who shares similar or same planet interchanges is much more difficult and needs much more privacy than the child or children who do not share this intimate contact. For example, a woman with the Sun in Scorpio square Mars, Saturn and Pluto has two daughters, both of whom have Sun square Saturn, in-herited directly from the mother (passed down the Capricorn line in the family). The elder daughter has the square from Sun in Capricorn to Saturn in Aries while the younger one has the square from Sun (and Mars) in Leo to Saturn in Taurus. This configuration is located in the *same degrees* as the mother's Sun square Mars, Saturn, Pluto – the younger daughter is very like the mother but found it much more uncomfortable to individuate into her twenties and accept being like her mother because she had to more actively reject her 'same as mother-ness' for her own personal self-discovery. In her maturity and having found her 'self' and her self-awareness and self-confidence, it is now fun to be like mother because it doesn't threaten to devour her own identity. Both mother and daughters enjoy their similarity while still loving their difference.

It is more difficult to become one's own self when one is *astrologically* very much like one of one's parents, especially the same-sex parent. All young people, especially in the adolescent years, need to be completely unique, dif-ferent and, sometimes, divorced from their parents. So finding astrological sameness between parent and child is not always an indication of a smooth road ahead! It takes supreme consciousness on the part of the older person and, eventually, responsibility on the part of the younger, to understand the fate of their cosmic connection and what it is saying to each of them.

It can be something as simple as a mother, daughter and granddaughter all having Venus in the same degree and sign. This 'means' that there is a powerful set of values which needs to be expressed in the same family through different means. This does *not* mean that these women are the same, or going to agree; indeed, it might mean precisely the opposite. Because the levels of expression of a sign, or a degree in a sign, are so vast, it really means that the family needs to have a great deal of emphasis on the underlying themes. By teasing out much of the meaning and expression those three women would be participating in a profound ancestral purification and possibly a maturation of an undeveloped aspect in that family. If something is literally repeated so precisely, it is because the family, the culture, the cosmos needs more refinement and individuation in that area. In this case it is Venus, which helps the archetype of Venus/Aphrodite evolve into even more human expressions. As we shall see as the book evolves, having planets in the same degree means that alterations, modifications, transformations will occur to one or more people at *exactly* the same time, but for personally different reasons. If it should be that it is the same planet in the same degree of the same sign, then each individual will undergo a variation on a theme. It is as if some secret force were at work to unite people in a diverse fashion. There is no doubt they are related, but they will always fight for their uniqueness.

There are occasions where a member of a nuclear family will resemble astrologically a distant relative such as an uncle or nephew – there are transfers of personal planets *across* families as well as down through bloodlines directly. Then, we have relatives who have a real affinity for each other and are much closer to each other than perhaps their parents or siblings are. Many times it is 'safer' that the astrological affinities are across lines into the uncles and nephews and nieces rather than directly descending from maternal or paternal grandparents or locked within a nuclear family. One friend of mine, a Gemini with a Pisces Mars, had a young nephew who had a Pisces Mars within three degrees of his, and both were computer specialists in the field of geography, but vastly different in those fields.

People are so often attracted to or attract individuals into their lives whose planetary placements are identical to their own family patterns. This phenomenon can be experienced in phases of types, where one is working through a particular family process or complex and thus energizes an affinity in that area, constellating a friend, colleague or lover with planets in the family places. This allows us to work through family issues in relative privacy and without the constant attendance of the family itself, thus on less charged ground. This is again a case where if it is familiar it is familial.

PLANETARY ASPECT-PATTERNS

Planetary aspect-patterns are also very common. Some patterns are more dominant than others, rather like brown eyes being dominant over blue, or green eyes being a recessive gene. There is no logical explanation for the dominance, but it does exist. The solar and lunar links are the most distinctive dynastic patterns which filter through family lines. Those patterns which are directly linked firstly to the Sun and the Moon are deeply embedded in the viscera, and thus transmitted genetically. They are very difficult to alter consciously, if not impossible. Then there are the more social patterns, such as Jupiter/Saturn, Mars/Jupiter or Saturn and so on. These patterns are equally familial; however, they form part of the conscious family pattern, the characteristics of families that manifest in characteristics that they are more likely to discuss among themselves as obvious family links.

Moon/Venus form strong dynastic aspects, ones which run through entire families and centre around such issues as relationships, inner feelings of self-worth, the feminine dichotomy which is inherent in the two symbols of maternity and femininity. Moon/Venus patterns are most commonly found transmitted through the maternal line, but can break pattern. A friend of mine *and* both her daughters have Venus retrograde – this is incredibly unusual, since Venus is the second least retrograde planet (Mars is the least retrograde of all planets) – and her youngest child, a son, has Mars exactly stationary-direct! Her daughters will need to further develop or process any of the unlived aspects of their mother's Venus retrograde. Since there are two daughters, and both have Venus retrograde in the tenth house, my friend has the bonus of having the opportunity to see herself refracted in multiple ways through both girls, and the maternal legacy will be transformed.

Sun/Saturn and Moon/Saturn is another dominant dynastic pattern which is difficult to transform because of the intrinsic nature of Saturn, and it being coupled with the Sun speaks of a paternal legacy which manifests in women as an issue with the masculine or definitive things in life, like authority, authenticity, ego development, success, autonomy, and so on. In men, it is found to be difficult for them to transcend the patterns of their own father's success story, and it is also very difficult, but not impossible, for them to move beyond the lowest common denominator in the family. They need to become 'circuit breakers' in order to crack the barrier between their maximum potential and possible self-limiting patterns which are dynastic.

The personal planets of Sun, Moon, Mercury and Venus in formation with the outermost planets, Uranus, Neptune and Pluto, are indicators that the family dynamic can lend itself to greater, collective service. What might be uncontainable in a small nuclear family is better used in the community or in the world at large. Very often, when individuals have personal-collective planetary configurations, they are 'too big' themselves to be contained within conventional boundaries and need to find special ways for the ego to encompass their grand inner life. Outer planetary contacts which run through families are too easily manifest as illnesses or complexes, and part of this, I am certain, is because the individuals are 'bigger' than their families and have to find unique paths to exercise their power. The family itself is too small an arena to work through their life-karma, and for health to predominate, a collective or altruistic purpose must be found and developed.

Certainly individuals with high-powered aspects chafe at the petty concerns which are part and parcel of normal family life. These major contacts between inner and outer planets speak of a conflicting history in the family, one which has caused much loss, pain, dissatisfaction and distress, because there has been no outlet for such high-wattage power. It is then incumbent upon the modern individual to find ways of transforming the eccentricities of the nuclear family legacy into something of value for the collective. For example, a man who has the conjunction of Mars/Saturn/Pluto in his ninth house experiences the 'international war' implied in this aspect, thus: his grandmother was a Campbell and his grandfather a Macdonald; the ninth house is grandparents, and one night the Campbell clan murdered the Macdonald clan in their sleep! His reaction to his family has been to turn away from all family and cultural ties and move to India, where he lives in an ashram.

Ideally, we look at each family member's chart for patterns which are replicated in some thematic form: for example, mother has Mars/Jupiter square, daughter has Mars/Jupiter square, her grandmother has Mars/

Jupiter quincunx, and the sister has Mars/Jupiter opposed. This kind of obvious patterning links a family to its sense of social adventure and to warrior/theological philosophies. However, patterns are often not that grossly manifest, but implicate themselves in more subtle ways.

NOTES

1. Bernadette Brady, *JigSaw*. See pages 377 ff.
2. Michel Gauquelin did a statistical research project in 1964–5 on planets and families, in which he says, 'The results show no trace of zodiacal heredity for the Sun, Moon and MC' (*Planetary Heredity*, ACS Publications, San Diego, 1988, page 42). He also says, later, that there is a tendency for children to be born when the Moon, Venus, Mars, Jupiter or Saturn are in the same diurnal zone (rising, culminating or outside) (ibid., page 47). Read this fascinating book.

4.

The Sun and Moon
in Families

'I am at two with nature.'   (Woody Allen)

ASTROLOGY IS NOT GENDER-BIASED

Astrology is not gender-biased. The planets are not discrete energies making us do things, nor do they have sexual gender as we understand it to mean males and females. Masculine and feminine do not necessarily always refer to men and women. If those statements are true, then we cannot say, 'The Sun is male and the Moon is female, therefore the Sun is our father-archetype and the Moon is our mother-archetype.' The common astrological conclusion reached here is based on cumulative and compounded fragments of selective information seen through the eyes and interpreted in the mind of whoever is in the thinking mode-of-currency at any given time in history. It is thought that myths arise spontaneously in cultures and have mysterious parallels with other cultural mythologies even when those cultures have never interacted or even in cultures which were not contemporaneous. There are many pre-Greek and other cultural myths that have sky-goddesses and solar heroines as well as Moon-gods and lunar masculine images.

It seems we astrologers are guilty of stretching and contriving interpretations of myths in order to render them useful to us. Very often this works well, especially if we take myth as allegorical, but in some instances it can be badly misleading, especially if the stories are biased towards male or female, which in turn will inevitably be translated into 'mother' or 'father' or 'daughter' or 'son'. In an astrology book on families, we must be scrupulous not to arbitrarily assign strict gender roles to planetary agencies, but to try to find relationships between the masculine and feminine archetypes and see how they are played out in the family dynamic among all members, and how they are transferred through individuals in the family regardless of their gender. Because archetypal images reach further back than our capacity to render them conscious, we may have founded dogma in modern psychological astrology based on compounded errors which restrict our perception, thus our potential to become increasingly aware.

To truly individuate, we must never restrict the possible human, the potential 'us', the essential being-ness of ourselves. If anything, astrology must liberate us from stereotype and instil a greater feeling of uniqueness, of individuality and originality. Our personal characteristics are shared and inherited but they are experienced and demonstrated in highly original ways.

With respect to the symbols Sun and Moon in the chart, we must be even more circumspect about not stereotyping or restricting their imagery. It is far too easy to designate parental roles to each of them because we have so much material which falls beautifully into place – and there are symbolic reasons that the Moon is more akin to the maternal line and the Sun the paternal, but it is *not* because the Sun and Moon are respectively masculine and feminine. However, we have to remember that the origins of the assignment of masculine to the Sun and feminine to the Moon are archaic, and from those origins, all our astrological interpretations have been extrapolated and overlaid with that information.

In astrology we continue to adhere to the cumulative symbolism of the Graeco-Roman myths, gods and goddesses. This is so partly because the names we used for the planets are of Roman origin and the Roman gods and goddesses were assimilated from the Greek pantheon and theocracy. But we tend to go no further back than that in modern natal astrology. Nor do we sweep the myths of the world to find a balanced equation – we swallow whole the myths of the Greeks and often then attempt to find useful and appropriate stories from other mythologies which will neatly fit our paradigm. Perhaps there is another way of looking at the symbolism – of an astrological origin.

In her book *Eclipse of the Sun*, Janet McCrickard[1] writes about many variants in solar and lunar origin myths. Ms McCrickard makes it clear that our current understanding of solar and lunar agencies has been powerfully shaped by the influences of social values as they have developed through history. This phenomenon – that of losing the primal source of current information through the passage of time – is a perfect example of how stereotypes overpower archetypes. Clearly, we have lost a great deal of information while creating 'new' myths which suit the current social trends. Hence, collectively, we tend to think in terms of lunar being feminine and solar being masculine. This is simply not true, but has some value in current thought today. So we have to approach this lunar/solar experience from many angles which encompass the archaic and the modern.

The first consideration before delving into the symbolism of the luminaries is that they each in their symbolic self are not confined to one or other parent. To relegate the Sun to the father and the Moon to the mother at best oversimplifies the imagery and at worse distorts completely our understanding of the full human person. *However* – and this is a major contingency – it is very likely that because of this stereotyping we *do* find our parents more one than the other. That is, we might find our mother more lunar than our father and vice versa or our lunar nature more influenced and represented by our mother and the solar character more enhanced by and embodied in our father. Then, based upon the interpretation of the Sun and Moon which is traditional now, we say our mother *is* the Moon and our father the Sun. From that, we interpret our charts, or worse, other people's charts, in that way. All aspects from the Moon tell us what our mother was like and all aspects from the Sun dictate our father's legacy to us. Knowing this tendency, we must include in our own bias the very real condition of our inner relationship to the outer world – we are very much a product of our own civilization and role-typing. There is a deep collusion between what we project and what we receive. It then makes perfect sense that we should relate to the Moon/mother and Sun/father doctrine. I myself have done it, do it and likely will continue to find it appropriate and fitting in most cases, on the archetypal level.

It does not follow, however, that we must swallow it whole or continue to do this by rote. We might consider opening the end of our bias and incorporating the possibility that *the Sun and Moon are our parents in the most archetypal sense*. How the Great-Mother, Hero-Father archetype is portrayed in mothers and fathers and is individuated through each person is where creative interpretation should allow for greater latitude of solar or lunar expression. That is, they are the symbols for the various ways in which we become increasingly ourselves; they are the images through which we might best picture the ways in which we experience our innate, collective human-ness. The Sun and Moon are the archetypal marriage and how we marry ourselves within ourselves is related to the Sun/Moon dyad in our

horoscope. How we mediate polarities within our psyche and mind is represented in the soli-lunar relationship. For instance, Sun/Moon opposition
people tend towards splits and mediation personalities. They experience dichotomy very intensely, and tend to cope with problems by mediating both
sides, having an innate awareness of the differences between the masculine
and feminine agencies; whereas, say, Sun/Moon trine people tend to have
an idealized vision of the 'archetypal parents' inherent within their psyche,
hence are not as prepared to deal with the possible difficulties that are
intrinsic within the masculine/feminine polarity.

This means we have to consider the Sun and Moon as distinct from the
planets in that they are unique from the planets and visually more evident
than the other bodies. Their imagery and symbolism is also much older than
the planets – collectively, we have been projecting a focus on them longer
and with more psychic energy than on the planets. That the Sun and Moon
have been so long in our consciousness means that there is stratum upon
stratum of unearthed information lying in the deepest recesses of our
mind. Periodically dogma is purveyed and accepted, and equally periodically
dogma is destroyed and rewritten. We see the Sun and Moon with all its
history and all the myths from aeons back, and underlying all that time and
past is a basic truth. This truth must be found.[2]

The Sun/Moon dyad is essential to understanding bi-polarism and options, differences and distinctions between experiencing the same things in
different ways – in other words, when an event occurs, we have it 'happen'
on many, many levels, and the Sun/Moon dyad presents a (rather simplistic)
way for us to understand two levels of experiencing the same event.

Dane Rudhyar was very clear on the Sun/Moon principle of unity in
duality: the astrological Sun and Moon are partners, pairs, a couple, as it
were, in relationship. His book *The Lunation Cycle* was a breakthrough in syn-
thetic astrology. He made it very clear that planets do not exist singularly,
that they are in relationship at all times. The significance of the soli-lunar
cycle was found in its waxing and waning cycles – the natural laws of relationship are fluctuating all the time, manifestly and subtly.[3]

There have been many theories about the natal lunation cycle and the
parental relationship: for example, the Sun and Moon in opposition 'means
that the parents were in discord or, at best, diametrically opposed in their
beliefs'. Which, then, is extrapolated out to be interpreted in the natal chart
as a psychological 'split' effected by this polarization of the parents (parental images of Sun and Moon) wherein the masculine and feminine sides

of the individual are not in unison. Well, when *are* they? Rarely, and when they are, a sense of perfect inner harmony is the result. Whether or not this is a consequence of the direct influence of one's mother and father is highly speculative. That it results from how we are innately *and* how we perceived our parents is closer, much closer to the truth. Which body, Sun or Moon, is best exemplified by mother and which is more father could vary in many ways at different times in our lives. We come back to the dialectic of nature and nurture.

There are characteristics which are distinctly lunar and others which are solar; if we consider various significant aspects of our motivating forces in life, for example, conscience, habits, responsibility, relating, ego-development, creativity, and so on, we might look upon the Sun and Moon and find in which way each of these bodies have played roles in the dominant way we achieve the end result of each of those character-building, individual components.

UNITY IN DUALITY

The Sun and Moon contribute equally to our ability to have reactions to and create life-patterns in various ways, but the following list comprises a short inventory of some of the most significant aspects of the Sun's and Moon's contribution to our character:

1. Conscience
2. Habits
3. Responsibility
4. Relating
5. Ego-development
6. Creativity.

This is a list of keywords to be associated with contemplating the value of the luminaries in the horoscope. They are not definitions for each body. We have both a Sun and a Moon, and two parents . . . the feelings associated with all of those can be combined or differentiated.

SUN	MOON
λογος-*logos* – name/word	εννοια-*ennoia* – seed idea
νομος-*nomos* – law	φυσις-*physis* – nature

social	instinctual
conscious	unconscious
ego	id
tradition	'now', present, current, urgent
structural	spontaneous
civilized	animalistic
thoughts	being-ness
ideas	irrational/non-rational
meaning	essence
libido	eros
desire	desire/permeating
celestial (solar system)	*chthonic* (earth's Moon)
regulated, constant	calibrated, phased
cerebral	visceral
order	chaos
democratic	anarchic
objective	subjective
individual/cultural	collective/global

THE SUN AND SOLARISM

In our current astrological reading, the Sun has been associated with the masculine almost exclusively. The cyclic movement of the Sun in the course of a full day is the basis for the myth of the hero – the Sun being equated with the hero's journey, rising out of the dark mystery of the night at dawn, bringing light, clarity, hope; culminating at the zenith to conquer sundry kings, leaders, tyrants; setting (off to the) in the west, abandoning the world to darkness and thence to undergo a mysterious ritual of monster-slaying, maiden-rescuing or treasure-recovering at the midnight hour, only to return each morning, carrying the torch of reason and knowledge into the daylight, undergoing the journey all over again.

The hero-figure is traditionally a man, attributed with traits such as objectivity, goal-orientation, capacity to seek-and-conquer, clarity of vision, ambition, personality, cunning, wit, courage, ascendancy and so on. All of these are accurate solar attributes, but are they particularly *male*? They might be archetypally masculine in orientation but most certainly they are not traits associated with men only. Today we read of very few solar-female figures in myth or in history – those that we are aware of are usually daemonic or skilled in the black arts. Witches, to be blunt. The heroic character is never portrayed in most myths through a woman (this polarization of characteristics is also discussed in the lunar section). Yet a woman can very easily parallel her cycles to the solar movement, and men can well identify with the Moon and its waxing and waning. There is a certain male rhythm which is associated with waxing and waning – the sexual act, for instance, has a distinct rise and fall, full (tumescent) and new (flaccid, hidden) pattern in his sexuality.

The Sun is the *focus* – the hearth-fire – of the solar system. It is our life-force and the central, organizing principle around which all the other planets revolve – earth and her Moon included. In the Gauquelin studies, it was found that the Sun had no 'attributes',[4] that is, it appeared to show no personality traits. Gauquelin drew from that a theory that the Sun was not a 'type', and with that I would agree. The Sun as a pure symbol has no boundaries nor does it have characteristics as such. What the Sun does appear to do is act as a lens through which personality and psychological traits are focused and filtered, to become distinct characteristics. The Sun/ego is rather like the emissary for the deeper Self which is the instinctual urge to become more of what one might become.

The Sun, in and of itself, can be associated with the ego in the purest sense – that is, our sense of 'I am-ness' – which is a vehicle for the soul or the deeper Self. The ego acts as both a container and a vehicle for the deep, inner impetus to display one's own self in the outer world. Ego is very important for functioning in the world and for self-worth and inner comfort, or security. Our relationship within our family helps shape and form our 'I am-ness', our ego; however, there is a predisposition towards a particular personality, which has been handed down through the family lines. The relationship of the astrological Sun with other planets in the natal horoscope shows how our ego will receive challenge and in what specific areas we will find consistent types of tasks or jobs that we will be required to address in the course of our lives – this function or task is part of our heritage. The Sun in the horoscope shows very clearly how the ego of the individual will interact with the various energies and agencies within the family context and what will be met in the form of developmental experiences. Our personalities are deeply enmeshed with the options and characteristics most commonly found threaded in the family system. But we must find individuality within that system, and the Sun is the key to how we go about doing that.

Ideally, we should attempt at all times to allow our deeper self to push our ego into greater and greater capacity, to become an ever-increasing container, until it becomes as great as the universe, until we become as much of ourselves as we could possibly be! This is not something that parents normally find easy to allow a child to do. The job of helping a child create a healthy ego is not about letting him do whatever he wants, nor allowing the natural childish instinct to manipulate and use the parents to his own end, but to teach the child by drawing boundaries around what they, the parents, will accept, and equally where they will bend towards the child's needs. It is rarely convenient to allow a child to explore his dimensions as much as the child wants or needs. Indeed, some of the restrictions, inhibitions and thwarting that take place in families inadvertently do challenge the developing ego in ways which are positive, and directly result in strong character. These are nature's blessings in disguise.

The thwarted child often finds creative ways of bringing out his being regardless of what his parents or siblings think or want. If the obstruction and frustration is not too damaging, it will become a tool for growth. As we see in all the cases illustrated throughout the book, there is a fate involved here. There is some selection process within which the soul has engaged that designates our families. From a family-dynamics viewpoint, this is entirely suited to enact or enliven various aspects which may lie dormant in the wholeness of a family dynamic – rather like filling in the blanks or rounding out an incomplete sphere. In that view, we are instruments of fate which are selected to awaken new aspects of the family which would remain unconscious if it were not for us. Our solarism, the development of our ego, is partly unique to us and to our own individuality, but it is also a fundamental element in the succession and extension – and possibly the continuation in some cases – of the family. As if each of us is a cell in an organic whole, not conscious of our role, but acting it out as the system itself demands. The Sun shows the type of energy, heroism and seed-ego that the dynastic family has given us to work with.

Our family environment is our primary encounter with a world immediately outside our own inner space. The circle of the family acts as the training and testing ground for the interaction our ego will necessarily experience later, when we are moving about in the extended world. How our ego develops has been, and continues to be, a lively discussion in all social-development fields, but is generally a confusion of theories and ideas. Let us just say that the formation of the ego is complex, highly specialized in accord with each individual, and undergoes peaks and troughs in its evolution. It is a force which radiates and asserts individuality regardless of whether or not we are conscious of it.

The Sun in the horoscope gives us a life-force which is apparent through our personality, but *is not* our personality as such. We radiate our deeper self through the Sun and out into the world. This is not always well received, and in the case of a real conflict of energy can result in a feeling of being rejected. If the Sun has 'prickly' aspects, that is, harsh angles between planets like Mars, Saturn, Uranus or Pluto, then, there is a raw energy which is highly volatile and needs to be crafted, matured and brought to a ripeness before it is civilized – it encounters wariness and discomfort in the environment. This is nature. For parents to nurture a child with a difficult Sun is trying, and takes a great deal of love, care, maturity and good-will on their part. However, at all costs and at all times the parents *must* acknowledge that their child has inherited that solar aspect directly through one or other of them – it cannot be totally unfamiliar. It is never out of character, the child is the family dynamic and thus is not acting out of accord with a bigger picture. If it is familiar, it is familiar.

Being born into a family is no guarantee of compatibility or of being well-received or, indeed, liking anyone. We are lucky if our Sun – our original statement of who we are – is well received and feels comfortable and non-threatening to our parents and other members of our immediate family. Naturally one assumes that since the parents are older, they must be more mature, but really, age and maturity seem to have little to do with comfort, compatibility, ease and grace in parent–child relationships. We tend to forget that children are people, too! And what if your child were your contemporary and you met him or her at a party – would you like him? Would you invite him or her back to your home for dinner or further cultivate the friendship? And the same might be asked of grown children – would you seek the friendship of your parents as people, should they be your peers? If so, under what conditions, in what way and what kind of relationship would that be?

How we experience our ego in its development is not a conscious thing at first. It seems clear that around the ages of two-and-a-half to four, the strength of self-will has a spurt and the thrust of identity begins to assert itself; the beginning of many of such peaks and troughs all through life. That time is not necessarily the point at which our ego 'develops', for it has been in development all along, and will continue to undergo change and modification throughout all our individuating life – it is when we seem to become conscious of ourselves and our impact on our environment and our relationship within the family. The Sun is about acting out, it is radiating one's inner self out into the environment. It is at this age that a child begins to ask if it is loved or liked, and usually it is comparing its *appearance* to another sibling, or family member. 'Am I as pretty as mother?' a small girl might ask her father, or 'as clever, brave, and so forth'; or similarly, a little boy might want to know if he is as loved as his sister or brother, or as brave as his hero of the moment. These are perfectly normal, healthy questions. How will you know if you do not ask? But by far and away more truthful and more deeply influential are the more subtle means of communicating feelings – you know how you are being received by the unspoken emotions that are directed towards you when you are 'being yourself'.

One of those insensitive parental statements, meant not to destroy but simply made out of annoyance, is: 'Oh, be yourself.' Well, what is that, who am I and what the devil do they mean by that? We have all heard it, and unfortunately, many have said it. A ten-year-old will probably not be provoked into a deep inquiry into existentialism, but will be made hurt, embarrassed, confused, angry and withdrawn by this offhand remark. And he or she will suppress it for later. The Sun is sensitive to criticism about appearances, actions, abilities, behaviour, and extraverted manners.

Sun/Neptune people are like sponges, they absorb the behaviours of others and often mimic in order to self-discover. Sun/Mars types are more insensitive to critique but instead feel the anger and shame of rejection. Sun/Jupiter can feel easily deflated or over-exuberant and have such great hopes for approval. Sun/Saturn always suffer the responsibility laid upon them, and feel strongly 'at fault' for problems in the home. Sun/Pluto are exceptionally vulnerable to undercurrents of power, which lends them the ability to manoeuvre and learn to lie, though by nature they are dedicated truth-seekers.

Sun/Neptune people tend to be deeply affected and absorbed by their environment and thus susceptible to becoming whomever they are with; rather like Woody Allen's character in the movie *Zelig*, they are like sponges, they absorb the behaviours of others and often mimic in order to self-discover. And Sun/Uranus types resist perturbations from the outside and are jarred by influence, being strongly self-orientated and invulnerable to suggestion.

By nature, some individuals are finely tuned and highly sensitive and have a difficult time interpreting what they are receiving; hence their capacity to radiate their inner self is inhibited. They might find themselves wanting when they compare to others – to some degree this is natural, to desire a trait that another has. To want to be like an admired (or envied) sibling or parent is normal and healthy; role-models are essential to self-discovery and development. To various degrees at different times, we all have uncertainty about our self-image, but if there is a serious block towards acting out one's solar urges, then it is worth considering what the family picture is, and how one might find one's individuality lurking in a hidden corner of the family. The next step is to liberate it! If an individual finds that his family has not been capable of supporting and encouraging his ego development, he will have to step outside the family and look at it from another angle.

The retrieval of the self from the bosom of the family is a lifelong project. It means periodically going back into the family and wresting bits of identity out of it, like the hero at the treasure-trove, and fleeing with it intact. The reclaiming of self from the collective of the family consciousness does *not* have to be an act of violence or violation – unless, of course, it was stolen from or bludgeoned out of you. It is a natural, evolutionary act – at certain times in life, when we feel stuck, trapped, engaged in a treadmill existence, we might need to go into the nest and claim more of our self to gain energy for the next phase in life. True individuation is a process, not an event, it is a job never done. It requires diligence, consciousness and courage – especially as one gets older and less adventurous. Chapter 11, 'Families in Flux – Transits and Moving Forward', talks about this kind of time and how it seems to come about.

If an individual's nascent ego is constantly countered early in life, and, because of this, he or she experiences deep insecurity and diminished self-worth, this will radiate into all areas of accomplishment and relationship. Looking deeply, then, one might find that one has constructed prefabricated barriers around one's deeper sense of self, preparing for rejection before it arrives. Some people were *born* that way, they were not created that way by their parents or by their siblings. Yet there is a degree of culpability in all this, regardless of innate tendencies – it is the unconscious collusion of the family to 'validate' the expectations of each and every member of the family.

For example, here is a real family Sun/Saturn pattern as it falls into a family dynamic of man, wife and three children. We will look at the middle child (4) as the main focus in relation to the elder son (3):

1. Father: Sun square Saturn.
2. Mother: Saturn singleton-retrograde on the occidental side of the horoscope.
3. Elder son: Sun in Leo sextile Saturn/Neptune – Sun in square to Mars opposite Jupiter. All planets but Mars *above* the horizon.
4. Middle son: Sun in Leo square Saturn – Sun/Jupiter/Mars in square to Saturn. All planets but Saturn *below* the horizon.
5. Only (youngest) daughter: Sun square Saturn.

A child with a challenged Sun is going to require more effort on behalf of his or her family than one with a rampant and less 'other-oriented' Sun. Using the above example, the middle-born child – a son – has a Sun-Jupiter-Mars conjunction in Leo, but all are in square to Saturn in Scorpio, and all his planets are below the horizon. Every time his inborn enthusiasm and exuberance for life threatened to emerge he somehow found it squashed! Inherently he tended to counter his own self as he grew. As a result, there grew a deep resentment for anyone else in the family who did not carry this repressed trait because he quickly learned to perceive 'others' as having more fun, freedom, power, energy, feedback, etc. And the sad part of this is that largely, his perception was true. His inherent tendency is towards shyness, to stop his own social enthusiasm and inner boundlessness from materializing before it gets a chance for rejection; however, it was reinforced by his ordinal position – second son and middle child, both being Leos – and by circumstances.

This then becomes a self-negating trait, setting him apart from others, thus confirming his worst fears. It sets a pattern for life – the message runs like this: 'Deep in myself, I am fun, free, and positive with an abundance of energy (Mars). However, when I put all that energy together (Sun/Jupiter/Mars) and encounter others, that trait is suppressed (Saturn). The obvious answer is to stop interacting with others, withdraw my light (Sun), initiative (Mars), and optimism (Jupiter) and have a withdrawn, resentful relationship within my family (Saturn), which will set the tone for my relationship and success patterns in all areas of my life.'

This young man's ego development seemed curtailed before it began, and when it peeked its head out was self-reinforced. This kind of solar picture is *very* difficult to correct or bring to balance without a great deal of self-consciousness and awareness. Often, it also requires someone else to see his positive side, if he can allow it, and to foster and nurture his Sun-Jupiter conjunction and try to help him use his Saturn in a new way. Indeed, he had a miserable first marriage, a child whom he still has a difficult time in seeing, and has now found a relationship with a woman who has borne him a second child and resents the child, him, and it seems the wheel continues to turn – no patterns have been broken but they have merely been rearranged.

The unconscious is a powerful instrument which is interacting with the unconscious elements of others in the family. His father had Sun in square to Saturn, and he died when the boy was around seventeen. The father–son bond was broken by circumstance, but he had always felt second-best to his older brother, another Leo. All this is in collusion with the fact that his older brother is highly independent and sunny in personality *and* has the exact same planet-interaction but in a very different configuration – the older brother, first-born, has Sun in the eleventh house square Mars opposite Jupiter and sextile Saturn. The older sibling not only got there *first*, but has a freer, more demonstrable Sun. Notice that the two brothers have the same planets in powerful, but entirely different configurations – Sun, Mars, Jupiter and Saturn. *This is the same theme played in different chords.* The elder son has refused his own shadow and his younger brother acts it out.

By looking closely at the Sun-patterns in families, there are always themes that play in different chords in myriad ways. The family I mention above also includes a sister (youngest of the three children by ten years) who *also* has a Sun-Saturn square, just like her father and the middle-child brother!

Now, the really fascinating aspect of this family dynamic is the horoscope of the so far unmentioned mother. All the children have powerful Saturn configurations with the Sun, just like their father; however, their mother has a singleton Saturn retrograde. In earlier generations than now, it was more common for Saturn to be carried by the father – archetypally it remains a masculine agency – and when Saturn is singleton-retrograde, it is highly projectable if only symbolically by its isolation and separation from the main *Gestalt* of the rest of the horoscope. It is as if Saturn is saying, 'I am all alone over here, none of my inherent authority as an individual is integrated within the context of the rest of the chart, thus I can abdicate from responsibility and/or put upon/allow others to carry it.'

Ultimately, the mother *had* placed very high expectations on the Sun/Saturn square father – all the children had picked this up from him and from her – but he died young, at forty-nine, leaving her to cope with Saturn on her own. He could no longer carry it. Shattered, she was not well prepared to take on the practicalities of life, and has had to fall on her own resources. However, this has in some way been a blessing – she has all the intelligence, authority and single-mindedness of the separated Saturn person, and has come to some sense of self-value and worth. However, a great deal of this has been through the agency of her eldest son, the one with the Sun/Saturn sextile. A long and very difficult learning period has brought peace and happiness and a measure of independence – she has now, at last, become her own authority. Her concern over her children remains, however.

It would seem that the Sun-links, the solar ties, in a family have to do with their capacity to allow each other to shine. The ability to feel comfortable with exploring new aspects of the unfolding self is essential to healthy ego-development. If we encounter derision, suspicion or indifference when we are growing, then our facility to exploit and utilize our solar characteristics is arrested or suppressed. That one member of a family can be more outstand-ing than another is appearances only – by comparison, we all fall short of the mark in some way, but standing alone with our best side lit, we can be just who we could be.

It is difficult to avoid blame, but as I have emphasized repeatedly throughout the book, there *normally* is no blame. In cases where the family situation is truly pathological, then, clearly responsibility and accountability must be brought forth. In cases of violence, sexual abuse, serious, consist-ent alcohol or drug abuse which shaped and formed – sometimes overruled – the innate characteristics of the individual, the work which must be done is far more difficult. It means clearly separating the self from the family and reclaiming lost or abandoned identity.

Summary of the Sun

The Sun is the centre of the solar system, and in the family of planets acts in just that way. It has high expectations of the others, and in itself, the Sun is the most powerful figure in the horoscope. As the focus, the Sun repre-sents how our life-force was received in the family and how our self and ego develops in accord with family values. The Sun can overpower other planets in the horoscope in quite primitive ways, when the ego-nature of the indi-vidual is stronger than and disconnected from his or her conscious sense of integrity or ethics. The nature of the Sun is to radiate, outshine and expose all things to its relentless light. It is the attention seeker, the planet which defies all, even Pluto, to check its power. The Sun has authority, but equally that authority can be undermined, thwarted or subverted by other planets, as it is a rare chart that has an unaspected Sun. The authority of the Sun can also dominate other planets, not allowing them to develop their full potential: just as a too-heroic or mythic-type father can weaken his children's power, a too-dominant Sun can obliterate gentler sides of an individual.

The Sun is the archetypal father-image, the heroic principle, and is usually associated with the male role-models in the family and the paternal line. The Sun in the chart can appear to stand alone. We must always keep in mind that the Sun is never really 'alone' because both Mercury and Venus are never far from this central figure, but it *can* be segregated from the *Gestalt* of the rest of the horoscope, in which case there are a number of other planets retrograde. This often shows an individual with an extremely unique way of being and one who finds it very uncomfortable relating to the average standards of his or her culture – particularly his or her family system!

When looking at the Sun in the chart with respect to family issues, it is very likely to draw immediate attention to one's own father and his unconscious imprint in one's psychic formation. The physical presence or absence of the father seems irrelevant in many cases, because the underlying archetypal expectation of the father is stamped in the solar figure in the horoscope. The father's unlived life can quicken in the soul of his children and thus become a powerful ingredient in the child's personality development. This is clearly both positive and negative – if we have to bear unrealistic expectations and must consciously overcome the failures of our father, we can suffer undue guilt and responsibility-feelings. Our Sun can be arrested in its development in order that the issues unresolved in our father can be transformed through us.

In contrast, the 'healthy' Sun can gently urge a child to emulate his or her father in positive ways, seeing clearly that his failures or successes are not their own problems. However, even the most basic psychological knowledge shows us that unresolved complexes in the parents are passed on for the children to seek solution. We will find that the solar legacy is one which most frequently runs down through the paternal line, and is then passed on through the next generations. Both men and women can carry paternal legacies – men identify more with the male principle through the Sun with respect to their sense of male-identity and desire to build, conquer and protect, while women utilize the solar legacy in their desire to control and conduct lives independent from the emotional zones of families and relationships.

Aspects formed by the Sun to other planets are often a literal image of how we perceived our father and his influence in our heroic – productive – life. As mentioned previously, the Sun *needs* challenge to develop its potential characteristics and assist in the development of the ego. Usually it is the father who enacts this kind of role-model for the children by being elusive, exciting, unpredictable in his appearances, big, strong, foreign to the nest, influential in the governing of the family, etc. This structure may *appear* to be archaic in its description, but then archetypes *are* out of time and lie at the base of our social and personal lives. Sometimes the father is strong in influence by his absence and conversely weak by his presence. Aside from our 'dad', we have a celestial-father image in our psyche, and the Sun shows what that is.

Individuals with the Sun rising or in the MC of the chart experience extraordinary pressure to succeed in whatever endeavour is undertaken. This can be fun if the person is allowed slowly to develop his or her own interests and is allowed to show off on a regular basis all that he or she has accomplished! If, however, the pressure is towards a skill or interest of the father's and not instinctive, or the expectation is literally received from the father, then the solar principle feels thwarted and the ego develops a shell or crust to protect the deeper Self from being hurt or damaged by this transgression of natural law. The Sun strongly placed in the angles like this does indicate a powerful psychological connection to the father, and the person carries the father with them into everything that is presented to the world.

An unaspected Sun is an indication that the individual will need to find a completely new way of using his or her ego to find something outside the family dynamic to pursue. There is a maverick energy with all unaspected planets, and it often indicates that a 'new soul' has come into the family to break professional, social hierarchies. The unaspected Sun person will find it exceptionally difficult to conform to the family, but will attempt to do so until a turning point occurs, allowing them to set off in their own direction. Often their father has not been traditionally paternal, has been a 'friend' or completely absent by circumstances or choice. There is usually a very strong longing for a father, or father figure, but because there is no aspect from the Sun to another planet, there is no clear image of the father in the psyche. Hence, the person has to become their own father, or to become their own authority. All the words that stem from the Latin *auctor* – author, authority, authenticity, and all derivatives – are especially significant for unaspected solar people. They must find inner validation rather than seeking it from without. This often means long periods of wandering, looking, seeking and searching for purpose and direction in life.

SOLAR THEMES IN FAMILY DYNAMICS

To preface this delineation, remember that these are *themes*, that is, they can manifest in either direction, overtly or covertly. They can also be made obvious by negation – for example, a Sun-Jupiter theme can be so inverted in one person that it results in one family member being very introverted, never travelling far from home, having narrow viewpoints and very little in the way of social energy, while another member of the same family travels widely, has a variety of activities, enacting for the others the exciting, dramatic and expansive life. Likewise, a Sun-Saturn theme can run from being terribly successful and goal-oriented to being downtrodden and melancholic, not fulfilling his or her fullest potential. Remember in families one can find a both/and situation – functional families are *not* static, are always flowing and continually finding new ways of accommodating, communicating, balancing, compensating and surviving. Truly and severely dysfunctional families do not allow for change, flux or dynamic action and the homeostatic principle is very strong and there is always an 'identified patient', someone who is carrying the illness of the family-theme – the scapegoat, the black sheep or the circuit breaker. With that mind, following are the energetic solar themes of family dynamics.

Sun/Mars (including solar aspects with Aries)

The family is heroic and adventurous, and often, competitive energies flow through the family psyche. This can produce high-achievers (or counter with strong conservatives and depressives if Saturn is part of the theme), executive types and self-made men and women. Each individual's ego development occurs in spurts and erratic characteristics abound; often, one member is the leader, the 'shining one', while another appears to haunt or darken the family collective. Individuating through the Sun/Mars family requires brute force – either mental or physical; the timid don't survive well emotionally, while innovators who have strong originality and a thick skin do. Wanderers, mavericks, renegades and individualists are lovingly, though occasionally grudgingly, respected. If combined with Jupiter, there is a manic-depressive atmosphere where someone is always countering or balancing the extremes – this family usually produces a mediator-type who trots back and forth or who suffers because of enmity between two others in the family whom she or he loves equally. One member may have to withdraw in order for the whole family to survive as a system. The balance of the family dynamic is tenuous and spark-filled, creating a sense of balancing and counter-balancing all the time. This family attracts nurturers, carers and, usually, quite stable relationship-partners to counterbalance the over-aggressive energy.

Sun/Jupiter (including solar aspects with Sagittarius)

Jupiter always brings a high moral tone to all situations; hence there is a strong potential for grandiosity and hubris lurking in each individual and within the family as an organic whole. Adventure is lauded, irresponsibility rampant, and high expectations and activity level are expected. The family is socially orientated – extraverted in expectation and activity. There is usually a strong religious theme in which orthodoxy is more likely than spiritualism or alternative religions. Because the thrust is gregarious and mobile there can be a '*puer/puella*' theme in the family system, wherein there is no real sense of having arrived at a stage of conventional adulthood; for example, professional sports-people, teachers (who never really leave school or university), itinerant types such as travelling sales-persons, lecturers, explorers and so forth. Courage, boldness, audacity and risk-taking are condoned and encouraged in the family. Ego development is encouraged through movement, travel and study. Individuation through the system is overtly encouraged – sometimes to an extreme, though it is not as 'cold' a system as the Sun/Uranus. Those individuals who are less adventurous and socially orientated in the family can become insecure and find their own contributions within the family appearing to be paltry and boring, where that may not be the case in another context. Sometimes the crossing of social bars is necessary to induct a fresh outlook or philosophy into the family system, in which case someone will cross the colour, class, religion or cultural bar and marry or involve themselves in counter-familial activities. The inherent need to import new and foreign energy is strong, but this is the shadow side of the xenophobic characteristic.

Sun/Saturn (including solar aspects with Capricorn)

Patriarchal and patristic societies are Saturnian in nature, and when a Sun/Saturn theme is dominant through a family-line, the masculine values of the culture are absorbed and become the mores and values of the family. They are socially conscious (relative to level of status) and sensitive to hierarchies both in their own small collective and in society at large. One of the main features is a high level of responsibility inherent in each member. As a group, they are family orientated, often harking back to the ancestors, which is rather nostalgic. There is a bi-polar motif in family expectation – either high-level expectations or 'poverty-consciousness' lies tacit in every family-rule whether this is spoken or deeply unconscious. Generally, the egos of individuals develop slowly, with time, and there can be a group of late-bloomers, who only feel and act mature when they are, indeed, well matured. Individuation through the system in the Sun-Saturn family requires courage and constancy, hard work, effort, clear, personal boundaries and constant self-awareness. Family values tend to be very traditional, often stringent but usually very simple, straightforward – if one knows the rules, it is easy to get by. Earthy practicality is valued and ostentation is discouraged – and anyone who wants to 'rise above' the family system will find that they have a harsh critic inside them, asking them who they think they are. This severe judge is not always a direct legacy from a parent's attitude, but lies in the archetype of old Kronos himself, who devoured his children through fear of being usurped, yet went on to sit as a benign ruler of the returned heroes in the underworld. He became a crusty old judge rather than the terrifying child-eater. Because of Saturn's mythological rulership over the long-ago Golden Age of Man, there is a tendency towards nostalgia and a re-writing of the past – as if once, long ago, the family was a great and golden thing which each person in this new family, today, must live up to and maintain. This is one of the strongest family links one finds in a working family – the frequency with which Sun-Saturn traits are passed down is startling, but characteristic of Saturn. Once a pattern with Saturn has 'taken', it will be repeated thoroughly in the individuals until it is necessary that it be broken. Obviously, the danger to the Saturnian family is that it will go the way of the unicorn and dinosaur, but the creative Saturnian family will live on in its dynastic influence if enough warmth is passed from individual to individual, encouraging him or her to have feelings, instincts and emotions even if they are tempered with restraint. (The other most powerful 'repeater' in family themes is the Moon/Pluto motif.)

Sun/Uranus (including solar aspects with Aquarius)

This is a signature found in the archetypal disengaged family we read about in Chapter 2. There is so much encouragement to be oneself at as early an age as possible that often the necessary aspect of repression and civilization for the sake of society is ignored completely. This is a highly unconventional signature for any group of people who wish to work together, unless it is through the Internet, or on the intercom, Cellnet or via satellite transmission. One would not think of this family theme as 'warm', loving or overly concerned about the feelings of others in the group. This does not mean that it is none of those things, has no feeling-tone or is sociopathic, but it will not appear to be a family in concert in that way. The best of the solar/Uranian energy encourages freedom of thought, action and in relationships. The path of finding one's own way is well developed, and those whose families have this theme might find it very difficult indeed, if they have subscribed to a more conventional, Norman Rockwell-type vision. Certainly, personal ego development is encouraged, but in fact it is deeply threatening to the Sun/Uranus family because there is an element of competitiveness necessary to individuate. What others might regard as eccentricity is regarded as a normal and valued trait. What appears chaotic or weird to visitors from outside the family is very likely a security system for the individuals within it. The privacy of each person inside a family of this nature ensures that no one *really* knows who the other is; each thinks he or she is the 'sane' one and everyone else is the eccentric – while, in fact, all are quite mad in their own way. Of all the human attributes, thinking is most meritorious; creativity and innovation is valued far above order; autocracy is essential to self-discovery and individuation requires repeated departures and returns to and from the matrix of the family. The inconsistency in itself is a form of stability; however, for any one individual who needs more attention, more nurture, more assurance, this is a very uncomfortable home and even a run-of-the-mill kind of emotional need can be seen as cloying, infantile behaviour. There do appear to be mixed messages floating around all the time – ambivalent feelings abound in the Sun/Uranus collective, and if this grouping produces a distant, cool and detached aura, then eventually it will freeze itself out of existence – which often is staved off by importing a Watery, emotionally expressive, yet cool person via marriage or through partnership.

Sun/Neptune (including solar aspects with Pisces)

The characteristics of the enmeshed family described in Chapter 2 are pronounced and specific in a family which carries the theme of Pisces, Sun/Neptune or strongly twelfth-house collective planets. This can manifest from the sublime to the pathological. For instance, there is always a high feeling-tone, though this nuance is not always clearly expressive of specific emotions or needs, and thus creates an aura of insecurity and 'checking' on what someone might *really* want or what people are *really* meaning. Anyone with a sense of independent identity in this family is mysterious, difficult to grasp, perhaps even lost in the family system. As with Jupiter, there is a religious theme, but this is largely mystical, metaphysical or even scientific in orientation. There are symptoms which are often received as negative, but in fact are part of a creative personality-type if well directed and channelled positively; these can be described as hysterical, psychic, visionary, empathic in nature, imaginative and singular. In such a family, independent individual ego development is *not* encouraged whereas dependency upon the family *is*. Because of this fact, individuation out of a Sun-Neptune family is difficult, because the complexes – which are the core-impetus of creativity – are shape-shifters and difficult to locate and anchor. For an individual in the Sun/Neptune family to come into a sense of separateness and Selfhood often requires a literal rebirth, cutting or severing from the family – re-enacting the cutting of the umbilical cord in a psychological and spiritual fashion. There is often much confusion about, which can be amusing, or chaos abounding, which is terrifying, depending upon the 'level' at which the family actually operates. There exists a lack of boundaries between family members – for example the mother might say, '*I* am cold, therefore *you* need to put on a sweater,' or the father might be completely unable to comprehend why his son does not want to (or simply cannot) follow in his footsteps and continues to witter on about how his son/daughter will be there to head the company, do the job, care for him, etc. when his time has come due. Because the feelings of lack of personal space in such a family are strong, it is essential for the individual to learn to erect appropriate and clear boundaries and self-definition in order to mature into adulthood. Very often saviour-types are attracted into the family sphere through marriage or friendly relationships to help one or other of the 'victims' – Sun/Neptune families often need to import earthy and solid types of people into their milieu for balance.

Sun/Pluto (including solar aspects with Scorpio)

This is a power-orientated family theme. As we know, power is neutral until it is given form and focus. If the Sun/Pluto motif is *genuinely* strong, that is, if there is a consistent Scorpio, Sun/Pluto or even eighth-house thread that runs back through generations and exists across the family lines and is centred within the nuclear family, we are looking at an exceptionally intense, highly volatile family theme. Plutonium is a by-product of a nuclear-fission reaction – the Sun itself is a series of nuclear reactions, and a nuclear reactor is a lethal container, surrounded by 'heavy water' as a coolant. Locked in the nature of Pluto is the power of the nuclear image – it can be life-giving or annihilating. Pluto is still relatively new for us, as it was only inserted into horoscopes after its sighting in 1930; however, we have come to know it well in a short period of time. In this type of family motif, mystery is highly valued and there are many skeletons in the closets. Often there is high drama, but it can be subtle, manifesting more as undercurrents, loaded silence, implications, subversions and emotional undertows. There is something terribly charismatic about this theme and though the family as an organism is tight, there is extreme individualism found within its walls. There is the water/fire combination which is a conflict of interest – there is the need for dynamic action and recognition, but the intense need for secrecy and power. Thus it can be difficult to establish boundaries, as the family acts not only as a protective space but also can become a prison in which personal power is subverted by the whole. Therefore ego development often requires stealth and secrecy; individuation out of the Sun/Pluto family requires the utmost of courage, self-knowledge and strength. Though truth is often feared, lies make members ill, literally. There are often themes or stories in the family that centre around separations, mysteries, deaths and dishonour. There is a tremendous life-force threading through the group which can annihilate individuality and result in one member withdrawing or 'blowing', causing the emotional equivalent of a nuclear melt-down. The emotions, especially passion and love, are powerful, and possessiveness towards each other is high. There can be great rifts, severing, disinheritances, feuds and so forth, all of which thread through the extended family and across lines. Very often the family energy attracts into it Uranian types of people, those who are unaffected by the power and have a strong, individual presence themselves, and are either oblivious to the undertow or are clean and clear enough to help freshen it up.

THE MOON AND LUNACY

The nature of the Moon comes out only at night – that is, our deepest, most hidden and mysterious well of feeling, intuition and emotion is something kept deeply interior. We are only truly aware of someone's lunar side when we know him or her well, and have felt their feelings, experienced their compassion and lived in their world long enough to have been nourished by and given nurture to him or her. It is the secret life, really, the dark side of the Moon. We take for granted our own feelings and we do not really *think* of them – often. To think of feelings is odd, unnatural and stilted. It is possible, just as it is possible to feel what one thinks, but it is an uneasy alliance we have between thinking and feeling. It is even more difficult to articulate a feeling – try it. It is enough to make one quite mad. People in the heat of passion, anger, feelings usually do sound irrational and lunatic. Trying to express feelings in a verbal way we are under the rays of the Moon, endeavouring to bring into solar clarity, deep, hidden, changing, fluctuating, emotional moods.

So we might stand in accusation of everyone, saying that they cannot express their feelings! Who can? Certain gifted people can convey feeling-tone through their art, but most of us might only be able to project a minute aspect of feeling or speak incoherently of the complexity of emotion swelling inside. Feeling-tone is more physical than mental, so we find our feelings are often mirrored in our bodies and how our bodies are behaving. We pick up other people's feelings in our instinctual levels: in our gut, in our muscles, in our viscera – we say people 'get under our skin', 'in our blood', 'up our nose', make us 'sick to our stomach', a feeling has 'gone to our head', that a characteristic is 'bred in the bone', that 'blood is thicker than water' – most of our deep, emotional metaphors and images are physical! The expression of feeling through body-therapy is millennia-old – the Chinese knew thousands of years ago that feelings (health) were in the body and found subtle measurements for variation on degrees of feeling being held in the assorted meridians in the body. The calibrations of health, ease-in-the-body and feelings are minute in acupuncture – what other medicine describes one's pulse as 'having the rhythm of a silkworm eating a mulberry leaf'?

As with the solar images, we have been indoctrinated to accept wholesale the idea that lunar is feminine. The Moon does have 'feminine' attributes in the sense that the womb, food, nurture, emotional life and security are all related to lunar imagery and the sign Cancer, which is traditionally considered the prime ruler of the family and the home, the biological origins of life and patterns of nature and nurture. It is true that the mother, the feminine, plays a greater role in the establishment of those bases in early life and helps form the foundations for our own abilities to do the same in our life. But it is not specific to women *per se*, nor could we say the Moon is female or feminine in its character. Our fathers play a tremendous role in our being free and clear enough to distinguish feeling from thought; and being strong enough to experience feelings without emotions diminishing or overshadowing action.

However, the primal lunar patterns are established in the womb and in the very first days, months and years of life. Those patterns are virtually impossible to break. If the reward is great enough, we can condition ourselves to delay or re-route instinctive responses – for example, if one has a fear of intimacy or emotional invasion one might be able to allow certain safe people in if one is sufficiently rewarded by them not abusing one's sense of safety – *and*, most importantly, if there is love and generosity in the relationship. In very specific circumstances we can adjust our responses through positive conditioning to individual people or specific situations, but the instinctual response will always flag itself first. We can learn new, more appropriate responses for special and particular conditions, but it seems we cannot change our instincts.

These instincts are very possibly encoded during the union of male and female, of sperm and egg. This act is beautifully symbolized by a conjunction between the Sun and the Moon – a New Moon. However, once the embryo is firmly implanted in its nest, it becomes wholly dependent upon its mother's body to feed and protect it, and *then* the instincts become intrinsically bound up with the mother's system – both psychic and somatic. The mother's hormonal system is affected by the pregnancy, and her own nutrients are passed into the infant. The symbiosis between mother and *in utero* child prepares them both for a new life: for the mother, the birth of the child marks a step across the threshold into a new life for herself, and the child has passed its initiation into independent life.

The pregnant mother is responsive to the embryo-as-future as well. Who the child is destined to become is already imprinted, its natal chart is already constellating and the moment of birth – which is yet to arrive – is in fact highly influential in this prenatal phase. In 'Rejected in the Womb' (page 290), we see how a mother is affected by her growing baby as much as her infant is *in utero*. There may even be a mysterious union on the quantum level that assures that the arrival of the infant will correspond to the appropriate transits for the parents to experience a dimension of themselves hitherto unexplored. In the case of Mohsin ('Who am I?', page 270), we see how the pre-natal eclipse pattern led him to his adoptive parents! The mystery and miracle of birth is boundless.

Just as with all the planets, the Moon does not make people *do* anything, nor does it appear to be the cause of anything psychological; however, the Moon is a receptacle that holds memory of all gestations and births down the line. This is why dynastic patterns which are associated with the Moon more frequently, but not exclusively, come down through the maternal line – because the influence of the mother's somatic mnemonic on the infant's is whole and profound. From womb to womb, the mothering, nurturing and symbiotic aspect of relationship is passed down, from generation to generation. Forming relationships as an adult, especially romantic relationships that involve a mutual emotional-survival dependency-web – which are not strictly procreative relationships, by the way, for example, homosexual relationships are *not* about breeding – usually hope to recapture this interdependence on the emotional level and re-create a relationship where two hearts beat as one. The precedent for this kind of relationship occurs in the womb. Men and women want to create this fusion for entirely different reasons. On the most instinctual level, women wish to form a fused union with a man to reproduce themselves and men want the same fusion to reproduce their relationship with their mother. Perhaps not with their mum, but at least with their mother's body-comfort.

Women-to-women relationships are very womb-like, highly organic – the embodiment of the 'gatherer' archetype – usually with lots of plants, pets, food, talking, emotional exchange and possessive togetherness, while men-to-men relationships largely tend towards the 'hunter' archetype, wherein there is lots of searching, looking, hunting, bachelorhood retention, competition, setting one off against the other, even in good, domestic relationships. However, even within this horribly blatant black/white stereotype that I am using as an illustration lies an archetypal dimension . . . men are men and women are women and they are very, very different. When they form loving relationships together, lifetime partnerships, the intrinsic, primordial, instinctive nature of the gender is thus doubly strong. Men's and women's relationship to the womb is vastly different – women are at home with it, and men are either longing to return to it or somewhat revolted by it.

The thought of an intimate relationship with his mother is usually and normally (sorry, Freud) an absurd, wholly unthinkable, physically repulsive concept to any man – *but* the need to have unconditional love, nurture and support is not. Men's bodies remember that maternal love and where it came from, and their desire to re-enter the womb is much more basic and readily, repeatedly attainable than a woman's – a man simply needs to have sex to get as close to the womb as he can, once having left it at birth, where-as a woman has to replicate her mother in order totally to recall her own intra-uterine experience – in other words, she has to become pregnant her-self. Hence, the lunar responses in men and women are entirely different from each other, and though they might have the Moon in the same sign in their horoscope, it will manifest completely different characteristics. Men who do not lust after women, and have found sexual happiness with other men, also long for the womb, but they do not wish to endure the emotional feedback loop that recreates the mother–son dynamic. Hence, they find womb-mates of a different order, and have relationships which exploit the male/female polarity within themselves.

The Moon shows how our mother acted as a conduit for our ancestral legacy in the emotional realm. What aspect of the family is being focused on in each of her children is shown by the position of their natal Moon. She has passed on not only *her* needs, but all needs from all time, but only a par-ticular facet will be highlighted in each child. The fact that all children in a single family do not have the same Moon sign, in fact all members of the family are likely to have different conditions around their natal Moon, at-tests to the complexity of this natural selection of recall. Just as our stories about our parents are going to be different from our siblings' stories, so are our planets arranged in ways unlike other family members – but there is always a connection. In large families of four or more children, the odds in-crease on replication of Moon signs. I have several large families in my files who include one or more children with the same Moon sign or the Moon in the same sign as one of the parents, or same lunation phase. This is not un-usual. The most common interchange in family horoscopes are the Sun, Moon and ascendant, as one might imagine.

The Moon in families can cause more discord than any other planetary arrangement. This is because our body-memory insists that what we see is not all there is. The Moon knows deeply what the undercurrents are in the family matrix, and it resonates on myriad levels to complex tones and feelings. To listen to the story of each child in a family, and their individual tale and experience of the parents and the family dynamic, might sound like they all grew up not only in different households, but in entirely different cultures! We have a bias at birth, and that bias remains constant – though it may open and allow new information to enter into the picture, evolve to incorporate more possibilities and alternatives, there is still the rigidity of the natal promise. The actual experience might be very, very different. This is where the split occurs – the split between what we feel and know to be true in our instinctual nature, and what is imposed upon us as truth by action.

Lunar themes mean just that – there is a *theme* in the family dynamic which holds all the instinctual, primal, visceral responses to emotional or survival issues. How those are enacted and translated into civilized behaviour, and whether or not one can be creative with the underlying theme, is entirely dependent on specific, individual people and situations.

The links that run through maternal lines don't have to be overly complex – simple is often better for true comprehension of a deep line. We often hear of same birth-dates in families, or marriage to someone whose birth-date is the same as a family member and so on. But if we find a theme with mothers and daughters that shows what is running down the line, we may find a solution to a problem. For example, a lunar-link:

In one family, looking at four generations of women, the grandmother was a Pisces Sun square Pluto in Gemini, her eldest daughter had Mars, Venus and Uranus in Pisces in the fourth house with Venus quincunx Neptune, and, in turn, *her* eldest child, a daughter, had a fourth house Sun and a Moon/Neptune conjunction. Then, her eldest granddaughter had Venus in Pisces opposite a Virgo Moon. She also exemplifies, in her Moon/Venus split, the long lineage of the maternal line:

1. *Grandmother*: Moon conjunct Venus conjunct Neptune late degrees of Taurus. (Sun 9° Pisces square Pluto in 4° Gemini.) (Husband had Aries Sun.)
2. *Her eldest daughter*: Venus 12°, Mars 9°, Uranus 3° in Pisces in *fourth house*. Sun Capricorn. Venus is exactly quincunx Neptune at 12° Leo. (Side note: she has Moon in Aries – and a younger sister with Sun in Aries – their father had Sun in Aries.)
3. *That woman's only daughter*: twelfth house Sun square Pluto; Moon conjunct Neptune in Libra, Pisces on IC, fourth house cusp.

4. *And her first daughter*: Venus in 6° Pisces opposite the Moon in 12° Virgo. Sun in first.

5. *And her younger daughter*: Moon conjunct Jupiter in the fourth house. Sun in first conjunct Mars (a bit of the Aries grandparent-line).

The Pisces grandmother (1) emigrated at the end of the First World War, and only once was able to return, when her eldest daughter (2), whom she had taken with her, was one year old. That eldest daughter had the 'heavy' fourth house, wherein she carried the unconscious recollection of the maternal family-of-origins. She was deeply affected by her mother's longing, sadness and anger (shown by her Mars/Uranus/Venus conjunction at the IC and in the fourth house) over never being in her own cultural milieu again in her lifetime. This longing (and repressed rage) of the grandmother was consciously transferred to her elder daughter, who became alcoholic later in her adult life and had great bouts of displaced nostalgia about her mother's birth-country! She then further passed on the astrological signatures – and the ancestral legacy – in a new strain to *her* daughter, who has the twelfth house Sun and Moon/Neptune conjunction ruler of Pisces fourth house IC (3).

Already we can see the permutations of the Pisces, Moon/Neptune and fourth house legacy from the maternal side, coming down three generations. This is further extrapolated into a Moon/Venus theme as it moves down another generation: this only daughter was to have a great rift with her alcoholic mother and not see her for eight years, only to return to nurse her, and do all the terminal care in her last weeks of life. (Inherited Sun/Pluto from the grandmother, and with her Moon/Neptune ruler of the Pisces fourth house, the maternal link settled in her to resolve.) Eventually, after her mother died and her own children had gone on to college and career, she went to the grandmother's homeland and became an immigrant herself, in the land of her Pisces grandmother.

The fourth generation: she had two children, both daughters, the eldest of whom has Venus in Pisces opposite the Moon in Virgo (4). Her elder daughter exemplifies the duality of the feminine archetypes, thus the need for bringing harmony into the female line (her Moon is in the eighth house of 'individuating the personal ancestral lineage'). So far she is working through much of the repressed independent female spirit of the grandmother and great-grandmother who preceded her. She does not want to compromise her values and her femininity for the sake of relationships. She does feel the split between the nurturing feminine (Moon) and the more exotic, seductive and erotic feminine (Venus/Aphrodite). This great-granddaughter is the latest of a long line of artistically inclined and talented but non-productive artists in the family and has actually become a very gifted practising artist. (Thus bringing the Moon opposite Venus into a blend, rather than a split, and working it through on a creative level.)

Her younger daughter (5) has no planets in Pisces and nothing in her twelfth house; however, she *has* received her legacy of Neptune in the fourth house and a Moon/Jupiter conjunction in the fourth house – in the *same sign* as her mother. She has inherited the mode of relationship (Libra) directly from her mother, but there is an interesting little twist: her father has a Moon/Jupiter conjunction in *Gemini* in *his* twelfth house, so she has got a bit of the father's personal and ancestral energy to carry around and process through her nuclear family house, and be the 'blend' between mother's personal legacy (fourth house) and father's more archetypal legacy (his twelfth house planets in her fourth house). She has no remarkable Moon/Venus relationship in her horoscope – this she escaped – she is a 'motion artist', a dancer, was a successful model, studied martial arts, and also has writing skills. She does not want to be responsible for the maternal line even though she has received much implicated material from *both* the family-of-origin ancestors (fourth house), and has absorbed a quality from both parents which speaks of her strong need for independence! She 'travels away' (Jupiter) from the responsibility for the maternal legacy in many ways, yet has clear traits in personality and attitude that are virtually identical to her mother (same Moon sign). Fortunately, her mother does not expect her to vindicate the sins of the mothers, recognizes that it all col-ludes individually, and is wholly supportive of her personal creativity and way of expressing her unique individuality. In this way her Moon/Jupiter in the fourth house signals the 'hopes of the mother-line' and all that implies, and coupled with the inherited factors from her father, mediates the mater-nal suffering to a great degree. She was also the first to have her own child.

Summary of the Moon

In the family of planets, the Moon is two things: mother and baby. It is the needy one *and* the caring one. The Moon is the 'planet' which gets attention by alternately whining, manipulating, insinuating, being moody, helpless, in-fantile, subtle – or affects other planets in the chart by being powerfully silent and suggestive, helpful, cautious, concerned, nurturing and protective. Its nature is to impose itself on other more linear planets in emotional ways – feelings, irrational behaviour and implications can even unsettle old Saturn! Although the Moon is reflective and implicitly related to the Sun (all its light is solar-reflection, or earth-shine), it is the most holistically influential body in the family of planets – and in the horoscope when viewed for family matters.

The Moon is the mother-image, the adaptive principle, and is *usually*, but not always, associated with the females in the family – mother, aunts, sisters, and the maternal line. The Moon is the container of the infant, its home during the formation of its body and deep instinctual nature. Lunar responses to life outside the womb can be traced back to the short intra-uterine experience. In the womb we *are* our mothers; we are not separate, but one. Her nourishment is ours, her heart-beat is tuned with ours, her emotions affect us, her body holds our body. This is the most significant body in the horoscope with respect to family dynamics, for it is the maternal line which acts as the conduit for generational transition. The Moon should be looked at as the primal, instinctual response to one's life-force. The Moon can be the weakest link in the chart – one can be strong, heroic, creative, amusing, innovative, brilliant and healthy but can be emotionally barren, hostile, tortured and impoverished.

The Moon in the horoscope shows how our environment affected us from the very instant of birth – and from that premise, how we perceive our environment and the people in it. The first contact with the outside world is meant to be the receiving arms of our mother. The infant, longing for re-connection to its source of life, is infused with this primal imprint for the rest of its life. The mood of the moment in astrology is the Moon – the Moon in the natal chart is the mood of life for us!

The Moon holds images of the fourth house, and in the fourth house lies the ancestral pool – not just the mother but the blending of maternal and paternal lines. This blend is held in the alembic of the fourth house, or the womb of the horoscope, and if the Moon is a very strong planet there are personal ancestral issues to be delved into. Only in conversation with ourself (or with a client with a strong lunar link) can we determine to what degree this is a maternal issue alone.

One very significant pattern in which the Moon can be problematic, and actually speaks of both parents, one by absence and the other by over-prominence, is the 'amputated Moon'. When the Moon is separated from the rest of the *Gestalt* of the horoscope – the handle of a bucket formation – it is very difficult for the person to be able to connect his or her feelings with behaviour, either of his or her own, or others. This lunar oddity usually indicates that there was a serious problem with the feminine in the family. It can indicate the only male in a family of women, or a family in which the father was particularly weak and ineffective. Men with this amputated Moon find it easier for women to carry their feelings than for them to be responsible for their own. It is absolutely necessary for the split-off Moon person to make every conscious effort to practise discovery of feelings. A typical scenario could run thus: a man has no idea what a woman is feeling and charges ahead with ideas, plans, expectations and assumptions and is shocked, horrified and dismayed to discover that she has no idea what he is wanting or thinking. Another issue could arise when the man is so disconnected from his own feelings that he damages the women around him by unconsciously 'using' them or their feelings to his own end.

Women who have this configuration find that they are oddly out of synch with their own feelings; they have tremendous intuition about other people, because they have likely grown up in an environment wherein they had to divorce their own feelings on behalf of looking after their mother's or their sibling's feelings. They find that they have a delayed reaction to emotional situations and are dissonant within themselves. These women are incredibly capable, reliable and have the potential for taking on very solar work, but suffer quietly, wondering why no man or woman will come to look after them.

The segregated Moon is like a hook; other people can hang their feelings on it, weighing it down, leaving no room for the owner of it to claim their feelings. This can be sad or it can be so unconscious that only their most intimate friends and, particularly, lovers will be aware of it. The image that comes to mind is this: if we were to fold the horoscope in half, thus 'folding' the Moon back into the other half of the chart, it would be integrated. On an emotional level, this needs to be done, and can be through conscious effort and awareness. There will always be an admirable capacity for emotional clarity and objectivity with this position, but its pathology is coldness, lack of empathy and delayed responses. It could be an ideal place for the Moon if it were treated in this way, using the metaphor of folding the chart in half, thus achieving integration.

LUNAR THEMES IN FAMILY DYNAMICS

Moon/Venus (includes lunar aspects with Libra and/or Taurus)

The receptivity to aggression is most powerful; there may be a strong maternal lineage which polarizes in the maternal/feminine dichotomy of the Madonna/Magdalene image of woman; that is, sensuality *versus* sexuality; maternity *versus* femininity; expressive, emotionally dominant, with a high level of romantic themes in relationships. There can be a confusion of values in the family, strong passionate agreement and disagreement on emotional and value-laden subjects. Feelings can dominate the rational capacity to understand what is expected of one. The function of creativity is very high and often encouraged, as both the Moon and Venus have to do with art and the senses. In the family, the emotional tone is the central principle, or at least the Moon/Venus person responds to the emotional tone powerfully. The nurturing, caring, controlling pattern is passed into both men and women equally, but for a man the Moon/Venus dichotomy can create a problem in sexuality wherein his wife ceases to be seen as his lover because the archetype of the dual feminine image is split. Moon/Venus splits are natural in the sense that there are two archetypal images of the feminine – the seductress and the maternal nurturer. However, when the Moon and Venus are in hard aspect, particularly the square and opposition, there are frequently problems in integrating the two faces of femininity. Very often, the women in the family have hidden one or other of their 'sides'. For example, the mother might have shown only the social, industrial and beautiful woman-face or alternatively suborned her 'seductress' by her maternal role, sacrificing her more exotic, erotic self.

Moon/Mars (includes lunar aspects with Aries)

The family has a line of emotional competitiveness. There can be a distinct lack of sympathy from the family at large when emotional issues arise. A deep rage runs a thread through the family which can become symptomatic in chronic headache, ulcers, colon problems, skin disorders (if Saturn is involved) and other angry physical manifestations. There is often a lack of boundaries or respect within the emotional zone, and all feelings are interpreted as threatening. There is a great need for calm and serenity, which paradoxically can be achieved through dynamic action such as athletics, race-car driving, and other intense challenges. When Moon and Mars are part of a family inheritance, the emotional climate is volatile and uncertain and there is a nervous energy about the home. It is not always externalized, but can lurk in the corners only to erupt under pressure. Generally, the family thrives on news, adventure, excitement and drama, holding adventure and revolution high in esteem. Often Moon/Mars is unspoken because the social implications are unpleasant – raging around the home is generally not considered a healthy expression of feeling, so many families suppress this rage or assertion, or fail to find healthy ways of using the energy, thus often the individual who inherits the Moon/Mars aspect is the one who carries the family rage. The emotional legacy may contain resentment and jealousy over status of other family members; it can show a line of maternal rejection in favour of the male line. Paradoxically the family is emotionally independent within itself, but needs the physical presence of its individual members for security. This is a strongly masculine aspect, and tends to be found in families in which the women are either very open about their needs for success and achievement, or alternatively have suppressed them, projecting their anger on to their children. (See Chapter 15, 'Rejected in the Womb'.)

Moon/Jupiter (includes lunar aspects with Sagittarius)

This contact shows a family in which there is a line of emotional wanderers, dreamers, artists, philosophers, politicians and moralists. There are usually very strong myths connecting generations, stories which are told and retold to reinforce self-belief. The playful, emotionally youthful side of life is emphasized, indeed, may indicate a family filled with generations of eternal youths and idealists who never achieve the *senex*-consciousness of the adult. For all its apparent benign traits, Jupiter has a cool streak – it can be insensitive and judgemental, passing moral arbitration off on all strangers – although this unpleasant trait is usually compensated for by a gallant and generous streak. The feminine line has strong masculine-orientated traits such as iconoclasm, adventuring, social conscience, career goals and so on. Moon/Jupiter is romantic and hopeful, desirous of relationships which bring cultures together, and there will be a line of mixed marriages, cross-cultural unions, vast gaps in relationships, possibly many relationships. Frequently the Moon/Jupiter is wanting in intimacy, but instead provides a friendly home environment which purports to be supportive and non-judgemental, encouraging new horizons. There is an instinctive drive towards independence and freedom, which can contribute to families who breed members who are incapable of emotional commitment.

Moon/Saturn (including lunar aspects with Capricorn)

This is a difficult and powerful family signature. Both the Moon and Saturn are parental images, one nurturing and the other devouring or restraining and controlling. The family legacy is usually fraught with suppressed and severely contained emotions. If Moon/Saturn is a strong and consistent family theme, then the line *has* actually suffered extreme hardship – culturally, politically, emotionally, vocationally or physically. The family system itself can appear to be cold and unwelcoming to an outsider, but in fact, might simply be very well contained and unaware of other than its own *Gestalt*. At some point along the line, a Moon/Saturn theme will produce a circuit breaker, a wild person, one who challenges the stifled feelings in his or her environment and thus splits off from the rest. Emotional aridity is found in a family system of people nourished by depression, difficulty, guilt, obligation and endurance. It is not lack of love that is indicated, but the ability to *demonstrate* or *express* loving feelings is diminished and, as a result, self-worth becomes an active issue for those who carry the signature through Moon in Capricorn or in aspect to Saturn. Creativity is given birth through effort and generally has pragmatic value; emotional separation is difficult to achieve; men are more nurturing than the women with this aspect, possibly because of the authoritative 'midwife' characteristics of Saturn; there is usually a problem about feeling authentic, solid, real, whole, equal – clearly this can manifest in over-compensatory characteristics of emotional tyranny, dynastic attitudes, imperious pretensions and excessive ambition. The hardships endured by a lunar/Saturnian theme often do produce very successful individuals once the balance between authority and authenticity is found.

Moon/Uranus (including lunar aspects with Aquarius)

Strong Uranian aspects from the Moon, or even the Aquarius Moon, shows a family in which emotional display is considered to be eccentric and rarely appreciated – unless erratic, flamboyant or dramatic flashes of emotionalism or sentimentality are present, which is also very Uranian. Generally, the

Uranus/Moon typology is non-maternal, very male and highly paternalistic in its values. There is difficulty in connecting the head with the heart – there is a natural, Cartesian split between the 'Ideal' and the 'Real' that family members are aware of, but might not be able to bridge. It is the signature of a non-domestic family, where the middle way is a chore. Because of this cool streak, emotionally 'needy' members are often ostracized and become scapegoats – in fact, they might be simply needy of normal emotional contact and display. However, by comparison to the heady, cool mood of the collective ethos, they appear infantile and are rejected by their 'independent' family. There is a streak of outrageousness and independence from others which can block the expression of feeling – this does not mean there are no feelings but, as with Saturn, the expression of them is difficult and unconventional. The father is frequently the passive-dominant parent; males do well in this emotional environment if they are secure, females thrive less well, unless they, too, need great spaces around them; emotionally disengaged, but generous, open-hearted and spontaneous; prefers collective activities to intimate family gatherings where emotions or feelings might arise; active, political, social in a humanitarian (that is, disengaged from the personal) collective fashion – i.e. causes, crusades, quests, movements are often part of the connection between Aquarian/Uranian type families.

Moon/Neptune (including lunar aspects with Pisces)

There is a distinct lack of emotional clarity in the family and it can be difficult to separate one person's mood from another's – no one knows who is feeling what because all members seem to swim in emotional circles within the family. There are strong physical hereditary traits. The Moon/Neptune Piscean family are largely dreamers, spiritualists, all longing to return to the womb and find numerous ways in which to accomplish this psychological state. Individuals are highly interdependent in psychic and emotional ways, seeking nourishment from the emotions and feelings of each other; however, it is a highly creative and responsive family ethos. Finding one's own identity is difficult, as members often feel they must actually leave the house and go into another environment to achieve emotional clarity. The mother is usually the apparently passive but actually more dominant parent; where her weakness is the hub of the family wheel, she may be ill, alcoholic, a victim, an immigrant, a second-class citizen in a real or psychological way. However, paradoxically, traditionally, women seem to have fared better than men with this aspect, perhaps owing to the softness and vulnerability of Neptune, though that could be changing with the times. Escapist tendencies are *very* strong – which are *not* always a negative attribute – and the desire to leave the world can result in highly imaginative, creative, poetic, musical, mathematical, technical wizards. As a theme, this might be the most difficult to understand, grasp and actually work with, especially if it is truly strongly configured throughout the entire family system.

Moon/Pluto (including lunar aspects with Scorpio)

Something hidden lurks in the family history; the emotional tone is intense, controlling and compelling. This is very likely a matriarchal line, wherein the women dominate by psychic and material management ability. This is the strongest indicator that there is a secret in the family, which will emerge through one of the hereditary members who has a Moon in Scorpio, in the eighth house, or hard aspects of the Moon to Pluto. The family line is loaded with healers and magicians, law-makers and law-breakers. Perhaps partly because of its incredible emotional endurance, a deep perceptivity, emotional maturing is achieved early, though usually this seasoned, even jaded attitude is directly related to some form of exposure to 'adult' experiences and situations, which are incomprehensible to a child-mind and catapult the individual into premature adulthood. It is often necessary for some form of emotional amputation to take place for the sake of survival, and always surfaces later. This characteristic threads through all Plutonian-theme families and, as a result, they are particularly sensitive to hidden agendas and always subject to emotional blackmail and fear of loss. Feuding in the family is very common, sometimes for a lifetime, but often just for the power struggle. Individuals in the family can experience feelings of loneliness in crowded rooms – for the family background is always present. There is always powerful psychic connection of the mother with other family members; the father can be hidden from view, but powerful in his emotional or physical absence. There can be strong attachment to revenge, lack of forgiveness, inability to let pride fall away in favour of harmony. Myths about the history of the family are populated with eccentrics, rebels, imperialists, invaders, renegades, cowboys/Indians, illegitimate kin, defrocked priests, lapsed nuns, mysterious disappearances, secrets and unexplained deaths.

NOTES

1. Janet McCrickard, *Eclipse of the Sun*, Gothic Image Publications, Glastonbury, 1990. This book is a breakthrough in many ways. Not only does it inform us in a clear, rational way, but also breaks down all locked stereotypes of Sun and Moon symbolism. I cannot recommend this book highly enough. It is a prerequisite for any astrological understanding of the luminaries and their *modus operandi* in the natal horoscope. It is written with a scholarly background in a clearly demarcated fashion, with numerous myths all succinctly written. It lacks the strident, desperate tone of much feminist literature, as clearly Ms McCrickard has a desire to balance an equation rather than create a new bias.

2. Howard Sasportas and Liz Greene, *The Luminaries*, Samuel Weiser, New York, 1993. In seminar-format, Howard and Liz explore the dynamics of the Sun and Moon and the parental images underlying and overlaying the lights. Highly recommended reading.

3. Dane Rudhyar, *The Lunation Cycle*, Aurora Press, 1993.

4. (a) Erin Sullivan, *Retrograde Planets: Traversing the Inner Landscape*, Chapter 1: 'The Sun', Arkana, Contemporary Astrology Series, London, 1992. Self-referencing is the highest form of nepotism; however, I *do* go into great detail about the Sun in the first part of this book. (b) Michel Gauquelin, *Neo-Astrology*, *passim*, Arkana, London, 1992.

5.

Mothers and Fathers:
Freud Had It Half Right

Although the separation of the World Parents is, strictly speaking, an integral part of the hero myth, the developments which, at that stage, could only be represented in cosmic symbols now enter the phase of humanization and personality formation.

With the birth of the hero the primordial struggle begins – the struggle with the First Parents. This problem, in personal and transpersonal form, dominates the hero's whole existence, his birth, his fight with the dragon, and his transformation.

(Erich Neumann, *History of Consciousness*)

PARENTHOOD — A STATE OF MADNESS

Becoming a parent immediately and instantly catapults one into a new status – there is no 'almost a parent', just like there is no 'sort of pregnant'. All the preparation towards that end, the hopes, wishes, antenatal experience, the final moments of labour and birth are *not* parenthood. That comes in an instant. The transits of that instant, that special moment of time, are forever impressed in the psyche and soul of both parents and embodied by the child. The child is a walking transit. From the second of the child's arrival, the effect of that moment – the baby – will be in relation to the heavens and their configurations.

This transition affects the entire family dynamic if there are children already, and if it is a first child the birth begins another branch. If it *is* a first child and the father is present, then the relationship as a couple has dramatically altered. No longer are they a couple, as such, but they are now a unit, a dynamic complex which reaches back far into their combined heritage, and old chords will be struck.

Freud had it partly right – he said that parents 'make' their children neurotic. Philip Larkin said, 'Your parents fuck you up', etc.; however, it must be considered that the arrival of a child into the lives of two adults has a powerful effect on the parents which can be akin to a form of madness. Have we ever considered seriously what the arrival of a child does to reasonable, relatively normal adults? It makes them temporarily insane. Parents are not in their right minds! They suffer from all sorts of neuroses which would never have constellated *a priori*. They become apprehensive, obsessed, over-cautious, future-orientated in the extreme, their bodies change, their priorities shift radically, their status in the world becomes wholly different – in short, they lose their past and gain an uncertain future. No wonder they are quite mad for a time. Whether or not they regain their sensibilities in time remains to be seen. On the whole, parents do adapt fairly well to their children, but very often they do not grow up with them, and in that way remain fixed in the (oddly normal behaviour in an abnormal condition) state of parenthood and lose their individuality.

Archetypes of parents – the World Parents – underlie our feelings and our expectations of our mother and father. Also, the Divine Child archetype underlies the feelings that parents have for their children. This is normal, healthy and natural. That it can conflict with the reality of life is the difficult part. There is a universality about parents and children which lies deeply in our inmost self, which comes into being in all parent/child relationships. There seems to be both a Good Parent and a Bad Parent archetype as well as the Divine Child and the Demon Seed. They both exist outside time. Thus, they are part of the psyche in a totally undifferentiated state. They emerge periodically and play havoc in our relationships in the family, and in relationships which extend outside the family when the old chords of early home environment are struck.

There are times when a child interrupts the lives of adults so drastically that they are unable to cope with their new status, and their own integrity as individuals and their personal relationship with each other deteriorates. There are children who, by some stroke of Fate, are indeed born to break the bond in the parental relationship, and sometimes in the entire family system. Modern horror movies have dwelt on this 'demon seed', the child of the devil, etc.; however, it is more likely that there is a necessity for this kind of challenge to enter the lives of the parents or family.

There are families in which a child is so psychologically removed from the family that his or her relationship is more within his own self and the parental status seems almost satellite-like (see 'Tobias – Touched by God', page 231)! Sometimes a child is so traumatized by his or her own birth that he never really recovers from it and is perpetually a burden to his family and parents. However, these are the more extreme and pathological situations which arise periodically. In the main, we deal primarily with the 'norm', that is, the majority of adults who find themselves in a temporarily acute, unique condition which abates with time and with the concurrent evolving maturity of their child and themselves.

There are also families wherein the child is born to be inadvertently victimized by his or her parents – where he or she is not allowed to develop in accord with his or her own instinctual nature and is constantly monitored or threatened by parental concern, and the child appears to acquiesce, but builds up a terrible inner rage. One or other of the parents is over-identified with the child and uses the birth of the child as an excuse to retard his or her (the parent's) own maturation and individuation process. This attitude, though highly unconscious, results in the adult's development being virtually arrested by the child's birth and the adult-parent appears to be thrown back into their own childhood, thus using (ab-using) their baby-child to help them recover something of their own lost inner child. In this case, we have a symbiotic development and the mother/child or father/child's charts are fused in some way.

We also see our parents through the specific lens of our own horoscope – what we see is what we need to see. We may not be able to resonate with a parent on a level which we ourselves cannot experience. Parents have as many personae as they have children. Many is the time I have talked to several adult children in the same family only to find that they had each experienced only a fragment of their parents or the other members of the family. Consciously, they had arrived at a relationship with the bare minimum contents of the mother, father or siblings. However, unconsciously, they are all part of the same pool, and in this way, the mystery of the unconscious acts out family drama in quite unexpected ways. The more open the lines of communication between parents and children, the more everyone in the family is allowed to expand their potentials.

I was explaining this to someone at lunch one day, and she was quite amazed. She had only just realized this phenomenon very recently in her life, when she and her sister were sharing memories of their parents. Her sister described her father and my friend recognized him, but it was 'not the father' that she had experienced. She still knew instinctively that she was right in her understanding of him from her own perspective. Both women had married men whom they recognized as being remarkably like their father, but each of their husbands embodied very *different aspects of the same father*. Because each of the women felt their father differently, each of them saw only what they would need from him.

Our parents are as multi-faceted as we ourselves are and as complex, in turn, as our children. There is no way that we can comprehend a whole person – especially since it is virtually impossible to comprehend our whole selves intellectually. Spiritually, this is another matter, but behaviourally, impossible. We have innate biases, lenses through which we perceive the world, and they are always shifting – both the quality of the lens and the perceived world. So we will, over time, see our parents and our children and, in turn, be perceived, in various ways – always leaving out some vital bit of information. Hence the danger of real misrepresentation and misunderstanding. All we can do is try to be as true to ourselves and as honest as possible, and hope like mad that we are allowing our important 'others' in our lives the same access to us as we would want of them.

Seeing, or rather, appreciating parents and children is rather like looking through a prism. We see many slightly variegated images of the same thing, depending on the angle of the cut and the cast of light refracting. Astrology delineates just what that angle is and the cut of the prism – by looking at the family horoscopes we can further differentiate what characteristics are more dominant to our perception and what traits we might be blind to.

However, as I said, on the whole, with the birth of a child, we are looking at fairly normal conditions which involve a major shock to the system – of both parent and child – which can be highly developmental and, indeed, cannot be avoided. The horoscope of a child is the transits of that moment in both parents' lives. We can read this transit as how the parents were feeling, what was going on in their lives and the entire emotional, experiential tone of the life at this period. However, this is one transit which will not pass and become history, but is a living, breathing entity which will be a constant reminder of a point in time. A time in which one person – the parent – became divided and dismembered into a new being – the child.

TWO NOT-SO-FAIRY-TALES

1. *The Good Mother*

Once upon a time an active, fulfilled, happy woman had her first child. When her baby was placed in her arms, she looked down upon it and fell deeply in love. It was so perfect, so beautiful and so much the embodiment of her soul and the love which gave it life, that her heart swelled with passion. She determined that she would do everything for her child and that it would want for nothing. There was nothing she would not do to protect, nurture, and contain her child. All her time and energy would not ever be enough, so she felt she must find a way in which to absorb herself into the child and give it everything that she had, including her very self if necessary. She fell into a great enchantment. Thus, she was so enamoured of her little baby, so in love with it, that *she swallowed it whole*.

2. *The Good Father*

Once upon a time there was a very ordinary, kind, nice man whose wife gave birth to their first child. He looked down at his beloved child and his heart swelled with pride and responsibility. He was filled with tenderness and love. Suddenly he was transformed from being an ordinary, very nice man into a demi-god, a hero who had an heir. Heirs must have something to inherit! Our nice hero-man knew he had no appropriate kingdom to offer his numinous new child and its now-holy mother, but soon it would be necessary to provide such a thing. He fell into an enchantment and raced off to create exactly such an empire to provide all the worldly goods possible, all the comforts and surrounds for his precious child and *was never seen again*.

These may seem odd and extreme for fairy-stories but really, they are quite appropriate for the behaviour of most of us to some actual or lesser degree. We have all heard of the 'devouring mother' and the 'absent father'. . . these are modern renditions of an archetypal condition which besets apparently benign and normal people upon the arrival of a child!

Now we do not really eat our children in any true sense of the word, but if we are honest, we do find that on occasion – perhaps more often than we like to think – parents have 'eaten' their creativity, 'swallowed' their spontaneity, 'devoured' their little developing selves. The deliciousness of the baby for the mother is an opportunity to eat it, to swallow it whole, so to speak, to devour it. Sometimes this is necessary, to prevent them running into the road or burning their hand; however, sometimes it is sheer convenience to keep a child from expressing itself at an awkward or inconvenient time. Mothers more than fathers do this, it would sadly seem, largely because they have more of a biological, gut-link to the child and, along with that instinctual pull, often more influence in the early development of the child. Women are more likely to be associated with nourishment and nurturing anyway, and they still spend a greater amount of time feeding, clothing and providing the basic, daily, nurturing life-necessities for their children than does the father. Thus, the mother *is* often the one who is the most impatient, the least indulgent and the one who will be closest in the most soulful, physical way to the child. Thus, both archetypally and practically, she frequently stands as a more psychically threatening entity to the development of the child's psychology. She will often require more holistic behaviour standards on a daily basis than the father will, whereas his behaviour requirements are as powerful, but more specific, as we will see later on in this chapter.

This responsibility for a woman to be the one who 'watches over' can be overwhelming and she can inadvertently become the devouring mother. She may feel that her responsibility to her children is such that she must never let up watching them, commenting on their behaviour and coercing them into becoming something they are not. The pressure on a woman, especially if she is not with the father of her child/ren, is tremendous. In the light of modern psychology, she is doomed, anyway, into the role of the covetous, Medea-like creature who is often (rightfully so at times) angry at the way things have worked out for her. Her life may not be one of high-level fulfilment in child-rearing, but one of suppressed ambition. Thus, her managerial abilities can be over-administrative in the family and directed specifically at the children. This is a situation which is often found to run down through the maternal line ... there is a generational link to the 'way women are' in the family. Certainly, the mother's experience is transmitted in a visceral, emotional, feeling way to the child *in utero* and in childhood and, long after, in adolescence and adulthood – to be seen again and again in the lunar aspects of her children and their children.

All of this leads us to think in terms of lunar experience: the one who watches over, who contemplates, who feeds, nourishes and reflects. The Moon is the 'light' of the night, the shape shifter and the versatile container of the Sun's light. Although in the chapter on 'The Sun and the Moon' it seems apparent that the Moon is not wholly 'female' and the Sun is not solely 'male', there still is the astrological symbol as we have used it for aeons – the Moon is still the mother and the Sun remains the father of the horoscopic family. We can 'degenderize' as much as we wish, but there are still the underlying archetypal essences, and that is very much what families are about.

The Moon in the chart speaks of the maternal line, the lineage as it goes back generation before generation – the women in the family, the mothers, pass on their legacy through the Moon and its aspects, even though we might find our actual father more lunar and our mother more solar by description. Moon and mother are still vitally linked and in that way we will analyse the relationships and aspects between the Moon and the planets in the natal horoscope with respect to our links to our maternal line. The mother lives outside time and her domain is the realm of feelings, moods, the inner matrix, instincts and soul, whereas the father has his manor in the outer world of time, space, accomplishment, mind and the mysteries of the expanding horizon.

Obviously, fathers do not immediately dart off into the forest (or the city) at the birth of a child, but our modern fairy-tale is not far from the truth. The responsibility of the father still seems to be material and not maternal. His role is largely one of a satellite support figure, who must sacrifice his own desire to lie about nursing the child. There is in some men a strong desire to do just that – to have the sole responsibility for the care and primary nurture of their baby, but it is rare. Mostly, it seems, men would rather not have that responsibility, and would rather provide the comfort, care and containment for the mother and child in the classic, archetypal male way – by not being there all the time, and bringing home the goods which will offer the family a better lifestyle. There is some positive truth to the 'absent' father – indeed, there may be a necessity and a vital link to solarization of identity in the elusive figure of 'father'. Again, though the Sun is not male, the Sun is the solar-heroic nature of an individual and we must find that in the masculine aspect of ourselves, in our own psyche, in our own soul.

Solarization of consciousness requires that we become increasingly compartmentalized and more uniquely individual – that we separate ourselves out from the matrix of baby-ness and oneness-with-all. The process of individuation – that experience of becoming increasingly who we are – demands that we become increasingly objective in our participation in our subjective experience. This appears to be a paradox, and so it is. The paradox of 'objectively observing our subjective experience' is vital to self-awareness. If we are constantly in the mood of life, in the feeling zone of things, then we are not capable of articulating our selves very well. We must pull away from feeling, step out of mood and become 'watchers' in order to be able to stand on our own two feet and declare an independent spirit and identity. This is where the father and his 'distance', his 'absence', becomes not only necessary but crucial in the development of our seeking-self. We must find the strength and the courage to step outside the comfort of our room, house, garden, yard and into the unknown area of community and world. Because we usually find father out there, he not only personifies the heroic jump into the world, he symbolizes our own need to develop a 'solar' consciousness.

So the Sun in the horoscope as the symbol for the father really means the impetus for outreach and accomplishment, because we know that the Sun is not about men nor is the Sun itself 'male'. The relationship of the Sun in the horoscope to other planets is, however, primarily the link to our paternal line. The Sun's position is never far from our heritage and from our father's relationship to us and, in turn, his own paternal experience. The inheritance from our paternal line is most important in finding the father within ourself. We must learn to be 'distant', 'absent' and seductive to our *own self* in order to be challenged from within, thus finding our own inner risks, trials, tests and demands to bring our solarism into full brightness.

6.

Family Themes:
Movers and Shakers
in the Family

There are distinct motifs to families, particular themes to which families love to hark back and which they perpetuate through their continuing lines. As well as the conscious patterns, there are the unconscious ones, those which are unspoken and implicit. It is these unconscious motifs that are the most fascinating. They can be either or both constructive and destructive.

A family pattern, or dynamic, bonds the family and establishes its identity, providing a container for each individual member to develop his or her own uniqueness within a recognizable framework. Psychologically, it serves as a protective space, allowing 'inherited' traits and attitudes to be accounted for and explained. Although in a positive way this dynamic acts as a refuge from the outside world and its influences, allowing each family member a safe place to become him- or herself, it can also act as a rigid structure which arrests an individual from developing his or her characteristics fully and completely as a separate identity within the family's system. The challenge of every family is to allow the individual person to become, as fully as possible, him- or herself, while still remaining recognizable as a member of the collective unit called 'the family'.

Although it is essential that a line of continuity thread its way through generations so as to maintain the fundamental imprint of each particular family, like a musical theme, it is equally important that each member be allowed to vary that motif or theme to his own particular resonance. In this way, the container of the family becomes a nurturing ground for greater expression of each individual within it.

Greater substance is added to a family by its ancestral tales, the stories which are the foundation upon which nuclear families continue to build their reality. By and large, the people in the family like these stories, they give them a framework to relate to which explains why they might be the way they are. The myths allow stability to be maintained while different people in the family might enact parts of a whole story.

Maintenance of these motifs, which are family myths – ancestral stories handed down from generation to generation – is the very substance of the family, but they must and do change with the times and with the advent of each new member of the family, whether that is through bloodline or marriage. The breaking and reformation of the family-pattern is essential to its continuation. This mutation is the substance of survival – should there be a stopping of this natural evolution towards new and more progressive ways of expressing the main theme, then the family stagnates and, if not literally, then psychologically, dies out.

Families need these stories and motifs, else they would not have their small 'cultural' bond among themselves. Just like nations develop their persona and history, so do families. Profoundly culturally bonded families such as Jews or Hindus or Navajos, or strongly tribal groups, for instance, incorporate their rich social myths into their personal collective. However, especially these days, it is common for families to have no such real connection to any cultural, religious, social or larger group. These families build up very strong interior myths, stories about themselves which enhance their sameness within their nuclear structure.

Family myths take many forms. Some of them are literal, others are romanticized versions of the truth, and yet others are what we euphemistically call 'secrets' – or family lies. In the ancient world, unconsciousness was not a consideration. In fact, the fate of a family was something we now call unconscious intent. It might sound like an oxymoron, but when we see the results of such apparent intention on the part of the family fate, or the deep unconscious of the individuals within it, it has the same ring as the story of Oedipus.

FAMILY ROLES

FAMILY SECRETS

Sometimes there is a family experience that no one talks about until well after the children are asleep, or that perhaps is never mentioned at all. These silent bits of knowledge are poisonous to the whole family, undermining the self-esteem, strength, and resilience of the entire system, and weakening each individual. This circumstance, though not uncommon, is not given enough recognition. First, we have to accept that there is no such thing as a perfect system or a perfect person, therefore we must strive always towards greater understanding. Obviously a certain degree of privacy is necessary and, too, children are not to be exposed to information which is beyond their comprehension – it is not that kind of secret. Children do need to know as much truth as they are old enough and mature enough to understand, and they always signal for it by behaviour or 'chance' remarks.

The unconscious has great powers of perception and knowledge, and in the individual members of the family, the unspoken carries a lot of weight. This is particularly true with young children, who uncannily know everything. It is ironic that it is in the name of 'protection' that families keep things from young children, yet it is woven into their psyches anyway, and will affect them whether it is on a conscious level or not. It is best dealt with in the consciousness rather than repressed or shoved down into the deep recesses of the mind, where it remains a kind of primitive force, forming the base of emotional difficulties in later life.

Family secrets will always emerge – there is no way that anyone does anything that is not characteristic in some way, nor completely outside the family mystique. As mysterious as some patterns of behaviour or traits appear to be, they can be traced to a source. The evidence of family secrets and their power to create and re-create the same pattern and scenario generation after generation is stunning. There are stories of the defrocked priest, the unwed mother, the homosexual uncle or great-grandfather, the mad aunt in the attic, the embezzler, the colonist who left for New Guinea and was never seen again, the horse-thief, etc. These stories, by the time they are diluted by generations, become legends and colourful history, but in some cases they are cause for great pain and remorse which is funnelled into each generation, creating unconscious guilt, tension and unaccountable fears in some members.

A positive result from an example of this kind of secret is found in the case of a client of mine, whom I shall call Colette. Colette has suffered from a lack of self-esteem all her life and has assumed that it is because her mother never thought her 'intelligent enough' or 'good enough' to confide in her. Her own mother, in turn, is a last-born, late child to elderly parents; she was raised in a cloistered environment and considered too young (always) to understand anything, so was kept in the dark. She was acutely aware of a certain 'something' being kept from her. For example, she recalls at the age of about eight coming into the sitting-room and having the whole family quieten and then volubly change the subject. This haunted her and made her feel as if she had done something wrong.

Colette's mother adored her own mother and thought she was perfect (the first mistake, but not an unusual one between child and parent). She treated Colette, her own daughter, the same way as she had been taught to relate by her mother – never confiding in her or sharing any intimacies or demonstrating human vulnerabilities. One weekend Colette received a message from her mother: she had found something out about her own mother which had upset her greatly but explained something completely, and she wanted to talk to her about it.

Colette rushed up to see her mother and was told that her grandmother had had an abortion and that's what all the covert discussions, secrecy and guilt had been about. This painful revelation for the mother ultimately worked to heal the rift that unconsciously had been between Colette and her mother, thus proving to be the turning point not only in their relationship, but in the relationship the daughter had with herself. It is true that secrets make you sick.

THE SCAPEGOAT

Scapegoating is an archaic ritual – in the tribes of Israel, there was a ceremonial day each year where the whole group would bring their troubles in the form of articles of clothing, dolls, rocks and various symbolic representatives to the edge of the village. They would have a purging ceremony to cleanse their families, themselves and their village of any evil influences that had caused their troubles to manifest. These troubles might be infertility, madness, loss of crops or animals, financial distress, lack of marriage partner for an elder daughter – anything that might beset any family or person in any time, culture or circumstance. They would then pile all their 'troubles' into a basket and place it on the back of a goat and drive it out into the desert. The goat then became the carrier of the evil, the figure of burden and the one who bore the troubles of the collective. Even as late as the sixth century, it was an Ionian practice to use scapegoat-magic to rid their villages of such burdens.

The ancient Athenians had a formal ceremony each year in which the citizens would inscribe upon an ostracon – a broken piece of pottery – the name of someone particularly odious to them or the community. It was largely a political ritual, but occasionally an ordinary citizen's name was found upon an ostracon. When the ostraca were all placed in a great vessel, they would be separated and counted. The person whose name was most frequently found upon an ostracon would be sent out of the city into exile for the year. Thus ostracized from his community, the citizen would have purged the city of its 'evil' person.

These rituals performed important psychological functions for the ancient peoples and they are still in effect today, though not in the recognized form of accepted collective activities. We experience scapegoating and ostracism all the time – in families and in our social sphere. We have very likely employed both of those techniques or have had them used on us at various times in life.

Scapegoating, for instance, is very common in families. In a flexible family system, the scapegoat always changes with the times and circumstances. However, in rigid families the scapegoat is frequently the same person all the time and becomes so burdened by the collective troubles that he or she becomes ill or disturbed. The scapegoat is not necessarily pathologically affected, but can simply be overworked and unrecognized and isolated. The scapegoat in the family is receiving all the troubles and has experienced the family pain in a more acute and conscious way. There are circumstances in which a member of a family 'volunteers' to be the scapegoat, and feels undermined and unrewarded, hence goes off into the desert all alone and maintains a pained distance from all other members, burdened by a family issue which he or she has taken on as his own personal problem. This volunteer scapegoat often worries the other family members and creates in them a feeling of guilt and unease, as if they have done something wrong.

Both kinds of scapegoat are victims in the sense that they are carrying the dynastic pollution, and both are volunteers in the sense that even in unconsciousness there lies a degree of responsibility. It takes a great deal of courage, and sometimes voluntary exile on the part of the scapegoat, to purge the family of its 'evil'. Evil and purge and exile are strong terms, but they are very real when people's feelings are involved.

In one family that was undergoing a crisis in the parental marriage, the two daughters were inadvertently pitted against each other. The member of the family who sought the consultation was becoming the scapegoat. She was the elder of the two daughters and very mature in her thinking – I shall call her Justine. She could see the situation that had arisen in the family very clearly, but this did not diminish her anger or her alienation. The parents were in the final throes of separation and the drama was running very high in the home.

The mother was depressed and the father overtly angry and directing his anger towards his elder daughter. Her singleton-retrograde Saturn, which was natally in her twelfth house, fell *exactly* on her father's Sun/descendant conjunction. With six planets in the seventh house, it would have been very easy for this father to find his own flaws in anyone else but himself. In an incident one night, the father turned on the daughter and blamed her for the breakdown in his marriage! His Sun on the descendant found the perfect hook in her Saturn. Though it was clearly irrational, her retrograde Saturn in the twelfth was ultra-sensitive to the father's pain and she would actually feel the responsibility though intellectually she knew it could not be true.

The lack of response from her depressed mother and the glee of her younger sister, who played on this dynamic, further encouraged the position of scapegoat. Born four years apart, the sisters have remarkably similar planetary placements in their charts: both have all planets under the horizon; both have the Moon in the same degree and sign, both have Venus in the same degree and sign and both have Mars in the same degree and sign. One would think that this astounding symbiosis of Moon, Venus and Mars would result in sympathy and understanding, but when there are splits in the family, it can result in precisely the opposite. The intimacy of the exact conjunctions becomes uncomfortable and cloying, competitive and resentful.

This kind of intimacy in siblings – indeed, between same-sex siblings or parent and child – so often results in one acting out the other's shadow function. Once this is pointed out and explained, it is often quite interesting to them, and a point of illumination and better understanding. I have found that when people are made aware of the most simple dynamic such as this one, they are fascinated by it and find it a source of endless discussion, which brings these unconscious and thus potentially lethal characteristics up to the surface for airing and civilizing. Unconsciously, each child feels compelled to act out the 'other side' of the other, so they swing back and forth, playing out functions or roles that each of them has within. When Justine was being the 'good daughter', her sister would act out the 'bad daughter' and both, being stubborn, would play this to the hilt. Sadly, the elder daughter was the more intellectually conscious – partly by age and very much by nature – so the younger one was more frequently seen as the 'good daughter'. Justine was too much in need of truth, and asked too many questions for the secretive parents to cope with.

Of the two sisters, she was the one who had natal Pluto at her IC. Her mother also shared this aspect – she, too had Pluto conjunct her IC, which she had inherited directly from her mother (who has Pluto at the IC, as well). This combination of dynamics left the father unconsciously to transfer his anger at his *wife* over to the daughter who he felt to be sitting in judgement of him – her Saturn on his Sun. In fact, it is highly likely that he always felt uncomfortable and inferior in some way to her, as, astrologically, she is more mature than him. Since her mother was the overt victim in all of this, she was also carrying some of the mother's unexpressed rage and certainly felt her pain. Justine's Pluto conjunct the IC does speak of her being the sister who was marked to transform the family fate, but specifically complexes left unresolved by her mother and the maternal line since this is the connecting link between them.

All of these circumstances were occurring when the transit of Pluto was going over Justine's Sun/Venus conjunction (at the same degree as her sister's natal Venus), bringing to light some of the darker, suppressed feminine elements in the family system. She and her mother both had natal Pluto at the IC – an inherited trait – and Justine was being 'scapegoated' for the mother's so-called inefficiencies in the whole family system. Although the younger sister was also having Pluto transit her Venus, she didn't have the added feature of the transit affecting her Sun. The fact that Justine's Sun *is* being transited affected triggers feelings of responsibility, awareness and consciousness of the situation. Justine's Pluto at the IC is also exactly conjunct her sister's Sun/Mercury conjunction, so the competition which was set up by the father had some validity to it. The sister eventually resorted to invading Justine's privacy by reading her journal and finishing all possibility of trust at that stage in their relationship. This is not engraved in stone, I must emphasize – change *does* happen, but only when every member of the family is in conscious collusion and is willing to undergo personal change.

So all members of the family were affected and implicated in the breakdown of the system, but one person felt particularly at the hub. In this case, Justine was not only scapegoated, but also psychologically ostracized. She was 'sent outside' the family and needed to find answers to her immediate and existential questions by seeking the counsel of friendly elders – replacing the traditional parents with tribal affiliations. There was a distinct feeling of being at the bottom of the pecking order and, as the one upon whom it fell to carry the burdens of the family, she had to step outside it to save herself. It was her mother who had the courage to help her daughter by having her chart done, and thus broke the line of suffering for her daughter. This took tremendous love and courage, and the young woman benefited not just from the session, but from the fact that her mother cared about her as a whole person rather than just as her daughter.

Scapegoats are not always Saturnian, but Saturn certainly fills the bill for characteristics: guilt, responsibility, burdens, etc., being the strongest keywords we have for it. And, oddly, Saturnian people do seem to collude with the world to accept the worldly cares and the psychological problems of those around them. This is part of the legacy that Kronos has left his descendants – that people of Saturn feel the archetypal accountability for which only Kronos himself should be responsible!

Other forms of ostracism and scapegoating can occur in families in which there is one member who is wounded in some way, and all subsequent problems seem to revolve around that person. This is more the Neptunian theme, where the hub of the family wheel revolves around a victim – either a handicapped person or an emotionally unbalanced one. Everyone in a group reacts individually to that person, some of whom can incorporate it into themselves, while others find it frightening, enraging or so alien that they abandon the situation wholly. Still another will find it feeds into their need to control the 'weak' one and thus become the saviour or the 'strong' one. Regardless of individual responses to the victim in the family, all are bound in deep, inextricable ways, for where there is Neptune, there are no boundaries.

THE BLACK SHEEP

Very often change comes in the form of a person, a family member who expresses entirely different characteristics from those the family thinks are 'theirs'. This is most fascinating, because it results in the black sheep syndrome, where everyone says, 'I don't know how Rupert got that way,' or, 'I can't imagine where Marigold gets these ideas!' If one looks back far enough (or sometimes even very close, in the case of a family secret), it can become apparent that black sheep are really just highly concentrated amalgams of an unspoken or hidden family theme. The black sheep is, in fact, a circuit breaker, whose arrival into the family offers variety and healthy diversion. In a way, these apparent interlopers prevent a form of in-breeding which eventually retards, arrests, or kills the family. Very often, families are secretly if not openly proud of their black sheep – depending on *how* black it is, of course! For example, they love to talk about how little Mavis is *so* different from everyone else, how determined she is to be herself and how unknown talents or abilities have manifested in her that no one would have dreamed in such a family. Or how young William has such superb skills with machinery while everyone else is a hopeless intellectual.

When a family becomes too complacement or has pointedly ignored signals to change or has had an experience thrust upon it for which it is unprepared, a black sheep will appear. This means that a former white sheep may begin to manifest behavioural irregularities, break his or her own patterns and behave in ways which are mysterious and 'different' from before. This is not always bad, indeed, it can be a very good thing because attention is being drawn to the need for change. If one member of the family becomes greatly out of tune, then, the harmony is shattered and the feeling-tone in the family is edgy, cautious, covert and very uncomfortable.

A black sheep can *also* be a scapegoat, a member of the family who carries the problems of the whole group on her shoulders, taking unconscious responsibility for the unspoken anger, sickness or distress of the whole system. In depth psychology this person is called the 'identified patient', that is, the one who by his behaviour makes everyone else look well. However, in keeping with the theme of the dynamic family, it is impossible for one part of the whole to be 'unwell' while all other parts remain unaffected – the angry, sick or depressed individual is merely expressing the anger, illness or sadness of all the others. In fact, acting out is often a release valve for the tension within a family, and when the truth is out, all are relieved that finally something tangible has been made manifest and now the work can be done.

All black sheep are not identified patients, however! And many of them are great fun and provide a release valve for everyone else, performing a function rather like the steam button on a pressure cooker. The other members of the family get to be part of something different while not taking any risks themselves. These black sheep are often the benevolent butt of family jibes and jest, act out accordingly and provide relief for the predictability of the other individuals.

Sometimes it is needed in the family to import a black sheep – this is done through marriage or adoption. More often than not, people adopt a child or marry a partner who conforms beautifully, if mysteriously, to the astrological family dynamic. This is particularly fascinating in the case of adopting a child whose horoscope flows alone with everyone else's, and the adopted parents *are* the parents in the child's chart – we know we cannot plan these things (see Mohsin's story, page 270). However, by importing a new ingredient, we refresh the family and bring a new line with it, adding more creative aspects and enhancing the productivity of the collective purpose.

This can be done by marrying someone of another culture, race, religion or socio-economic background. It is most commonly done unconsciously, and always shows astrologically. The marriage to a 'different' one is usually done by a person in the family who is a covert black sheep and needs the support of a partner to bring out the new theme – and the astrological signature of the resultant whole rounds out the family, adding a needed element of spice or, in the case of some families, some stability or earthiness.

Mars can be projected in families as well. All the anger – overt or tacit – which may weave through the family can be found nestled in one person in the form of the radical, the revolutionary, the one who 'causes' problems. It is highly unlikely that a Mars exhibition is a singular statement. The revolutionary in the family is acting on behalf of his or her more conservative or passive family members. Repressed anger surfaces in many symptomatic ways through illness and accidents. Mars can act as a warning, a kind of signal-flag to something more dangerous under the surface.

Unrealized or dormant characteristics can constellate powerfully in one individual, who then is compelled to act them out in order to cleanse, purge or simply more fully develop latent traits. Anything which lies sleeping for too long eventually rouses itself to dramatic action. Jung once pondered the mystery of why it was that one person was compelled to dramatically externalize a crisis and yet another appeared totally unaffected. Astrology seems to imply that there is a cumulative effect in planetary energy as it reappears in family horoscopes, which constellates in one individual in a family precisely at a time when critical mass in their collective psyche has occurred, and that one person then acts as the stimulus to bring the unlived aspect into fullness of being – black sheep are often the catalyst as well. In this way, he or she is propitiating or placating some family daemon.

Black sheep come in many colours.

THE MEDIATOR OR CIRCUIT BREAKER

There is a go-between in the family, the peace-keeper, the one who literally mediates between the various pairs or groups that form within the existing family. They facilitate communication while supporting the lack of the same across barriers that have been tacitly agreed upon within the system. There is a strong predilection for the Venus-type or Libran to be this person. Also, aspects of planets to Neptune can indicate a mediator. The sign Virgo is implicated in mediation as well, because of its capacity to absorb, digest, assimilate and understand situations which are confused and emotionally charged. Capricorns can become mediators simply because of their strong feelings of responsibility and family-loyalty traits. The mediator does eventually tire of the situation and has to find ways of slipping out of the role. It is part of their family system path to allow other people to work things out for themselves.

'Warring' factions can shift in families – first it is the mother and father who need mediating, then the brother and sister, or perhaps the situation will arise between the adolescent son and the father. There is much shape-shifting but often there will be the burden of communication lying on one specific member of a group. In the alcoholic family system it is called 'enabling'. The technique of the go-between, in fact, has a high degree of power associated with it. The anxiety that attends the power is debilitating and often overshadows the presenting symptoms of depression, anger and guilt, and the mediator will want to appear weak, victimized or vulnerable when in fact they hold considerable power over the family as a system, keeping it regulated. Should their role be replaced, then all hell would break loose – someone might speak for themselves in the family, replacing the mediator's role.

For example, in one family of four were a Capricorn father with Aquarius Moon, Scorpio ascendant; a Libra mother with Scorpio Moon and ascendant; elder daughter with Gemini Sun, Cancer ascendant and Moon/Pluto conjunction in Leo; younger daughter a Sagittarius, Gemini Moon and Capricorn ascendant. The elder daughter with the Moon/Pluto conjunction could not mediate between the alcoholic father and co-dependent mother – her Moon/Pluto tied in with their Scorpio ascendant, and she would get involved in the argumentative aspect of the family, while the younger daughter, the Sagittarius/Gemini with Capricorn ascendant, identified more with the role of mediator and, indeed, was the one who found herself caught in between all the family disagreements. The elder daughter had taken the role of rebel early on: she was a lesbian, became actively militant, a high-pressured academic who eventually failed to complete her Ph.D. work owing to alcoholism and depression – and her instinctual rejection of the ivy-league competitiveness of the academic world – and voluntarily entered Alcoholics Anonymous at her first Saturn return.

The younger daughter identified more with the parents as the caretaker – Capricorn rising with Saturn just into the twelfth house – and kept more of the family image and dynamic about her, especially of her father, whom she resembled physically and in her more sensitive nature. The elder, Gemini/Cancer rising daughter had the razor intellect of the father, but not the melancholic-feeling qualities he had passed over to the younger, Sagittarius/Capricorn rising girl. Her feeling of guilt, responsibility and degree of resonance was much higher, which does not mean that the older daughter did not feel it! She obviously did; having Cancer ascendant and a Moon/Pluto conjunction would have made her possibly more vulnerable to the devastation of the family, but it was the younger one who took on the caretaking, enabling role. This is Capricorn with Saturn only 3 degrees into the twelfth house!

One client said she really felt caught between her parents and would literally be sent from room to room, saying, 'Mother says this, and really means that,' then having to go to the other parent, saying, 'Father's response is such-and-such, but I think he really means this'. . . she had Sun, Saturn and Venus at the IC in Libra. She performed a balancing act between her parents, as well as being the mediating influence between her brothers and sisters.

In Fiona's story (page 317, 'What's Bred in the Bone'), we see that her Mars/Venus conjunction at the IC in exact square to Saturn on her descendant *almost* prevented her from being able to form a strong, equal relationship in her life. Being a Libra, she is the balance of the family, the one upon whom others rely to be fair, just, happy and soothing. Her family were such a responsibility and her response to them so profound that she 'had' to become ill and move away in order to break a powerful habit of being the one upon whom all relied. Her independence allowed everyone else in the family to break their own patterns and change. The problem with change is that everyone must do it, and that makes it very difficult for all to accept. A minor change in one person in a group requires significant change in all other members.

THE CATALYST

Catalysts fall almost wholly into the Pluto/Scorpio variety. There are many possible configurations of this signature – Moon/Pluto, lots of planets in the eighth house, Pluto rising, Sun in Scorpio, Sun/Pluto, Venus/Pluto and so on. Pluto is the unseen one, but the caretaker of souls. The catalysts are the ones in the family who walk into a room and everyone changes. People fall in love, get divorced, give birth, die, find new vocations – all due to the ministering and presence of this person. The true nature of a catalyst acts as the transformer of others, but they themselves do not change. The intensity of their being is enough to bring out hidden aspects of others, allowing others to show parts of themselves they may not even have known existed. The problem with this lies in the shock factor – the catalyst can become the brunt of attack and blame for family problems because they are the ones who have inadvertently opened the locked doors to let out the monster or the unknown.

Catalysts are often quite unconscious of this trait, until it is made known to them. They usually complain that they are always around when something of a disaster is coming down. And they are. They have a transformative quality, and thus are also the healer in the family system. It is always the catalyst that people turn to when they are in pain, in crisis or in some form of transitional state. They are the guides. However, to be truly and healthily in this role, they have to have no attachment – there has to be a degree of distance between them and the situation in which they have inadvertently found themselves implicated. They have to be particularly careful of giving advice or having strong opinions over sensitive issues, because it will backfire on them if they have allowed themselves to be caught up in the riot.

Ultimately the catalyst should walk in and out of situations unscathed. It takes time and age for this to become a safe role. They can easily become the scapegoat, especially if they have used their power in ways which have their own personal ends or needs in mind. Since it is a Plutonian experience, it has all the earmarks of a life-or-death level of experience; this is not always a comfortable role but it can be a very satisfying one, especially when the transformations have resulted in a stronger family system and a more honest one. They are never mediators because their stance is firm, unilateral and clear – others must change, there is rarely a compromise to be gained.

Happily, not all catalysts wear the dark cloak of Hades; some of them are transformers because they are so scrupulously honest and have the ability to allow others around them to be the same. Their energy can be so provocative and erotic that they create a sensation of love around them, giving others the freedom to express themselves in poetic and romantic ways. If love is a problem, or trust or freedom, the catalyst will always do something that creates such a stir that everyone has to pay attention to the core issue. Catalysts cannot stand suspense, they like everything out in the open. Living on the threshold is not their idea of a good life, they are very black-and-white. On some level, this is wearing. However, there are advantages to being so clear – if others are muddling their way through some issue or problem, the catalyst will come in and clarify the situation immediately with rather abrupt mannerisms and words.

Because they loathe pretext and subterfuge, they will attack anyone who is undermining the integrity of the family (or their tribe, for that matter) and demand openness. When a family becomes in need of deep psychological or spiritual change, a catalyst will be 'brought in', either through marriage, or through the birth of a child who has qualities that radically alter the perceptions of every single member of the family. Catalysts can be black sheep, for instance, the renegades who mock the hypocrisy of the status quo, thus allowing others to become more experimental. They are iconoclasts and have no reverence for *pro forma* rules and regulations – this does not mean they are criminal, but it does mean that rules have to be based on an ethical foundation.

7.
Families and Our Familiars

We all know the experience of meeting, or even just seeing, someone who feels very familiar and with whom we know instantly that there is a deep connection that must fulfil itself. Depending upon our individual natures, we will handle this in our own unique way. Some people's antennae are more sensitive than others, yet on a very deep level we *all* have the innate capacity to sense what a meeting is about and if it is to affect us profoundly. It is in the interpretation of the feeling, sensing or tone of the contact that confusion can arise – by using the intellect, when the viscera are more knowing, we often misconstrue or even distort a deeply honest message. Links between individuals are very easily translated incorrectly, and often are coloured by past psychological experiences and at times even badly mangled in the process of trying to work too hard on that mysterious energy that rises when we meet someone for the first time. By seeing the inside on the outside, we are really looking for the extended family in our friends. Good friends are family, and have astrological connections which, in many cases, are more cementing than blood-ties.

There are many ways of experiencing a positive connection, where we simply know that this person is destined to be our friend or lover. Equally, there are many ways of coping with what we intuitively know will be a difficult, trying or possibly even devastating relationship, whether that is through business, friendship or romance. All the information on the inner dynamics of the relationship is present in the first contact with any other person. The interface between individuals has a read-out. The relationship between two people is as unique as we are ourself, and the possible interactions between each of us and another can never be repeated or replicated in any other configuration of people. There are themes in relationships, but there are never two alike. In astrology, we do composite horoscopes to see what the meeting-place between individuals is like – we understand the meeting-place between them, the mysterious point of absolute interaction, the subtle yet highly assertive 'third-party' that a relationship really is. Astrologically it is the midpoint of two people.

That instant familiarity and instinctive knowledge does not always include the discretion to handle it with enlightenment and awareness. The tendency is naturally to find one's deepest intelligence overlaid and influenced by history, or received values. First *judgements* can be wrong – however, primal instincts *cannot* be wrong. In this way we are deeply animal and although we might overlay our instincts with civilized information, our gut will be the truth-teller. Many examples come to mind. For instance, you encounter someone for the first time at a gathering. You hate the person. Your vestigial pelt ripples. Your stomach contracts and you find yourself feeling irrational – and why not, it *is* a non-rational response, all relationships are irrational. You want to walk away from that person, but a little voice in your head says, 'Now don't be rude, give the person the benefit of the doubt.' In giving the person the 'benefit of the doubt' you well might be endangering your soul or your body. How many times have you later regretted befriending someone out of rational reasoning, when irrational feeling said, 'No!'

And, conversely, how often have you needed or wanted to go back into a situation to make a connection with someone you felt very attracted to at the time, but the little voice said, 'Now, now, don't be importunate/foolish/hasty/impulsive, etc. Control yourself, don't make friends too quickly, and so on.' This voice is the same as the one above which told you not to flee for your life for fear of being antisocial. This voice is often wrong. Your gut feeling is always right. It would be a good exercise to find the source of this voice and see if it is a familiar one – is it you or is it someone else's training-voice, a parent, perhaps?

There is also the reverse of this – when someone declares their undying love or friendship to you, if not instantly then close to immediately, do you not feel distrustful? Ask yourself why you feel that way. You may have good cause, the person may be mad, or desperate, but also, they may be right. They might recognize you first, as it were. Perhaps their instinctual nature has found its friend and they are simply rather gauche in demonstrating or making the connection. Feel carefully. Why are they approaching you? They might be 'projecting' – always a good excuse not to relate. It is all very complicated, this business of knowing what is real and what is not. Certainly we do not have all the answers and learning to trust one's own instincts is very important.

Instincts are remarkable. When we meet someone and form a relationship with them, we do not know their planetary positions, horoscope angles or lunar nodes. However, when we do look and know, the number of times that astrological signatures repeatedly appear in all our relationships is amazing. On a very simplistic level, there is a tendency to attract certain Sun-signs in certain periods in our lives. One might find oneself surrounded by an inordinate number of Geminis at one time, then at another phase discover a run of Capricorn people populating one's life. There is also the consistent theme, when there is a repeat of a specific Sun-sign that we know runs down through the family – say, Pisces – and we find ourselves involved repeatedly with Piscean individuals.

Then there is the more subtle aspect of astrology, where it is not the Sun-sign *per se*, but the *mode* or *quality* of Sun-sign: for example you are Fixed (say, Taurus) and everyone around you is Mutable (Gemini, Sagittarius, Virgo or Pisces). What do these things mean?

With respect to Sun-sign emphasis, it is very likely that there are times in life where an 'empty' space needs to be filled; periods of time when the deeper Self wants experience in an aspect of human nature which is not readily accessible to it, an aspect of ourselves which is deeply unconscious. We have all signs in our horoscope, but all signs are not occupied by all planets, therefore we have a distinct bias or lack of such in particular areas. A friend of mine, astrologer Jeff Jawer, once said that he would understand Taurus better if his Sun were not there! This is very profound – his simple statement is redolent with the implication that we are blinded by our own experience of ourselves. So sometimes we need others to come in and educate us and relieve us of our biases – sometimes rather harshly.

Other more complex issues arise when we have a strong natal aspect from one of the luminaries – Sun or Moon – to a planet. For example, a person with a Sun-Saturn square might attract Capricorns, other Saturnian types (ascendant, Moon, Venus-Saturn), or, in a more general sense, earth-element signs (Taurus, Virgo or Capricorn), who in turn are vicariously experiencing a sleeping aspect of themselves. There can be phases of this kind of attraction, 'clumps' of them in discrete times, or it can be a consistent theme. If it is a consistent theme it is likely that there is a need to compensate for a lack, to enhance another dimension of one's own self. A woman with Uranus in the seventh house wants the option of her own freedom in relationships and might therefore attract a man with an Aquarius Moon, or Sun/Venus in Aquarius. It is always valuable to self-awareness to consider whom one attracts and how they fit into one's own horoscopic pattern. One man I know has a Sun sextile to Uranus but everyone in his family, his mother, father, two sisters and one brother, has hard angles from the Sun to Uranus and the father has a Moon/Uranus conjunction in Aquarius. He himself is a warm and emotionally demonstrative man, but no one else in the family is. He married a woman with a Moon/Uranus opposition from Sagittarius to Gemini! We go for what we know.

A lack of Earth will attract Earth to it, lack of Air accretes Airy types, on through the elements of Fire and Water. When we lack an element, the deeper self will seek it out and find it in others so that we may have the benefit of it in our immediate environment. Speaking more psychologically, if we have an undeveloped or sleeping characteristic, it is very frequently 'projected' on to others who will collude in this projection and live it out for us. People who have difficulty expressing their deep feelings will find that people very close to them are often wildly emotional. This is natural, healthy and very human – it is not a problem unless it is a problem. If it *is* a problem, only then does it bear scrutiny and analysis.

When we attract our own type, for example if we have a fixed T-square (say, Leo, Taurus, Scorpio), and we fall in love with someone, or have a friendship with someone, or give birth to a child who has a strong Fixed cross in two of those signs or more, then we are meeting ourselves in our opposite. This can be very productive in that two people are saying the same thing, only differently, and although it is potentially combustible and volatile, it is deep, passionate and very real. It is hard to distinguish who is doing what to whom, however, and projection can be at its highest level in this context. Another potential difficulty with such deep similarity is the latent capacity for a *folie à deux* – where each individual feeds the 'madness' of the other and they become inextricably intertwined, finding it impossible to determine boundaries between them. In the case of Mutables with Mutables (Gemini, Virgo, Sagittarius and Pisces), there can be problems in decisiveness between the two people – or the group, if that be the case! Cardinal combinations (Aries, Cancer, Libra and Capricorn) have strong motivations to be on top and in control of every situation and this is one of the most difficult combinations between two people, creating a very competitive environment.

Naturally, the type of relationship itself is going to help determine the degree to which certain positive or negative characteristics emerge. A parent-child relationship has the deepest biological pull and is much more deeply rooted than a business relationship! Similarly a close friend is a different structure emotionally than a lover or spouse. Therefore, some relationships work very well and productively when there are stress aspects and others are disastrous. The horoscope will not say whether or not a relationship is disastrous, but will clearly delineate the energy patterns and tendencies for certain complexes to arise and under what conditions they are most likely to manifest. If those complexes are family-based, we are looking at something very fruitful in self-development.

We can be fairly sure that powerful relationships outside the genetic family are going to be tied into the family. If it is familiar, it is familial. People who have reasonably open horizons and who travel a great deal will find friends around the world who fit in with their family dynamic. Those who work in group situations with others in close and ongoing conditions – like boards of directors, steering committees, community work, collectives of any kind – will find that their family is often enacted around them by (apparently) emotionally uninvolved people! We will see ourselves no matter where we go and in what context we find ourselves. And, since we are made up of such a rich tapestry of characteristics and complexes which are fed by the ancestors, it is not surprising to meet your mother/aunt/sister in a group situation!

Family dynamics constellate whenever a gathering occurs – the longer the gathering is in relationship, the more intense the interaction. At a conference, for example, when people are interacting on a dynamic level, it becomes apparent who has been the oldest or only child, the abused child, the 'golden child', the mother/father-figure or the one who fell through the cracks. Our families are not just the people with whom we grew up, they are the inner population of aspects of the Self and we cannot help but see them – and really encounter them – outside our selves.

SEEING THE INSIDE ON THE OUTSIDE

On the subject of projection, which is considered to be a very bad thing in psychology, it seems that we cannot help but see ourselves reflected in the mirror of relationships. Lucretius, the second-century Roman poet, had a lot to say. Two thousand years ago he wrote a poem called *De rerum natura – On the Nature of Things* – in which he penned a famous classical diatribe against women. In this piece he writes hilariously about 'seeing the inside on the outside':

> It's easier to avoid the snares of love
> Than to escape once you are in that net
> Whose cords and knots are strong; but even so,
> Enmeshed, entangled, you can still get out
> Unless, poor fool, you stand in your own way,
> Forgetting, for example, in all those faults
> Your little darling has in body or mind.
> Desire is blind, desire is ignorant,
> And men can never stop this foolishness
> But keep on praising an attractive charm
> Which simply isn't there.[1]

I believe this is the first thorough treatise on the subject of psychological projection, and certainly antedates Carl Jung, who developed the theory of projection quite thoroughly. Setting aside the misogynistic tone of the passage – remember this was Rome – read carefully his admonition against 'seeing' what is not there. Although Lucretius is cautioning all (men) against the vagaries of romantic love specifically, we should further translate 'desire' into all forms of wanting relationships to be particular ways and our natural, innate capacity to overlook the warts on our parents, children, lovers, friends and business associates when we don't want to see them. And, then, the withdrawal of the projection and its subsequent disillusionment.

Jung wrote much on the subject of projection, varied his interpretations and allowed the activity of projection a great deal of life and latitude. He was fairly clear in his assertion that projection occurs in all relationships. Indeed, it would seem that to initiate a relationship projection is a requisite, and only the severely autistic lack the capacity to experience projection – as well as lacking the capacity for empathy, sympathy and emotionally bonding relationships. How those projections develop and are treated thereafter is then the penultimate issue in continuing and preserving relationships. A sudden withdrawal of all projections will result in the loss of relationship, but a gradual, healthy clearing of projections replaced with the actuality of the real person results in ongoing, developmental and 'healthy' relations. This serves in both family and friendly relationships.

Jung said, 'Everything that works from the unconscious appears projected on others. Not that these others are wholly without blame, for even the worst projection is at least hung on a hook, perhaps a very small one, but still a hook offered by the other person.'[2] At least there is *some* acknowledgement of reciprocal action, of relationship itself in this quote. He also said that a great deal of projection results from the contents of the unconscious being 'thrown out' and residing on the surface of another's psychological appearance. There is also the differentiation of the 'personal unconscious', that is, the storehouse of one's personal experiences that are contained deep in the psyche, and the 'collective unconscious' which is the storehouse for aspects of the unconscious that are common to all humanity. So we can project archetypally or personally.[3]

An archetypal projection would fall into various categories, such as a 'mother-archetype projection' – where the Great Mother, the all-giving, all-knowing mother, or the demon/devouring gorgon-mother, is projected on to one's own mum, or, conversely, one's mum is seen as the essence of Gaia herself, all nourishing and perfect.[4] Both are extreme. Then there is the personal projection where we might project our actual, personal experience of our own mum upon another person – usually a woman, but not exclusively. It all becomes terribly complicated.

However, in astrology we have our own archetypal symbols. For mother it is usually the Moon. The Moon *is* the symbol for the mother-archetype. How we experienced our *own* mother is also contained in the Moon, but it is further individualized by the quality of the Moon in the whole horoscope, its sign, house position and the aspects it makes to other planets. The experience of our own personal mother and the nurturing aspects of early life are logged in the personal unconscious and are readily available for projection upon any individual who even vaguely calls up archetypal images of mothering, whether that is another parent, a teacher, a friend or a lover. Therefore, there is Great Earth Mother and mother and mother-figure.

Similarly, we can project the archetypal father on to our own father; this is normal for a small child – he is the hero or celestial father who is all-knowing, all-powerful. Poor father, he could not possibly be these things really, but to his baby he is. Then the personal experience of one's father is overlaid upon the archetypal father so that how father really was becomes entwined with all father images. All persons of greater size, power and authority can become victims of our father-projections. If father was never there, then all figures who are elusive and unreliable become resonant with one's personal father archetype and are lumped into one category. This is neither fair nor realistic. The condition of our natal Sun will often talk about the overlay of real father on to archetypal father. The archetypal father is celestial, immortal and all-powerful, but real fathers are not, they are human, mortal. The archetypal father can be Woton, a relentless, ruthless god-image, or he can be benevolent and forgiving. The real father is likely a combination of those, only humanized, watered down. Therefore there is the Great Celestial Father, father and father-figure.

In attempting to determine what it *is* that is happening in relationships, we can over-analyse and thus destroy the spontaneity and nature of relationship itself. I personally do not recommend that anyone do this, but astrology falls victim at times to psychology and therefore it is important to understand how archetypal psychology has influenced some interpretation of natal and relationship type horoscopes. If we remain pure in our astrological imagery, then we do use archetypes faithfully, if we over-analyse and render relationships as totally symbolic, then we have no relationships with others, only with ourselves and our inner life. This is clearly very unhealthy. So, moderation in all things.

However, it is clear that when we find our friends, or create a relationship and move in a circle of people, wide or small, we are working in tandem with the family dynamic and experiencing ourselves in an extrapolation of the family system. We tend to attract to us people with configurations in their charts that are familiar and similar in flavour and sometimes are exactly like our own or a family trait. We are equally inclined to find opposites, exact opposites. If there is a theme of Pisces/Neptune in families, then one might be attracted to Virgo and earth to compensate for this, and balance our experience of ourself in this way. We are also inclined to have repeated relationship types (always, I must say) if unconsciously we are seeking to fill a deep need or replicate an early memory – this is not always a good thing, particularly for its tendency to dull the learning process in relating. However, we do get caught in cycles which have their own time.

TRIBAL FAMILIES

We seek out tribal affiliations because of who we are and what we are made up of. Naturally there needs to be a more in-depth look at the whole horoscope to really see the fullness of tribal affiliation, but there are some generalities that can be drawn about planetary/sign types. People with focal

Jupiter or strong Jupiter/Venus aspects have an inclination to travel around, looking for their families – this is the strongest tribal indicator. Not so much the Sagittarian, who is the maverick of the zodiac and remains staunchly loyal to affiliations which do not confine or require attendance.

Strongly Saturnian people are dynastically inclined and form relationships that grow and endure over very long periods of time, and their groups or tribes are usually based on a form of class-structure and ideology – should a friend change their affiliation drastically, they are likely to lose their Saturnian friend. Venusian people incline to the artistic tribe, and to people who are the social trendsetters, even radical-social trendsetters. In and of themselves, they are quite independent, both the Taurean and Libran variety, but are sensitive to the herd-mode and find that they are easily influenced by others and need to draw limits to their social activities.

Uranian/Aquarian types are not the loners that we might like to imagine – their tribes often lie in their work area, where they can have non-emotional ties, but strong loyalties towards their vocations. They often have a selection of friends who, if they all got together, would have nothing in common but their Uranian friend! Pluto/Scorpio people have Sicilian values and will endure anything from a friend but betrayal – should that occur, the friend simply ceases to exist. They are more inclined to passionate attachments which reflect current stages in their evolution; however, they will have intimate friends lasting for a lifetime.

Solar types, Leo types are the loners. They love people, are very good at projection and withdrawal, but are so highly individualistic that they can feel constrained by any group-bond at all. Moon people love family – friends are family and are treated as such, but there is a strong judgemental quality to Cancerian/lunar tribal affiliations. Their friends/tribe have to want to be mothered, fed, controlled and coddled – and to stay the same.

Neptunian/Piscean types of people float into relationships and find their tribe often through mutual needs. Fulfilling others' needs and working for the cause underlies the bonding needed for them – they love the arts, music and creativity, but they also love their privacy, so they can often be behind the scenes in their tribal affiliation, but with a great deal of power.

Mercurial/Gemini love the mental connections between people, and have very diverse needs in their interactions. Unless there are other more dominant aspects tending them towards grouping, they will, like the Sagittarian type, remain as free as possible from social or tribal structures. The Mercurial/Virgo type is fundamentally an introvert and enjoys the esoteric connections with other more mental types. Their adherence to families or tribes is not terribly strong, as they are the observers of people and relationships between people, enjoying the fact that they are part of the human race, but not responsible for it.

NOTES

1. *Lucretius, The Way Things Are*, Book IV, lines 1145 ff., trans. Rolf Humphries, University of Indiana Press, 1968. This excerpt is from a very long passage which becomes increasingly hilarious and absurd. It is part of his 'diatribe against women', which women classicists regularly haul out to demonstrate the absolute disparagement with which women have been treated since the rise of the Mycenean period in Western civilization which subsumed the goddess-based cultures, the Minoans. Unfortunately this is true, and the seeds for this were sown in the Greek soil over 3,000 years ago.

2. Carl G. Jung, *Collected Works*, Vol. 8, para. 99, Bollingen Series.

3. ibid., para. 270. Jung first used the term 'archetype' in this place. Before this work, he used the term 'primordial image'. The term *archetypus* comes much earlier in the work of St Thomas Aquinas – in much the same way Jung employed it.

4. Erich Neumann, *The Great Mother*, Bollingen, Princeton University Press, 1963. Weighty tome on the many faces of the mother archetype in myth, art, history and psychology.

PART II
Family Dynamics

8.

The Modal Family:
The Tension of Life

Modal patterns are based on angular stress. The three modes of being are Cardinal, Fixed and Mutable. All four elements are represented in the modes, and all are in opposition or square to each other. These emphases can go back several generations on one side of a family and settle into a nuclear family. As with the elements, there are patterns which form in families, but the structure is based on developmental conflict and opposition rather than the supine patience of agreeable elements. The family which has a dominant mode – any of the three – has a rigid infrastructure which, by the laws of nature, will produce or incorporate, through marriage or birth, an opposite. The modes are 'ways of behaving' – they determine how an individual or a family collective goes about getting things done.

Often there are compensatory or balancing acts which occur in family systems. For instance, a client with a grand cross in Fixed signs married a Virgo sign woman and has a Sagittarius son and a Pisces daughter. Clearly there was a need in him to expand his own dimensions into areas not inherently familiar, but deeply needed. I had said to him that perhaps, just maybe, he needed to understand more about flexibility, fluidity, mutability, and unpredictability! To have these people so intimately around him was to show him that he couldn't manage to control the universe by winding his own watch! Even though this is amusing, it is also very true. In turn, his little Mutable family will need to learn to find ways of charming this person so instinctually fearful of losing control into becoming more easy-going, and through him understand the value in being self-centred, fixed and rigid in some ways.

In contrast, when there is a perfect balance of modes, there is a fixed system which will crack at some point – a marriage, a new child, a powerfully influential experience will arrive to challenge the status quo. This is always a positive event and freshens up a tired, blocked or simply habitual

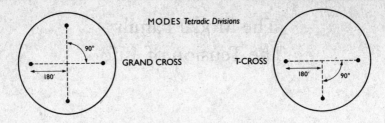

MODES *Tetradic Divisions*

GRAND CROSS   T-CROSS

Cardinal Involves the primal origins and creative thrust instinctively.
Fixed Involves the establishment of ego and stasis of the value system.
Mutable Involves the capacity for self-expression and comprehension of environment.

family system that is dedicated unconsciously to its homeostasis. Just as individuals meet and relate with others who will add a dimension to them or help balance them out, so do our family systems.

Creating equilibrium is one thing, maintaining it is another. The function of equilibrium is not static in the dynamic family. There is a constant flow and a hopeful possibility for change in both small and big ways. There are some family dynamics which are less inclined to change easily, and they are the more dramatic cases when breaks, schisms, and extremes occur. By and large, family dynamics are subtle and private – but no less profound for one family than another. In fact, it seems that the more subtle the 'problem' the more difficult it is to sort out. I have had many clients with fundamentally benevolent family backgrounds and no overt or violent aspects among them who find it more difficult to overcome their family neuroses than others who have been beaten or assaulted sexually, or have come from shattered families, single families, and so on. This might be because it is easier to deal with the obvious than the subtle – if one cannot make it to work one day, a broken leg is easier to explain to an employer than an anxiety attack.

Similarly, the more extreme the elemental or modal imbalance of a family system, the easier it is to analyse. Generally, there is a theme of Cardinal, Fixed or Mutable signs in families, just as there are the elemental weights.[1] What follows is a very general analysis of the core-themes of the modes of elements as they appear to work if they are emphasized or lacking.

Each mode contains a sign of each element and they are in a cross or opposite to each other, unlike in the elemental patterns where the signs are all in a trine, one of each mode. The square/opposition dynamic that is inherent in the modal syndrome talks about developmental tension, the kind of life-force which keeps life in a balance of perspective by opposition and excitement, tension and manifestation by square. Oppositions are 'split conjunctions' and always embody a polarity of elements which, by their very nature, are compatible. For example, Taurus is opposite Scorpio – Earth and Water respectively. Earth needs the Water to nourish and enrich it and Water needs the Earth to contain it, like the banks of a river and shores of the sea. Similarly, Fire is always opposed to Air and Air needs the warmth of the Fire for human-ness and for inspiration, while Fire needs Air for its very sustenance, to fan its flames.

In using these core-meaning interpretations, many variants could be employed. If you are using many, many charts, like over a dozen, including generations or cross-family charts, or a team of people, then you might want to isolate certain factors according to your interest in the extended family balance. In the case of a group such as a steering committee, or a board of directors, this could prove to be very fruitful in assessing the receptivity for change, cooperation, the 'warring' factor, innovativeness or adaptiveness, etc. If the birth data for a group is questionable or lacking, you could simply do planetary energy-patterns. For instance, you could do all the Mars in the family (or group) and see what the balance was, or all the Moons. Or all the planets *only*, without the angles, nodes, asteroids and other points, seeing only the planetary balances. Again, if all birth data were accurate, it could be done with just the angles being plotted in the elemental triangles or the modal crosses. Experiment with these and be creative!

CARDINAL
Aries, Cancer, Libra, Capricorn

Cardinality in families has to do with origins of the most organic kind. The Cardinal signs themselves represent the 'firsts' in life – the first breath of life and personality (Aries); the family-of-origin (Cancer); the first glimpse of relationship – 'others' and partners (Libra); and the initial contact with the social realm (Capricorn). The Cardinal signs, for all their apparent self-assuredness, are vulnerable to downfall and are deeply, unconsciously aware of this. Because the symbolism of being first implies an insecurity, the

Cardinals are signs of assertion and sometimes aggression. They all get their way in the end, and all are dedicated to being 'original'. The circuit of self, family, partners and the general public is largely a self-organized circuit which needs only inner impulse to create.

When there is a preponderance of Cardinality, there are often real issues that arise which are grouped around the origins and the organic nature in and of the family. This can mean a genetic trait, which runs down through generations and has variations on that theme. It is profoundly linked to the physical bodies of families, and if there is a strong imbalance – that is, a marked over-balance of Cardinal, there may even be something along the lines of a genetic problem. It can be as physical as asthma and eczema, which are connected: one member can have asthma and the other eczema, or it might skip a generation and not be known until it manifests in a member of the family. Dyslexia, too, can appear in the history, which mutates into other perceptual difficulties, or autism at the extreme end of that spectrum. There is almost always a genetic issue in a strongly predominantly Cardinal family.

More often, thankfully, it is a deeply rooted sense of ancestral lineage – Cardinal signs like to know they 'belong' to something or somebody. All the signs need to feel that they are leaders or very important in a movement or group. Their attempts at singularity are reactions to the insecurity of being untested and untried, like the more secure Fixed sign, or the sometimes jaded Mutable signs. Cardinal families like to know their origins, their ancestry and are fond of knowing their source. It is a highly social mode, very interested in society, their culture, group-consciousness and relationships.

Cardinality is an indicator of the self-starters, of the innovative and the groups who experiment with new places, people or ideas. There is insularity among highly Cardinal families, and they can become too condensed, too full of their own type, which produces a rigid feeling of having 'done it all'. Because Cardinality is an indicator of innovativeness, if there is too much, then all the freshness and innovation has burned out. Time for a change. In will come a new, likely a Mutable element to challenge the status quo.

A marked lack of Cardinality in a pattern is a lack of innovativeness. There is a likelihood of there emerging a genius of some sort, or a savant who incorporates all the lack of Cardinality and creates a whole new line of manifestation. *Mutatis mutandis*. This situation works well with existing modes of structure and makes the most of them, often being terribly successful as a dynasty by doing old things in entirely new ways. Carrying on family businesses, holding on to old heirlooms, passing on land, materials or solid 'gifts', are very important.

FIXED

Taurus, Leo, Scorpio, Aquarius

The Fixed signs are the midpoints of the Cardinal and Mutable signs and thus are the signs dedicated to holding-patterns. The Fixed signs form a syndrome which is associated with ego-creation and the building of self-worth and values, the capacity to invest those assets and, in turn, receive and give benefit from that circuit. Fixed crosses as a dominant family signature speak of a powerful homeostasis which overrules individual needs. The function of Taurus establishes the sense of values and worth; Leo the capacity for personal risk and investment of time, love or money based on the established value of self; Scorpio the capacity for collective value, joint assets – time, love or money – and thus, the corporate worth of the family; and, finally, Aquarius the capacity to realize a return based on the circuit of values – what does the family put back into the community or into the collective, and in turn, how accessible to change and input is the family as a group?

Fixity is not terribly innovative nor is it adaptive. It is the maintainer of the status quo. The circuit of worth, risk, corporate value and returns is one which does not allow for much change, but only for slight adaptation to the established movement. The circuit itself is self-perpetuating and requires little input from others, hence its self-inseminating quality. That is, its creativity is interior, internal, within the system itself. This is a strong dynastic indicator, where material things, and lineage both past and created for the future, are very important. This is not always a conscious intent in the group, but will show itself by evidence. Contrary to the conventional interpretations of Leo and Aquarius (both of which are loner-signs, as are Scorpio and Taurus), a group of dominant Fixed people are not very social outside their own milieu. They are an entity unto themselves. It is a closed circuit of high-powered energy. Remember, each of these signs is highly independent, and a 'group' as an entity would be the same – that is, independent within its own context – as if it were an individual loner.

A *lack* of Fixedness in a pattern would show a weak collective ego, a possible need to import a solid person or work within structures which are defined and rigid, giving a ready-made system. It strikes me that this would fit a long line of academics, for example, who need the structure of schools, universities and so on to give them a 'container' in which to place their work or ideas. The values of a family or group which was starkly weak in the Fixed mode would be adopted from other sources; their ability to invest or risk anything of value might not be the focus of their intent. There would be less concern about leaving behind a heritage, or creating a dynasty – not that it prohibits a dynasty, but it would be incidental.

MUTABLE

Gemini, Virgo, Sagittarius, Pisces

The Mutable signs are cadent, they 'fall away' from the two previous signs. As functions or modes, they are the communication circuit. They are the adaptors of the zodiac. The circuit is one based on both subtle and gross levels of communication and the processing of information. Gemini gathers data; Virgo assimilates and analyses; Sagittarius finds meaning and disseminates the 'information'; and Pisces distils this 'information' or input into a solution to the cycle of information.

A preponderance of Mutability is inclined to allow things to happen, to go along with what already exists and to adapt itself to conditions which are apparently unchangeable. They can change if the situation cannot. This kind of dynamic in an individual renders him or her the perfect support for others, and in a group is a nurturing indicator. However, there is no sense of adventure within the group itself; it needs to have external stimulus to be motivated. Usually there is a member of the family who is a maverick and is out charging around being innovative and extreme, who brings tales of the dangers of the outside world back to the home-hearth. In the Kennedy family data in the Appendix (page 376), there is a slightly higher emphasis in Mutability than in Cardinal or Fixed and a very small difference between it and Fixed, and, indeed, there has been a sequence of individuals who have broken the social-ethics barriers and have never suffered any retribution in a public sense, but have suffered horribly in their family collective. They live among themselves – this is accented by the fact that their group-elemental balance is almost perfect.

It would appear that 'justice' is visited to the Mutable family or group within itself; it is a law unto itself, and in that way is rather insular. Even with this insularity it is primarily a moral self-sufficiency, because this is the most social of the three modes by collective standards. Mutable groups are very influential in society because of their input, receptivity and interactiveness within their community or culture. They are the talkers, doers, mobilizers and networkers. They are not a 'loner-group'.

At the risk of being too literal, I would say this is the intellectual/mental circuit – not necessarily an indication of success at intellectual endeavour, but they are the thinkers of the modal types. The mind is important, aspects of the mental sphere and the psyche. Mental balance, emotional balance, psychological balance – all are factors in the Mutable cross. Here are the believers, ideologists, politicians, actors, mediators and adaptors. Taking ideas, systems and models that exist and creating something new from those extant sources is their facility. Keeping stability is difficult, but their intra-dependence helps, unless it has become too inbred and emotional instability is the outcome.

NOTES

1. See Chapter 9, 'The Elemental Family', page 158.

9.

The Elemental Family: Circuits of Being

ELEMENTAL PATTERNS

In saying that a family can be linked primarily by elements, I mean that there may be no other really powerfully obvious connecting link. This would be likely to be very rare, as the elements are added up by the planetary and nodal (sometimes ASC and MC) placements, so there is more likely a linking through the planets and aspects and signs as well. However, if it should be that the main and most profound link in the family dynamic is through elemental weight, then tacit agreement in the family is passive and receptive rather than aggressive or assertive. Strongly elemental families do not simply resist change; inherently they do not possess the inner anxiety to provoke it. This is not to say they are dull – on the contrary, they can be powerful, political, effective, efficient, strongly supportive of the community and the collective, but are an entity unto themselves. Their stresses remain internal to the network of the family, their successes equally so.

When there is a predominance of a particular element – Fire, Earth, Air or Water – the family has found a comfortable niche within itself. This shows that there is a special adherence to patterns which are easy. They can be incestuous and insular, finding the comfort of their own relations and actions to be sufficient. The elements are always in trine to each other. They form closed circuits in which all that is necessary for survival exists. When an entire family has a significant concentration in one element only, it is unconsciously longing for a change, a disruption. The family is complacent and will demand conflict. This conflict can come in the form of an event, a person or a social change which insists that new input be received. Very often there is one individual in the family who is different, who threatens the balance and composure. He or she can be a subversive, acting outside the element in common without acknowledging it consciously or openly. This is frequently the 'cause' of alienation or ostracism, when the person is

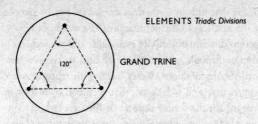

ELEMENTS *Triadic Divisions*

GRAND TRINE

Fire Involves the self-reliance and self-initiatory thrust in the sense of inspiration.
Earth Involves the sense of confidence and capacity to function by exercising the will.
Air Involves the socializing instincts and relating to others in a conventional way.
Water Involves the responses to stimulus on a basic and instinctive fashion – unconsciousness.

exposed or exposes him or herself to be the one who is threatening the status quo.

Elements are all saying the same thing, only differently. There is an underlying complacency in trinal relationships of any kind – they form a feedback loop. Triangulated energies always loop back to each other. Triangulated relationships form the underpinnings of transactional analysis, where the 'third party' present alongside the therapeutic dyad of patient and therapist-doctor is the invisible but powerful presence of another person or family member. The darker side of triangulation is the fact that they are rarely in harmony at the same time – there is always one left out. The relationship of 'the two' is dependent upon 'the other one' – these interactive relationships can create hidden dynamics. It is the basis of infidelity in love-relationships, marriages and also in friendships, where the triangle is in constant flux of balance.

In the Kennedy family, used in the Appendix as an example of the *JigSaw* program, we see that the graph showing their elemental balance is equal, with just a hair more Fire. This is actually quite unusual. The implications are that it is indeed a very well-balanced group which is self-contained and which only 'imports' those who will continue to hold the pattern or balance out and maintain the status quo. It is also a closed circuit in every elemental theme. It is well known that the Kennedys were exclusive to the extreme and instinctively selected people who would support the dynastic lineage – as well as the political and familial energy.

The elements are how we feel and how we instinctively respond to the world and what part of the world is more comfortable for us. If we lack Earth, we compensate for that lack by gathering around us Earthy people and earthing activities – if not, it is to the detriment of the whole. Similarly, an Air lack shows a need to develop objectivity, rationality and relatedness – to be able to think things through, to communicate and to receive new information are all part of Air functions. Water helps with trusting deep, instinctual feelings and values, and a lack of that element coincides in its extreme with a disregard for the feeling aspects of life or a lack of connectedness to other people's values and feelings – not to mention some difficulty with one's own emotional underpinnings. When Fire is weakly or not represented, there is often no concept of the future or the ability to act on things which will have future value. Fire connects things to the possible, and has much to do with the intuitive function which alerts us to something that will have significance in the coming times.

In the case of astrological patterns, there are very broad generalities that can be drawn across the twelve signs, but also within the elements of the signs. The four elements relate to types of experiences and ways of relating to the world. It is not unusual for families to have a predominance of one element in their collective astrology. The ascendant, Sun and Moon are very strong keys in family lineage; for example, often there can be a thread running through the family that has a Cancer-Sun father and Pisces-Sun mother, with a son who is, perhaps, a Gemini-Sun (Air) but with a Cancer Moon; and a Scorpio-Sun daughter with Pisces ascendant, but whose Moon is in Taurus (Earth). Regardless of the other positions of the planets, we would be looking at a 'Water family' because the majority of the personal signature is in the Water signs, and it provides the thread that is shared by *all* of them.

When we find the common or dominant element in a family, we can understand more about its inner life and thus how specific individuals might relate to the unspoken ethos of the family as an organic whole. The elements 'hold' the family (and the individual in it) to important unspoken ways of perceiving the world.

Grand trines – which is what the elements each form when there are planets in each one – are closed circuits. They can live in a system without each other. The energy runs round in a circle, like a feedback loop. They are terribly antisocial and a grand trine can shut out communication between planets in a chart or in a system which are outside the triangulation. In natal astrology, when a grand trine is found in a horoscope, there is usually a problem in externalizing the energy associated with the element, and the planets which are forming the syndrome are insular within the context of the chart itself. We look for a 'kite' tail, in that case, a planet which is in opposition to one of the planets in the grand trine, which helps the trinal energy externalize itself and provides an outlet for the pent-up energy.

By creating four separate triangles of each of the elements and placing all the individual's planets (in the family or group you are considering) at the apex of each of them, you will notice how much weight is placed in each of the elemental areas. The Appendix has the elemental bar-graph demonstrating an elementally balanced group in the Kennedy family. In their case, they *all* are black sheep, scapegoats, mediators, catalysts and identified patients! Such a balance is quite rare, and speaks of a powerful homeostatic principle centred in an enmeshed family fated to die out unless something or someone is destined to break the whole system up into something less balanced. Looking at that family will disabuse you of thinking that balance at all costs is the best thing!

As with the modes, you could isolate a particular factor in a group analysis – for instance all the Mars of a group, or the Moons. Perhaps only the angles, or using large groups of extended families where the birth times are unknown, just the planets themselves, without nodes or angles or other points or bodies. Play with these:

FIRE

Aries, Leo and Sagittarius

The characteristics strongly portrayed in families with a strong streak of the Fire element include spontaneity, inspiration, courage, high-risk or gambling natures, travellers, entrepreneurial abilities, pioneering spirit, freedom-loving, philosophical outlook, independence, passion, intensity, drive, volatility, change, stubbornness, wilfulness, self-centredness, power, apparent insensitivity, self-motivation, combativeness, competitiveness, strong values.

Predominantly Fire-families are volatile and expend much energy asserting to each other their own individual independence – which is highly amusing, considering that they are interdependent upon each other for this very same freedom! The tendency for hot-headedness and wilfulness is alternately admired and deplored within the family and frequently there are differences of opinion. This is often a source of misunderstanding because divergence and diversity is a fundamental signature to the family and it wants to be known as such.

Though all families tend to want to ascribe to some status quo, the Fire-type will only do it within its own code of ethics – which is an important theme: there is always some underlying code or standard that gives lip-service to 'doing your own thing'; however, because of the intensity of expression and strong will associated with Fire, there can be many diverse opinions on just exactly how this is done. A happy Fire-family rejoices in each of its members' uniqueness, as long as it is unique within the family myth! For example, if a long line of artistic temperaments produces a business-type member, there can be much suspicion around that person. It may well be that a balance must be struck and that the black sheep has come in the form of a commerce-orientated individual *who may express a very creative way of dealing with industry* and may, in fact, not be all that different at all.

Black sheep in Fire-families are often Earth or Water types, whose archetypal needs and fundamental essence are tied to another post – who find all that high-powered, energetic self-expression exhausting, time-consuming and over-dramatic. They are usually quiet, introverted and non-communicative, which threatens the outspoken, volatile Fire-family. The black sheep wants simple pleasures, security and a sense of domestic cohesion which might not be forthcoming in his Fire-family.

The family secret often comes in the form of law-breaking – somewhere in the family history is a renegade, a rebel or a political dissident, someone who has transgressed the laws of either the family or society. In some cases the failing comes in the form of religious apostasy, where the family has very rigid religious views and somewhere along the line a deep, unconscious need has arisen in the family system to alter this and give some flexibility to the expression of Fire. A new line may be started in this way, where the homeostasis of the family is shaken in order to test the strength and faith of the members, ultimately to stabilize and create new forms of the same myth.

The most important aspect to keep in mind with the Fire-family is their adherence to individualism and self-expression. Ultimately it is to the good that dissent and dissidence are allowed to exist, for in that freedom lies true happiness and trust for the family as a whole. The individual members need to feel that they are loved and appreciated for expressing what is, after all, a family characteristic.

EARTH
Taurus, Virgo and Capricorn

The element of Earth is precisely that: a grounded sense of being-in-the-world where fundamental life issues are taken in stride and all matters are dealt with in very practical, pragmatic ways. Characteristics which are held in high regard are: stability, reliability, practicality, steady ambition, achievable goals, privacy, security, self-control, containment, self-reliance, pragmatic skills, useful philosophies, harmony, precise speech, direct action, simple solutions, family-values, loyalty, feelings (as opposed to emotional displays, which are not a strong trait), faithfulness, constancy, steadfastness, fidelity, allegiance, devotion, ambition, success, greed, xenophobia, ignorance of others and pride in that attitude, conservativism, cautiousness, restraint, privacy, etc.

Families who comprise a very strong Earthy quality can often appear understated; they do not like overtly dramatic scenes associated with daily life, and getting on with it is the primary function. They enjoy the simple things in life and hold family-values very high in their code of ethics. Earthy families are self-contained and can be exclusive, even xenophobic in some extreme cases, not wanting anything 'different' to happen or to enter into their enclave. They seem to live in a closed circuit, though in fact they are no more closed to outside influence than any of the other elements, they are just more assertive about it. 'We don't need anyone else' is often the cry in adversity or fortune. This is a loyal family, one who will abandon no one, even when it is desired! They band together, facing the world as a solid unit. Meals together, family gatherings and celebrations of their union are all a must. The family history is usually dragged out and pored over on a regular basis, harking back to various outstanding members of the family who fit the current ideal.

Theirs is a working ethic, one in which no one gets anything for free. The level of ambition and its direction, of course, is going to be an individual family matter; however, there is a strong push for success and achievement in practical matters. Often the family story has emphasis in business matters, or the self-made-person theme, or having risen above the socio-economic status of the previous generations against all odds. The pride in these matters is palpable and forceful, encouraging all members of the family to exploit their practical and pragmatic character traits. The negative manifestation of the Earth-family myth is usually borne out through under-estimating one's capacities and a kind of 'shoot-yourself-in-the-foot' atti-tude. There is a certain pride in not rising above one's station; indeed, to undervalue one's abilities is lauded.

Being born into this kind of family theme could prove to be a problem for a dreamer or adventurer – this is where the black sheep is of the more Fire- or Air-orientated element, where thinking or wandering about with no real ambitious goal is evident.

In Earth families, the black sheep is almost always someone who has gone off to another country to explore new horizons, heedless of outcome or direction, or has aspirations to be a poet or artist, or is a thinker or intel-lectual who has 'airy-fairy' ideas and loathes the baseness of the family story. This does not include the academic who strives for great position in the world of letters or ideas, who is ambitious and covetous for recognition. The person who drifts aimlessly, follows his intuitions and operates on serendipity causes great excitement and alarm for himself and the family. The individual born into this fundamental, Earthy family who longs for adventure, excitement and risk will have to find the resources within herself either to carefully and respectfully depart from the family tradition or to sharply break the pattern and move forward, relying on the dependable loyalty of her Earth-bound family when push comes to shove. It can be done with the endorsement of the family if the black sheep can depart from the values-theme with love and respect for the family.

The family secret for Earth-families often involves someone who cheated or achieved ill-gotten fame or gains – in the case of an infamous ancestor, there might even be a secret pride in such a character because he or she achieved fame and did their 'crime' well! There might be an abject failure, or someone who ran out on his or her family at a time of great need whom no one speaks of, or who is regularly employed as an exemplar of how 'we don't act in this family'! The worst crime that could lurk in the ancestral line is one of irresponsibility for actions or others.

These characteristics imply a sense of duty-bound guilt as the negative manifestation of the basically good and healthy qualities of responsibility. There may be an undercurrent of anxiety over lack of production or meas-urable progress that weaves itself through the tapestry of the family. It would be difficult to simply 'be' in such a family, if the traits were undiluted. However, normally, there are other aspects to families, as there are with individuals, which provide an escape clause. But still, it is important for Earth-families to recognize that simply *being* is sometimes good enough, rather than always being *something*.

AIR

Gemini, Libra and Aquarius

The most striking aspect of Air-families is their love of relating. This is not an emotional state, but one of relativity and observation of life and its various aspects and participants . . . as a unit, they are made up of individuals who are strongly independent and value freedom. Some of the motifs that characterize classic Air-families are: eccentricity, disengaged feelings, independence, reliable unreliability, dispassionate objectivity, lots of space between members of the family, distance, coolness, experimentalism, diplomacy, discretion, savoir-faire, politeness, respect for individualism, carelessness in affections, multiple loves, ambiguity, indecisiveness, nerviness, fears, imaginings, rationalization, love of new ideas and ideology, academicism, studiousness, interest in the social or sociological, stubbornness, confusion of values or fluctuations of current values, versatility, multi-facetedness, etc.

The Air-family is probably best noted for its aura of abstraction and apparent disengaged attitude towards its very self as a group and as individual members. There is a strong mental bond between the members, but the emotional current is very low-key. Generally, the emotional tone may even be lacking to the degree that feelings are an area of discomfort and are considered 'messy'. This does not mean there is no love, as that is so very rarely the case in any family, but overt expression through emotional display, touching, or drama is not the personality of Air-groups, family or not!

There is a high degree of value placed on talking, sharing of ideas, thoughts and experiences, where members sit around and discuss things that happen. These confabulations may be rare, as the growing Air-family is usually very busy. A great deal of emphasis is placed on activities while the family is growing and there are a lot of extra-curricular and social activities constantly on the go – the children are usually always at lessons of one kind or another, music, dance, horses, languages, art classes, while the parents are often equally busy with careers, community work, social engagements and various projects both inside and outside the home.

Often the Air-family has to make appointments to meet, or the meal-time is the meeting-place when the various frenetic activities of the day are related! The fundamental philosophy of the Air-family is 'Keep busy, don't fret and the problems of the world will resolve themselves.' Clearly, this will not do for all members, for if there is a Watery or very Earthy person among this family-type, they will feel very different.

Thus, the black sheep of the Air-family will manifest unusual traits like needing to be alone a lot, needing to dream, or to lie about reading or watching television, or to wander in the forest or garden contemplating his or her inner world. The less gregarious individual in the Air-family might feel socially inadequate and incapable of keeping up the high-level extraverted energy patterns that the family seem to take very comfortably in their stride. In fact, the black sheep acts as the barometer of the emotional climate in the family and will often reflect what is really going on under the busy surface.

Black sheep are not always unhappy about their position – they are usually lovingly accepted if not really understood – but they always do feel that they have somehow been misplaced. A Watery or Earthy black sheep will feel that their bustling, busy Air-family is insensitive to feeling, possibly superficial and inattentive to 'the important things' in life, like soulfulness, emotional experiences, deep, inner feelings and the more poetic aspects of life. This may or may not be actually *true*, but there is an element of reality to this situation. In some ways this busy family dynamic can facilitate the quiet and contemplative life that the black sheep wants – they might be able to carry on their private, inner life in the midst of the furore of their family, feeling safe and secure in the knowledge that their secrets are protected because nobody will interfere with them!

In a family which is strongly, predominantly Air in its make-up, the family secret is usually no secret at all, for as in the oral traditions, the openness of the communication lines has likely passed on all the known information quite objectively. The psychology of repression, however, demands that there be something unspoken, unaired or unresolved, and with Air the tacit problem usually lies in the realm of emotions. Irrationality and passion is not considered 'important' – this is not a pose, but a truth. Normally, Air is not rife with inner emotional conflict – there may be problems with decision-making, but high drama is usually not the motif.

The type of family secret therefore is more likely to hold a highly charged irrational and emotional issue, involving passion, heat, romance or love –

which someone in the family always lives out. It can result in a situation where someone has enacted a Romeo and Juliet kind of scenario, sacrificing good sense and family unity for passion and love. Everyone else stands around wondering how this could happen and why there was no ability to control feelings, emotions or instincts.

The instinctual nature is not highly valued in the Air-family; it is often a thing of mystery if not of fearfulness. Mind over heart and matter can be the mainstay of the family motif, the principles of intellectual law over natural law. This is why the primal instincts do emerge through certain members of the family, in order for balance to be restored – the more truly understanding the family is, the more they gain from their black sheep and the less damaged they feel by the unspoken and repressed family secret, and the more enriched they are by the deep, emotional world of sensual feelings.

WATER

Cancer, Scorpio and Pisces

Water-families thrive on emotions, feelings, undercurrents, tides, storms, upheavals, love, passions, causes, spiritual dilemmas, religious expression, mystery, secrets, subtlety, intensity, depth, range of experience, exalted beliefs, romance, imagination, fantasy, dreams, poetry, music, helping, suffering, healing, ideals, hysteria, guilt, worry, confusion and chaos, humour, compassion, sympathy and empathy, intuitions, strong values, i.e. 'good' and 'bad' things, hints, implications, nuance, 'vibrations', etc.

Emotionally enmeshed and fused, personalities can become merged and identity lost in a strongly Water-sign family. There can be so much loving concern involved in the family that no one ever really achieves a sense of independence. This is not a problem unless it is a problem. Clearly, emotional expression has its positive side because one knows one is affected and has made an effect, but the darker side of it is controlling and upsetting. The subtlety of feeling is often hard to identify unless there is direct verbal communication. Water-families rely a lot on mind-reading, which they do well, but it is largely exclusive of others.

There is a natural affinity between the Watery members of the family which leaves a lot unsaid and can be unnerving, for instance, to an Air-type person, or can drown a Fire-type person. The depth of feeling that runs through the Water-family is profound and they are normally a very tactile group, always touching, stroking, cuddling and emoting. Equally, they can be remonstrative and punishing when feelings have been transgressed or crushed. Ideally, a Watery family should all discuss their dreams on a regular basis, for under the surface is a strong and equally powerful life which, when analysed, would make as much sense as their daily, mundane existence.

The loving, caring, supportive environment is very nourishing and fosters security and trust, always a good basis for forming and maintaining relationships – which is the primary motif of the element Water. The real problem that lurks underneath the loving concern is control and manipulation – this is not a prerequisite in a Water-family, but it can be a strong factor which, if addressed, is defused and clarified. Members of Water-type families really need to learn how to draw boundaries around themselves, see themselves as individuals and try very hard to retain an independent shape within the context of the family, and not identify too much with other members.

When problems arise in Water-families, the tendency is to suppress them and hope they will just go away. Rather than this being the case, the problems usually fester and grow, only to erupt at some other time, often inappropriately. Therefore, it is best for the issues to be aired as they surface. The negative manifestations of repression of feeling or emotion in Water families are hysteria, hypochondria or serious emotional disabilities. They need a lot of sunshine and picnics together.

The black sheep is usually someone who finds the Water-family smothering, rather than protective, and loathes all the cloying, invasive emotional content. They are usually more Fire- or Air-orientated themselves, and can appear stand-offish and distant, not wanting to take part in the family dramas or share their lives wholeheartedly with everyone else. Their needs for independence and freedom appear selfish and alienating to the more enmeshed members of the family, and although this has nothing to do with love, they really don't want to be watched or worried about all the time.

All families cannot be accomplished musicians, poets, artists or healers; however, an element of all these talents runs through the Water-family. There is a disproportionate number of doctors, nurses, psychoanalysts, police, detectives, religious and spiritually vocated people, writers and musicians that fall in the Water signs. Their affinity with the unknowable, unspeakable and invisible is powerful, and it is from this vantage point that their talents can be exploited in various themes.

In the Water-family the dark family secret can produce a mad person in the ancestral line, or a bunch of them. There can be an inherent instability which, in a healthy person, is simply a sensitive, highly-strung personality, but if there *is* a skeleton in the closet, individual members of the family might worry that they, too, will succumb to this mysterious madness. Like all family secrets, the likelihood of it repeating over and over precisely in the same way is very low, so to air out the damp closet regularly is a good idea.

There is always an element of secrecy or mystery in Water-families – they do tend to hold more secrets and hide things even when it is quite unnecessary. Other family secrets are likely to include abortions, out-of-wedlock children (now a fairly outdated concept, but powerful in history), mysteries surrounding deaths, religious fanatics or antisocial behaviour.

10

The Water Houses:
The Ancestral Eyes
of the Soul

The Water houses are the places of ancestral lineage. Although each house in the horoscope has its relation to the family, and all aspects of the horoscope are familial, these particular houses focus intently on three levels of ancestral relationship. The Water houses are the most mysterious of the twelve sectors; all of them symbolize varying levels of merging and bonding, feeling and emotion, body and soul.

I have begun with the twelfth house because that is the primordial womb, wherein lies our personal connection to the *anima mundi*, the world soul. In that realm, we are, indeed, all one. Where energy and matter are indistinguishable, we find the stuff and matter of the world redundant and the transcendant exists outside time. We are connected to the ancestral lineage, to the human race. This is the quantum-family house. From there, we incarnate through a specific womb, the mother, who houses us during the incubation of the body. In the fourth house we are the gene-pool of the family-of-origin, the astrological meeting place of the personal ancestors, wherein we become alive with our families all around and meet ourselves in the faces and souls of real people. In the eighth house we have the task of living with the dead; here is where we, as the incarnate soul, individuate our personal ancestors. They call us from that place, requiring that we receive our inheritance from them and use it wisely.

Transits through these houses will awaken their realms of experience, and bring us closer to the domain of the ancestral lines.[1]

THE TWELFTH HOUSE: THE COSMIC FAMILY SOUL

All consciousness separates; but in dreams we put on the likeness of that more universal, truer, more eternal man dwelling in the darkness or primordial night. There he

is still whole, and the whole is in him, indistinguishable from nature and bare of all
ego-hood.[2]   (Carl G. Jung)

In ancient astrology, the twelfth house was considered to be malign – it
was the house of hidden enemies, incarceration, insanity and self-undoing
brought on by influences outside one's own control – in short, a dreadful
locus. In modern astrology it is still mainly interpreted as such, in the sense
that the twelfth house is the house of sleeping characteristics and of self-
undoing, the shadowy realm where traits can remain unrealized, undifferentiated and not rendered in any way personal. It is seen now as the house of
the collective unconscious – a way of saying that it is the place where we are
deeply united with the greater ancestral line, that of the entire human race
back to its origins, and that we have no recourse but to fall into this primordial womb regardless of the degree to which we are conscious of this place.

There is a place in which the origins of all humanity reside, and they
dwell in the ancestral site. Perhaps this site is located via the reptile brain,
the pre-cortex brain which has record of the primal struggles for survival
and evolution – a place where our darkest survival instincts are still very
active and functioning. We know we have this place in us, as well as racial
memory, where we dream of gods, of monsters and of unknown skies
where three suns or eight moons are rising and setting. It is this place where
our recollection of the cosmic womb lies.

Somewhere in the deepest recesses of the soul in all people is a place of
perfect bliss – and a place of ultimate horror. This is the twelfth house.
Since the twelfth house represents the first couple of hours after birth, it is
likely to house the earliest recollections we might have after incarnation. It is
with great interest in this mysterious area that hypnotherapists, rebirth
workers and depth psychoanalysts try to help individuals reach back into
this realm. Lying in the twelfth house is the source of *Weltschmertz* – world
pain. That we are all connected to each other, we are all one, is the basic
tenet of the oldest religions, and although it flies in the face of logical posi-
tivism, it is fast becoming a generally accepted idea – that somewhere deep
in the genetic and psychic (spiritual) realm all individuals are connected to
each other, and to everyone who has gone on before.

It is in the twelfth house that we meet the ancestors of the entire human
race. And, very likely, the pre-human race, the organism of humanity. All
the ancient interpretations of the twelfth house have relevance if we see
it in this light. In that deep in our own psyche is our personal shadow,

stemming from the shadowy origins of humanity, it is the house of hidden enemies, as well as of guardian angels. Darkness came before the dawn, and our archaic memory of the Dark Age and the time before the bicameral mind resonates in today's freshly conscious person. The twelfth house contains the time-out-of-mind period of our human development, the time the ancient poets of the oral tradition sang of, the mythic realms when all was Night and Chaos, before the gods and long, long before man. When we are in the womb we are this prehistoric creature, unformed, with a tail and swimming around in a small salt sea, without consciousness, without reason and totally dependent on genetics (and fate) to keep us alive long enough to give birth to ourselves.

It is also the house of incarceration – if we take the literal meaning of the words *in carcere* to be in the flesh – and to be incarnated means to fold the soul into a body, which happens in the fourth house. But what happened before the soul incarnated, where was it incarcerated? This is the longest of the mysteries, the untraceable one. Whereas in the fourth house we can trace our known ancestors and in the eighth house we peel back the layers of our personal unconscious and our 'this life' connection to the ancestral line, the twelfth house offers no such rational exercise.

Certainly insanity falls into this house as well, because a person who has lost the tentative boundary between the personal realm and the deeper, archetypal realm enters the place which we call madness. But then madness and civilization have been a dialectic for aeons, and a discussion on madness and the twelfth house could be reduced to saying one thing. That madness is loss of differentiation, lack of individuation and complete disregard for the conventions of consciousness. It is being returned to the infantile state, or possibly even pre-infancy, to a time when gods, monsters and chaos were the state of being in the world. Through the twelfth house, we understand, though perhaps do not condone or accept, the horrors of the human condition and what people can do to other people to reduce them to ash – this is a house of amorality. It is through this understanding that we have the possibility of redemption of the dark side of human nature, as well. It is a very complex house, one not as easily rationalized as its counterparts, the fourth and the eighth houses.

The Platonic picture tells of the soul making a journey through the underworld after departing from the body, meeting various experiences and undergoing trials, all of which are tailored to the incarnate soul's previous experience and are designed to prepare the soul for its next reincarnation. One of the last trials of the liminal soul is to cross a blazing hot plain – the Plain of Oblivion – and reach a river of the same name (*Lethe* in Greek – the root of our word 'lethal'), where Plato's advice to the soul is to drink not too deeply from the river Lethe because it encourages oblivion (forgetfulness), which is lethal to consciousness in the next incarnation.[5]

This story is the underlying hypothesis of Plato's theory of recollection – that is, we spend our entire lives recalling what we knew before we were born – that we do not *learn* anything, but *recall* everything that exists in the realm of the archetypes. What we perceive as learning, then, is actually a process of midwiving already extant knowledge in the soul and bringing it to consciousness and applying it to the present. Though it is not stated as such, this philosophy implies a diachronous time, and that our souls live in this pan-temporal place, locked into temporality by the incarceration in the body. According to Plato, the highest achievement in life is to go about re-collecting the soul's knowledge (wisdom). This is the path of the philosopher. On a humorous note, someone once said that God invented time so that everything didn't happen all at once – this 'all at once' is the soul's time, not incarnate time!

In this region called the twelfth house, in this horoscopic place, the incarnate soul resides, deeply buried in the body, longing for recollection of the past and connected to the ancestral spirits of all humanity. Neptune is the twelfth house ruler, Pisces its sign and those two symbolized the cosmic womb, the place of pre-memory. In the twelfth house, things do happen 'all at once'.

The aspect of Neptune and all its domain which most interests me in this circumstance is its anaesthetic properties. Wherever we have Neptune is where we have natural endomorphins, pain-killers. The first pain is the pain of birth. The pain begins in the womb, when the foetus begins to reject the mother by releasing into her bloodstream, via the umbilical cord (which once was its source of life), hormones which then cause the uterus to contract – the uterus becomes lethal. This process continues until the foetus is expelled, the cord is severed and all symbiosis between mother and child has ceased. The ouroboric life has ended. This must hurt. In comes Neptune, for its first act, that of obliterating the pain of birth and initiating its role for the future: to divide consciousness from the archetypal realm, the world of unity-with-all and the oceanic state in which the preconscious being exists.

The infant is now an entity in itself, one which will long to return to Neptune, to the womb, to the collective undifferentiated state of being over and over again.

People with planets in the twelfth house find that they have a difficult time contacting the energies and agencies with which those planets are identified and are embodied by practical, conventional means. They seek and find myriad ways of reconnecting to the archetypal realm. The twelfth house planets are 'last to be born' as they reside in this Watery womb of the collective. Very often, the only way to connect consciously with the planets therein is to mythologize, spiritualize or universalize them. They find that it is easier to turn the embodied aspect of the planetary agencies into something outside the human experience, or at least the Earthy human experience. This is why heavily tenanted twelfth house people are hard to pin down; they find themselves hard to grasp, as well! They want to find cosmic order in the sordid aspects of human life.

That the twelfth house planets are last to be born means that it takes greater conscious effort to individuate out of the archetypal collective consciousness – the tendency to cosmologize the function of the planet renders it infantile and undeveloped in the psychological sense. Reason remains too far outside; it stays in the transcendent realm and thus does not come into the lower regions where psychology plays a role in transforming the conscious mind and working on the connection between the deeper layers of the recessed psyche and the upper air of the mental, intellectual realms. People with twelfth house planets are always speaking of their helplessness in the face of the larger reality, whether that is society, divinity or history. It takes great energy and conscious effort to make a thread of a bridge from the personal back to the collective and thus be personally conscious of being responsible for the collective.

Naturally the twelfth house planet wants to go back into the cosmic womb; the pain of being conscious and alive is often too great. It takes long periods of withdrawal and contemplation and small steps out into the harshness of the light (symbolized by the first house), and the responsibility for self and ego requires a cosmic purpose. Twelfth house planets do not so much speak of the family inheritance directly, as does the fourth, and secondarily the eighth, but more of the collective inheritance as it falls into the life of an individual born into a family in which there are many practical and physical difficulties. Twelfth house planets do speak loudly about secrets in the family, possible parental hatred or disgust with the child or the process of childhood, parents who were not cosmic enough and thus a child had to be born to take on the collective identity and become the cosmic one among them.

People with twelfth house planets often feel very lonely – and human relationships are not sufficient for assuaging that loneliness. Hence, relationships are formed with a divinity or a spiritual life. Blending these two apparently split domains is a life-path, for in the quantum realm there is no distinction between energy and mass, but our current development in consciousness maintains this gulf. This singularity is not the existential despair that besets the eighth house planet, nor the gripping, burdening isolation of the carrier of the family fate in the fourth, but the cosmic loneliness which is the making of the monk on the mountain. Twelfth house people might well have come from under the cabbages or down the chimney, brought by the stork, for all their connection to their family of origin. The fact is that they likely have jumped several generations and come in at a time when the family was becoming bereft of soul, and it befalls the twelfth house person to do the soul-work for them. They are deeply connected to their nuclear family of origin, but have been given the inordinate responsibility of spiritualizing for the entire family, as far back as it goes to the priest, nun, monk, or novitiate.

Therefore it is essential for the twelfth house planets to become connected to the body somehow. If not, the person can suffer body-symptoms and emotional disconnection. The body is always a bit of a problem with the twelfth house person anyway, because of the nature of the house itself, and its polar opposite, the sixth. The sixth is the body and the twelfth is the soul or psyche . . . the combination of *psyche* and *soma* in some form or other is the function of incarnation. Hence, the psychosomatic dis-ease which can so easily and readily befall the twelfth house person. Care of the soul is necessary for us all, but it is the guarantor of health and life for the strongly twelfth house person. This is why many people with the personal planets in the twelfth do have weak constitutions, especially in the first developmental years of their lives. Their souls are not terribly connected to their bodies.

This can be because the mother herself was disembodied during the pregnancy or during the labour and delivery. My younger brother was born within minutes of his mother being administered a new, experimental drug of the times called 'twilight sleep' (1962). It provoked horrible nightmares and an almost satanic reaction to the doctor and delivery-room staff on her part, and it also slowed the contractions. All this as Neptune crested the horizon in Scorpio! These people are haunted by the shades of the ancestors and are called back and back again to find the harmony or chord between the now and mythological times. They are the mythopoeic voices of our times. A friend of mine was born as Uranus was just into the twelfth house, and he was delivered in the car, in the car-park of the emergency entrance to the hospital. Uranus in the twelfth provokes radical attempts to move away from mass psychology, to break from social movements so as to find individuality outside the collective. Many people with Pluto rising almost die at birth, literally, or their mothers almost die or get septicaemia . . . this is truly the endangered heroic birth! Their connection to the archetypal realm is profoundly teleological – they are always looking for the end, to find meaning in death. On a very, *very* deep level, one which is quantum and thus without blame, the child with outer planets rising is not wanted, or is inconvenient and is a child of the collective, not of the family. Hence, the sense of alienation and isolation of such people.

The most profound recourse to this kind of personal yet not-personal rejection is to find their larger family. They are children of the universe, and must assume the burden of that role. In shamanic cultures, these are the people who bear the burdens for the collective, heal the wounds of the tribal consciousness. It may take half or over half the lifetime to find the special purpose, but it is there. These people are tailor-made for collective identification and work in the collective. Some of them simply must do work on behalf of many – even the inner work, the philosophical and personal psychological work benefits the collective. This can be very difficult to say to someone who is suffering personal pain for a collective or family debt – to say, your own suffering and understanding of that suffering will reduce the world-suffering by that much. Some of the people with these major configurations simply do not have the voltage to cope, and become victims of the many, rather than workers for them. In the case of criminals or madpersons, they have been swallowed by the collective, they were overcome, their energy and *nous* not capable of battling with the massive forces at play with the outermost planets.

As for the age-old tradition of putting all twelfth house planets in gaol – literally, in prison – there is some justification for that. As there is justification for the substance abuser being found in the twelfth house, along with the mad person. All of the above conditions remove ego. There is no identity in the strongly individuated sense for a prisoner, a mad person or a stoned person. They have all been swallowed by the collective. The role of a prison-mate is to be one of many, they are a mote in a body of criminals, a number not a person. A mad person has slipped between the crack of the contained, Saturnian manor of the conscious horizon and entered the twilight zone of the collective archetypal realm, wherein there is no differentiated personality as the ego describes, and there is no conscious control over the external environment. On the purely psychological level, this is a problem. On the spiritual level, it is a problem within society as we know it.

There has always been and there will always be those who live outside the bounds of proscribed values, behaviours, beliefs and move beyond the limits of society and the times. And there will always be times of the day or night when planets are cresting the eastern horizon, passing through the twelfth house. This is the quietest time of day, the time when most animal activity is at its culmination and the earth has a quality of freshness and newness to it. It is a transcendent time of day; just as twilight, near sunset, is a time when the spirits can slip in and out of the reality zone, so they do at the moment of sunrise. The twelfth house planet is the connection to the spirit realm, wherein there are no morals, there is no psychology and there is no boundary between the conscious and the unconscious.

The Sun in the twelfth is an indicator of the reluctant incarnate, he or she who would rather never have left the safety of the womb, but whose need for solar-system individuation was so overwhelming that their rejection of the cord of life was ultimately of their own choosing. Because the Sun in the twelfth speaks of an endangered origin or an insulated life, it means that there was an initial sense of adventure about being born, then a deep regret for such a foolish decision. The rest of the life is spent contemplating existence through a veil or at worst, the very worst, through bars of one sort or another.

Mercury in the twelfth house finds the most complicated way to say the simplest thing. There must be a cosmic reason underlying every single act of creation and being. Often, Mercury in the twelfth find it impossible to articulate the knowledge they have, because they live in the boundary of the conceptual and archetypal. They need to find a vehicle through which they might bridge those two split realms.

Venus there will have a mythic frame of reference around relationships, a fantasy of the perfect relationship – this might translate into a relationship with god or a fairy-tale relationship with the feminine embodiment of Venus. There is a strong relationship with the divine order of things; hence it is monastic and has ties to spiritual love. Also, they need to be alone to find contact with this level of ancestral life, before being able to relate to individuals.

People with the Moon in the twelfth house often try to elevate primal feelings to the most spiritual level. Because part of them, the emotional aspect of life, remains in the cosmic womb, they can have doubts about their human feelings or emotions. The most pathological expression results in reducing human feelings to sordid, atavistic behaviour, whereas the other extreme elevates their feelings to a class beyond the realm of human experience, to the divine love. They often feel an emotional bond with a country or culture which is not their culture-of-origin, but a spiritual heritage coming from ancestral sources.

Mars can love or hate the collective, fight with his or her own immune system, spiritualize the most fundamental of desires, rather than come to terms with the human need to aggress, draw boundaries and declare war and territorial dominance. I think that Mars in the twelfth can be haunted by ancestral spirits and find it difficult to give birth to their own individual ego without it being attached to a collective 'institution'.

I have referred to Jupiter there as an 'archangel on the shoulder, a guardian angel', and it is, in the deepest sense. One's social urges are rising from a collective desire to follow the divine guidance in life; hence the priest or novitiate consciousness, which in its most negative manifestation, comes through as messianic (Jupiter/Neptune, as well).

Saturn in the twelfth is like having the body inside the soul, rather than the other way around. There is something about the person that gives them the feeling that they have a collective debt to pay. Often there is a feeling of a huge, intangible authority figure standing in judgement on the puniness of life's endeavours. Indeed, there is some authoritative organizational principle of a cosmic nature – the Greek word *cosmos* literally means 'order' – *but* it is impersonal and has no judgement on individuals. But Saturn is so easily assumed to be one's own father when, in fact, here it is the archetypal father. The personal father is not the judge, however; the inner author of one's destiny is.

The twelfth house planets bring us to the point of ego development. This is where the outermost planets must be employed in new ways to contain the ego. They become very personal planets. We have called them transpersonal too long; they are not 'beyond the personal', but are more personal than the Sun and Moon when an individual is required to incorporate them into the identity. The outer planets are the threshold of the new consciousness which is still, in 1996, in its infancy. As a mass, we are still in process of individualizing them. When they are in the Water houses, *especially*, one is required to incorporate them by using them in ways which will benefit the masses, the collective, thus personalizing them through their own spirit.

Uranus requires that one do something personally about the collective – be involved with supportive groups, global organizations which connect cultures with other cultures, or work with the disaffected and disabled in whatever sense appeals to the individual him or herself. Individuation through the collective is the only real answer to the existential longing. It can literally mean developing new ways of perceiving the invisible, networking the masses, and finding personal meaning in mass psychology.

Neptune here actually hears the music of the spheres. It is a sign that the individual will remain very closely connected to the primordial energy of the cosmos. Often there is a quality of being haunted, of living in a crowded room even when alone. It is partly because there is no individuation in this house, and Neptune is right at home – look to where the sign Pisces falls for clarification of where one's cosmic origins can be earthed and grounded in a practical, incarnate way, else a lot of wandering about among the constellations occurs. Part of the individual remains unborn, and deeply connected to the ancestral realm – hence, it so often is a devotional aspect where the individual must find succour in the divine.

Pluto, having risen into the twelfth during the course of the last stages of labour and birth, illustrates an endangered birth and thus a challenged life. There is a constant struggle to maintain individuality in the face of collective entropy. Symbolically, these people are likely to have known what it was to be burned at the stake. It is a radical, revolutionary placement because the argument with the cosmos is about life-or-death issues. One's relationship with the divine is deeply connected to the origins of the universe. On a practical level, working in the collective with those who are confined, entrapped, facing death, living in inhuman conditions and having to fight for life will lend them the strength of their convictions.

THE FOURTH HOUSE: THE ANCESTRAL FAMILY OF ORIGIN

Full circle, from the tomb of the womb to the womb of the tomb, we come: an ambiguous, enigmatical incursion into a world of solid matter that is soon to melt from us, like the substance of a dream.   (Joseph Campbell)

In the strictest sense of the meaning, the fourth house of the horoscope does mean our home; however, in the global community, 'home' might not mean the fourth house in the chart. That is, we may not live in the land of our nativity. The old saw, 'We are judged in the land of our nativity', means that no matter where we go, there we are, fourth house and all. In fact, our fourth house is bigger than we think – it is tenanted by family members who have passed on before us and those who have not yet been born. It is the house of the ancestors and the progeny of our own lives.

The fourth house is the house of greatest personal mystery. Experiences occur there which never reach consciousness and clusters of planets around the IC can add to the mystery of it, rather than fully explain it. Like the roots of a great, ancient tree, our own source of deep earthy nourishment and life-blood is underground, hidden and protected from the light of day. That roots continue to grow and seek new ground in accord with the sprouting of fresh branches and leaves implies that our ancestral linkage is itself enriched with each new addition to its chain – and with each conscious step forward, we excite the ancestors into new life. In the same mysterious way as the tree, our own lives grow and branch and our roots sink deeper and more resiliently with each day, adding to our lives an inestimable measure of enriched life.

Many cultures place great emphasis on the ancestral spirits. Their daily lives include their forebears in ways which might seem superstitious or sentimental to some. Yet a majority of cultures pay great homage to their ancient pasts, not out of fear and oppression by ghosts, but because they are aware that within each of them as individuals lie the souls of all the ancestors who went before. Through this mainline to the souls of family lineage the peoples of aboriginal cultures are strengthened and fortified emotionally, physically and spiritually. They *are* the spirits of the ancestors incarnate. Walking with the dead is taken for granted and great respect is paid to these foundations of lifeblood; they are religiously involved with their progenitors.

That is not to say that we of the Western civilization are not respectful of the ancestors – after all, we are more than proud of our great-grandfather who started his own company, for instance, or of grandmother who courageously left her homeland for a new country, thus starting a fresh line of settlers. We are indeed! However, when we are considering aspects of an individual's nature and concentrating on his or her natal horoscope, we might run up against some mysterious blockage which we cannot 'explain'. There may be a haunting or a deep sadness which may not be completely accounted for in the psychology of the immediate family. Also, there may be a longing for a path or direction in life which is quite outside the expectations or understanding of one's immediate family. Sometimes there are inexplicable feelings of obligation towards maintaining a family situation or ritual which no one appeared consciously to require from you.

We might be considerably more healthy if we had our ancestral linkage present in our nuclear family structures in everyday ways . . . that is, by bringing in the grandparents and their history we are one step removed from the immediate parents. This can reduce the emotional charge of the immediate parents and siblings. We are too close to our parents fully to appreciate their impact on our psyche, and it is often only when we reach our own mid-life that we truly see who they are, and by then they are very old, sometimes dead. The proximity can be blinding. It can either deify or under-appreciate the parents as people themselves. This is part of the nature of things, that the parents are merely a link to the past and a biological step forward into our future. However, if our myths, our history and our ancestral line were more emphasized we might find more objectivity in the family structure.

Even more mysterious is the situation where an individual feels called to go back to a root-religion abandoned by the family for generations. There are many cases where the person did not even know of their spiritual origins and was mysteriously drawn towards expressing a religion or to a calling towards a place or idea! In a large family, there may be one person who carries the message of the ancestors and feels an obscure but unequivocal mandate to fulfil that inner command. The fourth house can shed light on such situations, and add a rich dimension to one's awareness of participating in a very large family.

The fourth house is both womb and tomb – it is the fertile source of our own life and harbours the past shrouded in dignified mystery. We too often pass it off as 'mother' (or father in some cases), 'real-estate', or the address at which we live. It is all of those but more – it is where we live, where we find life and it is the root of all our longings to be. It is out of the fourth house that we individuate and become increasingly ourselves. We must continually go back into that labyrinth to wrest out lost or unborn aspects of individuality and bring them into daylight for foster and care and maturation. This is a lifelong process and one which must never be abandoned in the name of being 'all grown up'. If the process of individuation is as it appears to be, it is never accomplished, but is transitive and ongoing.

The Moon and the sign Cancer are the rulers of this house, and the Moon represents the personal womb, as different from the twelfth house, the collective womb. These are very physical symbols, the Moon and Cancer. The personal container for our incarnation was our mother, and her nurture brought us to the brink of life. Once severed from her, the fourth house then becomes our place of containment for the early years of life, a place where all the family patterns and influences from generations past settle in our psyche. The sign Cancer is the most secretive sign of all, in that it can function with complete unconsciousness of its visceral – gut-reaction – motives, yet primarily operates by this intuitive and instinctual function. Cancer is deeply concerned with its territory, its manor, its home. The fourth house is how we respond on a deep, physical level to the world around us, based not only on our immediate nuclear family, but on the ancestral pool from which we are comprised. So the Moon and the fourth house then later becomes the foundation for the extension and procreation of the continuing family line, as we grow older, make our own homes, create our own families and so on. All of which is based on the mysterious combination of hundreds and thousands of ancestral bodies and souls.

Nestled in the fourth house is the soulful recollection of everything related to the blood-line, one's dynastic family of origin. It is easy to transpose the fourth house as the mother because our mother is the vehicle for our incarnation; she houses us in gestation while our bodies mature mysteriously and secretly to term. (In ancient astrology the fourth house was the 'house of confinement', when a woman was pregnant and hidden from society.) When does the soul enter this body? We do not know the answer, but it is sufficient to say that the soul is an often reluctant dweller in the body and its longings are to go home – somewhere, wherever 'home' is. As we read in the twelfth house, this home is a very large place, indeed.

Naturally, the actual conditions surrounding one's immediate family –

parents, siblings – and one's created family – partner, children – all are found in this mysterious house. But they, too, are all part of this great reservoir of genes, codes, blood and bones. We are deeply entrenched in the web of the family and it is necessary to define oneself as separate from but belonging to a family. To a greater or lesser degree, depending upon how closed the unit is, liberation from the family is necessary for personal development. This may take the form of a simple maturation process, or perhaps the discovery that one is carrying a gift from the family lineage or holding the charge of neurotic family complexes.

I have found that the more complex the immediate family is, especially if it is extremely malignant, the more important it is that the fourth house be considered as a *larger container* than just that immediate family. We are trained to think that all our problems (and blessings) come directly from the interaction of the nuclear family in which we spent the formative years of our lives. This is patently not true. That way of thinking is fast becoming outmoded and by the time we are well into the twenty-first century will very likely cease to be a major consideration. The fact is, we are part of a much larger collective and are increasingly intertwined with global issues. The fourth house must also contain the history of the entire family pattern. If there are very hard aspects or several of the outer planets in the fourth house, there may be some characteristic that has been passed into the individual to transmute for the entire family lineage.

A word-play in ancient Greek is particularly profound in this sense: the Greek words for body and tomb are remarkably similar – body = *soma* and tomb = *sema*. The quote from Joseph Campbell on page 180 highlights the *soma/sema* analogy; whether that is deliberate or not, I do not know. However we perceive body and soul, the Platonic view is thus: the body is the grave of the soul and its liberation is not only necessary but desirable. But the soul's journey after springing free of the body and its journey through the liminal place between incarnation is complicated and arduous. This we know from reading the twelfth house, in which crossing the river Lethe required the soul to drink not too deeply from this 'river of forgetfulness'. This fourth house soul is the family soul, where we are intuitively connected to our ancestors and from whence we begin our incarnate journey. It is how we remember our history and what it has to offer us this time round.

The soul itself does recollect the past, but does the *mind*? If the mind does not recollect then the body will – and through the body of one's own self and the body of the family and the ancestral past, we recall ourselves and the innate wisdom of all that has gone before. We can only achieve this 'knowledge' of recollection in soulful ways – through feelings, dreams, images, urges, vocations, longings, hopes, fantasies, love, intimacy with one's own deepest self. We can only listen to the soul in the privacy of our own senses and bodies and minds. We might be reminded of our soul's path through another person or an experience, but we are never knowledgeable, we never understand it in the intellect. The soul is not the intellect. The process of finding the ancestors and digging into the archaeology of the family psyche can bring us to the purpose of our life.

Because the houses are reflexive, that is, they incorporate aspects by implication from the opposite house, the tenth house is also important as a family place. As the fourth house is the most secret, the tenth house is the most public. Often we can see more clearly by reflection something that is too glaring or too deeply unconscious. A person fulfils his or her creative impetus based upon the security of self-discovery in the context of the family. If that foundation is shaky or disruptive, or the person has to work through dynastic patterns to get to his or her own essence, then arriving at personal creativity and security can be a major struggle.

The tension of the IC/MC and fourth/tenth house axis rests on a longing for a sense of continuity of past and urgency towards the future. They appear to be at odds, but when we really think of life and its paradoxes, it is this very tension which gives meaning and thrust to being alive. If one or the other becomes overwhelmingly dominant, a real spiritual crisis occurs. That is, if one is inclined to ignore the longings of the soul to retreat in favour of the demands of the outer world, then the soul sickens and withers. If the soul has ascendancy to the extreme, there is no excitation of the body/mind and a dullness, an apathy towards the world, ensues; a loss of *thumos* – life-force, libido – arises and depression can result. Having a relative balance requires both body and soul to conspire and collude in what appears to be a transitory but highly interesting life.

A basic psychological premise proposes that we 'project' interior secrets in very public ways – we can measure our inner selves in the outside world by reflecting on the deeper, hidden meaning of our actions, accomplishments and associations with others. Planets in the fourth house speak eloquently about the foundations of our security and the relationship we have with the family as our personal fate.

When the Sun or Moon is in the fourth, it is the individual's very purpose in life to get to the essence of the family matrix. They enjoy it, unless there are very hard aspects to the lights, and if Venus and Mercury are also there, then there can be a general fascination with genetics, family patterns, history and the whole issue of families as a subject. They have been required to spend a great deal of their creative energy feeling secure – this is not automatically a security placement, but one in which security must be acquired through trust. Normally, an introverted signal, home, family and native roots are essential to their health and well-being. One can either carry on a family tradition in vocation or, on the contrary, there can be a need to individuate right out of the family-system in order to become wholly independent. By nature this person is a dependent person – his or her identity is bound up with the whole family as a persona, hence the need to do one or other extreme.

Mars brings all the wars in the family history into the psyche of the person; they experience the inner war, and often are the rage-carrier of the family. There are some erotic overtones here, as well, and though not an indicator of incest (there is no single indicator of any pathology), this person picks up any unresolved sexual issues which are dormant or repressed in the immediate family. There may have been a sexual issue in the ancestors – secret homosexuality, prostitution, illegitimate children, and so forth – but all that must be brought into the open, and this is the one in the family destined to do that.

Jupiter in the fourth is the necessity of finding one's roots and cleansing them of all social guilt and ills. (See Rosemary's story in 'The Procession of the Ancestors, page 356.) This is a joyful end, but can be a long, tortuous and multicultural exploration. The person who undergoes this journey willingly has the reward of freeing the family from its own curse, should there be felt to be one. There has been a very powerful religion influencing the family, likely to be an ethnic one, or a history of oppression either by the family or of the family by cultural coincidence; a strong moral conditioning lies at the foundation of the family. The person may need to travel widely or leave their native land to complete this task.

Saturn in the fourth talks about feeling the responsibility for being the sole carrier of not only the parents' but also the ancestral guilt. The child grows into the adult who feels the need to expiate the burdens of the family system. There is often a confusion about the parents' roles – where each of them is, for instance, who the nurturer is and who the provider is. The birth parents will be likely to have neglected to realize that this child is inherently anxious to please and 'knows' he or she is marked by a responsibility, and thus they can damage his or her sense of personal authority by demanding too much regard for them as authorities or by forcing upon the child their values or opinions. As adults they will be fascinated by history and their own origins.

Neptune in the fourth shows a fear of being lost, sacrificed, ignored or victimized; there is a sense of boundlessness which breeds fear of disappearing and very often that was compounded by real-life events. There may have been any number of circumstances that fed the sense of insecurity: alcoholic parent(s), ill parent – especially the mother – too many relocations in childhood, illness as a child resulting in isolation, or living, somehow, 'at sea'. There is a psychic fusion with the ancestors, and a sense of vagueness about the immediate nuclear family; people with this placement experience odd moments of atavism where they are cast out-of-time, and they are frequently uncomfortable with contemporary society, though often gifted at portraying themselves as being in synch with the *Zeitgeist*. Their deep, inner vision of the world is not contemporaneous, but is beyond temporal bounds.

Uranus in the fourth symbolizes a strong need to individuate beyond the bounds of the immediate family. It will require strength and courage in adolescence to progress. Very often there is a renegade in the background, a grandparent or ancestor who was very inventive or ingenious in some way, who failed according to his or her own lights, and the new chance rests in the soul of this person, his or her next opportunity to change the direction of the family. This is so often indicative of a total split between mother and father, where the child carries two vastly different family lines and they meet in him or her. Hence the radical, revolutionary need to break out of both lines of the family which are meeting in such a conflicting way, and to do something entirely different, to challenge and shock the nuclear family.

Pluto in the fourth speaks of a secret, of something hidden in the ancestral closet. There can be undercurrents in the family system which are dark and mysterious, casting long shadows. It makes for an inquisitive child and a truth-seeking adult. If the family secrets are indeed dire, the Pluto/fourth person feels strongly his or her responsibility for purgation – of both his or her own personal soul, and the souls of the ancestors. Being carried along on the river of family secrets inevitably lends a feeling of helplessness, something the Pluto/fourth house person abhors, but has to cope with. Contact with the dead, the ancestral realm, the rituals of the past and also rituals of the present, like religious expression, healing, counselling others, and so forth, seem to be effective paths for these people. They are truth-seekers. They frequently are fascinated by genealogy.

THE EIGHTH HOUSE: THE ANCESTRAL LEGACY — MEMENTO MORI

If you can't get rid of the family skeleton, you might as well make it dance.

(George Bernard Shaw)

In the eighth house we find the inheritance we have been left by our ancestors. Collecting that inheritance has stringent rules. As with all points of law, one can only receive one's due process by applying through the right system. As with the previous Watery domains, the twelfth and fourth houses, this house speaks of our family lineage but does so through symbols, ciphers and metaphor. All the Water houses are particularly cryptic, but none so dedicated to the use of synchronicities, images, messages, ciphers and so forth as the eighth. We do connect deeply to the archetypal collective symbology in the twelfth house of dreams, but in the eighth we are one with our personal ancestry. The ancestors come through in many voices, many languages and have become an aggregate of the complex of family archetypes. Periodically, one will individuate enough to speak lucidly, with specific messages and meaningful intent; however, it is mostly a cacophony of residual tones from our personal ancestral history that resound in the eighth house.

The eighth house is the *pontifex maximus* – the big bridge – between the ancestors and the deeper Self and ego. In the Catholic religion, the Pope is considered to be the pontifex, and the Pharaohs of Egypt were the same – they were the personal representatives of god, and thus had special dispensation for interpreting the messages or the *logoi* of god. In actual fact, we are all this to some degree, but strongly eighth house individuals, people with planets in the eighth, are specifically both blessed or cursed with this bridge-making role.

None of the Water houses are rational; no state of synthesis is achieved through reason. And to reconcile the dead with the living, symbols are used. Symbols connect one half with another. The word 'symbol' derives from the Greek word σνμβολον, which was an object such as a bone or stick which would be broken in two and each half given to two people, such as members of the same secret order or society, who could then identify each other by fitting both halves together. This fitting of the two halves brought about a meeting in which mysteries known only to them and their higher order could be shared. They would then speak in the secret code, bringing together the necessary components to create communication.

Obviously the holders of each half knew themselves to be 'true', that their own piece was true, but only when the two pieces were fitted perfectly would each then know that their opposite was true also. It is in the meeting that recognition occurs. Carl Jung felt that the two extreme moral poles of good and evil were capable of reconciliation – that suffering the tension of opposites in full consciousness could bring about transcendence of both. In the *mysterium coniunctio* a marriage of opposites brought about fullness and wholeness. Reconciliation of opposites occurs in the eighth house. The transcendent function is achieved symbolically through sustaining this tension of opposites, which generates the problem of the split between the ego and the Self to a higher order where conflict is resolved. Good is reconciled with evil, and a state of renewed synthesis follows thus between consciousness and unconsciousness.

When life meets with death, a symbol arises. The symbols we employ to resurrect the dead – pictures, talismans, heirlooms, mementoes, icons, totems, and so forth – are not sentimental, but sacramental. The use of such materials for religious and spiritual purposes brings about a change in consciousness. In the eighth house, we can ritualize our daily lives and live in accord with a long line of our progenitors, thus creating an inner sense of social harmony. Because Pluto and Scorpio are associated with the eighth house, it is a *memento mori* – a reminder that we will meet the end, the terminus, and thus need to live in harmony with that reality.

The eighth house is the place in between. Its position lies between the initial contact of oneself with others (seventh house) and the divine realm of the gods (ninth house). In the in-between world, there is access to the haunting of personal and cultural ancestors. Cultural ancestors do enter in through individuals – why do we have affinity with some cultures not our own and not with others? Some people are drawn to the Maya, others to India, some to China, yet others to the equatorial or other 'foreign' aboriginal cultures. The eighth house connects us not just to our own cultural ancestors who appear on our family tree, but occasionally to specific ancestors from other cultures who have found us to be a channel or cross-connection to the corporeal world. People who are dedicated to the helping and supporting of cultures other than their own are probably called to this work through ancestral voices coming through them. Perhaps they have the means and the skills as well as some deep link to them. Most people have no rational source, but usually a deeply emotional or spiritual feeling for their dedication to helping indigenous or persecuted cultures outside their culture of origin. It then leads directly to the twelfth – not only is it the house 'in between' others and god, but it is the house in between the personal, family-of-origin ancestral line and the archetypal collective realm of all humanity. The eighth house links us in myriad ways from our home to our cosmos. The eighth house is the meeting place of the συμβολον where the personal and the collective meet and match.

Those ancestors who do settle in our souls and want individuation through us can only use the ancient ritual of symbols and signs to do so. We might find ourselves performing little rituals without knowing why. They are also earthing routines, little acts which in their repetitiveness assure us of our existence. Freud would have termed this experience death anxiety – that compulsive, repetitive habits were a process by which we staved off death (or the consciousness of it, that is). This adherence to ritual can so easily become neurotic, indeed it is a particular type of psychosis when carried beyond consciousness. Jung tells of a man who had a peculiar hand gesture, a tic which flung his hand to and fro. When asked why he was doing it, the man replied that if he didn't the planets would stop revolving around the sun. Pathological obsessive-compulsive disorders are ritual observers *in extremis*.

Heavily eighth house people are highly ritualistic and are always on the lookout for signs and symbols. They are exceptionally susceptible to being taken over by the ancestors and thus are looking for ways to protect themselves from being absorbed by their unconscious. They tend to be very observant of ritual and are usually called into professions with a high level of order and procedure with historical lineage attached. This necessity for ritual can manifest in a fondness for all sorts of work in the world, from banking and economics with its secret codes and order of procedure, to law and its cryptic language, high ritual, due process and adherence to precedent, medicine with its arcane history and its magical properties, or even linguistics if the mystery of communications in other cultural orders is a strong pull. Adept Jungian analysts are eighth house Plutonians, and astrologers, too, are favoured through the eighth house because theirs is a world of symbol and their work the translation of the word of the stars – the labour of the ἀστρολόγος is to find truth in the heavens by interpreting ciphers.

In this vein, eighth house people are always probing the far inner regions, being dangerously susceptible to total ego loss or high inflation resulting from having dallied too long at the threshold between the upper air and the nether-world. Traversing the limen of these worlds is fraught with peril. When Aeneas sought entry into the underworld, he solicited the advice of the oracle. The Sibyl warned Aeneas of the hazards lying ahead of him in his impending descent into Avernus (the Roman Hades, which literally means 'birdless'):

> facilis decensus Averni,
> noctes atque dies paret atri ianua Ditis
> sed revocare gradum superasque
> evadere ad aurus,
> hoc opus, hic labor est.[4]

> The descent into Avernus is easy,
> Pluto's door is open, all the day and night
> But, to recall the steps, to escape to the upper air –
> This is the work, that is the labour!

To bring back the knowledge of the ancestors is the hero's quest – always it was Hermes, the psychopompos, who took them to Pluto's underworld realm to speak to their ancestors, to receive their orders or to clarify something necessary to continue with their task or life purpose. Mystery religions are eighth house – where death is enacted in life to prepare for the inexorable great crossing. We use symbols to connect us to the ancestors to hear what they have to say.

The image of peeling back layers of the personal unconscious to get to the core of family complexes is fitting, here as well. We might apply that process to the various levels of atmosphere in which dwell our personal ancestral spirits, between which are veils preventing transmission except by passing through first one, then another, and so on. Each of these strata become increasingly rarefied the more removed the ancestral being is from life, itself. On the psychological level, we can become neurotic and fixate on one of these levels. Neurotic complexes are often fundamentally very creative – they give us a nucleus of energy which allows us to revolve around it, orbit it, so to speak, and develop strong ideas and theories. This house of ritualistic behaviour stems directly from the fourth house of family origins and the habits which were inculcated in childhood, but become deeply rooted in the subconscious as our own.

Thus, we are only able to contact the ancestors through various rituals, designed to help us communicate beyond the veils, the boundaries between personal relationship and divine relationship. The eighth house is the first house of true merging of self and others, and leads towards the house of 'the higher mind', the ninth house, where we formulate strong beliefs and receive dogma about spiritual, religious matters. It is the eighth house where we dwell in the mystery of union of body and soul. The eighth house is a place for communing with the ancestors – use of chant, prayer and trance and analysis (breaking whole down into parts for reassembly) of symbols in dreams, for example, all prepare the ego for a relationship with the Self, which in turn finds contact with one's familiars.

The eighth house is territorial and guarded by various *daemonion* – these are both lethal and benign. These chthonic beings are sacred and have taxes that they extort. As one pays the ferryman, Charon, crossing the river Styx into Hades, so we must pay a price for traversing the threshold of the ancestors. The price is usually precisely what we have in our pocket, or in our home, or in our legacy from our ancestors. It is a matter of discovering just what exactly is the right object, talisman, icon or memento that will allow safe passage and encourage relationship with our guide and guardian.

Planets in the eighth house signal special duties assigned by our ancestral spirits; the more planets in there, the more necessary the contact with them. Certain talents that have been highly specialized and overdeveloped, or have never been fully manifest in families, can come through an intensely eighth house person, as if there is an unlived aspect of a spirit making itself alive in the person.

The Sun and the Moon are signals that there is a direct link to the ancestral realm which will surface periodically in one's life. The Sun speaks of a paternal legacy which has probably lost its brilliance and suffered an amputation from its source, or roots somewhere along the line, and it is up to the individual to reconnect this bond – to be the συμβολον. The father may well have lost his 'inheritance', or leaves no continuation of his family line, whereas, with the Moon in the eighth, we are seeing the maternal link being associated with earth-mysteries and religions that pre-date the sky-gods. One's emotional root is planted in darkness, in the ancestral womb, and the emotions and feelings are profoundly deep, complex, volcanic and very, very intense. Feelings arise apparently from nowhere. By doing family work, this is much less tiring and compulsive and people with these placements are liberated.

Hermes – the astrological Mercury – is quite at home here, his guise as psychopompos – soul guide – being dominant in the eighth house. Hermetic people are always flitting to and from the threshold of the conscious and unconscious. This is not always comfortable, nor is it safe; however, they have a facility, a gift, for translating ancestral knowledge into some form of art or work. The family history is rich in mystery, and the search for the ancestral roots productive. They think about death a lot, and often work with it productively.

Venus can find love in the darkest places, but love is a form of ritual for them. Love should bring one closer to one's primal self. The sexual and reproductive urge is deep and instinctual and, to be fulfilled, often crosses cultural, social and religious bars. Venus is amoral here, she listens only to the call of the whole person, which can be socially awkward. There is also a love and fascination with the mysteries of life, a capacity to guide others towards their own deeper self, and a compassion for lost souls. There are long bouts of sexual abstinence, of celibacy. It is also a placement symbolizing the vestal virgins, those holy women who enjoyed ritual sex but never gave their soul to a man, never married.

Mars is the warrior, and when it is in the eighth house we find that there is often the most difficulty in interpreting and directing anger. There is often a maverick rage without focus, anger with no outlet, that can be mistaken for personal anger. In fact, this is a place for the spiritual warrior, one who can use anger to appease the restless spirits. However, the person with this has to take care not to go rushing about in areas of the spiritual realm in which he or she might find danger! This is a high-risk placement at the best of times, and one in which the only real thrill in life is to stand on the abyss and look over. A friend of mine with Mars in Pisces in the eighth house was forever, all his life, thrilled by the underground. When he was in his early teens, he spent hours walking the train lines in the deepest tunnels in the New York subway, plucking out the ultra-violet light bulbs and giving them to friends. These 'light' bulbs had the property of sucking light out of a room – and he called himself 'Johnny Appleseed of Darkness'.

Jupiter protects the individual from himself – there is a fascination with why people do things and why cultures develop the way they do. There can be a strong calling to work with people who are at the terminus of their lives, to help them cross over the threshold to death. One of Jupiter/Zeus's epithets was 'Zeus Chthonius' – he was the god who took Oedipus from his tortured existence to the underworld, a rare activity for the Olympian sky-god, but Oedipus was a tragic victim of dynastic pollution, of the family fate, the transformer of the cursed house of Laius. Jupiter protects and guides those who atone personally for the sins of the ancestors.

Saturn in the eighth house *is* difficult – there can be such a strong barrier between the day world and the night world that the night world achieves a numinosity and power that it does not fully deserve. Fears and anxieties about death and the dark can prevent one from making the most of his or her ancestral legacy or literal inheritance. It could be taken away, restricted or unavailable. It can also mean that one's ego, the boundary between the deeper Self and the transcendant self, must undergo a complete dissolve at some stage in life before one is allowed, or allows oneself rather, to acknow-ledge the depth of power which lies in the realm of the ancestors. It is the mark of a sceptic.

Uranus in the eighth house specifically requires that the person use the mysteries to free him or herself from the grips of obsession and employ the collective and the ancestral realm to individuate. They will be called repeat-edly to the gateway of life and death, heaven and hell, to mediate between the two realms, and to use this experience to modify their own life and be-haviour as well as to help others and their own ancestral line. This is a very anxious place for Uranus, for as the god of the heavens, he is deeply un-comfortable in the realm of the Furies. This placement is one which re-quires tremendous consciousness and goodwill to work towards a positive end.

Someone many years ago told me Neptune in the eighth house meant 'fear of drowning'. Perhaps this is a symbol thrown across from the twelfth house to the eighth – a message to the individual to distinguish personal anxiety from collective *Angst*; to differentiate between one's own individual fears stemming from personal history, and the collective fear of losing per-sonal identity in mass integration. Especially since the Uranus/Neptune conjunction in Capricorn, there has been much confusion over who is doing what to whom and how. That is, the individual has been made increas-ingly aware of his or her involvement with the collective experience, and has gained increasing independence but lost a certain amount of ego signifi-cance in the Big Picture. People with eighth house Neptune tend to be acutely aware of their insignificance as individuals, but can turn this into a healing gift. One man I know, a priest cum Jungian analyst, works with AIDS patients as analysands, and takes groups to Lourdes.

Pluto in his domain – lord of the eighth house – this is the most mysterious harbour. If Hades today is a state of mind, but archetypally remains a place, then what and where is this place? I have known people with Pluto here who have had near-death experiences and retained clear recollection of the journey. They did not die, so they do not know death, but they have seen the way to the gate. This *does not mean* that if you have Pluto in the eighth, or your child does, a near-mortal experience will happen! However, it does mean that there may not be a clear route to the ancestral legacy – whether that is through inheritance of money, land or life-force. It can sometimes mean being cut off from it, removed or relieved from the responsibility.

NOTES

1. See Chapter 11, 'Families in Flux: Transits and Moving Forward', page 195 below.
2. Carl G. Jung, *Collected Works*, Vol. 10, para. 304, Bollingen Series.
3. Plato, *The Republic*, translated by Robin Waterfield, Oxford University Press 1993 (Book X in some translations), ll. 621a ff., page 379.
4. Virgil, *Aenid*, translated by Allen Mandelbaum, Bantam Classics, 1961, Book VI, ll. 176–80.

11.

Families in Flux: Transits and Moving Forward

The seeds of future events are carried within ourselves. They are implicit in us and unfold according to the laws of their own Nature.

(Lawrence Durrell, *The Alexandria Quartet: Clea*)

Change – how frightening! Even the most exciting change which has been effected by a positive event is stressful. It is said that in levels of stress, extremely happy events are as stressful as extremely tragic ones. The quality of the change is the only difference. In a family system, change is brought about in two basic ways – first, if there is an interior experience within the family, such as an illness, a breakdown, a death, a birth, a marriage, exciting promotions, successes, age-points and status changes, and second, if there are external events which affect large groups of the collective and the fabric of the society itself, such as'war, revolution, natural disasters such as floods, earthquakes, volcanoes, or a stock-market crash, mass redundancies, or any major shift in cultural experiences which affect the family. Examples are the 'communist scare' in the United States in the 1950s, which affected millions of ordinary people and closely affected certain families in high-profile positions, some individuals being forced out of their work and their country; the major wars; the depression of the thirties; changes in government or economy; all of which affect individuals, their families, the culture and have sweeping effects on whole networks of culture.

As any organization of people endures over long periods of time, whether it is a couple in relationship, a family, a league of individuals with a common goal, or even an entire culture, its members come to act in synchrony with each other, finely attuned to each other's energy, experiences and inner life. Much of this is deeply unconscious and eventually becomes virtually biological in that their bodies and psyches are in collusion at the quantum level of being. There is no rational explanation for this phenomenon, but it is clearly evident and generally accepted. Astrologically it can be explained by the development of many years of sustained and constant simultaneous transits to specific points in their horoscopes which bind them individually to a common experience. The individuals still retain their sense of separateness and unique identity, but they increasingly flow with their group. The attraction of people to each other – their 'elective affinity' – is deeply rooted in familiarity and knowledge. It is the kind of knowledge which is deeply rooted in past, present *and* future – for not only are we made up of the past while existing in the present, but also we are drawn towards the unknown horizon by the pull of eventual configurations in the heavens which enliven our natal charts with promise for a future life.

Families, therefore, have an elastic-adhesive property which keeps them revolving around core points which do shift and change with events and time, but there is also the powerful homeostatic principle which brings them up short and freezes them in a fixed place when crises occur. When life is flowing smoothly, there is much more freedom and movement for exploration and loosening of this stability factor. However, should there be a sudden radical change, the system seizes up and constellates around the most rigid focus. This is why it is often said that if people can move through the difficult times together, their true essence emerges. People long for change and growth, but something deep in the core of us does not want to have to change. An old axiom says that everyone wants to go to heaven but nobody wants to die! To a great degree this is true. Our individual homeostasis kicks in when we are forced to give something up. This is hard enough to reckon with, so the complexity of groups, families, undergoing collective change and staying in some conformation together is vast. Even when families do alter drastically, for example through divorce, death or relocation, their threads, tentacles, hold and touch, so that even when we are no longer with someone with whom we have a blood tie *we* are affected by and affect them.

When looking at a family as an entity, we see a remarkable frequency of synchronous timing with major turning-points in *all* the horoscopes of each individual. All are affected, but often not in the way we might imagine – each person is not necessarily receiving the same transit. It is unlikely that all the members of the family are experiencing a Uranus to the Sun transit when they are required to move to a new city or country because of a career change in one of the parents' lives! However, since families all share certain similar traits, and equally share certain orbs of degrees in accord with the modes Cardinal, Fixed and Mutable as well as with the elements of Fire,

Earth, Air and Water, it stands to reason that transits will occur simultaneously. It is very unusual for such an intimate group not to have a common degree-point or, at the very least, a common orb of degree connections – within about 6–10° maximum spread. This means that the closer in orb the contact planets are (or midpoint to planet) the more closely bound the family is to the very lengthy transits of the outermost planets, Uranus, Neptune and Pluto, should they all be receiving them. Those planets' work is deep, long and often invisible until a transit of Saturn arrives, or even Jupiter, which can blow something into sight which has been subterranean.

This means that if there is this common link, and one member of the family is receiving a hard-angle Uranus transit while everyone else is about to have Saturn transit his or her planets in the course of that same year, we might well be looking at the Uranus person being the 'focus' and the Saturn people having the satellite experience. For instance, a family with a young daughter, who had struggled with leukaemia since the age of five, had Uranus come to the square of her natal Venus at 23° Capricorn for three passes over an eighteen-month period. Her parents *both* had Pluto transits – the mother to her Moon at 29° Leo and the father to his Sun at 28° Scorpio – during the same period of timing. Her younger brother by two years had Mars at 27° Leo (also receiving the transit of Pluto) and the other sibling, a younger sister by several years, had a stellium of planets from 9–27° Cancer which would receive a long transit of Saturn over a period of about eighteen months – indeed, did so – and the final transit of Saturn was opposite to her natal Mercury about one year after her sister died, showing that she was deeply depressed about it and felt not only the loss of the same-sex sibling but also the deep mourning of her parents, which for her meant a multiple bereavement.

The child with the illness had the Uranus transit, while mother, father and brother had a Pluto transit, but the younger sister had Saturn – this implies that *her* personal experience of the loss required suppression of her own growth during that time, something that is quite natural in those conditions. When such a crisis occurs to someone else, all other problems recede into the background, and probably she was ignored inadvertently during that time because of the extreme circumstances, *not* because she was unworthy. Saturn can often bring guilt, especially, in these circumstances, survival guilt. Her parents, however, are very enlightened and understand this, and will support and work with her over time, as she will have to work through many levels of these feelings. With support and help from her family, she will come to understand it better as she grows.

So each person in the family will experience a death in very personal ways. Each member of the family will have significant transits and progressions, but they will rarely, if ever, be the same transit, as we have seen. There always appears to be a collusion of transits, and occasionally there will be a spate of the same planetary transit, but even so, it will be to various planets in the natal horoscopes of each of the people involved. This is individuality bound into the collective – the cells of the organism responding and resonating in their own way to a shock that requires them all to shift together to a new order of action and response.

Therefore, we have to look very carefully at the *meaning* of a transit in this way of seeing things. That is, we might all be experiencing the same event – say, one family member has come to awareness of how deeply traumatized he or she was by the family system and confronts the parents or has symptoms like alcoholism, ME or a depression, thus changing the internal structure and forcing a re-evaluation and examination of the whole picture. Each member of that family, the children, had the same parents, but clearly experienced them differently and must now, because of the one in the whole, look at him or herself anew. The 'symptomatic' member might be receiving the most shocking of transits, but all are experiencing it.

Deeper considerations from a harmonic or midpoint view *do* produce fairly consistent coherence in transits, in which case it is important to look at this multi-dimensional correlation between the 'members of the system', that is, the comparison of family charts, if one wants to examine remarkable collusion in dynastic or family lines. For example, all Jupiter/Pluto midpoints may be 'hit' in one particular harmonic of all family charts when a major event occurs, such as a birth, a marriage or a death. This is the most subtle and most cognitive area of chart relating in groups or systems.[1]

All personal transits are transits to the family system – we are not alone, and our so-called independence is hard-won and only a surface veneer. Deeply, viscerally, psychically and ancestrally we are bound to the network of the family. If we are affected deeply by an experience, we can be assured that it is resonating through the family whether we are living at home or whether we have moved across the world. This is a fairly unique way of observing personal transits, and requires a new mind-set – away from the self as 'only' and towards the group as 'part of' the self and vice versa. We are inextricably woven into a fabric, and if one thread in that fabric is pulled or torn, the entire pattern has altered by that much. In turn, that rent radiates outwards from ourself into the collective, the community and our friends, associates and colleagues.

In the event of a critical family upheaval, it is extremely helpful to have a look at each member's horoscope and see what the main focus is by transits. In this way, the collective allows its individuals their uniqueness and aloneness in the situation. Differentiating the individual out of the collective while still acknowledging his or her participation in the whole experience offers greater insight into how the incident is uniquely affecting *the person*, how it will continue to affect him or her, and most importantly, will explain and support his or her behaviour during the transition. In this way, the whole might be healed or restored to a new balance. In the story of Fiona (page 317), we read about family transits and how they affected each member of a nuclear family during a separation of the parents.

Therefore, we affect and are affected by all resonance in varying degrees of significant experience. This is why, in the following family, the death of the father brought to the eldest son a better capacity to have a deeper relationship with women in his life. To the wife it brought greater interaction in the community and in extending herself into business, and to the daughter a greater sense of her own greatness and worth – which will inevitably benefit not only her, but anyone with whom she comes into contact.

For example, in the case of a family whose father was about to die from cancer there were a significant number of transits in all the members' charts. The family consisted of Jules himself, his wife, Marie, and their two children – a twenty-four-year-old son and a daughter, nineteen. The father had been under the pressure of the on-and-off Saturn-Pluto square to his Moon at 23° of Leo in 1993, but then Saturn went on to oppose his Sun in Virgo in 1994. His diagnosis of prostate cancer occurred in the first pass of Saturn opposite to his 13° Virgo Sun in June 1994. Jules was treated, but the cancer had spread to the lymph nodes (often said to be ruled by the Moon, which was the natal planet so heavily leaned upon by Pluto and Saturn all through 1992–3). By the October period of 1993, Saturn had stationed-direct opposite his Leo Moon, while Pluto was still in square to it, and the cancer had spread already by the time it was diagnosed much later, in June 1994.

His wife, Marie, a Capricorn, with the Moon at 12° Pisces (opposite her husband's Sun), was experiencing the Uranus/Neptune conjunction on her natal Sun all through the same years – Sun at 19° Capricorn! She was experiencing a complete dissolution of all her solar power – in her case, very much placed in her family and with her husband – along with the cold fear and responsibility to fall upon her with transiting Saturn finally conjoining her Moon, after the first pass in June 1994, and the final pass in February 1995, which is when Jules died. Marie's legacy from her husband was to find something in herself which would allow her to realize her dreams. She had always been an excellent photographer and had done many amateur-status portraits for friends, family and acquaintances but had never had the courage or inner authority to set herself up in a business. She had languished after the children had reached the age where they were much more independent – her son had left home seven years ago, and her daughter was very resourceful and busy and in university by the age of seventeen. So Marie was home alone much of the time until Jules fell seriously ill, and she had been deeply dissatisfied with her current life. It was time for her to change, anyway.

It was not ever thought that death would force this change upon her, but it did. She would probably have made more of her hobby eventually, but the loss of Jules gave her added incentive. Focusing on creativity helped her with her devastating loss and loneliness, and it also forced her to develop some of her 'Sun', which her successful husband had, in a sense, 'done' for her! The transits in the family did not speak of death to me at all, but then I tend not to look for that unless it is something imminent. The transits for her and Jules (and the children) did speak of a major family shift, one which would affect each of them independently, but clearly, as a unit because they were all major transits and they were all coinciding in the same time-frame.

The eldest child, a son, twenty-four years old, had his Sun at 15° Gemini with natal Saturn at 28° Taurus which was opposed by his Moon at 27° Scorpio. The same transit of Saturn and Pluto was affecting him as it was affecting his father – and, being the eldest child and a son, the transits were appropriate to his legacy. He found that his father's death was obviously a sad personal loss but would also put him in the position of 'head of the family', which in the natal picture is clearly stated as a promise. By nature, the Moon opposite Saturn suggests that he, at some point, must feel responsible for his mother, and the Saturn square to his natal Sun at the time of his father's diagnosis and then death nine months later is the legacy of losing his father while at the same time gaining his own authority and authenticity. He had always been very akin to his father, felt 'just like' him, as he said, and was never very comfortable with his mother until Jules fell ill!

Then, his protective and authoritative side (Moon opposite Saturn) came into action, and once he felt he could be protective of his mother and in charge of something emotional, he stopped feeling alternately smothered and rejected by her. He always felt that his mother competed with him for his father (Moon opposite Saturn), and his greatest negative feeling at the death of Jules was guilt that he might have been wrong about his perception of this facet of his mother. There is lots of time for him to discover a new way of relating to his mother – and to all women, in fact.

The daughter, the youngest, age nineteen, had the transit of Saturn in a sextile to her Sun/Jupiter conjunction at 8–9° Taurus through 1994 into January 1995 (a month before her father died), while transiting Uranus was in opposition to her natal Saturn at 26° Cancer square Mercury at 26° Aries! In the time of Jules's diagnosis, illness and death she fell into the protective mode, looking after her father and nurturing her mother all during the decline, and though she was herself very sad and grief-stricken, she was not at all shattered by her father's death. She had seen her father as a benevolent but highly dictatorial man to whom she had not been able to relate since childhood, but whose impending death brought them very, very close indeed. The natal Mercury/Saturn square does speak of her feelings of inability to express herself, or receive positive feedback from her father, but the Uranus transit broke all that up – which it would have done in some way, anyway, even if this had not been the time of her father's death – and during his illness and subsequent death they became closer to each other than could ever have been imagined. The transiting Saturn sextile to her Sun/Jupiter conjunction brought her the kind father she imagined he really was, and his legacy to her was a greater sense of herself as a whole or solar-type woman. In the end he gave her what she needed – to feel needed, supported, wanted and worth talking to!

This family was dynamic – is dynamic, I should say, for they still are a family. The entire system was hit by a blow from the outside, so to speak, and each of them experienced it in his and her own way. Not only were the relationships of wife, daughter and son radically altered, which is clear, but the purpose, the nature and the intent of the deeper self in each of them quickened and brought to life aspects of themselves which had been in reserve until the transits and the coincidental death of the father occurred. Both sides of the transits were experienced: the dark and the light, the negative and the positive. If we were to use metaphorical and descriptive language to talk about what kind of changes will occur within families based on each major planetary transit, we would come closer to understanding what the deeper intent of the family is in our own individual process.

Even when we are adult, that is, not living with our original nuclear family, maybe with our own created families or on our own, having moved outside the family circle, we can look at our transits as if they were telling us something about ourself and our current development with respect to the family dynamic. No matter where we are, there they are! And all transits mean all things. If we examine a transit and keep in mind that we are looking *only* for family indicators, we can make use of them in this way. As each individual unfolds in accord with his or her inner intelligence, so will those closest in astrological bond.

It has been suggested in astrology books that certain transits, and even then only of particular houses, or planets, have to do with families. Because we are systemically involved with the family no matter where they or we are, all of our transits will have to do with family issues. There is so much implicit in family systems and so many levels that we would be better off to look at it as an open system, in which there is a multiplicity of meaning, layers and spheres of impact, in a single event or experience. With respect to transits and families, we need to explore the archetypal meaning underlying a transit with specific regard to how that transit might affect our ancestral link, our current relations in a family system, our potential for creating a family in the future, etc. We cannot say only certain transits mean family matters are at issue, but we must look at the transits (and progressions) for family matters specifically if this is what we are needing to focus on. It matters whether we are paying attention to them in that way or not.

Having said that, I might add that there *are* certain transits that do recall family matters absolutely. I only want to emphasize that all transits are all about families but some transits are specifically about certain particular aspects of families. Those are any major transits of Saturn through Pluto over the fourth house cusp (IC), the Midheaven (MC), through the twelfth, fourth and eighth houses, to the Moon and to the Sun. Those are the main transits which scream, 'Pay attention to the family dynamic and find out what it is that wants to be known.'

In the situations I have mentioned above – wherein the system has been shattered, altered or brought closer into its common or nuclear purpose – in each individual case the transits have *not* been consistent. That is because we all experience our lives for different ultimate purposes. The only thing that is consistent is that every member of the family is getting a strong hit of planetary action *at the same time*. The same event will not have the identical impact on or meaning for any two people, no matter how close they are psychologically or biologically. There may be threads, as in Marie and Jules's family when there were more 'hits' to Saturn/Capricorn themes, and Jules, the father, died, and we can sense that the status quo and regulating force of the family has undergone a breakdown in its relationship to Saturn – they all lost their 'authority figure', the person who most represented stability and homeostasis in the group. But we cannot predict this, nor can we judge it, we can only talk of the quality of the time for deeper understanding.

In the story of Mohsin (page 270), we shall see that Pluto transiting over his IC occurred when he was longing to resurrect his 'dead' family, and find his mother, his roots and his culture. Roots, mother, culture, the seed of identity and the matrix of life all lie in the fourth house. The situation for him resulted in a period of killing off his adoptive family until he could reconcile the two points of origin for himself. In the course of reconnection, his adoptive mother died. Other people's transits of Pluto over the IC have produced no less extreme conditions – but the events are significant only to the individual and in the context of their lives. The *character* of the transit is what we must absorb. We have to dig deeply into the archetypal essence of the transiting planet to discover what is being born or freed in the individual with respect to his or her bond with the family. Ultimately it is a rebirth transit – the act of giving birth to our Selves is no less real than the original birth of our bodies. After many years away, a close friend of mine moved back to her birthplace when Saturn went over her IC and her father had just been diagnosed with Alzheimer's. Nine years later, Pluto transited the IC and he died, released from his infantile prison; the entire family moved on very rapidly, but no one more than my friend, who was, of all five children, the closest one to her father on a deep, psychic level. His life experience was reflected in her horoscope.

Fiona's family, in her story, 'What's Bred in the Bone' (page 317), shows how transits affected the family at one time because they shared 24–26° of Cardinal signs. The degrees in question had accumulated a history of experience, and then, years later, when the same degrees were transited by Uranus, further developments in the same theme occurred. Seeds of individuals, seeds of families – all unfold according to their own nature.

It is important to realize that in the course of our lives we have to return, many times, to the bosom of the family in order to wrest out some lost, forgotten, stolen, or still unborn trait to which our fullness of being is essential. Without this to-ing and fro-ing there is no point of reference for the individual. She is more capable relating to her larger family, her tribe, culture or global family, once she is able to pull her individuality increasingly out of the family nest and more into herself as an individual. It is not for purely self-centred reasons that this process of self-reflection and analysis should be undertaken periodically, but for the collective, as well. For each of us who increases our own level of truth, we have aided the collective by that small amount.

So we look back to the ancestors and our archaic forebears, our nuclear families and into our own selves, and outward to the collective and the future. We need to do this in the attempt to pass on more creative ways of dealing with complexes to our own children – or, in the event of not having children of one's own, on into the community-tribe in some vital way. Knowledge is communicable and infectious, and can spread rapidly, moving through entire cultures by epidemic. Consciousness seems to be implicated in every action made by every individual which resonates both forward and backward, both inward and outward. The outer planetary patterns have shown us that we are linked to our past and are the medium to future generations. That which is left undone now is to be done in the future; the planets move on, as do we individuals, and as the next generation takes up where the last left off, the work one does now affects the future in that way.[2]

When a family undergoes a radical shift and the system seems to reel under the change, the transits that each member is experiencing help her or him to come to terms with the personal experience of the collective event. The following is a way of looking at transits to see what the meaning is in a family event.

Conversely, by looking at the transits in one's own chart one might gain greater access to the family's experience of oneself and how the family might – even deeply unconsciously – be changing and moving in accord with one's own inner life.

Transits also 'prove' that immortality is real. When, in the natural course of events, parents die and the adult children live on, transits to the deceased parent can still affect the children. When Uranus and Neptune were in the same degree as my mother's Sun in Capricorn, I dreamed of her almost every night, and I hadn't dreamed of her since the week after she died in 1986! They were very healing dreams and I could not think why she kept emerging during that time until I realized that *she was having a transit*. Now in reality, I was experiencing the transit because I am the one living with her in my psyche, her Sun degree – and horoscope – being imprinted in my own being (her natal Sun is in the same harmonic-degree as my Sun/Moon midpoint). Our relationships with our parents continue to evolve even after they are long gone. This is a blessing, for the healing and communication process is kinder and more universal in those levels than they are on the gross physical level. This is not to say one should leave their relating till after death, but it does say that it is not over when one dies. So we could look at deceased parents' (or grandparents', uncles', etc.) horoscopes for transits and relate them to deep inner experiences of our own.

The ancestors do not often appear in dreams, thank goodness; however, when they do, it is time for change. They come to help one move on, to create something for them and to bring transformation to the line. They get restless and, if one is chosen to act on behalf of a family line, it is incumbent to listen to those messages. In Rosemary's story (page 356), we see how she was guided by her ancestral forebears towards liberation on both the collective and the personal level. Reflected in her, we see the personal connection to the collective consciousness of a culture in radical transition. Her transits are in accord with changes that occur in the most mundane affairs of a nation in crisis and transformation; she experiences her life not only personally, but in the cultural, familial and ancestral spheres.

So we might ask our deep inner self, or our immediate family or our ancestral guides, to interpret our transits and our dreams for us. Some of the aspects of the following transit-guide will help with this work. For example, consider how the planets Saturn, Uranus, Neptune and Pluto might represent particular members of your family or situations which are arising in the family; also, if there are transits prominent in other family members, how those transits will affect the person in change – what is the family doing when an individual is getting the transit?

There are some aspects which are more related to 'others' than to 'self'; that is, when a conjunction from a transiting planet occurs, it is the person himself who is instigating the change, rather than someone else. The transiting planet can be translated literally into the type of change, mood or experience which is being undergone. For example, Saturn is about better organizing and ordering one's life, creating effective limits and boundaries; Uranus is for clarity and separation, for compartmentalizing and breaking into new territories; Neptune talks about reconnecting with a more cosmic whole, or dissolving into an amorphous collective for a while; and Pluto speaks of dying and being resurrected, of seeing the truth in everything, and cutting ties that bind. If we look at those core-meanings and extrapolate them out into a group dynamic, into the family system, we can get to the issue at hand.

Our natal charts, as we now know, *are* our family-patterns. Therefore, transits to the natal chart reawaken and reactivate our infantile and developmental selves in relation to the family. In a sense, all transits are about the family within ourself. To read transits as family-pattern markers, try to see the planet that is being activated by the transit and look at it with *only* the family or ancestral influences in mind. By training the mind's eye on that planet in this way, you will find a depth to your self-understanding that is based on your origins in the deepest possible sense. For there is layer upon layer of influence underlying each planet in the chart, each of which holds memories of the family, its members and the ancestral line far back.

If you share a degree of the zodiac in common with other members of the family, try to determine first what you are experiencing, then look at what they are experiencing. It is very likely that you share a common degree point, but not necessarily the same planet in it (although same planet, same degree does happen frequently – as the story in 'Rejected in the Womb' (page 290) illustrates) – which means you are experiencing a similar impact in a very different area in your lives.

Also, if there *is* a major family event in progress and you are looking at your own horoscope to find personal meaning in a collective experience, this guideline will help unravel the complexities which family and ancestral events bring to bear upon our consciousness. If you are looking at another family member, make every attempt to withdraw your own projections upon that chart, for you yourself might be the transit that that person is experiencing!

The duration, like all the trans-Saturnian planets, is fairly long – from one year to eighteen months before the exact degree is left behind. This seems to be the cosmos's way of making sure that the changes occur on the cellular level – it is not a mood, it is a process and, ultimately, a change in lifestyle. Hence the cautionary tone to making changes in haste. First we look at core-meanings of natal planets from a family and early environmental viewpoint, then at the transits of Saturn, Uranus, Neptune and Pluto.

NATAL PLANETS AND ANGLES:
FAMILY CORE-THEMES

The following core-meanings are a guide to what kinds of family-related matters might be surfacing or needing examination during long transits to natal planets from the trans-Saturnian planets.

The Sun

The relationship with one's father; inheritance from paternal line, material or psychic/emotional; one's purpose in life as it was encouraged/discouraged in the family; one's own life-force, libido, drive, energy level; one's status in the family, one's ordinal placement and what that meant, i.e. first, eldest, only, middle child, etc.; sexuality as an exciting experience; health of body (libido); truths related to the core of the family's image in the greater society; one's ability to 'shine', succeed, be heroic, take on challenges – all of which are rooted in the development of the ego in the earliest years of life; capacity to undergo changes and revision of egoic needs and expression.

The Moon

The relationship with one's mother; inheritance from the maternal line – psychic/emotional or physical; one's ability to nurture and be nurtured in accord with how it was demonstrated and experienced in the bosom of the family; the women in the family; the demonstration of affection and feelings; sexuality as an extension of nurturing love; children of one's own or feelings about children in one's own family, step-children, children in general; literally, one's home or sense of roots; genetic factors relating to health, well-being, glandular or immune-system structures; ability to be flexible or durable in the group-mind (emotionally based, always).

Mercury

Siblings; relationships to fraternal or sororal friends; relatives such as aunts, uncles, extended family members; mind-sets according to family guidelines; ideas, ideologies; the earliest received information and skills; feelings of inferiority or superiority and how they can be adjusted with renewed perspectives; one's capacity for change, openness to new vistas; relationships with pedagogues, teachers, guides and sudden turns-of-events; the ability to trust chance, fate, one's own intuition, as one was 'taught' in childhood; capacity to learn new things.

Venus

Women as independent creatures; one's mother as a female person; sisters in specific, women in general based on the feminine-factor in the early family; love and values that were demonstrated in the family context; security needs as were rooted deeply in the body as an infant, and fostered in the nuclear family; one's own femininity and feelings of beauty, love and contentment; sexuality as an extension of sensuality; the ability to receive accolades – comfort with praise, applause and so forth – all based on one's 'reception' and acceptance in the family as a beautiful, lovable person; degree of comfort with one's body (based on its treatment as a child).

Mars

The ability to say no. This starts about two years of age. Capacity to draw boundaries, declare effective war, be assertive; brothers in specific, men in general, based on the maleness-factor in the family-of-origin; concerns about one's own masculine aspect and comfort with that; creativity in the crafts-sense; follow-through, how you were encouraged to complete projects, etc.; sexuality as a function; the ability to self-create or self-inseminate, based on the support and trust of one's parents in childhood; the winner-consciousness; how to get out of bed and get dressed.

Jupiter

Uncles; avuncular relationships and benefactor-relationships; how to receive benefit based on self-worth; how to be benign, generous but not a doormat, under duress; how one reacts to adversity based on childhood history; advancement; adventurousness; trusting in god; believing in one's own self (based on instilled self-trust as a child); capacity to grow beyond one's domestic, cultural or educational limitations; ability to say yes; ability to be wise, not full of information; desire to expand within the context of circumstances, again directly related to early growth and parental acceptance; capacity for accepting new and strange things.

Saturn

The parents; grandparents; adulthood; maturity; all authority based on exemplars in childhood and especially in adolescence; ability to accept real limits; capacity to know when something is really over, and how to allow the homeostatic principle to reorganize around a new centre or focus; ability to be successful *because* of one's own limitations and not becoming depressed; ability to be depressed without being suicidal – based on the experience of small failures as a child/adolescent and the support system of the family or parents; the ability to accept oneself for who one is without undue self-criticism – self-critique is healthy; endurance under stress; productivity; meeting deadlines based on historical knowledge of one's own capacity, in turn, based on the guidance of one's elders – tutors, parents, teachers, authority in general; grace to age in seven-year cycles; appreciation of the past, but not nostalgic; nostalgia (literally: the 'pain of recall'); ability to allow old walls to crumble and new ones to be erected based on real-time conditions, not old-time conditioning.

Uranus

The Great Father archetype arises with transits to Uranus – the distant, unattainable masculine power of imagination which stirs our *genius* to life. Our ability to change, based on the degree of trust given us in gradual degrees as young people; our own need for individuation out of current situations based on childhood and adolescent patterns; the society around us as an extension of the family; the culture as our family perceived it; ability to be creative, wildly experimental, challenging to the status quo; ability to be distant, objective, clear, divorced from emotional charge; capacity to distinguish between the Ideal realm of the imagination and the Real circumstances in which those ideals can be realized; ability to perceive ourselves as separate from our family but integral to it; capacity to be creative without fear, based on originality; to live without approval from others.

Neptune

The Great Mother archetype arises with transits to Neptune – the longing for 'earth's sweet flowing breast'; ability to be romantic; capacity for creative fantasy; ability to dream, and to analyse those dreams; love of beauty; capacity to endure pain; separations; to merge, fuse, bond deeply and where those urges come from – from the natural womb-memory or from a fear of being abandoned or rejected? Our relationship with the divine force; capacity for magical thinking; ability to hear one's ancestral voices; capacity to be alone and not lonely; capacity to endure pain without resorting to oblivion; conversely, to become oblivious when necessary but not habitually – again, all 'taught' in childhood; the awareness of divine discontent – the unscratchable itch.

Pluto

How to cope with the *terminus*, with entropy; existential longing; capacity to be lonely and know that everyone is; capacity to trust in the cosmic order which is in constant death/rebirth; how to deal with loss, based on how losses were presented to us as infants and young people; how to grow out of being 'abandoned', rejected, hated, misunderstood and maligned – whether it is true or a misconception; grace in the face of an ultimatum; how to age gracefully; where our resources are most resilient and to realize that it is the adversities in our lives that provided the strength for endurance and creativity in the eleventh hour; finding creative ways for coping with small or large obsessions and working through them; knowing that you will never get it all done anyway and accepting that; being still in times of chaos; not masking fear with anger; being passionate without embarrassment; erotic needs; survival instincts arise in times of threat.

TRANSITS TO THE ANGLES: THE ASCENDANT AND IC[3]

The Ascendant

This recalls the moment of birth. The transit, having passed out of the twelfth house, brings with it memories of the earliest kind – a feeling of rawness, newness, and a 'soft' ego results. It has a dream-like quality in which we are still very connected to the Great Umbilicus, where our soul is in the threshold, and we are in the limen of who we used to be and who we are on the verge of becoming. There is a feeling of 'having no skin'. It is a time for slowly reconnecting to new symbols, meaning and direction. A meeting of opposites occurs, wherein all that has lain dormant, incubating in the twelfth house, arises to be looked at openly. One's horizons seem endless and almost too open, there is no place to hide. The *persona*, the masque of protection, is virtually non-existent until about one year after the transit has passed – in the case of Uranus, Neptune and Pluto, much longer. Situations arise which test one's ability to undergo a rebirth. A battle for life in a new form ensues, in which we might encounter the so-called 'hidden enemies' in the twelfth house, which are usually our own worst inmost fears.

Implicitly this transit incorporates its opposite, the descendant, thus relationship issues arise spontaneously – we find that only the strongest and most durable of our alliances will survive this transit. Our family affiliations are in question – this is the test of origins. We are often haunted by the collective ancestral heritage, the ancestry of humanity itself – that is, we are more susceptible to hooking into social, collective and global (group) concerns, thus are vulnerable to mass psychology and crowds, and tend to avoid them. Health is marked simply because this is an organic place; the ascendant is the very moment when the umbilical cord was cut, and our resources for life became ours alone, we acquired no more nutrients from our mother. Transits to this point are thus tests of our resources, physically, mentally, emotionally, psychically and environmentally. As the transit matures into the first house, a renewal of the ego takes place, a sense of self-identity is more solid and based on current, rather than historical traits. We can break out of old family patterns after about one year of the transit occurring, establishing an identity based on who we are in process of becoming rather than who we have been.

The IC, Fourth House Cusp

We begin to find our foundations shifting radically. There is a strong need to find the base of our life. The roots, history and ancestral line become urgently necessary to locate and stabilize. There is an anguish about this transit, only because it is natural to undergo an exploration of the darkest recesses of the soul periodically. This is a long night. The IC is the most mysterious place in the horoscope, holding the genetic line of the paternal and maternal inheritance. This inheritance needs to be claimed – it can be physical, psychological, material or creative: reclaiming ancestral roots; going back into an ancestral religion; buying a home; selling a home; marrying; divorcing; having a child; a parent dies; one finds out a family secret; the search for 'Home' wherever that may be. The family-of-origin and its legacy is of the utmost importance. This is always felt in advance, in the last stages of the third house transit, and usually takes about a year at least (perhaps the whole fourth house transit in the case of Saturn) to actually come to any conclusions. The family is at issue, and one's role in it is undergoing sharp review. Here is where the hero goes into the cave to slay the dragon, or Theseus into the labyrinth to face the minotaur, a half-man, half-beast creation of Zeus's – these acts are symbolic of reclaiming power, taming the instincts and understanding one's dual origins – differentiating one's self out of the family-group. A process of individuation based on separation from the family in a healthy fashion can be most productive – going back into the matrix of the family in order to reclaim parts of oneself left behind is an ongoing process.

Implicitly, the MC is involved in this transit – how we are manifest in the outer world and how our parental heritage is reflected in our vocation, social status, public face, and self-confidence. One's parents and their influence on our vocational response and our ability to embark towards new horizons will be strongly affected by reflection. If there is a cultural revolution at the IC, the MC will undergo a change in leadership – that is, if we have discovered a new bond at the IC, whether that be via a home, a partner, a parent or a child, then the conditions of our social *persona* will undergo change as well, in response to and as a reflection from the new knowledge of our roots.

TRANSITS TO THE NATAL HOROSCOPE AS A FAMILY DYNAMIC

With those natal planet core-meanings, and the awareness of the angles in relation to our ancestral and family origins in mind, let us now look at the transiting planets in relation to our context of family; how these planets bring old feelings from our family framework into the present circumstances – offering us the opportunity to reframe the fundamental structure of our being.

SATURN

Transits from Saturn to the Natal Chart

A Saturn transit inevitably brings one into contact with the past – the procession of ancestors and all that have gone before us parades through the psyche. The intent of Saturn in the family context is to create an awareness of how rigid the homeostasis is in the family, and how difficult it is to make a change without shattering that pattern. Strength at its most resilient is tensile, it bends with stress and pressure; however, if it is crystallized and rigid, it will break or crack. A Saturn transit will focus in on one's sense of responsibility in the 'family' sense, whether that is to the family of humanity or one's own parents or one's parenting ability – in other words, how well do you look after others? How do you react to pressures that are directly related to collective problems or needs? Even if the events around one are not specific to family but are, say, related to one's work conditions, a cursory self-examination will reveal that the reactions to the situation are directly linked to how one was raised to deal with limits, responsibility, leadership, organization, control, authority and so on.

A strong Saturn transit brings to bear all the habits that were created out of security needs, how our family taught us to 'keep our shape' and develop our inner authority in the face of limit and adversity. A Saturn transit brings an opportunity to reform old teachings into new ways of climbing over walls, scaling mountains and blocking energy-draining situations. Boundaries around our selves are obviously necessary, but we outgrow certain ones and need to create new ones periodically. When Saturn is actively hitting planets or angles, it is time to refocus on the appropriateness of our methods of drawing parameters around our needs and make adjustments as they are demanded by circumstances. We are so often acting in ways historically necessary but currently outmoded that Saturn helps focus on what is history and what is going to be appropriate for the future.

Have we created emotional and personal boundaries which are overpowerful because they were needed in the family environment, but now prevent us from finding personal happiness? Are we so caught up in the work life that there is no real quality to the personal life? A Saturn transit almost always brings someone into focus who is demanding attention – either because they don't have it and they are fed up, or because fate has decreed that they absolutely need this attention from you. Only in these situations do we find out just how effective – or necessary – are our personal boundaries. If, as a child, it was essential to defend or protect oneself from one's mother for some reason – she was 'dangerous', that is, hysterical, cold, harsh, scattered and ambivalent in her feelings, not-present, helpless, bereaved or possibly simply a weak woman – then we will have created around us an impenetrable barrier to the subtleties of other people's emotional range. But when Saturn transits remind us that there are others out there who want something from us, we may find ourselves ill-equipped to deliver. So, the old instinct is to withdraw.

Therefore, it is important to explore the family dynamic for motives underlying all defensive or protective behaviour-patterns. Do you look after people because you were taught to and feel you have no other choices? Or might you find another way to use your sense of responsibility in a productive way? Does guilt play a role? Was it easier for a parent or elder sibling to 'do it her/himself' than to allow you to fend for yourself, resulting in you tending always to oversee other's actions or behaviour? Or, conversely, were you left too much alone to try to discover how to look after yourself because you were abandoned in some vital way? This is an excellent opportunity to extend one's boundaries and limits and allow ineffective ones to collapse, while more contemporaneous and useful ones can be erected.

When Saturn is transiting a planet, someone in the family circle seems to require extra attention, very possibly a parent, especially if the transit is to the Sun or Moon. There is a strong pull towards helping someone else, but there is often an equally strong reaction of anger and guilt at not wanting to have to do this act. Essentially we are 'stuck' with Saturn and the transit reminds us always that on some deep level we do not have choice and control. Saturn is very close to fate – his scythe midwived the Furies, who come into play in the psychological sense, as our conscience. Saturn transits are double-edged; like the mythological Kronos and his adamant sickle, there are two sides to the knife. On the one hand one must do what is put before one, but on the other hand Saturn is about choice. Once there is a situation, one has to decide which side of the cutting-edge to work with. Do you go with the old family values, or do you try to midwife your own inner authority?

Depression is inversely proportional to the amount of energy being suppressed. This is the ideal time to address how deeply one's rage might penetrate into parts of oneself which are dormant. Something has a lid on it; there are old family patterns afoot which are infuriating and have always been self-limiting, and by looking at how the rest of the family has dealt with Saturn, and one's own natal Saturn, and if anyone else in the family is having either a Saturn transit or other strong 'hits', one can help open the door to see what it is that lurks.

There may be a need to transgress hierarchies – that is, if one is in a cultural or familial strata which as an individual one has outgrown, it will take extra effort to work oneself out of that level. All the homeostatic principles will kick in to 'stop' one from doing this radical act; it may take the entire transit for it to occur, especially if Saturn will retrogress back over the degree or point in question, giving birth to the new potential after a nine-month cycle of 're-training'.

URANUS

Transits from Uranus to the Natal Chart

Uranus symbolizes change, clarity, freedom, uprooting, separations, revolution and so on. Uranus transits to a planet or angle can last for up to one and a half years if Uranus traverses retrograde and direct over that point in the horoscope. This allows for a considerable amount of time and possibility for many things to change, but very often it is the first pass that gives the clue to what is about to undergo the process of separation and clarification. Uranus says that some condition (which is symbolized by the planet it is contacting) in the system must radically shift in order to allow the parts, the individuals, to move into a new level. This is normally produced by a sudden shock, a radical shift in perspective, away from the safe, comforting nest of security.

We are always required to look back to the first separation we endured – that of the moment of birth. If we look at our natal Uranus and find its inherent meaning and message, we are somewhat closer to understanding what Uranus wants us to give birth to. In the family context, Uranus is our ability to individuate out of the family matrix and into the world. There are always times in life when we would like to fold back into the family, either our real one or some mythological family of our fantasy. However, nothing is more clear than a Uranus transit to show that we need to move yet further away from old familial patterns – if only temporarily – to find our own individuality to offer back to the family.

Uranus is the symbol for the disengaged family. If one is receiving a

Uranus transit, it says that someone in the family is in line for a break-through – although it is often the Uranus person who is the instigator of the change, it is not always. The shake-up is to assist the entire family structure to release itself from a rigid homeostatic hold – this all being done through the person receiving the transit. The person having the transit is changing and we now know that one person in a system cannot change alone, but in-stigates change in all. It serves to have a long, cold, distant, clear look at the planet being transited, and locate the source in the family of what is being challenged, and to approach that challenge with clarity of mind and the will to allow the separation to occur.

Be it breakthrough or breakdown, the homeostatic principle in the family is being threatened by the person who is having the Uranus transit. It is an opportunity for the entire pattern to shift. Sometimes it means there is a divorce in the air, or a child who is fed up, acting out all the unspoken iconoclasm in the family, or perhaps it is about the mid-life crisis of one or both parents! The black sheep all come out of the closet under Uranus transits.

There are some implications of ancestral linkage when Uranus is making strong aspects to natal planets. There may be a need to look further back in the family for a stifled creative urge, and the Uranus-person is suffering from frustration at not having the opportunity to live it out in his or her life. Certainly if a majority of a family group are receiving a Uranus transit, there is a long-range collective shift in process and it will have something to say about the family patterns and ancestral links. Was there a renegade in the closet and has another one now appeared? Does the family have to face up to uncomfortable truths? Will the Uranus person or people be the harbinger of a fresh, new revolutionary way of being?

Truly, catastrophic or not, this is the transit that has everyone in the family talking to each other. Usually about the Uranus person, but still, they are talking! This in itself can be the revolution that wins the war against the family dying out through lack of connectedness. The Uranus person elec-trifies and energizes the family, forcing it to confront its rigidity or lack of acceptance of certain members of the family or their behaviour.

Uranus leaves profound clarity and realization in its wake. There is an air of idealism that moves in the transit – this might be completely unrealistic in the long run, but all things need to be considered as possible during this time. Give every thought at least five minutes' consideration, mad as it might appear to be. If it is meant to take, time will bring its fruit. Caution should be exercised only because the tendency is to behave rashly, radically and suddenly, only to reflect on the wisdom or lack of it later. Families tend to scatter themselves about and contemplate serious changes in structure, location and relationships within their context – and if that is done with the future in mind, rather than just the excitement of the present, then it is an excellent opportunity that has arisen.

NEPTUNE

Transits from Neptune to the Natal Chart

Under Neptune, we are more aware of emotional enmeshment and dependency patterns which are related to our earliest home environment. One might even experience recollections of birth, of being close to mother, or even of losing her. One is more conscious of patterns which have brought one to seek oblivion and avoid life situations. Wherever Neptune is in the natal chart, and its conditions – aspects, house placement, etc. – holds a message for us when it is in transit. How do we find release from the bonds of the worldly plane?

Neptune awakens longings for divine experiences and to replicate our womb-condition, that of total fusion, enmeshment and bonding with a person, idea, thing or place. That we cannot return to the womb does not mean that there are not ways to attempt to re-create this idyll. It is good to look back on the ways in which we were encouraged to escape, to fantasize, to create something out of nothing. If we were thwarted in the areas of the arts, then transiting Neptune can awaken a sleeping desire to be more creative; conversely, if there were unhealthy ways of escaping given to us as family examples, such as alcoholic parents, a chronically ill mother, or an invalid sibling, then we would have to take special care not to slip into those old family patterns of dependency and victimization ourselves. However it was that our family environment 'used' Neptune is how we are inclined to receive and employ it ourselves. With Neptune, ultimate care must be taken not to become entrenched in habits which were or which we perceived to be negative in our parents or in the family-system as a whole.

Neptune offers the opportunity to go back into a secondary womb and incubate an aspect of one's own self. This is in the hope that a new level of one's self will be born. Neptune is a cloudy transit, wreathed in fog and mist, so there is usually something very uncertain about the family network all during the main part of the transit. Like Uranus (and Pluto) this can be a lengthy gestation! For as long as eighteen months, Neptune can affect a single degree while it undergoes its retrograde process. Even if only one person in the family is experiencing the Neptune transit, I have never seen it occur but that there was something afoot deep in the entire family system – where there was an uncertainty, a dissolving, or a loss or sacrifice being made.

In the course of the year and a half of one young woman's Neptune transit over her ascendant, multiple levels of family meaning occurred: her mother moved to a foreign country a quarter of the world away, her only sister was also abroad, her first significant relationship was in a state of confusion, her own identity was in crisis and, circumstantially, she was in a totally new city undergoing a crisis in education, and the girl with whom she shared her house had a psychotic breakdown and broke everything and left her with all the bills! She later described it as 'living in a fog', having no one to turn to and feeling disconnected from everything. It seems as if everyone she was related to, including friends, were also in a fog of a type. She has Neptune natally in the eleventh house – all her hopes and dreams of fulfilment fell by the wayside for a time, to be realized about two years later, after the fog had cleared, by which time the family had recombined in a tangible way, and her creative work was much more solid.

Neptune is the symbol for the enmeshed family, and a Neptune transit can bring one closer to a person in the family from whom one has been separated. Boundaries are often muted, resulting in stronger psychic connections to blood-ties. Obviously this can be sad; if there is a person in the family who is ill, unhappy, depressed, in crisis, this means that one can be more empathic and experience another's pain as one's own. This can happen by other-dimensional means – visitations from ancestors, dreams of reunion with a lost sibling, fantasies of the perfect mother, are all part of Neptune transits. But it can also be exalted, and a spiritual union can occur between distant family members; the longing to 'belong', to bond and merge with family, establishes itself.

This leads to another caution: attraction to surrogate families can be powerful, especially if they fulfil parental roles that were not strong in childhood. This is a cult-transit. Folding into a family of loving or religiously based groups as a family-substitute is not a particularly good idea – unless, of course, it happens that it is a true vocation. If this is part of the experience, the family of origin will find your transit weird and become alarmed – you then become their Neptune transit and all their fantasies of loss and sacrifice arise.

Neptune seems always to involve triangles – Oedipal situations can arise, especially if they replicate the mother/father/child scenario. If one parent played the other one off when one was a child, it established a deep attraction to or fear of triangulated relationships. So often an affair is undertaken during a Neptune transit. This is definitely a family affair. In the sense that the 'outside person', the 'other-person' in the triangle is standing on the sidelines, unfulfilled, he or she is repeating a familial scene. Somewhere in there will lie a terribly important message about belonging, of having one's own family and the sense of safe love and security.

People can have visionary experiences under a Neptune transit – this has to be clearly distinguished from delusionary visions. This, too, speaks of ancestral links, especially if the individual has a strong Neptunian feature in their chart natally. It would be one of the best times for a vision-quest, in search of ancestral history and spiritual links to family members. On page 290 is the story of Anne, who rejected her mother *in utero*; she underwent a form of (deeply unconscious) rebirth when Neptune transited all her fourth house Capricorn planets, and became very independent after it was done. But first she had to become very self-absorbed and indulge herself in herself. Interestingly, young Anne's family (her father's) was deeply enmeshed, and Anne loved it – until Neptune (and Uranus) came along to change her relationship with the family from loving safety to smothering enmeshment.

Neptune can dissolve family connections – the person who is having the transit might well fade away, simply drift off from the family for a while. Clearly, if there is a tendency towards drugs, alcohol or emotional imbalance, this could be a time when it threatens a person with those experiences. Everyone who has a Neptune transit does not become a religious fanatic or a drug addict, but if it is in the family, this is the time to break the family chain. It takes the utmost will to deny access to the darker, more accessible traits in the family history, and Neptune is rather enervating and undermining. It can simply erode self-will and self-worth, but only to the degree that it has been wanting in the past, and in the way in which it was learned from the family.

There are times when our Neptune transit says that someone *else* is drifting away – that one of our family-members is slipping out of sight. We might be more conscious of a parent who is ageing, or a sibling who is distancing herself, and try to reconnect with that person. Also, if there has been a 'lost' person in the family, a Neptune transit can make one more empathetic with that person and soften relations so that a reconnection is made. Victims in family systems play strong roles when there is a preponderance of Neptune transits. It is very difficult to be clear about who is doing what to whom when Neptune is angled to one or more planets over a long period of time; ultimately it is best to enjoy the part of it that brings out the inspiration, the muted boundaries between the harsh world of the everyday and the softer world of dreams and imagination. People usually have profound dreams under Neptune transits, and those dreams are more likely to reveal one's deepest connection to the mother, to the collective unconscious, and thus to the parade of ancestors. Occasionally a sacrifice needs to be made on a ritualistic level or even on a practical level in order to correct a balance which has been tilted in the family.

PLUTO

Transits from Pluto to the Natal Chart

Pluto transits are painful, no matter how we look at them – personally, collectively, transcendentally, familially or however! They are all about truth, no matter how we have painted it or had it fed to us in small, sweet doses. Anything that has lurked under the surface or has lain in wait for us will rise up under the transit of Pluto. Because Pluto moves so slowly, we can expect a single transit of it to take over a year, or even two if it will retrograde back and forth a single degree in the horoscope. Thus the entire phase is not racked with agony, but, periodically, help from the gods is necessary.

This is the ideal opportunity for the ancestors to come in to offer guidance, and often they do. I have often said that under a Pluto transit the gods (hence, spirits) are kinder than people. Because the area in which ego forms relative to the planet that is being 'hit' dies, there is a sacredness, a spirituality to the loss. For example, if Pluto is transiting Venus, our values go out of the window, we become obsessed with something unusual or even dangerous to our whole well-being. Whatever is being taken is so huge that the gap left is vast and remains a vacuum for quite some time. The family context is usually around death or divorce, discovery or mourning for something or someone. It might be that the integrity of the family is broken by circumstances. In certain charts I have seen it coincide with the downfall or invasion of a homeland, the destruction of a sacred place, idea or icon. Certainly, if there is something nasty in the woodshed, it will be seen and never mentioned, unless put under the spotlight.

One woman's father died under the first transit to her Sun. Nine months later, at the retrograde pass over it, she discovered that she had been cut out of the family legacy and off the family tree! The whole family had conspired in this and had known for ten years it would happen at his death, but only under Pluto's glance did she discover her true place in that family. At its direct pass, she had broken the spell of the father's gaze.

Pluto dredges up all secrets and hidden agenda which left in the dark would eventually spread a miasma among the family. In the case I mentioned earlier (page 197) of the little girl who died, the whole family was awaiting this event on some deep level, and her father and mother were both having Pluto transits – him to his Sun (fathering) and her to her Moon (mothering). They both knew the death would come some day, but the stark clarity of truth did not arise till it occurred. Pluto is inexorable – in this case, people knew it would happen, but lived as if it wouldn't until it did. Pluto is healthy denial. If we wandered around waiting for Pluto then we would be pathological. If we could accept Pluto transits as truths waiting to come out, we would be less intellectually devastated by them.

Wherever Pluto is in the natal chart is where we are existentially alone. No family in the world can fill this gap. The unseen one is just that – lord of the other world. There is a part of all of us which has no love – it does not give or receive love. This is the biggest problem-point in familial and familiar relationships. Because we once were fused with another (our mother) we still want that. But because we were cut from her incisively (Pluto) we have already experienced a death. To be born is to die. When we have a Pluto transit, we are reminded that no matter what our family situation is like, we are alone.

However, as we read in the section on the eighth house (page 187), where Pluto is, so is the order of the ancestors. We can become direct channels for ancestral truths and, through that process, be it via dreams, visions, ritual or inheritances, we individuate our ancestral links. Immortality acts in this way – we have responsibility not only for our future selves and for our progeny but also for our history and our ancestral line.

Pluto is the death/rebirth point in the horoscope and its transits demarcate life's little deaths. Because so much can be dredged up when someone is having a Pluto transit, it is difficult for the family to lie about anything. Pluto coincides with one become absolutely ruthless for truth. Superlatively, it can also coincide with a bout of paranoia, where all knowledge is exalted and blown out of proportion and if there is a small secret somewhere – as there usually is – the Pluto-transit person can dramatize it beyond its real power.

Pluto is about obsession – and finding a good obsession is absolutely necessary during a long transit of Pluto. Rather that than it finding you. Regardless of what form the focus of deep desire takes, it is the most thorough of experiences. Certain forms of ritual under Pluto transits help appease the situations or circumstances which are concurrent with its lengthy transit. Certainly no stone is left unturned in self-discovery. Very often it means pulling away from the family in order to mature in private. It is important to undergo rituals of death and rebirth in extreme privacy, and emerge renewed and refreshed. Mysterious transformations of the entire family system take place when a focal person is having a Pluto transit.

There is something erotic about going underground – the marriage of Persephone and Hades has an attraction – and a relationship with someone who is outside the family sphere is not unusual, or one which seems to go against the grain of one's own ethics (which are usually family-based) or culture. One might discover a secret relationship occurring in a family, or the sexual orientation of a relative might be finally opened up.

If there was the loss of a parent or close member in the nuclear family in one's early or formative years, a Pluto transit can bring up retroactive mourning – a very healthy cleansing of the psyche and soul. The opportunity for ancestral clearing has arrived and it is the nature of Pluto to be sweeping in its breadth and depth, hence the feeling of global or universal grieving can present itself under this transit. Often it appears that the experience of 'mourning' under a Pluto transit is groundless, but it never is – it is worth staying with the feeling, exploring it deeply and finding the source. The grieving process may not be for a person, but for a part of oneself, passed on, extinct or outmoded, and wanting a proper burial. Perhaps it is the mourning of a collective sort, a *Weltschmertz*, an existential experience which is being undertaken on behalf of others in order to deepen and enrich one's own self, and reclaim submerged or suppressed material from the depths of one's soul.

NOTES

1. (a) M. Harding and C. Harvey, *Working with Astrology*, Contemporary Astrology Series, Arkana, London, 1982. (b) Also, see the dramatic graphs and diagrams for the

Kennedy family in the Appendix, generated by the *JigSaw* PC program for analysis of group/family patterns. This material is also generated for my story of Toby, the young autistic man, in Chapter 13, 'Tobias: Touched by God', page 231.

2. See Part I, page 3, for the generational flow: 'The Big Picture'.

3. See Erin Sullivan, *Saturn in Transit: Boundaries of Mind, Body and Soul*, Arkana, London, 1991, for a thorough understanding of Saturn transiting the angles of the horoscope (and the houses in sequence).

PART III
Dynasty

12.

Real Lives, Real People

LIVING IN THE FAMILY

This last section of the book is the most significant – because it is about people, not theories or models. All the stories link the personal, the collective and the corporate ancestors of the families in these scenarios. From beginning to end, the stories deal with birth, childhood, adult life, death and the ancestral realm meeting the personal experience. Read this like a novel, for it has a beginning, a middle and an ending. However, as with all endings there is a beginning, just as the tail of the serpent-of-eternal-life is taken into its own mouth; thus we have the never-ending story.

Writing depth-cases is difficult but rewarding work. It requires a great deal of sensitivity on the part of the astrologer to know what will be of value to the reader and to what degree the person or family should be explored and exposed. In all the cases I have written, I have moved through the process with the client. Because publishing books is a protracted experience, the case-study begins a year before the book goes into the publishing machine, and in the course of that year, very often stimulated or catalysed by the process of working on the case, my clients will undergo dramatic changes which are directly linked to the case-writing process. I am acutely aware of this before I begin, and I ask only certain people if they wish to take part in this.

The inexplicable, non-rational result of this case-work is the number of synchronicities that occur which are directly connected to the interviews, the writing, the exploration that the person does on his or her own self and family – all this activity contributes to a quickening of process for them. They are required to plumb the depths of their soul and mind, and I am required to explore the astrological and emotional, psychological levels. This amazing experience of moving through experiences is often dramatic. In the case-story of Mohsin, the adoptee, for example, I asked him to come for an interview and, unknown to us, the date chosen out of convenience for both of us several weeks beforehand was already laden with fate. While we were going through the work together, taping our interview, Mohsin's adoptive mother died at that very same time (a fact unknown to us then), immediately changing the dynamic with which we were ostensibly working.

The mobility and fluidity of a single individual's personal experience is exacerbated by the sheer numbers when we are working with the family dynamic. When working on an individual case alone, the variables in what is happening, what is going to happen, what will surface as a direct result of the work I am doing – all alone in my 'writer's cell' (I think!) – are difficult enough to chart and funnel into the limitation of words; however, when we are doing the family-work, it becomes phenomenal. People are born, die, divorce, marry, move and so on and – I don't think it is my imagination, for I couldn't create such drama if I tried – things move more quickly and more deeply for people when I am working on cases with them.

This phenomenon is partly to do with the fact that clients are forced to activate an aspect of themselves which they might not have done otherwise. Partly it is to do with the fact that I might reach an agreement with an element of them that up to now has not had a relationship with someone where such objectivity has been allowed to enter into the scheme of their life. And partly it is to do with the magical side of consciously and actively engaging in a process with another person who is going to offer them the opportunity to see themselves in a bigger picture, and the fact that their story will help other people. The story-telling side gives a quality to the psychic life which deepens their connection to a dimension of their own nature which might continue to lie dormant without the catalyst.

So in some way I act as a catalyst in these proceedings, an agent for the mysterious psychic self – it is the very knowledge that I am doing this that makes the work sacred and responsible. The clients who have agreed to work with me have found the process to be invaluable – as have I. I am saying this not to make myself look amazing and wonderful, for that is not likely to be the case at all, but to point out the tremendous responsibility that the astrologer as counsellor has and the power that the astrologer holds in his or her work. The major cases take a lot of emotional energy, and one has to enter into an agreement with the individual whose story is being lived and told – not just on a conscious level, but on a deeper level, the level which Geoffrey Cornelius delved into in his book, *The Moment of Astrology*.

He says, 'However objective we astrologers try to be about our material, however much we may experience it as a clockwork machine, there is always something else going on just beneath the surface. When our astrology is really successful, it can be as if some unexpected blessing or providence has led us to our conclusions.'[1] Essentially, Geoffrey is saying that in a successful horoscopic reading, the function of genius, daemon or numen in each of the individuals – astrologer and client – must come to some mysterious, tacit agreement with each other. Once that agreement is achieved, and this is the 'moment of astrology', the truths begin to flow. This is magic. It takes time, and trust, but when the daemons agree to confer, there is a magical sequence which proceeds, and continues throughout the entire time. And, in the case of writing, this will go on for about a year. The client and myself are not engaged in some kind of therapeutic work – I am not a practising psychologist or analyst – nor are we on the phone constantly or in each other's laps. We might communicate periodically, but fundamentally, once the work on the case is done, we resume a fairly normal astrologer–client relationship and see each other professionally for sessions just as before the 'case-study' (which I prefer to call 'their story'). However, we are both enriched and have shared something special. And, in presenting the stories of my clients, I am reverent towards this process which occurs in some other dimension than in my consulting-room or between me and the client as we *think* we are.

In the case of Toby, the young autistic man, his mother has been a tremendous source of information for me, and her story is the telling of a dynastic congestion which she sensed and which the astrology confirmed, relieving her further from natural feelings of guilt and unhappiness. The truth is in the stars, and if it is rendered as clearly as possible by the interpreter – the astrologer – it is a metalogue wherein that which is being discussed is also arising.

In Laura and Anne's story, 'Rejected in the Womb', the completion of the writing of the story coincided with Laura's trip to see her daughter Anne and her own mother, during which time she found time and appropriateness for using the process of our story-work to further develop, perhaps quicken, their own family-work. Also, Laura herself had done much family-work, both personally and in her career training as a psychospiritual 'midwife' for families, but mainly for unmothered people.

In 'What's Bred in the Bone', Fiona was in a stage of healing; there was a minor relapse of her health, directly related to the material we were working through. She was more able to see this in its family-related context, and don her protection without anger or fear, but with a sense of rightness, knowing that it was for the best, not just some selfish motive on her part.

My last story, the story of Rosemary and the ancestral linking, is most profound. In the telling of that story, our appointment to discuss the whole thing together took place (arbitrarily) just as the planet Mercury was at 18° of Gemini in June 1995 – and that degree, as you will see, is potent. It is a degree loaded with ancestral memory and was the pre-natal station-retrograde of Mercury in Rosemary's natal chart . . . and Mercury, as we know, is the psychopompos. Hermes guided the souls all through the telling and the writing of the tale.

NOTES

1. Geoffrey Cornelius, *The Moment of Astrology*, Arkana, Contemporary Astrology Series, 1994, London, page 190. The chapter on the Daemon, and chapters following, are of interest in this phenomenon.

13

Tobias: Touched by God

The following is quoted from a letter Barbara, Toby's mother, wrote to me in April 1995 after the main body of their story was written:

'I have received your chapter, read it through and was moved to tears, how glad I am that I met you and that you have helped me with this miracle child of mine. What you have written brings everything into an incredibly sharp and beautiful focus, I always knew my life made sense somewhere even if it appeared to be a maze of contradictions and difficulties from an earthly viewpoint, you've slotted the final piece into place and now the pattern dances and sparkles and it can work with anything. I cannot believe that I have two such amazing souls as my children, all that crap of life doesn't count for anything when I look at that.

Will you please, please put somewhere in your book how good your advice and help has been to me, to all of us, and how happy I am about that.'

Done, and let me say that I have learned much about myself and others, and feel humbled by my work with Barbara herself.

In the spring of 1991, Barbara came to have her chart and her son's compared. She was trying to resolve some difficulties between herself and him, having become convinced that she was the 'representation of the devouring dragon-lady in Toby's life', and she needed to have some perspective on this.

Indeed, looking at their horoscopes, I came to quite a different conclusion. I looked at the Moon, Sun and Venus contacts between them, to isolate the parental and feminine contacts between them. Toby's Venus, at 26° Virgo, sits exactly on his mother's ascendant, while her Moon at 27° Leo is Toby's Sun · Moon midpoint – the 'giver of life'. Also, Toby's Moon at 22° Gemini is his mother's Moon · Mercury midpoint (and also within two degrees of her Moon · Venus midpoint). If anything, this Sun, Moon, Venus interaction resonates with a strong image of the archetypal lover-mother, as

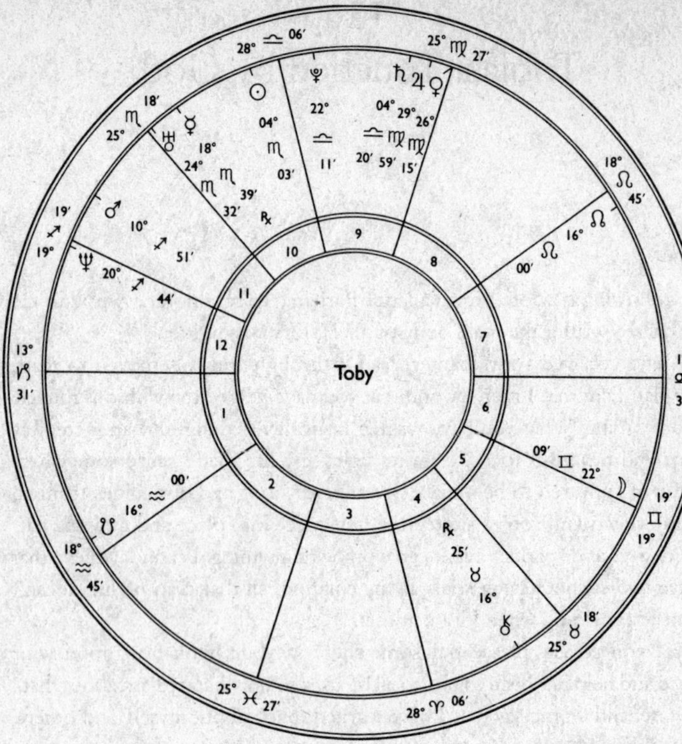

Midpoint Sort

☽/Asc	02°♈50′	♃/♄	02°♎09′	☿/♄	26°♎29′	☉/☿	11°♏21′	♂/♅	02°♐41′
☽	22°♊09′	♄	04°♎20′	♃/♅	27°♎15′	♄/♆	12°♏32′	♇/Asc	02°♐51′
☽/♀	09°♌12′	♀/♇	09°♎13′	Mc	28°♎06′	☉/♅	14°♏17′	☿/♆	04°♐41′
☽/♃	11°♌04′	♃/♇	11°♎05′	☉/♇	28°♎07′	♂/♇	16°♏31′	Mc/Asc	05°♐48′
☽/♄	13°♌14′	♀/Mc	12°♎11′	♄/♅	29°♎26′	☿	18°♏39′	♅/♆	07°♐38′
☽/♇	22°♌10′	♄/♇	13°♎16′	☉/Mc	01°♏04′	♂/Mc	19°♏29′	☉/Asc	08°♐47′
☽/Mc	25°♌08′	♃/Mc	14°♎02′	♀/♂	03°♏33′	♀/Asc	19°♏53′	♂	10°♐51′
☽/☉	28°♌06′	☉/♀	15°♎09′	☉	04°♏03′	♆/♇	21°♏28′	♂/♆	15°♐48′
☽/☿	05°♍24′	♄/Mc	16°♎13′	♂/♃	05°♏25′	☿/♅	21°♏35′	☿/Asc	16°♐05′
☽/♅	08°♍21′	☉/♃	17°♎01′	☿/♇	05°♏25′	♃/Asc	21°♏45′	♅/Asc	19°♐01′
☽/♂	16°♍30′	☉/♄	19°♎11′	♂/♄	07°♏35′	☉/♂	22°♏27′	♆	20°♐44′
☽/♆	21°♍27′	♇	22°♎11′	♅/♇	08°♏22′	♄/Asc	23°♏55′	♂/Asc	27°♐11′
♀	26°♍15′	☿/♀	22°♎27′	☿/Mc	08°♏22′	♆/Mc	24°♏25′	♆/Asc	02°♑07′
♀/♃	28°♍07′	☿/♃	24°♎19′	♀/♆	08°♏30′	♅	24°♏32′	Asc	13°♑31′
♃	29°♍59′	♇/Mc	25°♎09°	♃/♆	10°♎22′	☉/♆	27°♏23′		
♀/♄	00°♎18′	♀/♅	25°♎24′	♅/Mc	11°♏19′	☿/♂	29°♏45′		

Figure 4

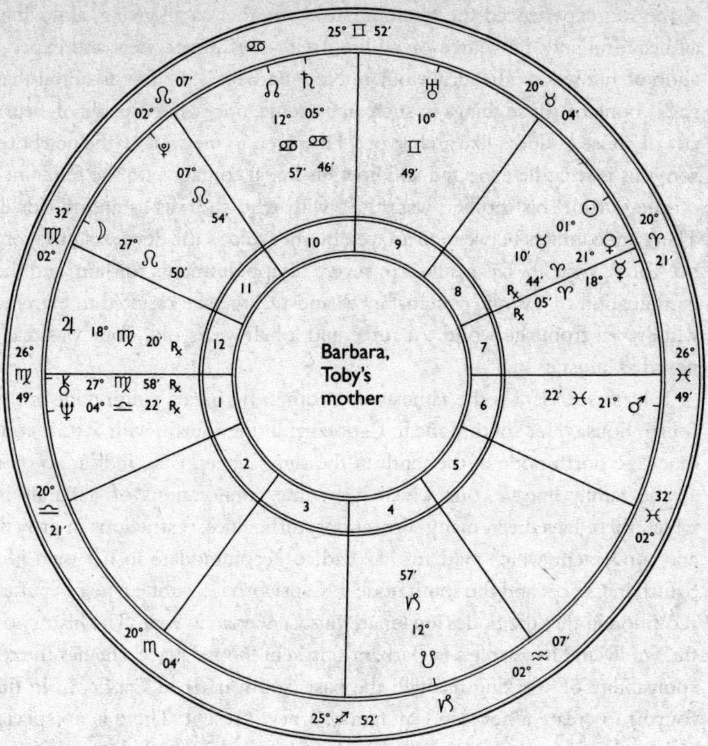

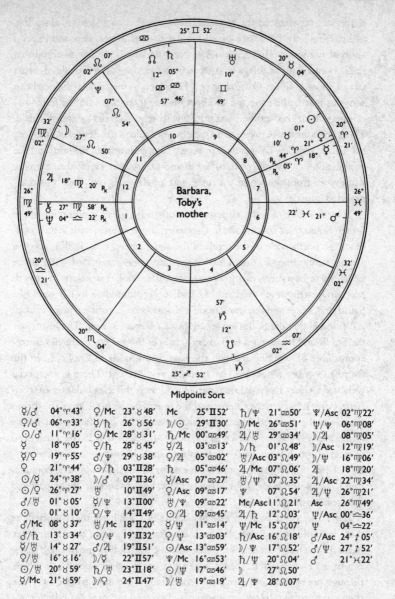

Midpoint Sort

☿/♂	04°♈43′	♀/Mc	23°♉48′	Mc	25°♊52′	♄/♇	21°♋50′	♇/Asc	02°♍22′
♀/♂	06°♈33′	☿/♄	26°♉56′	☽/☉	29°♊30′	☽/Mc	26°♋51′	♆/♇	06°♍08′
☉/♂	11°♈16′	☉/Mc	28°♉31′	♄/Mc	00°♋49′	♃/♅	29°♋34′	☽/♃	08°♍05′
☿	18°♈05′	♀/♄	28°♉45′	☿/♃	03°♋13′	☽/♄	01°♌48′	☽/Asc	12°♍19′
☿/♀	19°♈55′	♂/♇	29°♉38′	♀/♃	05°♋02′	♅/Asc	03°♌49′	☽/♆	16°♍06′
♀	21°♈44′	☉/♄	03°♊28′	♄	05°♋46′	♃/Mc	07°♌06′	♃	18°♍20′
☉/☿	24°♈38′	☽/♂	09°♊36′	☿/Asc	07°♋27′	♅/♆	07°♌35′	♃/Asc	22°♍34′
☉/♀	26°♈27′	♅	10°♊49′	♀/Asc	09°♋17′	♇	07°♌54′	♃/♆	26°♍21′
♂/♅	01°♉05′	☿/♇	13°♊00′	♅/♇	09°♋22′	Mc/Asc	11°♌21′	Asc	26°♍49′
☉	01°♉10′	♀/♇	14°♊49′	☉/♃	09°♋45′	♃/♄	12°♌03′	♆/Asc	00°♎36′
♂/Mc	08°♉37′	♅/Mc	18°♊20′	☿/♆	11°♋14′	♆/Mc	15°♌07′	♆	04°♎22′
♂/♄	13°♉34′	☉/♇	19°♊32′	♀/♆	13°♋03′	♄/Asc	16°♌18′	♂/Asc	24°♐05′
☿/♅	14°♉27′	♂/♃	19°♊51′	☉/Asc	13°♋59′	☽/♇	17°♌52′	♂/♆	27°♐52′
♀/♅	16°♉16′	☽/☿	22°♊57′	♇/Mc	16°♋53′	♄/♆	20°♌04′	♂	21°♓22′
☉/♅	20°♉59′	♄/♅	23°♊18′	☉/♆	17°♋46′	☽	27°♌50′		
☿/Mc	21°♉59′	☽/♀	24°♊47′	☽/♅	19°♋19′	♃/♇	28°♌07′		

Figure 5

if the son experienced the feminine in his mother as all-giving, all-loving, all-beautiful and the source of all life itself – his innate view and expectation of her was of the ideal woman. Now Barbara is the first to admit that she is none of those things in such an extreme, nor is she capable of being any of those goddess-like archetypes. However, to the soul of the newborn son, this is what he expected and how his initial contact with the feminine-on-the-outside, his mother, was fused with who she was as an individual. There are conflicts between them, yes, but her role as the devouring-dragon, no. Toby's own life has resulted in severe disappointments for him, and the combination of events, circumstances and reality have resulted in extreme withdrawal from the world. At three and a half years old, Toby was diagnosed as autistic.

Toby's ascendant is the same as his mother, Barbara's, south node in the fourth house. Her south node in Capricorn in the fourth, with Saturn conjunct the north node in the tenth in the sign Cancer, is an indication of a strong family lineage, one which has some connotations of a family in which there have been many separations, difficulties, restrictions in growth and movement which Barbara has had to accommodate in her own life. Saturn in Cancer and the south node in Capricorn is a subtle type of mutual reception in that the nodes are lunar, thus Cancerian in tone. The history of the family and its past lies in Barbara's present 'home' place; she has the responsibility of working through the past (south node in Capricorn in the fourth) to create a new kind of family, a new present. There is no special weight on either maternal or paternal side with this combination of configurations; however, the Cancer and the fourth house node leans the thread slightly to the maternal line, but we shall see that her own father and Toby's father are very much involved in the purge. It seems that Barbara will need to work through some of the links in the family history to unravel the mystery of her son, whose ascendant – his point of incarnation – is in conjunction to her south node. Toby is the last link, both the result of the past and the creation of the future.

Indeed, in a conversation with her before he died, her father told Barbara that he thought she was the 'human catalyst'. Barbara says, '[however, before] I felt like a barrier to the past which could only come through to the future as I changed it.' She'd had to process other people's 'rubbish' through her system, and turn it into something nourishing to give away; she then wrote to me, 'How wonderful to discover I am actually fulfilling my purpose!'

Toby's birth was fine, quite normal. He was born three weeks earlier than the due date, but strong and healthy. He was received joyfully by his mother, loved by his older half-sister, Zöe, who was fourteen at the time of his birth, but resented by his father. Toby's father's Moon · Neptune · Pluto midpoint is 26° Leo – all the father's own fears of his own mother-devouring are present in the Moon of Barbara and in his son's Sun · Moon midpoint. He instinctively felt shut out, yet he has and will continue to play a powerful role in Toby's emergence from his interior world (see Figures 4, 5, 6, 7).

Toby was loving and receptive, and Barbara recalls his remarkable eyes when she breast-fed him; she says he would take hold of her breast and devour her with his eyes, staring deeply into them, feeding on all levels, as it were. The eyes, typically a Scorpio trait, are a dramatic feature in Toby – intense and searching, seeking behind the veil of the flesh. It seems that Toby was born with an overwhelming need for nourishment and deep-level contact from the instant of his birth, even, perhaps, with a reluctance to being born. Let's go back to the beginning and work our way forward into Toby's nuclear family and then back into the ancestral line.

Toby was conceived on Valentine's Day in 1980, the result of a deep, passionate love affair between his mother and father. But at ten to eleven weeks Barbara began spotting, almost miscarrying. She was given a series of male-hormone injections over a period of six weeks to stop her uterus from contracting. At six weeks – if we look at Toby's birth chart and at the pre-natal experiences of the time – we see some remarkable connections.

> Pre-natal eclipses from conception forward to birth
> 1. 16 February 26° 50′ Aquarius . . . total eclipse of the Sun
> 2. 1 March   11° 26′ Virgo . . . appulse full Moon
> 3. 27 July   4° 54′ Aquarius . . . appulse full Moon
> 4. 10 August   18° 17′ Leo . . . appulse new Moon
> 5. 26 August   3° 03′ Pisces . . . appulse full Moon

Because we have the conception date, which is often obscure, we are lucky to know that the first pre-natal eclipse after Toby's conception occurred two days later – at 26° 50′ Aquarius – a total eclipse of the Sun. Remember, this is Barbara's Moon degree and Toby's Sun · Moon midpoint. It is also his father's Moon · Pluto midpoint. Very early on, Toby's own life-force was threatened and his mother's emotional tie to him jeopardized by a total eclipse of the Sun. Symbolically, a total eclipse of the Sun is the feminine principle obscuring the masculine principle. In actuality, the Moon

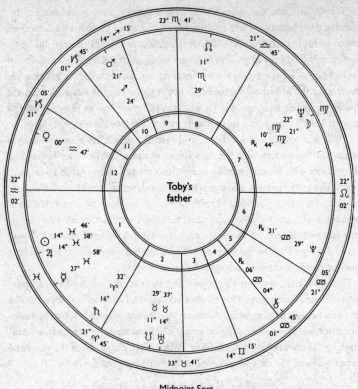

Midpoint Sort

☉/♄	00°♈39′	♅/♀	22°♊04′	♆/Mc	03°♏12′	Mc/Asc	18°♐09′	♅/Mc	29°≈26′
♃/♄	00°♈45′	☽/☿	24°♊51′	☽/♂	06°♏34′	♂/Asc	21°♑43′	♂/♃	03°♓00′
♅/Asc	03°♈20′	☿/♆	25°♊04′	♂/♆	06°♏47′	☉/Mc	29°♑31′	☉/Asc	03°♓24′
☿/♄	07°♈15′	☽/♄	04°♋08′	☽/♀	26°♏16′	♃/Mc	29°♑37′	♃/Asc	03°♓30′
☉/♅	14°♈42′	♄/♆	04°♋21′	♀/♆	26°♏29′	♀	00°≈47′	♀/♄	08°♓40′
♃/♅	14°♈47′	☽/♆	18°♋10′	☽/Asc	06°♐53′	☉/♂	03°≈05′	☿/Asc	10°♓00′
♄	16°♈32′	♅/♆	18°♋23′	♆/Asc	07°♐06′	♂/♃	03°≈11′	☉	14°♓48′
☿/♅	21°♈17′	♆	29°♋31′	Mc	14°♐15′	☿/Mc	06°≈06′	☉/♃	14°♓52′
♀/♄	00°♉09′	☽/♇	25°♌37′	♂/Mc	17°♐49′	☿/♂	09°≈41′	♃	14°♓58′
♄/♅	00°♉35′	♆/♇	25°♌50′	☽/☉	18°♐15′	♀/Asc	11°≈25′	♄/Asc	19°♓17′
♀/Asc	10°♉47′	☽	21°♍44′	☽/♃	18°♐21′	♄/Mc	15°≈24′	☉/☿	21°♓22′
♅	14°♉37′	☽/♀	21°♍57′	☉/♅	18°♐28′	☿/♄	18°≈58′	☿/♃	21°♓28′
☉/♅	22°♉08′	♆	22°♍10′	♃/♆	18°♐34′	Asc	22°≈02′	♀/♅	22°♓42′
♃/♇	22°♉14′	♀/Mc	06°♎53′	♂	21°♐24′	☉/♀	22°≈47′	☿	27°♓58′
☿/♇	28°♉44′	♂/♆	10°♎27′	♀/Mc	07°♑31′	♀/♃	22°≈53′		
♄/♆	08°♊02′	☽/Mc	02°♏59′	♀/♂	11°♑06′	☿/♀	29°≈23′		

Figure 6

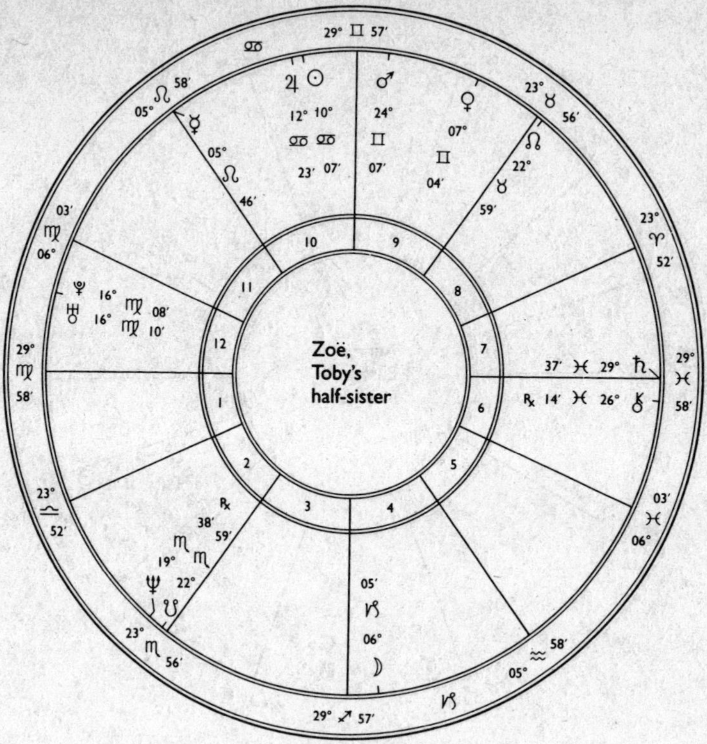

Midpoint Sort

☽/♂	00°♈06′	♂/Mc	27°♊02′	♀/Asc	03°♌31′	♀/♆	28°♌21′	♅/♆	17°♎54′
☽/Mc	03°♈01′	Mc	29°♊57′	♂/♇	05°♌08′	☿/Asc	02°♍52′	☽/☿	20°♎56′
♀/♄	03°♉21′	☉/♂	02°♋07′	♂/♅	05°♌08′	♂/♆	06°♍52′	♆/Asc	24°♎48′
♂/♄	11°♉52′	♂/♃	03°♋15′	☿	05°♌46′	♆/Mc	09°♍48′	☽/♇	11°♏07′
♄/Mc	14°♉47′	☉/Mc	05°♋02′	♇/Mc	08°♌03′	☉/♆	14°♍53′	☽/♅	11°♏08′
☉/♄	19°♉52′	♃/Mc	06°♋10′	♅/Mc	08°♌04′	♃/♆	16°♍01′	☽/Asc	18°♏01′
♃/♄	21°♉00′	☿/♀	06°♋25′	♂/Asc	12°♌02′		16°♍08′	♆	19°♏38′
☿/♄	02°♊42′	☉	10°♋07′	☉/♇	13°♌08′	♅/♇	16°♍09′	☽/♆	12°♐52′
♀	07°♊04′	☉/♃	11°♋15′	☉/♅	13°♌09′	♅	16°♍10′	♄/Asc	29°♐47′
♀/♂	15°♊35′	♃	12°♋23′	♃/♇	14°♌16′	♇/Asc	23°♍03′	☽	06°♑05′
♀/Mc	18°♊31′	☿/♂	14°♋56′	♃/♅	14°♌17′	♅/Asc	23°♍04′	♄/♆	24°♑38′
♄/♇	22°♊53′	☿/Mc	17°♋52′	Mc/Asc	14°♌57′	☿/♆	27°♍42′	☽/♄	17°♒51′
♄/♅	22°♊54′	☉/☿	22°♋57′	☉/Asc	20°♌03′	Asc	29°♍58′	☽/♀	21°♓35′
☉/♀	23°♊36′	☿/♃	24°♋05′	♃/Asc	21°♌11′	☽/☉	08°♎06′	♄	29°♓37′
♂	24°♊07′	♀/♇	26°♋36′	☿/♇	25°♌57′	☽/♃	09°♎14′		
♀/♃	24°♊44′	♀/♅	26°♋37′	☿/♅	25°♌58′	♆/♇	17°♎53′		

Figure 7

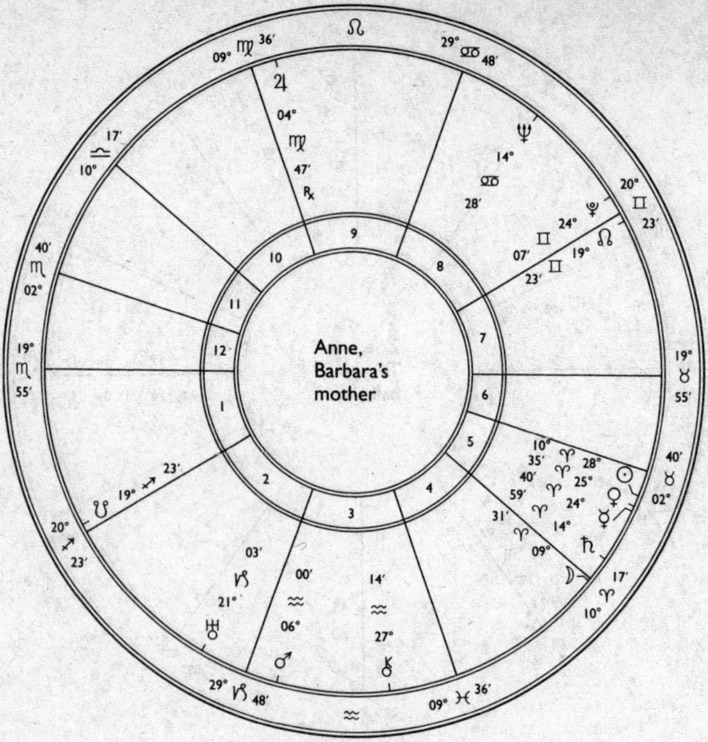

Midpoint Sort

♅/♇	07°♈35′	☉/☿	26°♈25′	♃/♄	24°♊53′	♃/Mc	07°♍11′	♂	06°♒00′
☽	09°♈31′	☉/♀	26°♈53′	♄/Mc	27°♊18′	Mc	09°♍36′	☿/Asc	07°♒18′
☽/♄	12°♈15′	☉	28°♈10′	☿/♃	29°♊44′	♆/Asc	17°♍11′	♀/Asc	07°♒45′
♄	14°♈59′	☽/♇	16°♉49′	♀/♃	00°♋11′	♃/Asc	12°♎21′	☉/Asc	09°♒03′
♂/♇	15°♈03′	♄/♇	19°♉33′	☉/♃	01°♋28′	Mc/Asc	14°♎45′	☽/♅	00°♓17′
☽/☿	17°♈06′	☿/♇	24°♉24′	☿/Mc	02°♋08′	♃/♅	12°♏55′	♄/♅	03°♓01′
☽/♀	17°♈33′	♀/♇	24°♉51′	♀/Mc	02°♋36′	♅/Mc	15°♏20′	☽/♂	07°♓46′
♅/♆	17°♈46′	☉/♇	26°♉08′	☉/Mc	03°♋53′	Asc	19°♏55′	☿/♅	07°♓52′
☽/☉	18°♈51′	☽/♆	27°♉00′	♆/♇	04°♋17′	♂/♃	20°♏23′	♀/♅	08°♓19′
☿/♄	19°♈50′	♄/♆	29°♉44′	♆	14°♋28′	♂/Mc	22°♏48′	☉/♅	09°♓37′
♀/♄	20°♈17′	☿/♆	04°♊34′	♃/♇	29°♋27′	♅/Asc	20°♐29′	♂/♄	10°♓30′
☉/♄	21°♈35′	♀/♆	05°♊02′	♇/Mc	01°♌51′	♂/Asc	27°♐57′	☿/♂	15°♓20′
☿	24°♈40′	☉/♆	06°♊19′	♃/♆	09°♌37′	♅	21°♑03′	♀/♂	15°♓48′
☿/♀	25°♈08′	☽/♃	22°♊09′	♆/Mc	12°♌02′	♂/♅	28°♑32′	☉/♂	17°♓05′
♂/♆	25°♈14′	♇	24°♊07′	♃	04°♍47′	☽/Asc	29°♑43′		
♀	25°♈35′	☽/Mc	24°♊34′	♇/Asc	07°♍01′	♄/Asc	02°♒27′		

Figure 8

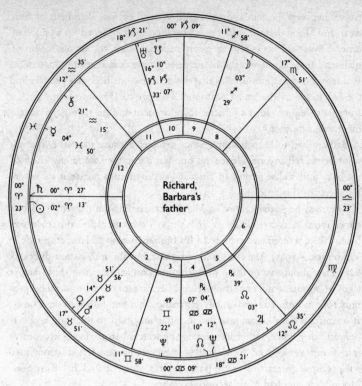

Midpoint Sort

Asc	00°♈23′	☿/Ψ	28°♈49′	♂/Ψ	06°♊23′	♃/♅	25°♎06′	♅/Asc	23°♒28′
♄/Asc	00°♈25′	☿/Ψ	08°♉27′	♀/Ψ	13°♊28′	☽	03°♐29′	♄/♅	23°♒30′
♄	00°♈27′	Ψ/Asc	11°♉36′	♂/Ψ	16°♊00′	☽/Mc	16°♐49′	☽/♀	24°♒10′
☉/Asc	01°♈18′	♄/Ψ	11°♉38′	♀	22°♊49′	☽/♅	25°♐01′	☉/♅	24°♒23′
☉/♄	01°♈20′	☉/Ψ	12°♉31′	☉/♃	24°♊15′	Mc	00°♑09′	☽/♂	26°♒43′
☉	02°♈13′	♀	14°♉51′	♂/♃	26°♊48′	♅/Mc	08°♑21′	☿	04°♓50′
♅/Ψ	04°♈41′	♀/♂	17°♉24′	Ψ/Ψ	02°♋27′	♅	16°♑33′	♀/Mc	07°♓30′
☿/♀	09°♈51′	☿/♃	19°♉14′	Ψ	12°♋04′	☽/♀	19°♑09′	♂/Mc	10°♓02′
☿/♂	12°♈23′	♂	19°♉56′	♃/♀	13°♋14′	☽/Asc	01°♒56′	♀/♅	15°♓42′
♅/Ψ	14°♈19′	Ψ/Asc	21°♉14′	♃/Ψ	22°♋52′	☽/♄	01°♒58′	☿/Asc	17°♓36′
♀/Asc	22°♈37′	♄/Ψ	21°♉16′	♃	03°♌39′	♂/Mc	02°♒29′	☿/♄	17°♓39′
♀/♄	22°♈39′	☉/Ψ	22°♉09′	☽/Ψ	13°♍09′	☽/☉	02°♒51′	♂/♅	18°♓15′
☉/♀	23°♈32′	♃/Asc	02°♊01′	☽/Ψ	22°♍47′	☿/♅	10°♒41′	☉/♀	18°♓31′
♂/Asc	25°♈09′	♃/♄	02°♊03′	☽/♃	03°♎34′	Mc/Asc	15°♒16′	Ψ/Mc	26°♓29′
♂/♄	25°♈12′	☉/♃	02°♊56′	Ψ/Mc	06°♎07′	♄/Mc	15°♒18′		
☉/♂	26°♈04′	♀/♅	03°♊50′	♃/Mc	16°♎54′	☉/Mc	16°♒11′		

Figure 9

passes between the Sun and the earth, in such perfect alignment of Sun, earth and Moon that the solar fire is obscured and blackened for a period of time. A solar eclipse is also an insemination, a dark, mysterious union of male and female wherein the feminine principle dominates the masculine. In a family context, this implies that the maternal line becomes primary and the link to the mother most profound. This pre-natal eclipse seems to be a foreshadowing of Toby's father's abandonment and his own deep attachment to his mother.

Barbara had to keep her pregnancy a secret because the father did not want her to tell anyone. Hence, no one but her immediate family knew of the baby until the beginning of August – seven months pregnant and a very big secret by this time.

The next pre-natal eclipse in March occurred at the degree of Toby's conception Mars-retrograde at 10° Virgo ('coincidentally' this case was being taken, written and explored with Barbara during a Mars retrograde in Virgo cycle – 1995). Mars was still retrograde, but about to station-direct six days later, about two or three weeks before Barbara began to show danger signs of spontaneously aborting Toby. There are no more pre-natal eclipses until four months later, when he 're-attached' himself fully into the womb.[1] It seems that the soul can take its time attaching itself to the body, and may hesitate for a while, rather like testing the waters before diving irrevocably into its new vessel. And Toby's soul seemed very earnest at first (strong total solar eclipse interacting with both parents' Moons and his own Sun · Moon), but later had some second thoughts.

The difficulty would have begun around Barbara's own solar-return, the anniversary of her own birth, and continued on for a critical six weeks. Her solar return of 1980 had Mars at 27° Leo square Uranus retrograde at 24° Scorpio, and certainly the transit of Mars could have triggered the bleeding in this early stage of pregnancy, considering that she conceived when transiting Mars was retrograde and it had only just gone direct and was then conjunct her natal Moon! Coupled with the square of Uranus, there was danger all about.

Barbara's treatment with male hormones had unknown side-effects, but certainly it prevented her losing her baby, and when the July eclipse occurred at 4° 52′ Aquarius, it seems that Toby had become involved with his future self – however, at a conflict level. With his natal Sun at 4° 03′ of Scorpio, there is a tension between the experience in the womb at this time and the mysterious purpose of his incarnation – there are both the dark and the light forces to contend with, to which Toby is extremely sensitive. He connects very deeply with people and 'knows' what they are feeling – this is terribly uncomfortable for him and he almost cannot bear, perhaps cannot bear at all, the flood of feeling that comes from others into himself.

Somewhere around the end of the hormone treatment, at 'three to four months' pregnant, Barbara had a dream in which a man came to her and she was running through various names, but the man said his name was 'Toby'. When the baby was born, the family was looking through lists of family names and Barbara put down Toby, and everyone agreed – and it is not a family name! When she looked up its meaning, it was 'touched by god'.

Toby has a Moon · Neptune opposition from the sixth to the twelfth house, and this is a very strong hint of him being a 'reluctant incarnate' – his need to remain in the womb, fused with his mother, is intense, and his capacity to emerge into his own identity would have taken a great deal of assistance and support from both parents, but particularly from his father. If his father had been present, accounted for, in some deep way more 'there' for him and his mother, then Toby might have had more inclination to move out of the oceanic state of the womb, infancy, and toward toddlerhood and eventually independence. However, this is not the case. This is not to indict the father, but to show how remarkably manifest symbolic images can become.

If we look at Toby's father's horoscope, we see that he has a Moon · Neptune conjunction in a general opposition to his Pisces planets, and in very tight opposition to his Mercury. Toby's father is not that well connected to the earth mode, himself, and with the Sun · Jupiter in Pisces, is given to flight. Though he has taken much of the financial responsibility recently and has become as involved as he can be at this time, in the beginning and for the majority of Toby's life his father has been virtually 'absent'. This is a reflection of Toby's father's own lack of strong fathering and of how the distant, escapist father is very much part of the maternal family line. We shall see this Neptunian imagery abounding throughout the family tree on both sides, but primarily in the maternal line.

Infant Toby was loving and very attached to his mother, seeking nourishment from eye-contact and responding to affection and love. But, after many ear, nose and throat infections and general poor health, by the time he was a year old Barbara began to notice 'something'. She said, 'It was as if Toby had come down the straight road and at about one year old he started to become confused and not responding to signals well. Maybe it was the illnesses, his father, something like that, I don't know.' Somehow, Toby was losing his footing in the world and was not experiencing himself in his environment very well.

By eighteen months he was still not talking, becoming hyperactive, and by five he was 'demonic'. Raging, not talking; in short, completely out of control. Terrified and distraught, Barbara returned to England to seek advice and help which was not available in the country in which they were living. There began a long, painful eight years for her and for Toby. To add to the strain, Toby's father left them at that Christmas in 1985, leaving the onus of responsibility entirely upon Barbara. Also, Zöe had reached the age of adulthood, beginning to move out into her own life, though remaining close to her mother and very attached to Toby. Zöe's Moon is seven degrees behind Toby's ascendant in Capricorn, and Toby would see her as a maternal figure; certainly Zöe's feelings for Toby are loving, motherly and responsible – as a Cancer woman with Sun · Jupiter opposite the Moon in the fourth house, her feelings about her own maternity might be bound up with Toby. That she shares her mother's ascendant would add to Toby's easy identification to her as another mother. Toby could be Zöe's son, they are so alike in looks.

Barbara says of Zöe's feelings about having a child: 'Something in Zöe longs for a child, really aches and yearns, but she is not like me – she has sense! Part of it is that because of her own missing father she needs to feel totally secure in a relationship and know her partner wants a child as she feels unable to bring up a child on her own, and part is that she has seen the hard time I have had with Toby and doesn't feel that she could cope with anything like that, and part is the type of sacrifice mothers make does not appeal to her. She enjoys luxury, her own space, her own time and creativity. It may be that one day she will decide to have a child, but it could equally be that other things will be her "children".' Now, this is very astute: to me, it implies that Zöe is not repeating the family fate in the maternal line, she is more in touch with herself than all of the women, she has deep sensitivity, love and caring for both her mother and her brother, but she will not, and should not, sacrifice herself for either of them. To her mother's credit, Barbara has surely had a hand in giving Zöe her independence, and, in keeping with her 'circuit breaker' mode, has not gripped her daughter out of resentment for the young woman's free spirit.

AUTISM: WHAT IS IT, AND WHY IS TOBY THAT?

In Oliver Sacks's book, *An Anthropologist on Mars*, he says, 'Autism, clearly, is a condition that has always existed, affecting occasional individuals in every period and culture. It has always attracted in the popular mind an amazed, fearful, or bewildered attention (and perhaps engendered mythical or archetypal figures – the alien, the changeling, the child bewitched).'[2] Autism was medically identified simultaneously by two individuals in the 1940s who named it independently.

Autism is what it implies: self-ism. Isolation, mental aloneness, disregard for others, being internally stimulated, being withdrawn, and so on, are all characteristics of the autistic person. There is a characteristic ability to focus and regard something for long periods of time, a kind of fascination or fixation on an object or things, repetitive actions and movements, ritualistic behaviour and narrow preoccupations. One of the explorers of autism, Hans Asperger, said, 'They do not make eye contact . . . they seem to take in things with short, peripheral glances . . .' This certainly did not describe Toby when he was in his first year, nursing at his mother's breast, gazing intently, raptly, searchingly into her eyes! However, at some point he receded and became alienated and enraged, where, as Asperger defines, 'The use of language appears abnormal, unnatural . . . the children follow their own impulses, regardless of the demands of the environment.'[3]

Now in some way and to some degree we are all autistic, incapable of seeing outside ourselves, involved in small obsessive activities which exclude the environment. Highly creative people have a strong streak of this trait. Profound autism is unique, however, and moves well beyond small fetishist hobbies, interests or even obsessive behaviour. Profound autism results in as many types as there are autistics! In Chapter 2 I spoke of extremes – of Uranian and Neptunian 'types' of family-systems. Autism can present in any type of family, either Neptunian or Uranian, and it can also appear to relate in both or either Uranian or Neptunian ways. When we see the various family charts in Toby's family, we are clearly getting a plethora of Pisces, Neptune and twelfth house and Water signs – an overwhelming majority of weight lies therein – but there are also family patterns forming with Uranus, particularly Sun and Moon hard aspects, in several of the individuals.

Neptune is the oceanic state, the psychic ouroboros, wherein no separation between self and others exists, where subject and object merge and the fusion between the physical and the psychical or imaginal world is complete. In a sense, the world and us are one ball when we are 'in Neptune'. When we are in the womb we *are* one with the nourisher, but when we are born, Neptune holds the shock of separation and in Neptune we have the symbol for the constant longing that lurks in the hearts of people to re-create this intra-uterine bond. Natal Neptune acts as the receptacle for all the shock and trauma that occurs at birth, and all subsequent blows that even vaguely recall that event! Neptune is soft, saline, misty, feeling, fused and synaesthetic, wholly in *participation mystique* – indeed, a kind of cosmic womb. We all have Neptune in our charts, and it represents the place we 'go' to blur the harshness of the world and its sharp edges, a panacea from reality as we encounter it on a daily basis. Some people go to Neptune via drugs, others through religion, others through art, relationships, rituals, work, and so on. There are as many diversions from hard-edged life as there are people to create these. All people with Moon · Neptune have difficulty relating to a world in which strong boundaries are needed – their sensitivity level is ultra-acute and it ranges from the shaman to the madman. Fortunately, the average Moon · Neptune person falls somewhere in between the extremes; however, all share the same difficulty – that of recognizing or creating boundaries between themselves and others, between their subjective experience and the so-called objective reality.

For example, Toby's Moon is opposite Neptune. His interior world of feelings is so completely fused with his experience of the environment that it has created the need to be emotionally and relationally completely severed from his surroundings. He has been unable to separate *or* contain his responses to life, vibrations, feelings, moods. The total apparent withdrawal and rejection of the outer world has become necessary because there is little capacity to compartmentalize or rationalize what is going on around him. What is going on inside him comprises his whole world – to such a massive degree that he appears not to participate in his world with any feeling. His feelings have always been apparent to his mother, but she has a main-line to his psyche; to the vast majority of others, however, he is not present.

In contrast to Neptune, Uranus represents separation and shock – the split from the world rather than the fusion with it. Uranus is the symbol for the irrevocable divorce between the ideal world and the real world. Uranus is cold, unfeeling, hard, compartmentalized and clear, very much a witness to life rather than a participant. We are psychically separated from the part of our self and feelings that is represented by Uranus, rather than the undifferentiation between various feelings which is created by Neptune. When we have strong Neptune aspects to the personal Planets – Sun, Moon, Venus or Mercury – and at the same time strong Uranus aspects to the personal planets, there is a profound schism between two worlds, two distinctly opposite psychic states. The collision of fantasy and reality is jarring, clashing, clanging and very likely overwhelming in the sensory realm. Toby seems to be the meeting point of the two worlds in his family system. Oliver Sacks speaks of Temple Grandin, an articulate autistic woman, and about her experience of the world around her: '[it is] one of sensations, heightened, sometimes to an excruciating degree (and inhibited, sometimes to annihilation): she speaks of her ears, at the age of two or three, as helpless microphones, transmitting everything, irrespective of relevance, at full, overwhelming volume – and there was an equal lack of modulation in all her senses.'[4] This heightened sensitivity to sound, touch, taste, smell and so on is a Neptunian quality – Toby's mother, Barbara, says that she 'hears with her skin', her own sensitivity being acute and synaesthetic to a large degree. She has Neptune rising – and its only major aspect is the square from Saturn, which rules the skin as a surface, a container of the body.

About that, Barbara wrote: 'I've had to really work hard to understand boundaries, between myself and others, the world, the universe! At one point in my early forties, I thought I would go quietly mad because I couldn't shut anyone or anything out, I think it was probably because I'd opened up so many channels to try and understand Toby's problems that I nearly drowned in the resulting influx. Even now I have to have techniques so that people don't get into me and I don't get into them. I keep the radio on all day to keep my focus at a low level, I try not to have a deep conversation with anyone face to face with nothing in between us, I can't drink or take drugs – I go off my head. I even have to wear clothes that touch me all over so I know where I begin and end.'

Toby's Moon · Neptune opposition is connected to the MC/IC axis – the parent-axis – in an intricate way, saying he must find ways to clear himself of his family complexes and move into his own world. If Uranus is the planet of individuation, of becoming increasingly who we are, then Toby's Uranus is especially intricate. His natal Uranus is involved in a complex of midpoints: it is the direct midpoint of Neptune and the MC at 24° Leo, but that involves the Moon · MC midpoint as well, which implies that his ability to come into his own, to develop his unique place in the world, requires him to undergo several kinds of 'psychological births' – the initial emergence from the womb will need to be re-enacted several times over to give birth to himself repeatedly. His need for individuation out of the family system is strong with Uranus as the connecting planet to Moon, IC/MC and Neptune, but the ties to that family matrix are in strong competition and require superhuman strength and courage. We shall see that this self-birth is not just a fantasy in a psychologist's mind, but a reality in Toby's life.

For all Toby's apparent disengagement from the world, he has acted as an anchor for his mother. Barbara feels very strongly that if Toby had not been born, if she had not had him, she would have 'drifted off', she might not even have lived! His Saturn exactly on her own Neptune has seen to it that he places the burden of responsibility on her desire to float away and acts as an anchor to reality. The work, effort and time involved with Toby's life has both required and given Barbara tremendous strength – she recognizes this. As a transit himself, Toby is her Saturn on Neptune – his birth was a stark reminder that life will not allow Barbara to escape.

Toby's Sun has no major aspects; we might say that it is virtually unaspected but for the exact semi-sextile to Saturn – his solar purpose is not well-formed nor his ego-capacity very strong. When the Sun is unaspected, there are no specific or easily identifiable challenges to the ego to grow and contain the Self. If one has a Sun · Saturn square, then one's solar purpose has a strong, hard and very tangible challenge to it, similarly if the Sun is square to Mars – the Sun's aspects symbolize our capacity to see ourselves in some 'form', in a defined role, a stereotype replicated on an archetype. However, Toby is more in the archetypal realm and has not found a stereotype for his Sun/self/ego. He lives in the world of his deeper self and finds encounters with the external world repulsive and harsh; he has not been able to develop a solid ego, a container for this overflowing self. Since the father-archetype and the personal father himself is associated with solar imagery, then we would have to say that his father was not fated to provide the boundaries which would help his son climb out of the womb and into the world.

Toby's father is a Neptunian man himself, a Pisces Sun in opposition to the Moon · Neptune conjunction. The Sun · Jupiter conjunction is a key to his own desire for flight and is rather childlike, even puerile in some ways. Although he now is paying for Toby's education, and coping with that level of responsibility, still he is unable to create the paternal structures Toby himself declares he wants. At Christmas, 1994, Toby said, 'Why is Daddy so far away, like God in the sky – I pray to him, yes, I pray to him.' This was after a very difficult Christmas when mother, father and son were together. With a Sun · Jupiter in Pisces father, it would not be difficult for such a boy as Toby who literally dwells in the mysterious, archetypal world of symbols, myths and images to see this father as a celestial figure, a Zeus-Poseidon type. Such a father could easily appear to be in the heavens and shape-shifting, both compelling and fearsome! Toby had decided at that time that he did not like the sound of his father's voice – one wonders if it sounds like Woton! The sky-god booming down at him. Toby longs for this myth-ical father, yet fears him – truly the hero's legacy!

As we shall see, Toby is not the only one in the family with a mysterious father or no sense of origins – in fact, Toby's father might just be an im-provement in the line, and Toby, himself, both the mystery and the solution to a long line of enigmatic family secrets.

FAMILY SECRETS

There is a mystical streak in the family, a hidden factor, and every so often Scorpio or Pluto emerge (Barbara's mother Scorpio rising, her half-brother Moon conjunct Pluto, and finally Toby himself, a Scorpio). Primarily, the consistent thread is attached to Neptune and Pisces, a planet and sign as-sociated with the collective unconscious; the great sea of life; the 'sleep' zone in the zodiac; the end of a line; an elusive, shifting reality; the suffering victim or the saviour; the axis of the soul and body – where the soul and body are in some way profoundly emphasized. The Water family system always has an emotional undertow, with some members of the family either succumbing or mutating into an Earth or Fire dominance. There is also a strong Aries streak – Barbara's mother, grandmother and father are all Aries with Neptune/Uranus aspects – plenty of energy, with either nowhere or too many places to go.

Let's look back at the family line into which Toby was born: Barbara de-scribed her family as a 'collection of individuals'. On the surface it appears she has come from an extreme Uranian-type family – totally disengaged – but there is an undercurrent of unspoken messages, hints, subtleties and psychological manipulation which is characteristic of the Neptunian (and the Water) family. Both of these diverse family-types are present in the ex-treme, creating a deep schism in the collective, family psyche. Though the

Neptune theme is stronger by planet and sign, both family-types are fairly equally represented by aspects to Uranus. On the one hand there seem to be no boundaries between the deeper, psychic moods shared in the families and the mysteries. There is a deep, unconscious bond between all members of the family down the line, through enigmas and concealments in the history – each individual is enmeshed in the collective distortion. This self-deception and secretiveness is like a glue between the individuals in the family, and with each generation it grows geometrically and must, at some point, lodge in one member who becomes the 'symptom'.

But then, on the other hand, there is also a distinct sense of disengagement, as if no one really cares about anyone else and the family 'encourages' distance, separation, alienation, isolation and rifts between each other (Uranus). There exists between all members a profound subconscious, uncontained emotional bond, BUT when there *is* volition, action and motive, largely it is to disguise and hide people from each other – to separate them. It is as if feeling and experience are split off from each other. People in this family system cut other family members out, sever them from their lives, divorce or abandon them and either pretend that they never even existed, or re-create an existence which is based on falsehood!

Barbara does not speak to her mother or brother now, and the father, Richard, Toby's grandfather – the man who 'kept the family together' – died in 1988. In the maternal line no one now relates to anyone else, neither Barbara, her mother nor her brother. Barbara's family have always been feudal, in that sense, and she suffered terribly as a child and young woman from this lack of consistency. Let us now look at Barbara's mother's horoscope:

Barbara's mother, Anne (Figure 8), has a stellium in Aries starting with the Moon · Neptune square ending with a Sun · Uranus square! Barbara's father said she was an 'unattached motor' – quite a brilliant metaphor. With the exception of the generational Neptune in Cancer, Anne has no Water planets in her horoscope but has a Scorpio ascendant in the same degree as Toby's Mercury (which is conjunct Uranus). She has no solid contact with her feelings, as they are always shifting and changing. She appeared to be frightened of her feelings and, as an Aries, anger was a way of dealing with the fear. It is very likely that Anne has a deep revulsion to emotion, which results in the hot/cold aspect of her nature. The Scorpio ascendant alone, with no planets, in Water signs can be terribly manipulative and controlling of the people around her. Often when we see only Water on the ascendant and no planets in Water signs, the person is born to learn about feelings, they have no trust in their feeling-self, and find it very difficult to relate to highly emotional people. As a result, they compensate by attracting Watery types of people to them – marry them, give birth to them, and so on – and wonder what they are always emoting about!

Anne's inconstant, hysterical behaviour is born out of fear of her *own* feeling function, and her intense desire to avoid being the recipient of others' feelings. Barbara says her mother's moods were 'vast', wildly changing, she was a hysteric, to be short. This verdict is easily accepted when we see her lunar-emotional enmeshment in her own self, while at the same time her solar energy is erratic and wild, electrical and unpredictable (Moon square Neptune versus Sun square Uranus). Barbara wrote about her mother:

'I don't know if my mother was frightened of her feelings, she used to frighten the shit out of everyone else though, and I know she was terrified of her sexuality. After I told her I had been sexually abused by a neighbour (who I am convinced was also her lover, although I have no proof of this), she tried to smother me with a pillow, and the rage and fear I felt coming from her were worse to experience than the sensation of airlessness and death that my physical being was undergoing, and after this she quite deliberately made me (at three to four years old) carry the sexual and sensual side of her nature. She regularly beat me with anything that came to hand because of my 'knowingness' (!). I was the impure member of the family and she tried to make me feel guilty for it. Needless to say, I felt very confused, but guilty, no I certainly didn't. I was too little to know *why* the lie was, but I knew *what* it was and I wasn't taking it on.'

The time in which Toby was born was for Barbara a time of 'truth' – she was finally very angry with her mother, Anne, and the birth of Toby marked a virtual divorce, a separation with the mother who never acknowledged Barbara's 'truth of being'.

That Toby was born when Uranus had just been passing over his grandmother Anne's ascendant speaks of the year prior to and during Toby's birth as being highly disturbing – and also of the 'divorce' from her daughter. Toby's birth also brought Mercury to Anne's ascendant, and through Toby she was 'hearing' some news, getting some information, or perhaps Hermes/Mercury was about to play a trick on her through her grandchild. She herself had been a tricksterish mother, shape-shifting and secretive: Barbara has an elder brother, but his own biological real father is unknown to him. For the sake of confidentiality, I will call him John. He was born to

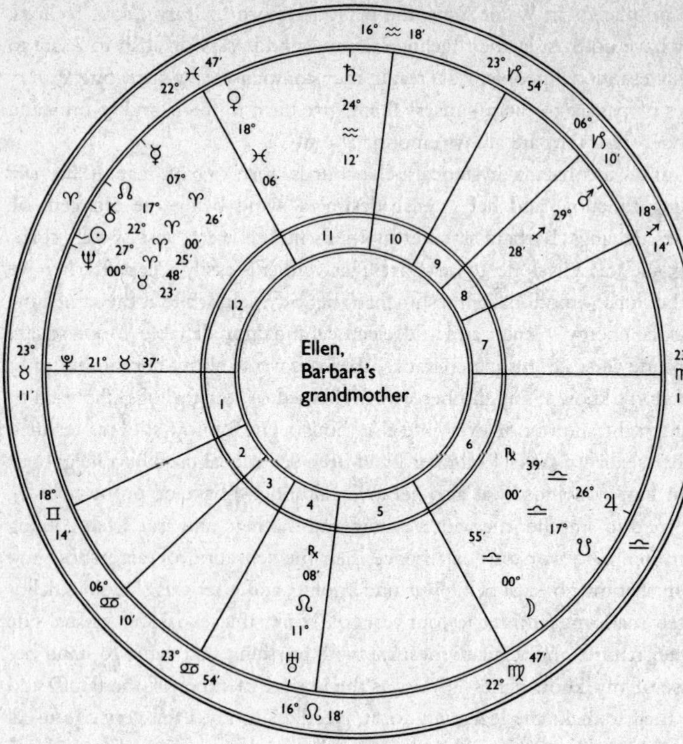

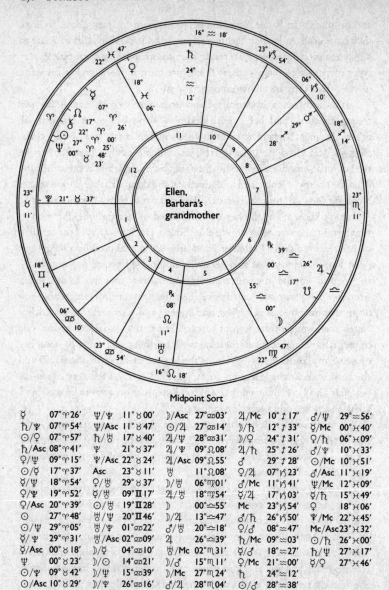

Midpoint Sort

☿	07°♈26′	♆/♇	11°♉00′	☽/Asc	27°♋03′	♃/Mc	10°♐17′	♂/♆	29°♒56′
♄/♇	07°♈54′	♆/Asc	11°♉47′	☉/♃	27°♋14′	☽/♄	12°♐33′	☿/Mc	00°♓40′
☉/♀	07°♈57′	♄/♅	17°♉40′	♃/♆	28°♋31′	☽/♀	24°♐31′	♀/♄	06°♓09′
♄/Asc	08°♈41′	♇	21°♉37′	♃/♇	09°♌08′	♃/♄	25°♐26′	♂/♇	10°♓33′
♀/♆	09°♈15′	♇/Asc	22°♉24′	♃/Asc	09°♌55′	♂	29°♐28′	☉/Mc	10°♓51′
☉/☿	17°♈37′	Asc	23°♉11′	♅	11°♌08′	♀/♃	07°♑23′	♂/Asc	11°♓19′
☿/♆	18°♈54′	♀/♅	29°♉37′	☽/♅	06°♍01′	♂/Mc	11°♑41′	♆/Mc	12°♓09′
♀/♇	19°♈52′	☿/♅	09°♊17′	♃/♅	18°♍54′	☿/♃	17°♑03′	☿/♄	15°♓49′
♀/Asc	20°♈39′	☉/♅	19°♊28′	☽	00°♎55′	Mc	23°♑54′	♀	18°♓06′
☉	27°♈48′	♅/♆	20°♊46′	☽/♃	13°♎47′	♂/♄	26°♑50′	♇/Mc	22°♓45′
☉/♆	29°♈05′	♅/♇	01°♋22′	♂/♅	20°♎18′	♀/♂	08°♒47′	Mc/Asc	23°♓32′
☿/♇	29°♈31′	♅/Asc	02°♋09′	♃	26°♎39′	♄/Mc	09°♒03′	☉/♄	26°♓00′
☿/Asc	00°♉18′	☽/☿	04°♋10′	♅/Mc	02°♏31′	☿/♂	18°♒27′	♄/♆	27°♓17′
♆	00°♉23′	☽/☉	14°♋21′	☽/♂	15°♏11′	♀/Mc	21°♒00′	☿/♀	27°♓46′
☉/♇	09°♉42′	☽/♆	15°♋39′	☽/Mc	27°♏24′	♄	24°♒12′		
☉/Asc	10°♉29′	☽/♇	26°♋16′	♂/♃	28°♏04′	☉/♂	28°♒38′		

Figure 10

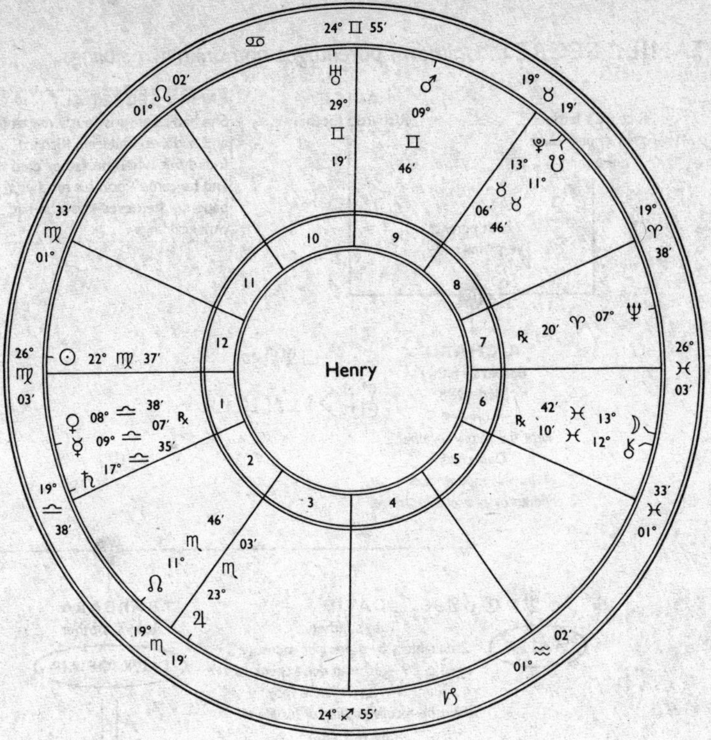

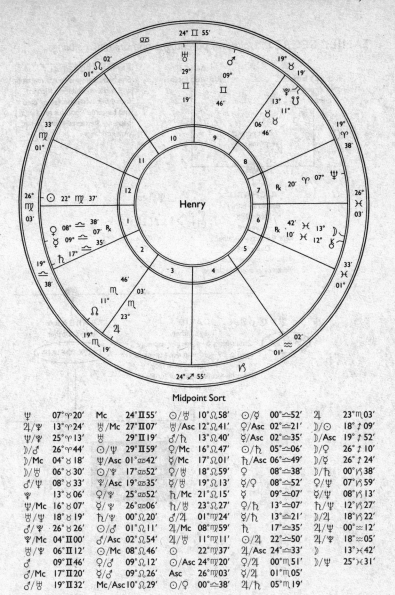

Midpoint Sort

♆	07°♈20′	Mc	24°♊55′	☉/♅	10°♌58′	☉/☿	00°♎52′	♃	23°♏03′
♃/♇	13°♈24′	♅/Mc	27°♊07′	♅/Asc	12°♌41′	♀/Asc	02°♎21′	☽/☉	18°♐09′
♆/♇	25°♈13′	♅	29°♊19′	♂/♄	13°♌40′	☿/Asc	02°♎35′	☽/Asc	19°♐52′
☽/♂	26°♈44′	☉/♆	29°♊59′	♀/Mc	16°♌47′	☉/♄	05°♎06′	☽/♀	26°♐10′
☽/Mc	04°♉18′	♆/Asc	01°♋42′	☿/Mc	17°♌01′	♄/Asc	06°♎49′	☽/☿	26°♐24′
☽/♅	06°♉30′	☉/♇	17°♋52′	♀/♅	18°♌59′	♀	08°♎38′	☽/♄	00°♑38′
♂/♆	08°♉33′	♇/Asc	19°♋35′	☿/♅	19°♌13′	☿/♀	08°♎52′	♀/♆	07°♑59′
♇	13°♉06′	♀/♇	25°♋52′	♄/Mc	21°♌15′	☿	09°♎07′	☿/♆	08°♑13′
♆/Mc	16°♉07′	☿/♇	26°♋06′	♄/♅	23°♌27′	♀/♄	13°♎07′	♄/♆	12°♑27′
♅/♆	18°♉19′	♄/♇	00°♌20′	♂/♃	01°♍24′	☿/♄	13°♎21′	☽/♃	18°♑22′
♂/♇	26°♉26′	☉/♂	01°♌11′	♃/Mc	08°♍59′	♄	17°♎35′	♃/♆	00°♒12′
♇/Mc	04°♊00′	♂/Asc	02°♌54′	♃/♅	11°♍11′	☉/♃	22°♎50′	♃/♇	18°♒05′
♅/♇	06°♊12′	☉/Mc	08°♌46′	☉	22°♍37′	♃/Asc	24°♎33′	☽	13°♓42′
♂	09°♊46′	♀/♂	09°♌12′	☉/Asc	24°♍20′	♀/♃	00°♏51′	☽/♆	25°♓31′
♂/Mc	17°♊20′	☿/♂	09°♌26′	Asc	26°♍03′	☿/♃	01°♏05′		
♂/♅	19°♊32′	Mc/Asc	10°♌29′	☉/♀	00°♎38′	♃/♄	05°♏19′		

Figure 11

FAMILY SECRET: *Unknown parentages and unknown siblings*

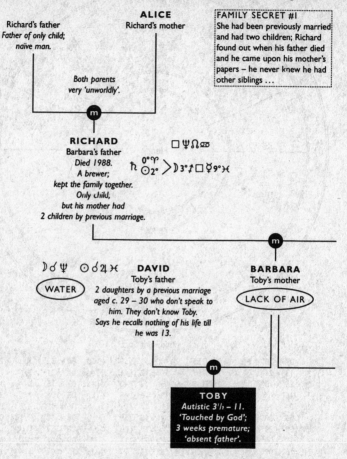

ALICE
Richard's mother

Richard's father
*Father of only child;
naïve man.*

*Both parents
very 'unworldly'.*

m

RICHARD
*Barbara's father
Died 1988.
A brewer;
kept the family together.
Only child,
but his mother had
2 children by previous marriage.*

DAVID
Toby's father
*2 daughters by a previous marriage
aged c. 29 – 30 who don't speak to
him. They don't know Toby.
Says he recalls nothing of his life till
he was 13.*

WATER

m

BARBARA
Toby's mother

LACK OF AIR

m

TOBY
*Autistic 3½ – 11.
'Touched by God';
3 weeks premature;
'absent father'.*

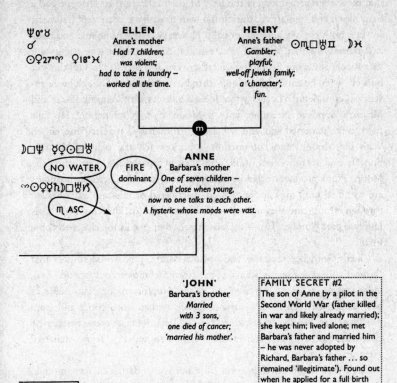

Ψ0°♉
♂
☉♀27°♈   ♀18°♓

ELLEN
Anne's mother
Had 7 children;
was violent;
had to take in laundry –
worked all the time.

HENRY
Anne's father
Gambler;
playful;
well-off Jewish family;
a 'character';
fun.

☉♏□♅♊   ☽♓

ⓜ

☽□Ψ ☿♀☉□♅

NO WATER

FIRE
dominant

♒☉♀♄☽□♅♈

♏ ASC

ANNE
Barbara's mother
One of seven children –
all close when young,
now no one talks to each other.
A hysteric whose moods were vast.

'JOHN'
Barbara's brother
Married
with 3 sons,
one died of cancer;
'married his mother'.

> FAMILY SECRET #2
> The son of Anne by a pilot in the
> Second World War (father killed
> in war and likely already married);
> she kept him; lived alone; met
> Barbara's father and married him
> – he was never adopted by
> Richard, Barbara's father ... so
> remained 'illegitimate'). Found out
> when he applied for a full birth
> certificate.

ZOË
Toby's half-sister
Difficult birth, mother almost died.
Unknown father;
very close to mother;
14 when Toby born.
Didn't get on with David (stepfather);
went to Australia to make new life.

Anne during the war. The father was a pilot who was killed and it is likely that he was a married man at the time of their relationship. That she had a baby alone and unmarried, during the war, must have been very traumatic for her, both socially and emotionally. However, when Anne met and married Barbara's father, Richard, they raised the boy without ever telling him that Richard was not his biological father. The boy was left to find this out himself when he applied for a long-form birth certificate! Though his horoscope is confidential, I can say that John is a Pisces with Venus in Pisces and Mercury opposite Neptune, with a Moon·Pluto conjunction! He falls right in the maternal line, and not distant from Toby's paternal line, either. With his Moon·Pluto conjunction, John has felt the pain of the dishonesty and secretiveness of his mother's Scorpio rising. Very often the Moon·Pluto produces a family secret of this nature, where birth origins are withheld until they are unearthed, discovered or in some way revealed through stealth, and the mother is the holder of a 'dark' secret. But this is family secret Number Two – there is yet another one in the closet to come forth!

Clearly, with her secretive and volatile nature, one would suspect that Barbara's mother must *also* have come from a complex background. And, indeed, Anne's parents *are* involved in this Neptunian·Uranian theme as well, as can be seen from a cursory glance at their horoscopes and from the Planetary Family Tree (pages 252–3). Let's look at these parents of Barbara's mother, Ellen and Henry (Figures 10 and 11), Toby's maternal great-grandparents.

Ellen had seven children, one of whom was Barbara's own mother, Anne. One problem with very large families is that the individuality of each child is often lost in the crowd – the parents simply don't have the time or the resources or the energy to foster the development of each child so specially. Anne's mother, Ellen, was a hard-working woman who, though married to a Jewish man from a well-off family, had to take in laundry and extra work to make up for the losses of her fun-loving, easy-going, gambling husband. She, like Barbara's mother and father, was an Aries, but with the Sun conjunct Neptune, and Venus in Pisces. Apparently she was physically abusive to her children, violent and obviously terribly frustrated, taking it out on the children, who banded together, becoming very close in that way while still at home, though that shattered as they each went their own way.

Ellen had a horrific death – she had fungating breast cancer which grew and grew; Barbara says, 'And that's where all that fire and energy went –

into that rampaging cancer that didn't eat her away, but ballooned her body hugely until it split. If I hadn't known all this, when I had cancer myself, I'd never have made the connection and would not have changed. And if I hadn't changed that's probably what would have happened to me.' (Another indication of 'circuit breaking' on Barbara's part.)

Ellen's husband, Henry, Anne's father, very likely has a Pisces Moon and very definitely has Venus · Mercury in opposition to Neptune! I am sure if we continued even further back with the family maps, we would find this Watery trail into infinity. The fun-loving Henry had a Pisces Moon and a Sun · Uranus square – is this where it all started or is this just part of an enduring theme? Henry, with his devil-may-care attitude towards family, money and time, was a real 'character'. He was fun, playful, called the children by various nicknames – Anne was 'Nancy' for instance – in short, he was a child himself! He was clearly the quicksilver Virgo whose wife became the victim and continued to perpetrate victim-females down the line. We see a hint of the rage that likely underscores the maternal line here with Ellen, where she, long-suffering, puts up with the silly husband and raises seven children, hand-washing other people's underwear. An Aries? What about the fire, the excitement, the executive power? Clearly it was never developed to the degree that she found an arena for her aggression, and it was meted out to the children through violence and abuse.

Skipping over to the paternal line, Barbara's father, Richard – married to Anne (see Figure 9) – has a Sun · Saturn conjunction in square to Neptune from Aries to Cancer. Of her father, Barbara says that 'he kept the family together'. Richard has several strong solar aspects, showing him to have a sense of duty and purpose, clearly applying his Sun · Saturn to the family objective, keeping the ties together, working very hard and taking on a great deal of responsibility. As an only child (so he thought), with his marriage to a woman who came from a seven-child family and who also had a son previous to meeting him, he falls into a fascinating place. Barbara describes him as a 'gentle, kind' man, his Sun · Saturn likely softened by the square to Neptune. Barbara has inherited his Saturn square to Neptune which is rather like being the 'holder (Saturn) of secrets (Neptune)'. Definitely Richard was the more benevolent parent for Barbara, and his contacts with Toby are also tied in with Saturn – between him, Barbara and Toby, their Saturns form a T-cross in cardinal signs – Aries, Cancer and Libra.

He was a brewer (Neptune) by profession later in his life, but a fireman when Barbara was born. We know a little about Richard's parents. Barbara remembers them, her paternal grandparents, and describes them as 'unworldly, naïve', rather not of this world; even the name 'Alice', as in Wonderland, was apt for her grandmother. Richard's father died first, but when his mother died, he discovered among her papers that she had not only been previously married, but had had two children! He knew nothing of this through his entire life, and by the time he discovered it, there would have been no point in pursuing it, as he was well advanced in his own age! Richard had two half-siblings whom he never knew. What other secrets they had will never be known now.

So Barbara's mother had had a son during the war, and raised him as Richard's child with his knowledge. It was kept a secret from the boy until he found out by accident when applying for a full birth certificate. And, back two generations, Barbara's own father's mother had had *two* children by a previous marriage, and *he* didn't find this out till his mother died and he came upon her papers. The family secret is the unknown father and mysterious children.

BACK TO TOBY: PRESENT TIME

It is as if all these mysterious secrets have been pooled into Toby, the Scorpio with the Moon · Neptune opposition ... he has become the 'circuit breaker', the one who carries the entire family complex and has upon him the onus of breaking the family fate. The resolution of the secrets, the openness of the family as it continues to work through Barbara, Zöe and the father, can only help to bring Toby out into the world. Toby seems to have been born to carry a great deal of this mystery – he is the only Scorpio in the entire family, although there have been hints of it coming down the line through Moon · Pluto, Scorpio ascendant, and his own mother's Sun · Pluto square.

When Barbara and I first met to discuss the relationship between her and Toby in April 1991, Pluto was transiting his Mercury and I felt that, autistic or not, his horoscope was a place of truth. The astrological realm does not know if the chart is one of a tree, a person or a project. If the chart is 'radical', that is, alive and breathing, then it works. Pluto over Mercury is a deep realization in all sensory layers. Pockets of information, knowledge, understanding are brought to light during its lengthy transit, and between that time and the autumn of 1993, there was a struggle to find Toby's place in an educational format that would assist in the birth of his sensory connection from the world inside him to the world outside him. At the same time, in 1991, the transit of Uranus was at Barbara's south node in the fourth house – it struck me that she was getting towards a point in unearthing the unknown fate which had beleaguered her family since as far back as we might go. Toby's ascendant is also 13° Capricorn, and his image, his persona, was shattering. An autistic persona is as good as any, but it seems that even *it* has to change! Toby was arriving at a point in his life where the process of individuation meant separating from his mother – just as with any ordinary pre-adolescent boy, it was time to begin the journey away from the mother and move towards a more independent environment. Although she appeared to be facing a fairly bleak couple of years of hard work and rejection by the system, her natural strength and her Sun · Pluto square was in motion – both she and Toby were beginning to reach a point of breaking.

However, a couple of endings and beginnings occurred in the autumn of 1993: Toby's sister left home and went abroad to work, and Toby was finally admitted to a Steiner school as a boarding student. The struggles with the various educational authorities while Pluto was still in his tenth house provided absolutely no support for him, but when the final pass of Pluto went over his natal Uranus and into his eleventh house, he was admitted to an alternative school where his needs are understood, his development encouraged and they are preparing him for the next level of his life with a long-range plan. The plan will continue through to the transit of Saturn over his ascendant, and his renewed sense of self and the ability to carry out responsibilities and act with volition seem now very possible.

October 1993 brought Saturn in Aquarius almost to the exact square to Pluto at 24° Scorpio – by January 1994, the final square of the eighteen-month process took place – right on Barbara's Moon. The long years of stress and aloneness had taken its toll. She began to have physical symptoms; her time alone, her time of release brought all the symptoms into the body while Saturn transited her sixth house through 1994 and 1995. Whereas Toby seems to be in a slow process of self-discovery, his mother's body is experiencing the retroactive effects of suffering and of being the victim of the family's suppressed anger. Her Mars at 21° Pisces in the sixth house fits right into a tight T-cross with Toby's Moon · Neptune, and undoubtedly there is a considerable amount of the family rage being felt through and because of Toby's own withdrawal and unwillingness to reach out and relate. Her own Aries planets, Venus and Mercury – both retrograde – are exactly conjoined her maternal grandmother's north node and Chiron. The woman who had the seven children and produced Barbara's raging mother has something to do with this. As things can skip a generation, the suffering of the pioneering woman lies unrewarded and her hardworking nature has been handed on to Barbara (Barbara's Mars in Pisces opposite to Jupiter in Virgo is tied into her grandmother's Venus in Pisces, as well).

The teachers at the school have tested Toby and feel that he has not been formally autistic since he was around eleven, that he is slowly coming towards himself in a way which will allow him to be productive and more involved in his world. In Oliver Sacks's book, he makes an interesting comment: '. . . in a strange way, most people speak only of autistic children and never autistic adults, as if the children just vanished from the earth. But though there may indeed be a devastating picture at the age of three, some autistic youngsters, contrary to expectations, may go on to develop fair language, a modicum of social skills, and even high . . . achievements . . .' It is likely that the adult autistics have all been institutionalized or marginalized to the degree that any abilities or talents they might have had inherently have lain dormant and made them quite crazy. Sacks goes on to say that there are two primary types of autism; that in one of them, Asperger's, individuals can go on to tell us of inner experiences, feelings and perceptions, while those with classical autism cannot. Toby *is* a communicator – he *does* have an inner world which is beginning to be shared. He tells his mother and sister how it is with him, and he is beginning to sort out his inner self with respect to his feelings about his parents. This is all quite normal behaviour for a thirteen-year-old boy. He is not doing it in the consensus 'right' way, though. He has a complex psychology and a very perceptive nature, and, though he is more than likely to develop a gift, an interest and become part of the world, he is very likely not ever to like or relate to the outer world as much as the safe place in which he corrals himself.

Sacks also says that autism is connected to historical oddities in families, like dyslexia, obsessive-compulsive disorders, attention-focus problems, Tourette's syndrome and so on.

What we don't know enough of is the astrological patterning in cases of autism, and the family connections in that way. However, there is a sense with Toby's astrological family tree that a build-up of escapism (Neptune) finally needed a psychological container. One gets the feeling that Toby, rather than just growing up to yell at his children or drink and gamble or have seven children and be angry and long-suffering or have children that no one knew about, and so on, may have just decided to defect from it all and say to everyone, 'Go figure.'

Further, it is said that autism does not 'go away', regardless of development beyond the isolated, withdrawn, raging level of the young autistic. There always remains a removed aura, a touch of other-worldliness, perhaps a god-like lack of human emotion. Uta Frith, another person well-versed in autism, has postulated that there is a kind of rarefied purity to the socially developed autistic, and that it is possible that very unsullied, high-level intellects and saints might just have been this way; that there is a 'sort of moral or intellectual intensity or purity, so far removed from the normal as to seem noble, ridiculous or fearful to the rest of us'.[5]

That the autistic person finds touch, emotion, relationship and all forms of intimacy repulsive sounds like a family trait *in extremis*, a kind of condensed, concentrated psychic product which has lodged itself in the psyche and body of Toby. There is a distinct development in the family line towards something that will find an extreme way of expressing the revulsion and rejection of family issues. There are hidden children, children given away (or died?) and not talked about, mothers who abuse their children, fathers who don't want or understand their children, and so on. Toby's father has two adult children from a previous marriage, for instance, whom he has no contact with.

This is very Uranian-sounding to an astrologer. To be 'pure', removed, elevated and without the mortal tie to emotion is to be with the god Ouranos, who was repulsed by the world of form, by the sheer physicality of his monstrous offspring – the Hekatonchires – whom he refused birth. His wife, Gaia, straining under their urgency to be born, employs her first-born son Kronos – Saturn – to castrate her husband, Ouranos, and allow the monstrous beings birth. Uranus, the planet, stands for that kind of emotionless, cold, distant, observant but inhuman form of relating.

Toby's family has this touch of Uranianism – a distaste for familiarity, for intimacy, a fear of emotion, abandoning each other, an indulgence in self-absorption and very little capacity for generosity or growth through relating. His Taurus mother has been a kind of Gaia, an earth-woman with a child unwanted by his father, giving birth to him anyway, with the midwife as Saturn (Toby's Saturn is on her Neptune), as if to say, 'I might not suit the ideal fantasy of my father, but my mother will have me no matter how I am.' Toby is imperfect, unacceptable, possibly frightening and repulsive to his idealistic father. In turn, Toby has acted very like Saturn in that his birth has been the divorce of the earthy mother (Taurus) and the celestial father (Sun · Jupiter in Pisces); while his imperfections are repellent to his father, they are in fact, a deep connection to his mother.[6]

Autism might, in fact, be normal. To an autistic person, *he* is normal, other people are not. There is much negative focus on the problems that autistic people have in their environment, and their behaviour is very frightening to their parents – parents don't like to be rejected, either. There is so much of this fear and negativity that a great deal of the potential positive in the autistic person does not get focused on and developed. The possibility that their social defects have outweighed their potential gifts seems quite likely. Ours is a world of convenience. Autistic people are inconvenient. They will not behave. However, now there is a greater understanding of the relative norm, thanks to R. D. Laing, who was quite mad himself. And today there is much more likelihood that the autistic child can become the autistic adult, a functional, contributing adult in a world of millions of types.

Summary

o The family picture is eloquent, both in the horoscopes presented and in the *JigSaw* graphs included to dramatize the collective pattern as it emerges through this family as an organic unit.

o We have seen an inordinate amount of Moon/Neptune and Pisces, but also the dominance in the ancestral line of Aries and Mars. This is why the Elemental Graph and the Modal Graph of *JigSaw* comes up with the Cardinal and the Fire as being dominant.

o Though the 'weak element' is earth, Bernadette Brady (creatrix of the *JigSaw* program) wrote to me, in a letter accompanying her graphs: 'With Toby, the lack of earth in his group is not very significant re statistics. X^2 result of only a one in five probability, however, the tenth house stress in his family is VERY significant. Too much stress over *too* many generations. Fits in with your title, *Dynasty*.'

o The Cardinality and the tenth house manifestation of too much weight, and Toby's major configurations occurring in that house, mark him as the one who has become the turning point in the 'too much stress over too many generations'.

o Recall that in the 'Fourth House' section (page 180) I mentioned that the product of the fourth lies in the tenth – well, here it is. The secret, inmost place, the fourth house will 'out' in the tenth. Whatever the family is holding in its genes or psyche will demonstrate itself in our tenth house of public awareness. We project our unconscious IC into the MC for tangibility. A Capricorn, Cardinal, Earth house, ruled by Saturn, the planet of incarnation and embodiment, is the solid reality-frame of the mysterious Cancer, Cardinal, Water house ruled by the Moon in the house of deep, personal ancestral lineage. As Melanie Reinhart (author of *Chiron: The Healing Journey*) said about the fourth house: 'We should call the IC the "I don't C".'

o Most importantly, we have seen how a woman has come to terms with her own self, and in doing so, her son has become communicative within his own very close boundaries.

Addenda

The following figures are the graphs from the *JigSaw* program and a brief delineation of them follows:

FIGURE 12 The harmonic scan shows a Venus/Saturn link with all members of the included family (primarily maternal line) in the sixth harmonic. This is a boundary problem, one which needs to be established firmly – Venus and Saturn – but in the sixth harmonic implicates the function of creativity and communications. The harmonic creates a series of sextiles. Toby has an out-of-sign conjunction of Venus and Saturn. He has created a wall, not a boundary. (Bernadette Brady said, after the fact of this case, that she has also found Venus/Saturn in autistic families.)

FIGURE 13 The house emphasis of the group is tenth – 'too much stress over too many generations' – and we find this in the Kennedy family (page 378) as well as a strong secondary weight. Basically, the family needed 'outing'; the closet of the fourth house was getting pretty crowded.

FIGURE 14 This is the zodiacal sort, resulting in a dominance of a zodiacal degree. Each of the points actually equals five degrees (to make it easier to see, therefore multiply each number by five, coming up with the dominant degree). In this case, 5 × 6 = 30 which is 0° Taurus as the dominant collective degree of the zodiac (ruled by Venus, but also very close to the last degree of Aries, which shows as a strong focus by Element and Mode). 25° Taurus is the second 'spike' in this graph (Toby's Uranus is at the 25th degree of Scorpio) – breakaway, individuate out of the family matrix and break the patterns, shatter the composure and rigidity of the Taurus sign type. Of them all, he is the 'individual shaman'.

FIGURE 15 The elemental weights are not remarkably imbalanced – a slight leaning to the Fire, with Earth being less occupied. Actually, this is a signature that too much homeostasis has endured for too long. (Again, see the perfect balance of the Kennedys – something has to give.)

FIGURE 16 The modal weights show Cardinal as the main occupied zone – this speaks of something in the genes, something organic in the family blood-line that will out in some person who has embodied the congestion in the family. (See Chapter 8, 'The Modal Family', page 151.)

FIGURE 17 This graph is a bit more exotic than the bar or wheel-type graphs. And it also requires a more careful look. It portrays the sixth harmonic signatures of Venus and Saturn, which the computer actually finds itself. The data is entered and the computer scans every harmonic along with the planets of the entered data of the whole group (family and powerful events, and so forth). It then produces a chart such as this, where we can look at each individual, or event, and see what is its strongest harmonic connection to the whole.

Initially, I had thought there would be a Neptune/Mercury or Moon contact to thread through the family; however, what has come out is a Venus/Saturn contact in the sixth harmonic. This is interesting on several levels: first, the sixth harmonic implies that something is workable, that there is a level of communication which has creative potential. And second, it tells us something about autism – that it is *not* a communication problem (as we would expect with, say, Mercury/Neptune) or a 'disability' *per se* or a form of madness. It is an indication of alienation and limited ability for relationship. For all the overt Moon/Neptune and Piscean/Mutable themes in this family complex, the intra-dimensional tie is Venus and Saturn: sadness, love denied, alienation, lack of relatedness, and so forth. And Toby, who has Saturn in Libra and a 'split-off' Moon, has embodied the collective alienation of generations of lost fathers, family secrets and missing siblings.

See the Appendix and the graphs for the Kennedy family for some further notes on *JigSaw* graphic patterns. (page 376)

NOTES

1. See the case on adoption in Mohsin's story, page 270. The sequence of pre-natal eclipses is very closely bound up with the adoptive parents.

2. Oliver Sacks, *An Anthropologist on Mars*, Picador, London, 1995, page 181.

3. ibid.

4. ibid., page 242.

5. ibid., page 241.

6. For further information on autism, see the Bibliography, page 388.

JigSaw 1.0 – Family/Group Research Report

Project Title: **Erin Sullivan's Toby data**
SubTitle: **Enabled Records**

Tropical Zodiac – Geocentric Coordinates – True Node

Search Pts: ♀ ♄ ♀/♄
Harmonics: 6 to 9 – 1st Harmonic Orb = ±10°00'
Position: Any
Matches: 3+ To Any Combination of Search Points

Selected Match
6th Hm – 5 Hits – 5 Charts – 59°46' ±1°40' – 2 4 1 6 3

Charts in Match
2 – ♀/♄ at 58°45' (28° ♉ 45') Barbara – Toby's mother
4 – ♄ at 59°37' (29°♓37') Zoe –toby's half sister by another father
1 – ♀/♄ at 0°17' (00°♎17') Toby Autistic son
6 – ♄ at 0°29' (00°♈29') Richard – Toby's maternal grandfather
3 – ♀ at 0°47' (00°♒47') Father

Data File: **C:\JIGSAW\USERDATA\TOBY.DAT**
Saved: **Jul 7 1995 4:32 pm**

List of Enabled Records

1. Toby Autistic son	27 Oct 1980	USZ3 −04:00
11:40 am, 25N18 055E18 Dubai		
2. Barbara – Toby's mother	21 Apr 1945	BWT −02:00
5:45 pm, 51N31 000W10 Croydon UK		
3. Father	6 Mar 1939	GMT +0:00
6:00 am, 51N31 000W10 London UK		
4. Zoe –toby's half sister by another father	2 Jul 1966	BST −1:00
12:20 pm, 51N31 000W10 Croydon UK		
5. Anne –Toby's maternal grandmother	18 Apr 1909	GMT +0:00
9:00 pm, 51N31 000W10 London		
6. Richard – Toby's maternal grandfather	23 Mar 1908	GMT +0:00
7. Ellen –Maternal great grandmother	18 Apr 1875	GMT +0:00
8. Henry –Maternl great grandfather	15 Sep 1864	GMT +0:00

Figure 12

Jigsaw 1.0 – Research Polar Graph

Project Title:	Erin Sullivan's Toby data				
SubTitle:	Enabled Records				

Zodiac:	Tropical	Divisions of:	Houses	Harmonic:	1
Coords:	Geocentric	Division Type:	House	Modulus:	360°00'
Houses:	Placidus	No. Divisions:	12	Total Charts	8
Node Type:	True	Anchor Point:	n/a	Points Used:	300

Avg Count = 25.00
Division = 10th House
Count = 60
Chi Sq (11) = 49.0
Prob. = 1 in 1083385

ALL POINTS

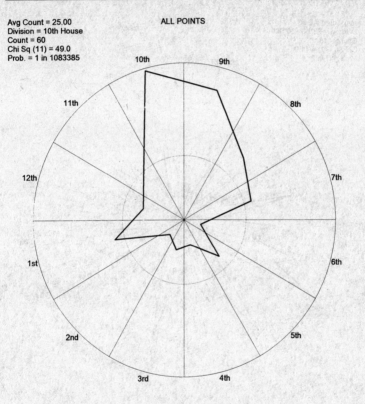

Figure 13

JigSaw 1.0 – Research Polar Graph

Project Title:	Erin Sullivan's Toby data				
SubTitle:	Enabled Records				

Zodiac:	Tropical	Divisions of:	Longitude	Harmonic:	1
Coords:	Geocentric	Division Type:	User Defined	Modulus:	360°00'
Houses:	Placidus	No. Divisions:	72	Total Charts	8
Node Type:	True	Anchor Point:	0°00'	Points Used:	470

Avg Count = 6.53
Division = 25°00'–30°00'
Count = 15
Chi Sq (71) = 11.0
Prob. = 1 in 2

ALL POINTS

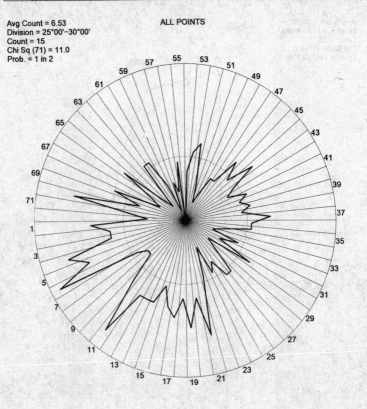

Figure 14

JigSaw 1.0 – Research Bar Graph

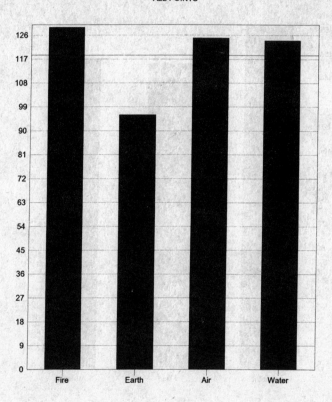

Figure 15

JigSaw 1.0 – Research Bar Graph

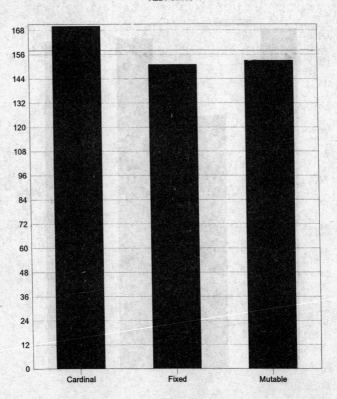

| Project Title: | Erin Sullivan's Toby data | | | | |
| SubTitle: | Enabled Records | | | | |

Zodiac:	Tropical	Divisions of:	Longitude	Harmonic:	1
Coords:	Geocentric	Division Type:	Mode	Modulus:	360°00'
Houses:	Placidus	No. Divisions:	3	Total Charts	8
Node Type:	True	Anchor Point:	0°00'	Points Used:	474

ALL POINTS

Figure 16

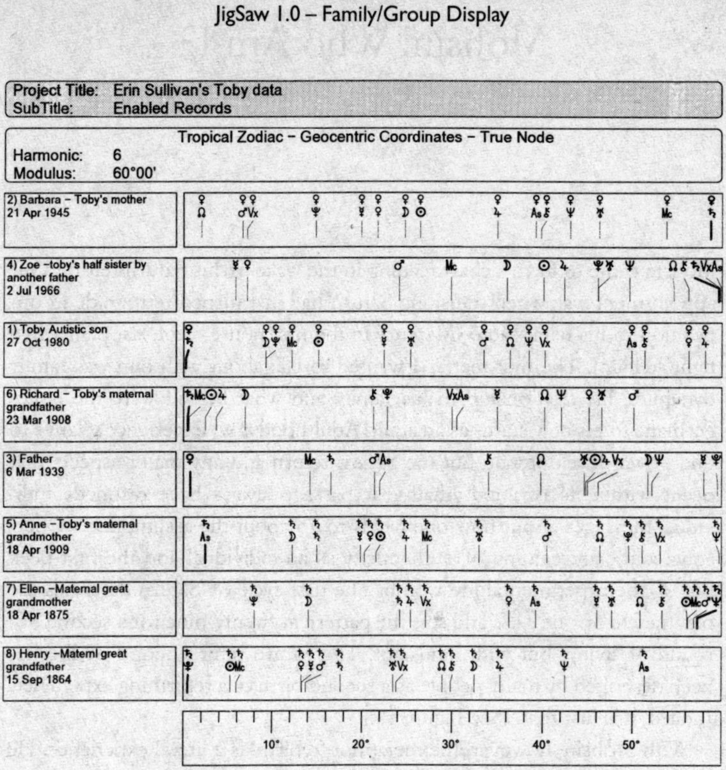
JigSaw 1.0 – Family/Group Display
Project Title: Erin Sullivan's Toby data
SubTitle: Enabled Records
Tropical Zodiac – Geocentric Coordinates – True Node
Harmonic: 6
Modulus: 60°00'
2) Barbara – Toby's mother
21 Apr 1945
4) Zoe –toby's half sister by another father
2 Jul 1966
1) Toby Autistic son
27 Oct 1980
6) Richard – Toby's maternal grandfather
23 Mar 1908
3) Father
6 Mar 1939
5) Anne –Toby's maternal grandmother
18 Apr 1909
7) Ellen –Maternal great grandmother
18 Apr 1875
8) Henry –Materni great grandfather
15 Sep 1864
10°
20°
30°
40°
50°

Figure 17

14.
Mohsin: Who Am I?

Mohsin came to have a chart reading in the wake of his Saturn return. Our appointment was when transiting Saturn had just turned retrograde in opposition to his natal Pluto · Mercury in the first house – the last planet in a tight stellium. The first matter I wanted to talk about with him was family dynamics, his relationship to his family and what he felt were the issues germane to his new status as an adult. Adulthood is an experience relative to one's own development, but the Saturn return and any major aspects that occur within its two-and-a-half-year passage always have distinctly individual messages about how one needs to go about the assumption of personal authority, gaining of authenticity as an individual and the first peek out of the experimental life-womb. The first cycle of Saturn describes the parameters of one's life and sets the pattern at twenty-nine for a second go-round of living, but with hindsight. The Saturn return period of life has been described by many people as a second birth or a rebirthing experience. Indeed, it is just that. (See Figure 18.)

With Mohsin, however, the metaphor 'rebirth' is a literal experience. He has Neptune at the IC at 15° Scorpio, Sun rising in opposition to Saturn and the Uranus · Mercury · Pluto conjunction following the Sun – all in the first house. The first house is one's arrival on the planet and one's encounter with the world. It is also one's status in the family – the angles are the origins of life, but the ascendant in particular talks about one's reception into life and one's place in the family. Considering the astrological context in which the initial consultation was occurring – Saturn had just stationed in opposition to his natal Pluto and would pass back over it for the final transit in the last week of February 1995 – I wanted to be especially careful about uncovering too much, too soon, and since the Saturn cycle is so closely analogous with the gestation cycle (nine months long) and we were only at conception, it was essential to be cautious about implanting negative suggestions and act more as a midwife of potential.

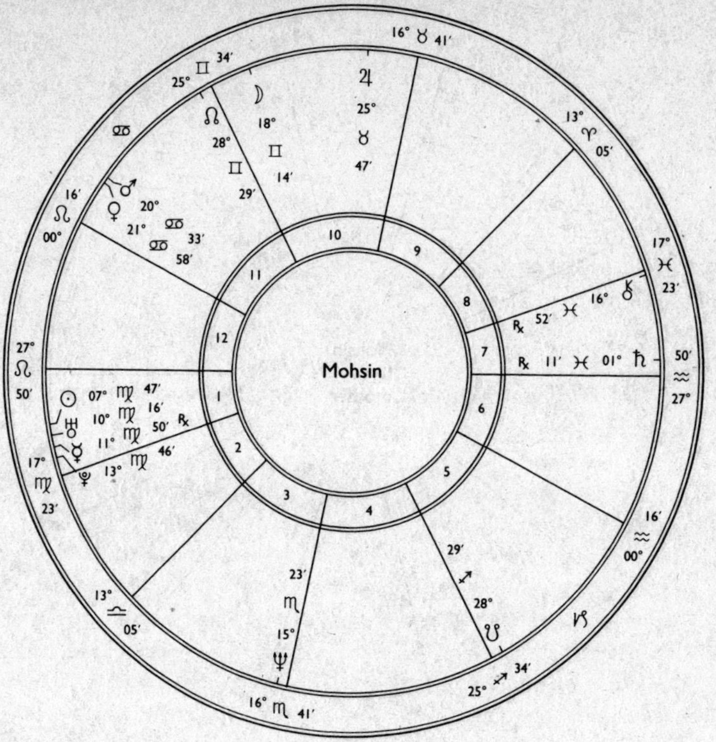

Midpoint Sort

♄/Mc	08°♈56′	☽/♂	04°♋24′	☽/☉	28°♋01′	Asc	27°♌50′	♂/♆	17°♍58′
♃/♄	13°♈29′	☽/♀	05°♋06′	☽/♅	29°♋15′	☽/♆	01°♍49′	♀/♆	18°♍40′
☽/♄	24°♈43′	Mc/Asc	07°♋15′	☽/☿	00°♌02′	☉/Asc	02°♍49′	♆/Asc	06°♎37′
♂/♄	10°♉52′	♃/Asc	11°♋48′	☽/♇	01°♌00′	♅/Asc	04°♍03′	☉/♆	11°♎35′
♀/♄	11°♉34′	☉/Mc	12°♋14′	♂/Asc	09°♌12′	☿/Asc	04°♍50′	♅/♆	12°♎50′
Mc	16°♉41′	♅/Mc	13°♋28′	♀/Asc	09°♌54′	♇/Asc	05°♍48′	☿/♆	13°♎37′
♃/Mc	21°♉14′	☿/Mc	14°♋15′	☉/♂	14°♌10′	☉	07°♍47′	♆/♇	14°♎34′
♃	25°♉47′	♇/Mc	15°♋13′	☉/♀	14°♌52′	☉/♅	09°♍02′	♆	15°♏23′
♄/Asc	29°♉31′	☉/♃	16°♋47′	♂/♅	15°♌25′	☉/☿	09°♍49′	☉/♄	04°♐29′
☽/Mc	02°♊27′	♃/♅	18°♋01′	♆/Mc	16°♌02′	♅	10°♍16′	♄/♅	05°♐44′
☽/♃	07°♊00′	☿/♃	18°♋48′	♀/♅	16°♌07′	☉/♇	10°♍46′	☿/♄	06°♐31′
☽	18°♊14′	♃/♇	19°♋46′	☿/♂	16°♌12′	☿/♅	11°♍03′	♄/♇	07°♐28′
♂/Mc	18°♊37′	♂	20°♋33′	☿/♀	16°♌54′	☿	11°♍50′	♄/♆	08°♑17′
♀/Mc	19°♊19′	♀/♂	21°♋16′	♂/♇	17°♌09′	♅/♇	12°♍01′	♄	01°♓11′
♂/♃	23°♊10′	♀	21°♋58′	♀/♇	17°♌52′	☿/♇	12°♍48′		
♀/♃	23°♊52′	☽/Asc	23°♋02′	♃/♆	20°♌35′	♇	13°♍46′		

Figure 18

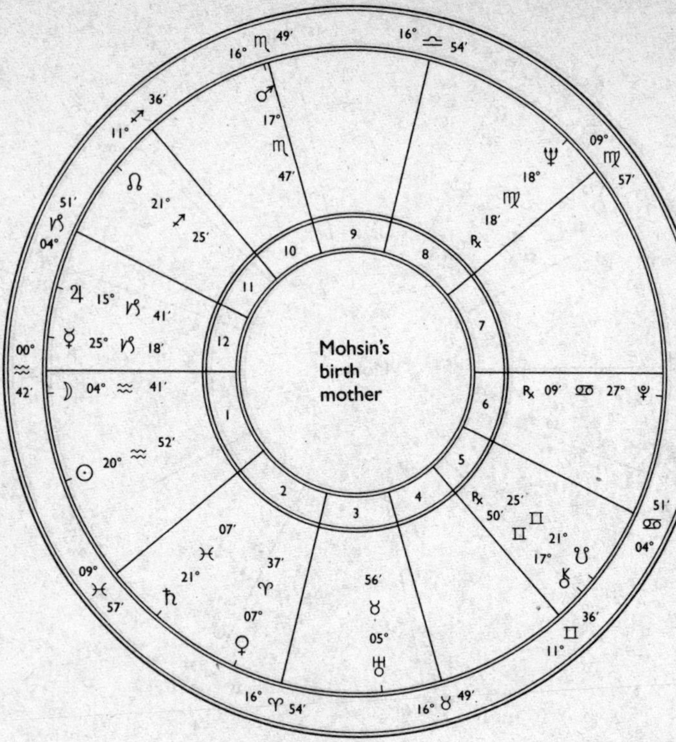

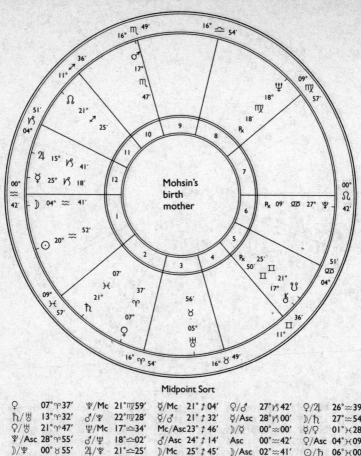

Midpoint Sort

♀	07°♈37′	♇/Mc	21°♍59′	☿/Mc	21°♐04′	♀/♂	27°♑42′	♀/♃	26°♒39′
♄/♅	13°♈32′	♂/♇	22°♍28′	☿/♂	21°♐32′	☿/Asc	28°♑00′	☽/♄	27°♒54′
♀/♅	21°♈47′	♆/Mc	17°♎34′	Mc/Asc	23°♐46′	☽/☿	00°♒00′	☿/♀	01°♓28′
♇/Asc	28°♈55′	♂/♆	18°♎02′	♂/Asc	24°♐14′	Asc	00°♒42′	♀/Asc	04°♓09′
☽/♇	00°♉55′	♃/♇	21°♎25′	☽/Mc	25°♐45′	☽/Asc	02°♒41′	☉/♄	06°♓00′
♅	05°♉56′	☿/♇	26°♎13′	☽/♂	26°♐14′	☉/♃	03°♒17′	☽/♀	06°♓09′
☉/♇	09°♉01′	Mc	16°♏49′	☉/Mc	03°♑51′	☽	04°♒41′	♃/♅	10°♓49′
♄/♇	24°♉08′	♃/♆	17°♏00′	☉/♂	04°♑20′	☉/☿	08°♒05′	☉/♀	14°♓15′
♀/♇	02°♊23′	♂/Mc	17°♏18′	♃	15°♑41′	☉/Asc	10°♒47′	☿/♅	15°♓37′
♅/♇	16°♊33′	♂	17°♏47′	♄/Mc	18°♑58′	♅/Mc	11°♒23′	♅/Asc	18°♓19′
♄/♆	19°♊43′	☿/♆	21°♏48′	♂/♄	19°♑27′	♂/♅	11°♒52′	☽/♅	20°♓19′
♀/♆	27°♊58′	♆/Asc	24°♏30′	☿/♃	20°♑30′	☽/☉	12°♒47′	♄	21°♓07′
♅/♆	12°♋07′	☽/♆	26°♏30′	♃/Asc	23°♑11′	♃/♄	18°♒24′	☉/♅	28°♓24′
♇	27°♋09′	☉/♆	04°♐35′	☽/♃	25°♑11′	☉	20°♒52′	♀/♄	29°♓22′
♆/♇	22°♌43′	♃/Mc	16°♐15′	☿	25°♑18′	☿/♄	23°♒13′		
♆	18°♍18′	♂/♃	16°♐44′	♀/Mc	27°♑13′	♄/Asc	25°♒55′		

Figure 19

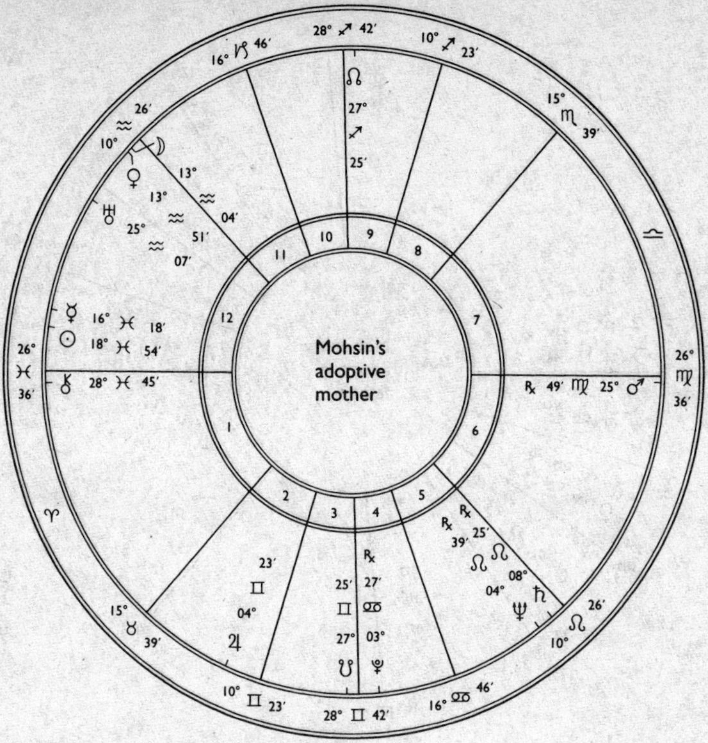

Midpoint Sort

☽/♃	08°♈43′	♇/Asc	15°♉01′	♂/♃	00°♌06′	☉/♂	22°♐22′	☽/☉	00°♓59′
♀/♃	09°♈07′	♄/♅	16°♉46′	♆	04°♌39′	Mc	28°♐42′	☉/♀	01°♓23′
♃/♅	14°♈45′	☿/♆	25°♉29′	♄/♆	06°♌32′	☽/Mc	20°♑53′	☽/Asc	04°♓50′
☽/♇	23°♈15′	☉/♆	26°♉47′	♄	08°♌25′	♀/Mc	21°♑17′	♀/Asc	05°♓13′
♀/♇	23°♈39′	☿/♄	27°♉22′	♂/♇	14°♌38′	♅/Mc	26°♑55′	☿/♅	05°♓43′
☿/♃	25°♈20′	☉/♄	28°♉40′	♂/♆	00°♍14′	☿/Mc	07°♒30′	☉/♅	07°♓01′
☉/♃	26°♈38′	♆/Asc	00°♊38′	♂/♄	02°♍07′	☉/Mc	08°♒48′	♅/Asc	10°♓51′
♅/♇	29°♈17′	♄/Asc	02°♊30′	♂	25°♍49′	Mc/Asc	12°♒39′	☿	16°♓18′
♃/Asc	00°♉29′	♃	04°♊23′	♇/Mc	01°♎04′	☽	13°♒04′	♃/Mc	16°♓32′
☽/♆	08°♉52′	♃/♇	18°♊55′	♆/Mc	16°♎41′	☽/♀	13°♒28′	☉/☿	17°♓36′
♀/♆	09°♉15′	♂/Asc	26°♊12′	♄/Mc	18°♎34′	♀	13°♒51′	☉	18°♓54′
☿/♇	09°♉52′	♇	03°♋27′	♂/Mc	12°♏15′	☽/♅	19°♒06′	☿/Asc	21°♓27′
☽/♄	10°♉45′	♃/♆	04°♋31′	☽/♂	04°♐27′	♀/♅	19°♒29′	☉/Asc	22°♓45′
♀/♄	11°♉08′	♃/♄	06°♋24′	♀/♂	04°♐50′	♅	25°♒07′	Asc	26°♓36′
☉/♇	11°♉10′	♆/♇	19°♋03′	♂/♅	10°♐28′	☽/☿	29°♒41′		
♅/♆	14°♉53′	♄/♇	20°♋56′	☿/♂	21°♐03′	☿/♀	00°♓05′		

Figure 20

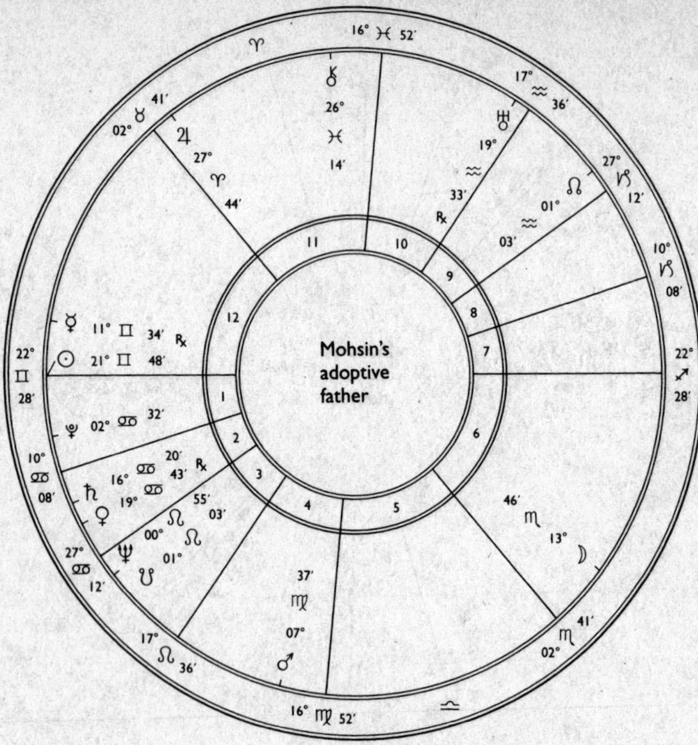

Midpoint Sort

☿/Mc	14°♈35′	☉/♃	24°♉46′	☿/♀	00°♋39′	♄/♆	23°♋37′	☽/♀	16°♍45′
☿/♅	15°♈34′	♃/Asc	25°♉06′	♇	02°♋32′	☿/♂	24°♋36′	☽/♆	22°♍20′
☉/Mc	19°♈42′	♃/♇	00°♊08′	♂/♃	02°♋41′	♀/♆	25°♋19′	☽/♂	10°♎41′
Mc/Asc	20°♈02′	♃/♄	07°♊02′	☉/♄	04°♋04′	☉/♂	29°♋42′	☽	13°♏46′
☉/♅	20°♈40′	♀/♃	08°♊44′	♄/Asc	04°♋24′	♂/Asc	00°♌02′	♂/Mc	27°♏37′
♅/Asc	21°♈01′	☿	11°♊34′	☉/♀	05°♋45′	♆	00°♌55′	♂/♅	28°♏35′
♇/Mc	25°♈04′	♃/♆	14°♊19′	♀/Asc	06°♋06′	♂/♇	05°♌05′	☽/Mc	00°♑41′
♅/♇	26°♈03′	☉/☿	16°♊41′	☿/♆	06°♋14′	♂/♄	11°♌58′	☽/♅	01°♑40′
♃	27°♈44′	☿/Asc	17°♊01′	♄/♇	09°♋26′	♀/♂	13°♌40′	☽/♃	05°♒45′
♄/Mc	01°♉58′	☉	21°♊48′	♀/♇	11°♋08′	♂/♆	19°♌16′	Mc	17°♒36′
♄/♅	02°♉57′	☿/♇	22°♊03′	☉/♆	11°♋21′	☽/☿	27°♌40′	♅/Mc	18°♒35′
♀/Mc	03°♉40′	☉/Asc	22°♊08′	♆/Asc	11°♋41′	☽/☉	02°♍47′	♅	19°♒33′
♀/♅	04°♉38′	Asc	22°♊28′	♄	16°♋20′	☽/Asc	03°♍07′	♃/Mc	22°♓40′
♆/Mc	09°♉15′	☉/♇	27°♊10′	♆/♇	16°♋43′	♂	07°♍37′	♃/♅	23°♓39′
♅/♆	10°♉14′	♇/Asc	27°♊30′	♀/♄	18°♋01′	☽/♇	08°♍09′		
☿/♃	19°♉39′	☿/♄	28°♊57′	♀	19°♋43′	☽/♄	15°♍03′		

Figure 21

I felt that the 'gestation period' of Mohsin's new Saturn-return self was in the most nascent stages and that the most illuminating time was yet to come. A premature delivery is never a good thing. Exposing the infant psyche is not always a method of strengthening it! However, Mohsin was not only astrologically fairly literate, he had already been delving deeply into the very things which I felt to be sensitive and volatile – in other words, he was ready to be conscious, yet again, of another level of his search for identity.

The fourth house (IC) is the soul of the chart, the ancestral line of the family of origin, the history of the family and the individual's relationship within that dynastic line. Family secrets; genetic disposition – DNA; psychological lineage; patterns of parenting – including one's own future parenting issues; one's family fate and one's job within that; one's treasure of self-identity; all these things, and more, lie in the nadir of the horoscope.[1] With Neptune there, in the middle degree of Scorpio, I suspected a mystery, something unknown, perhaps a veil over or a cloud around his conscious knowledge of his family history or lineage. Also, Neptune might mean coming from a different family of origin than one had thought. I might add that there is some danger in wading in with this kind of information, initiating a first-time consultation with such a ripe topic, but I already knew that Mohsin was himself an adept if novice astrologer, so he would be expecting real astrology.

Starting the consultation openly with Neptune and privately worrying about the first house configurations all opposite Saturn singleton-retrograde on the horizon, I asked him if there was a mixed message to him from his parents, his father in particular, about his capacity to achieve – I suspected on one hand that his father had had great expectations from him, but undermined them as they were expressed. Rather like saying, 'You can do anything you put your mind to, son, but I rather doubt you will.' That kind of message. Indeed, the response was yes. His separated Saturn openly reveals his sense of isolation and his 'ivory-tower' consciousness, walled-off from others and feeling as if he is the odd one out, peering in through the windows at other people's happiness – Saturn in Pisces also creates the fantasy of other people's happiness in contrast to one's own imprisonment in solitary confinement. However, there is always some unconscious collusion in the family system which validates such innate characteristics, and his isolation and loneliness were very likely amplified in childhood. I then went straight to the IC to attempt to penetrate the veil which lay there, preventing full understanding of what it was that corroborated his apparent lack of identity, and seeming search for self. What lay at the base of his origins?

Certainly the immediate presenting aspects of Sun · Uranus · Mercury · Pluto opposite Saturn on descendant were hard to delineate without sounding thoroughly dismal and sombre. From the looks of Mohsin's arrival on the planet, his incarnation was perfectly aligned with the 'hero's birth' – endangered upon arrival, isolated from the family, of mysterious origins and with a task set at birth to retrieve something valuable for the culture and himself.

When I asked him what it was about his family that was so mysterious (Neptune · IC) he said that he did not know *who* his family was – that he had been adopted; and not only that, but cross-culturally assimilated from his probable Indian, Asian or Persian origins to an English family of older parents who had three older children, the youngest of whom was a girl aged sixteen. From that moment on, I was a partial participant in his journey towards self-discovery.

Mohsin's birth-mother was twenty-seven, single, and apart from her birth data very, very little is known about her – the birth information was retrieved from Mohsin's birth certificate. It is only in reflection on the past and his search for origins that anything at all has come to light. That which has emerged still leaves his IC, his origins, enshrouded and mysterious, but his search has resulted in some remarkable insights and self-discovery. For often when we look to the outside for an answer, it arises within. His search for identity in the world has resulted in a greater sense of identity in himself. (See Figure 19 – Mohsin's birth-mother.)

When Mohsin was eight, the first awareness of his family status was brought to his attention by neighbourhood children taunting him, saying he was adopted! He rushed home to ask his parents about this, hoping they would acknowledge it openly, tell him everything, the truth! But they told him his father had been killed in a car accident, and that his mother had died at his birth. Not until he was seventeen did any more information come to him. He was searching through private papers and came upon his birth certificate and his adoption records, which said he had been legally adopted on 25 September 1965. His adoptive parents had taken him home on 4 April 1965. Where had he been from birth to that day in April, almost eight months later? We had to peel back Neptune's veil.

Mohsin says he recently had an awareness of himself as an infant who at about six months old had to begin to work seriously to find some parents.

Time was running out and the pressure was increasing. His own mother had been able to keep him for six and a half weeks, because benefits were allowed for that time; then, apparently, she had to give him up. It is possible that she wished to keep him and, in that six-week period, realized she could not. What has happened to her since remains a mystery, and although the father's name is known, Mohsin has not been able to trace him.

Mohsin's search for his origins began in earnest in 1988 and resulted in his legally reclaiming his birth name on 25 September 1989 – by 'coincidence' legally given on the anniversary of his adoption, twenty-four years later. He also withdrew completely from his adoptive family at that time, rejecting them in order to undergo his own incubation and rebirth. In the course of that time, his life has undergone a tremendous change, and he reconnected with his adoptive family in a new way in 1995 – as an individual in his own right, with a great sense of himself and his place in the world. But that story comes a bit later.

The big question in adoptive cases lies around the relationship of the baby's horoscope and the adoptive family. There are no mistakes, there are no coincidences – very often we find horoscopes of children in a family who seem to be outside the family system, and they were *born* into that family. But equally often we find adopted children with more contact with the adoptive family than could have been arranged by a planet-search! Since we have only Mohsin's, his adoptive parents' and his birth mother's charts to look at, let's begin with the adoptive mother, father and their new baby, Mohsin. (See Figures 20 and 21.)

It struck me at once that Mohsin's parents adopted him to fill an empty nest, their other children grown and fairly well gone. His mother was forty-seven and his father forty-nine when they brought their new son home. Clearly he was adopted because he was wanted; however, the conscious motives are not always as clearly demonstrated on the surface as they are revealed in the astrology of things. Mohsin's name was changed – anglicized; he was completely assimilated into the 'foreign' culture and his natal identity subsumed by the very nature of the 'benign middle-class English family system'. From the beginning he was not who he was. But Mohsin was already seven or eight months old by then! What had happened in the meantime?

For this story, we want to look very deeply into the more esoteric sides of birth and life – when there is a question of origins and possible fated experiences before birth, during the birth and the early infancy states, it serves to look very closely at the lunar themes in the charts – the lunations, pre-natal eclipses and nodal contacts and their interactive relationships between the infant and its parents. In this way we have a partial glimpse into the dimension of life which eludes consciousness and exists in the pre-conscious state. With Mohsin, I think it is good to look at his life before birth and his complex relationship with the whole issue of incarnation. This quickening and enlivening aspect of creation and existence is very closely associated with the nodes, Moon and all aspects of their cycles, because they symbolize the time spent in the protection of the womb. Eclipse points which fall on inter-dimensional levels (midpoints and harmonics) in the charts of all the people in a group speak of a 'multiverse' in which decisions are made long before we consciously call them ours. Eclipses are a line-up between the earth, Sun, Moon all falling along Moon's nodal axis – this is like an expressway into a manifestation of events, or, in this instance, the movement of the soul into the body.

Mohsin's intra-uterine life is very exciting – there is a series of pre-natal eclipses which begin a month after conception would have been and continue right up to about seven weeks before he was born. The pre-natal eclipse prior to birth is considered to be the 'final' stage of soul-entry – the point of no return, so to speak. His most recent pre-natal eclipse point was at 17° 16′ Cancer (occurred 9 July 1964), which is very close to Mohsin's natal Mars · Venus conjunction at 20° and 21° Cancer respectively – more significantly, that eclipse had fallen on his adoptive father's Saturn · Venus midpoint – in fact, closer to the conjunction of his Saturn! By converse direction, his sixth week before birth relates to his sixth week after birth – Mohsin was given up by his mother at six weeks old.

His enduring love affair with the mysterious, exotic and missing mother is reflected in his Mars · Venus conjunction in Cancer. The pre-birth eclipse also falls exactly on his adoptive father's Saturn · Venus midpoint. The Saturn · Venus conjunction in this man's chart is a very lonely configuration, which trines his Scorpio Moon. He has deep emotions and passions all of which are probably under a very tight control. Venus with Saturn is impoverished – the Aphrodite archetype is not given free reign, neither for her more erotic and lusty quality, nor for her nurturing, fertility characteristic. She was amputated from him, and he feels it very much.

Mohsin himself has had a difficult time modulating his emotional expression, probably because of the influence of this Venus/Saturn father on his Venus/Mars. Too much control in the paternal example – he needed to have more expression and truth than his father was capable of demonstrating during his growing years. He is also much older than the average father – another Saturnian signature. Mohsin's 'frustrations' at his father's knee will be likely to have influenced his uneven emotional communication. As he said, he lets it all out at once, intensely, overwhelmingly. He wants deep, meaningful relationships, with lasting value, not casual, passer-by contacts. Often the Venus person will attract others to him who deny those deep, substantial and solid values and see them as being 'too intense' or too demanding and reject them. It takes years, time, maturity for the Venus/Saturn person fully to appreciate himself, then to allow others of the right calibre to come into his life.

That Mohsin's pre-natal eclipse falls on this midpoint of his father's conjunction shows that he would love his child, but might not be able to convey it well. And the interaction of Mohsin's Mars · Venus with his adoptive father's Saturn · Venus is like a brick wall between them – surmountable, but with effort. I think, too, that the pre-natal eclipse on the adoptive father's chart talks about him experiencing the loss of his *own* children, his loneliness and his need to continue to nurture by fatherhood – a man with many planets in Cancer finds it hard to let go of the paternal role!

This pre-birth eclipse also triggered the Mars · Saturn midpoint of Mohsin's birth-mother – that seven weeks before her baby was born, the eclipse fell on her 'death axis', and seven weeks after he was born, she gave him away. What pain she must have felt, and such a death to her and to her baby – for she probably had to pretend that was, indeed, what had happened, that he had died. Ebertin calls the Mars · Saturn midpoint the 'death axis'.

However, to backtrack over all the pre-natal eclipses from birth to conception is stunning in relation to all the charts: pre-natal eclipses have to do with the soul's gradual adherence to the foetus, and its final resting place in the infant. In accord with the baby's ongoing gestation *in utero*, they are indications of transcendent experiences which will continue to mark the incarnate life of the person as he grows to adulthood . . . future transits to the points of pre-natal eclipses are very sensitive, as we shall see with Mohsin's life to date. Also, we shall see the relationship of the adoptive parents' charts to these mysterious points, who ostensibly do not know of his imminent arrival nor of their adoption of him in the future! It is likely that his parents had discussed and worked towards adoption for possibly four years before his birth, but it wasn't until 16 October that they filled out the application forms for adoption.

The Pre-natal eclipses are as follows – from birth backwards to conception:

1. 9 July 1964   17° 16′ Cancer (new Moon: partial)
2. 25 June 1964   3° 30′ Capricorn (full Moon: total)
3. 10 June 1964   19° 19′ Gemini (new Moon: partial)
4. 14 January 1964   23° 43′ Capricorn (new Moon: partial)
5. 30 December 1963   8° 01′ Cancer (full Moon: total)

At nine and a half weeks before Mohsin's birth, he had a pre-natal eclipse at 3° 30′ Capricorn/Cancer – a total eclipse of the Sun. Mohsin's adoptive mother's Pluto is within *three minutes* of that eclipse, in her fourth house – is she preparing to rescue this child fated to be abandoned soon in the future? Somewhere in her own soul she is 'seeded' by the future of her adoptive child, whose Moon · Mars midpoint is at 4° Cancer. So, by 25 June, everyone is preparing for the coming event – in the unknown future. Mohsin's adoptive father is perhaps unconsciously preparing for father-hood, again, late in life – his Sun · Saturn midpoint is 4° 04′ Cancer and his Mars · Jupiter is 4° 25′ Cancer. With (unconscious) expansive hopes he awaits his son. The birth-mother's Sun · Mars midpoint is at 4° Capricorn which is opposite the adoptive mother's Pluto – both mothers are already deeply in collusion.

In fact, when Mohsin was legally adopted by his new family on 25 September 1965, *his progressed Moon was at this very degree – 3° 25′ Cancer* ! ! ! Mohsin's progressed Moon had arrived to his adoptive mother's natal Pluto in the fourth house when she assumed the role of his protector and nur-turer – albeit a borrowed role.

Pre-natal eclipses happen to the infant while still in his mother's body – therefore they are a form of transit to the mother via the foetus's life. The eclipses falling in the Cancer/Capricorn axis speak of a strong soul-need to embody oneself through the earth parents, rather than the celestial parents. Here we see where the Moon · Mars midpoint sits on the full-Moon eclipse axis – the birth mother is virtually relegated to a heavenly position, a celes-tial creature; certainly not a real woman, but a goddess or a demon. The problem *is* that his future adoptive mother's Pluto will sit right on the baby son's Moon · Mars midpoint and it will be impossible for him to accept her as a substitute – ever. She has 'stolen' him somehow, just as Pluto himself rushed up to steal away Demeter's daughter, Persephone, leaving the mother wandering the earth, searching endlessly for her abducted child, and the abducted child forever longing to return to the nurture of the earth above. This motif also is amplified by Mohsin's progressed Moon being on her natal Pluto when he is legally adopted by her, which highlights the baby's emotional anxiety via the Moon·Mars midpoint. Mohsin's mother told him that this was, indeed, a time in which she was very worried.

Mohsin's pre-natal eclipse cycle is in Cancer/Capricorn because the nodes were in that axis during his gestation, with the exception of the 'blip' in Gemini. The eclipse 'blip' into Gemini falls right on his natal Moon at 18° 14' Gemini! And he was destined to follow a long search for his mother – his birth mother, the one who held him in her body for nine months of Cancer/Capricorn eclipses. Now this odd-eclipse-out, Gemini, on 10 June 1964, strikes me as the moment of final arrival of the soul into his fully-formed foetal body, when he 'agreed' to be in the world, and his future natal Moon was already in agreed position at this time.

Mohsin's nodes are 29° Gemini/Sagittarius, right at the beginning of the next two-and-a-half-year cycle. However, that this pre-natal eclipse falls right at Mohsin's natal Moon and his birth mother's Chiron·South node speaks of the deep wounding his own emotions felt at his mother's pain of giving up her child (Chiron in the fifth house at 17° 50' Gemini). Though he has not seen his birth-mother since he was seven weeks old, he is still emotionally tied to her eternal wound of losing her child – her nodes are conjunct Chiron, squared by Saturn (in Pisces, again like Mohsin), and in the same sign axis as Mohsin's nodes, only reversed – her north is his south node. She'll never have forgotten him, but probably her circumstances prevent her from ever contacting him – cultural and circumstantial barriers are powerful. The adoptive mother's nodal axis is the same as the birth mother: south node in Gemini/north node in Sagittarius – her being almost a full nodal cycle older than the birth-mother. Also, considering that the *birthchart of the child is the transit chart of the parent*, Mohsin's natal Moon is the transit at the time of her delivery of the Moon to her Chiron·South node conjunction and her Saturn·Neptune midpoint. Again we have another indication of the painful wounding of being fated to lose the child. A more subtle implication is that Mohsin is the nodal 'midpoint' of his two mothers.

The next pre-natal eclipse back fell in January 1964, at 23° 43' Capricorn (a new Moon). This degree is Mohsin's Moon·ascendant midpoint – his connection to the mother (Moon) and his emotional commitment to development and eventual birth (ascendant) – there is no connection to any point of high note with the exception of that eclipse falling close to his adoptive father's nodal axis. A fairly weak eclipse. But the first pre-natal eclipse after conception is even weaker: the pre-natal eclipse which occurred immediately after his conception-time fell at 8° 01' Cancer/ Capricorn – a total eclipse of the Sun. It fell right at Mohsin's ascendant · Midheaven axis midpoint – which is the incarnation midpoint, the place of arrival at the horizon and meridian. This degree is the adoptive father's Saturn · Pluto midpoint, the adoptive mother's Jupiter · Saturn midpoint, while *making no overtly significant contact to the birth-mother's horoscope* (though square to her natal Venus) in a way which fits into this Moon/node/eclipse womb symbolism. So Mohsin's first pre-natal eclipse after conception is not connected to the body which will nurture him for nine months *in utero*, and for seven weeks in infancy, and never see him again. This is not a good sign for a strong bond with the mother – it seems as if the connection immediately following conception is frail, tenuous and more connected to his future, unknown, adoptive parents than to his birth-mother.

All the pre-natal eclipses increase in strength by contact to all three known parents as his intra-uterine development increases – he becomes increasingly committed to incarnation, but more painfully connected to the birth-mother and more responsibly connected (lots of Saturn, Moon, nodes) to the adoptive parents as he grows! What does this mean?

So Mohsin is born, and his arrival is fraught with the depression of his mother having to give him away – there is a mysterious gap between seven weeks of age and around seven and a half months. Records have him in foster care, in a nursing home and in various places – the foster-mother, found by Mohsin, is confused. She doesn't recall the woman whom Mohsin describes as the woman she thought to be the mother; but she also does not have the same recollection of time as he. He truly does not know what happened. But on 4 April 1965 his adoptive parents brought him home, and from that time right up till 25 September there remained the uncertainty of the birth-mother's rights – he was not legally 'theirs' until that date.

He must have been very insecure until that time, waiting for his legal adoption and his life to settle down – it was Mohsin himself who said to me that he felt that he was pretty young to be 'working at getting parents, but what's a baby to do?' Mohsin's progressed Moon was 26° 39' Gemini on the date of his first arrival to his new home, just past the square to his adoptive mother's Virgo Mars and his adoptive father's Pisces Chiron. We also see in the adoptive mother's horoscope the same anticipation-anxiety replicated while Saturn transits her Pisces Mercury and Sun weeks later, after the adoption has taken firmly and she has become his own mother. (She was to die in December 1994 under those same aspects.)

Now, 4 April 1965 had Saturn at 12° 01' of Pisces, in June it stationed-retrograde at 17° Pisces, and it traversed back to 12° 27' Pisces by the 25th of September! Then, by the end of December, Saturn made its final, direct, pass over the twelfth degree of Pisces. With so much emphasis, and in the context of his experience, that degree – and any of its harmonic relatives – remains forever imprinted in Mohsin's psyche – and we shall see the magnitude to which this is profoundly significant in his rebirth.

As mentioned above, it happens that my first contact with him, on 10 July 1994, was when Saturn had *just* gone retrograde and was 12° 10' Pisces. And when I was in the middle of interviewing him for this story, Saturn had gone direct and was passing *back over that degree* – almost exactly to the minute, recollecting the Saturn experience of all those years ago.

As we have seen, Mohsin's desire to know his origins simmered for many years, emerging at a time which impacted the entire family system, showing the deep sympathy which permeates a long-established unit. There is always doubt in the mind of an adoptee about his or her self-worth and value – there is an intrinsic feeling of unworthiness and taint, as if they might have done something terribly wrong. This feeling is not rational, so it cannot be reasoned with and must be accepted until the adopted person finds himself to be a person of worth and value based on his own evaluation and inner nature. But what triggers the action towards finding one's birth-parents, and do all adopted people feel that need? To varying degrees they do, but it does entirely depend on their circumstances.

For example, a close male friend of mine, whose high-school sweetheart had had to give up their child for adoption when they were both sixteen, found a strong need to find his adopted son when he contracted terminal cancer – he hoped to find him before he died. Knowing the horoscope of the boy, who would have been twenty-seven at the time, we saw that Saturn was transiting the boy's Capricorn Moon in his fifth house and the father's ascendant (the same), during the time his father was wanting to find him.

Both my friend and the mother of the son agreed to make themselves available to 'parent-finders' and make every attempt to find the long-given-up son. They never did find him before my friend died, though I wondered if the boy was not undergoing some urge to know his birth-parents but was content enough (or fearful enough – Moon in Capricorn) to maintain the status quo. Unbeknown to the boy, his father was dying when Saturn was transiting his Moon, and his birth-parents were colluding to find him (a Saturn · Moon collusion) – clearly, the family is inextricable from one's natal chart. Whether or not he was consciously engaged in the death of the father, the event was evident in his horoscope.[2]

It was an important part of Mohsin's rite-of-passage out of his lunar return towards his Saturn return to undergo the search. The transit of Pluto began to edge towards his IC in 1988–9 (his birth-mother's Mars · MC) and he became increasingly alienated from the family and moved out. He spent time drifting, not having any real focus, but became increasingly organized in his search, contacting various social services and agencies and instigating his own research, all the while continuing to cut the ties to his adoptive family.

Mohsin had been robbed of his birthright. He felt annihilated. He was not English in his bones. He rightfully needed to take back his heritage, go into his roots and find his soul before any thought of generosity towards this family who had taken care of him like their own children.

He had to get to the root of things, and penetrate the veil between who he was and who he appeared to be. Pluto transiting Neptune is a painful experience – it is as if the anaesthetic has been turned off and all pain is accessible. Birth-pain is the one thing we all share, and Neptune is the 'holder of the birth-pain' – it is as if the trauma of departure from the comforts of the womb (Moon/Neptune) and the severing of life-support from the mother are so devastating that we cannot recall it. Neptune is the river Lethe in the unconscious, it allows oblivion and forgetfulness to wash over us, so we might go to Neptune in the chart over and over to wash us free from the pain of birth. The position of Neptune in the horoscope is simultaneously both the place where we might seek this oblivion and the place where we need to be awakened. For Mohsin, the transit of Pluto shut off the anaesthetic dulling the bald realization that he had been given away and could *never be connected to his mother* – ever.

The resonance of his Pluto transit was also happening simultaneously to his birth-mother – she was having Pluto transit her natal Mars all the while her unknown son was experiencing the rising pain of loss and the determined reclamation of his ancestral roots with Pluto going over his IC. We don't know what his birth-mother was experiencing, but from my understanding of morphic resonance and family systems, she was likely to be undergoing some recollections herself. All of this was following Mohsin's move away from home and his descent into the underworld of his own making to undergo the quest for self-identity.

After he reclaimed his birth-name and separated from the family on 25 September 1989, he saw them only twice after that until 1994. Simultaneous with his leaving and taking back his origins, his adoptive mother developed Alzheimer's disease, and began to fade from life. She was re-entering her own womb, moving back to infantilism. Pluto was squaring her Moon and Venus while it was creeping up to Mohsin's Neptune. She was losing her identity, her life force and retreating back into an infantile state of her own, while her adoptive son was beginning the long, arduous process of giving birth to himself as an adult. Things were turning inside-out. On the date of his legal resumption of his name, Mohsin's progressed Moon was at 17° 45' Taurus, precisely at his MC, and had opposed his natal Neptune just two months prior – his identity and nationality were in a state of dissolution, and a renewed status, place in the world (MC) and sense of identity was born out of the time. So we have his adoptive mother re-entering the womb as he climbs out of a secondary-womb, all with his Moon and Neptune playing major roles in the nativity play.

This secondary birth would not need a mother's womb but would require great nurturing from himself and the capacity to endure long, mysterious happenings in the deeply unconscious regions of his own psyche. He would need to enter his own Neptune, and transit his own fourth house, into his own soul – but that would require at some significant point a return to that family to reclaim his identity left behind there, and put both past and present together, creating a whole. This small family system is reeling with individual transits all occurring synchronously – and I am not including the elder three children of the parents, all of whom were also undergoing family dynamic crises, as well.

Mohsin's adoptive father had just had transiting Uranus station-direct opposite his Pluto at 2° Cancer when his son disowned him and his wife was diagnosed – and Neptune in transit was at the Saturn · Pluto midpoint. The transit of Pluto was at 13° Scorpio – conjunct his Moon. All hell was breaking loose for him and his mainstays were collapsing, his wife retreating into her Pisces Sun · Mercury finally and for ever, and his loved adopted son mysteriously heading into the underground!

However, the transit picture from 1989 onwards shows a slow, deliberate movement of Pluto towards Mohsin's IC – towards the place of reclaiming ancestral support, slaying the inner dragon and retrieving lost treasures of identity. In November 1989 Pluto entered his fourth house for the first time; it passed back over it retrograde in April 1990; then entered it finally in October 1990 only to retreat back again to 17° and station-direct at that degree in July 1991. It was a long process, during which time he remained on his own, working, in therapy and almost completely without relationships. Mohsin had entered his secondary-womb and was in total incubation.

During this time the transit of Saturn had moved into Aquarius, resonating through the small family unit of mother, father and son – and reaching to the absent birth-mother as well. Saturn was to oppose the adoptive mother's Neptune and slowly descend into her twelfth house, sealing her off from the world and containing her in her dream-like consciousness – Saturn through the twelfth house always involves a necessary loss of identity, but Alzheimer's is a total deconstruction of the ego. His adoptive father was having Neptune transit opposite his Saturn – all his structures dissolving – and Uranus would be quick to follow in its wake, to pass over all his Cancer planets, south node, and station in opposition to his Neptune at 00° Leo by May of 1995. (Mohsin's Sun · Moon midpoint – 'the giver of life' – is 28° Cancer, which is his adoptive father's south node, and it is likely that there is a deep understanding that lies between the two of them, unspoken, but present in feeling.) It seemed to be a long haul ahead, but then it was to be.

With Pluto firmly in the fourth house, and Saturn about to enter his sixth house, Mohsin was becoming increasingly existentially adrift. Pluto's entry into the fourth also speaks of 'the end of the matter' – he never did find his mother, but he also made his last attempt to do so in the summer of 1993. That summer he ran into a dead-end, a closed door: he had found someone with the same last name and contacted him and this produced a suspicious cold shoulder. Mohsin let go. Saturn was in the last degrees of Aquarius, but would pass back over those degrees again, for a final sweep, in January 1994. Meanwhile he continued with therapy to come to terms with the loss of his mother, and made no contact with his parents.

By the time we had our first consultation, on 10 July 1994, there had been some progressive movement towards resolution for Mohsin. He was wanting to reconnect with his family, see his parents, perhaps somehow help them in some way and go and see his other, older, siblings. He was still very nervous about it, and unsure of why he wanted this, but he had let go of his mother and had felt he'd had time to reconnect with himself – to the degree that it was 'safe'. His father had been rather passively understanding about his taking back his name, passively curious, but not rejecting.

At the end of November 1994, I realized I wanted to explore Mohsin's experience more deeply and I contacted him to set up an interview where we could see how his life could contribute to the book. I had been deeply touched by his story, and also very impressed with the way he was working with it. Also, the astrology was brilliant, irresistible.

We had an appointment for 6 December 1994. Mohsin came and we delved deeply into the past, the timing and all the circumstances around his childhood feelings, his adolescent discovery of his real parentage, the subsequent break from the family, his search and where he found himself at present. At the time of the interview in December, Mohsin's progressed Moon had reached 29° Cancer – just entering his twelfth house and conjunct his adoptive father's south node. The transiting Sun was 14° Sagittarius (the degree area of memory-sensitivity, and in square to his natal Pluto), and the transiting Moon was in Aquarius, right over his adoptive mother's natal Moon and Venus – and Uranus. She was very ill with bronchitis – Mars had been in opposition to her natal Uranus just three days before that. Transiting Uranus was in opposition to his own Venus in Cancer, further sensitizing and clouding his feelings about relationships and his needs for care and nurture. It was also a time in which he was preparing to leave his female therapist, as they were mutually agreed on a four-month 'withdrawal' and then they would conclude.

One month later, I received a letter from Mohsin – his adoptive mother had died on 6 December 1994, the very day we were sitting reviewing his life and moving through some of the more emotionally difficult experiences in his life. Coincident with the catharsis of having his life raked over in detail, his mother died, unknown to us at that time.

Mohsin's father wrote to him, and he went to the funeral; since then, he has reconnected with the family in a new way. The relationships with his older siblings, his father and himself are now on a vastly different plane. The death of his mother has released him – when our parents die, there is sadness and grief and loss, but there is also release and a legacy of freedom from them. While parents remain alive, they remain active participants in our projections, they are substantial, manifestly present 'hooks' for the archetypal parental projection. One maintains expectations and can sometimes find it difficult, if not impossible, to take responsibility for one's own fate. Upon the death of a parent, the mother or father ceases to be solid, and is then more easily assimilated into the psyche as an aspect of one's own self, thus becoming integrated more fully into one's own identity. Parental relationships, like all deeply bonded relationships, do not die but continue to evolve. We are still deeply enmeshed in the collective ethos of the family system, and continue to work through the family as we grow. This is quickened at particular times, especially under strong transits when there are new and greater steps forward in the 'inner family'.

When Mohsin and I met in March 1995 to go over the final discussions for the story told here, Saturn had reached that significant place between 12° and 14° Pisces which marked the end of the nine-month gestation that was heralded at our first meeting. Although new and fragile, Mohsin was feeling positive and grounded. He was much more secure within himself, and finding a new way of seeing his life.

After I completed this story and after he had read through it, Mohsin said that his life at this stage was a threshold (mid-1995) – the ending of an old cycle and the beginning of a new one: 'With this major cycle of my life now complete, I have at last found a sense of stability and security in the world – upon which I am able to build.'

Summary

We have seen how pre-natal eclipses can foreshadow parental relationships. We have also found that adoptive parents are indistinguishable from natural parents, and in this story how they are more involved on an inter-dimensional level with the child than the birth-mother was.

We have seen a strong enlivening of the fourth house, search for origins and roots. The transits are startling and the relationship between them and the events are classic.

There has been a validation of the deep, inter-dimensional aspect of family dynamics; how we do not operate alone, but in groups. We also see how people in enmeshed families don't change unless they are forced to do so.

All through this final stage of Mohsin's story, his sister was undergoing a divorce, and other changes were taking place in the family. Mohsin had a great effect on this family dynamic, and they had to adopt him to incorporate the system-breaker!

Transits have been precise, and connecting people with events consistently – the 'family in flux' is strong.

NOTES

1. See Chapter 10, page 170, for deeper understanding of the fourth house.
2. See Chapter 11, page 195, for delineations of transits to individual natal charts and their implications in the entire family dynamic.

15.

Rejected in the Womb

LAURA: HER FAMILY OF ORIGIN AND
ANCESTRAL HERITAGE

Laura came to see me in July 1994 to go over her horoscope in a fairly general way and to talk about what transits and progressions to work with in the coming year or so – in particular the movement of Uranus and Neptune over her descendant and Saturn through the ninth house, opposing her Moon and stellium in Virgo. She was in the middle of a training programme to become a psychoanalyst, having begun, literally, a new life in 1991.

Laura's psychotherapeutic work was centring around family matters, especially the 'good-mother' and reworking that with people. As we shall see, this is not surprising. The session went very well, but in the last fifteen minutes a remarkable statement was made. Laura said that her daughter Anne had rejected her while she was still in the womb. This was certainly an about-face from what we are normally told – usually we talk about mothers (or fathers) rejecting their children, but as I had already developed some strong ideas on the possibility of a child rejecting its parent, I was more than interested in how this might pan out astrologically, if this were the case, why and how and to what purpose. (See Figures 22, Laura, and 23, Anne.) However, before fully exploring Laura's fate and hence her daughter Anne's, let us look at Laura's own parental and family background.

Laura's horoscope is unusual in that it presents Jupiter singleton and retrograde in the MC opposite Saturn at the IC, with Uranus just having crested the horizon, in its station-retrograde. Uranus was virtually motionless and just about to move backwards, having stationed four days before her birth, hence just quivering for adventure. All other planets are beneath the horizon, and with the Sun and Mercury in Scorpio in that most secret of houses, I assumed that she had undergone more than one major

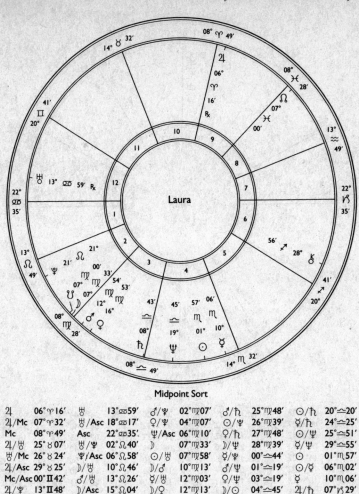

Figure 22

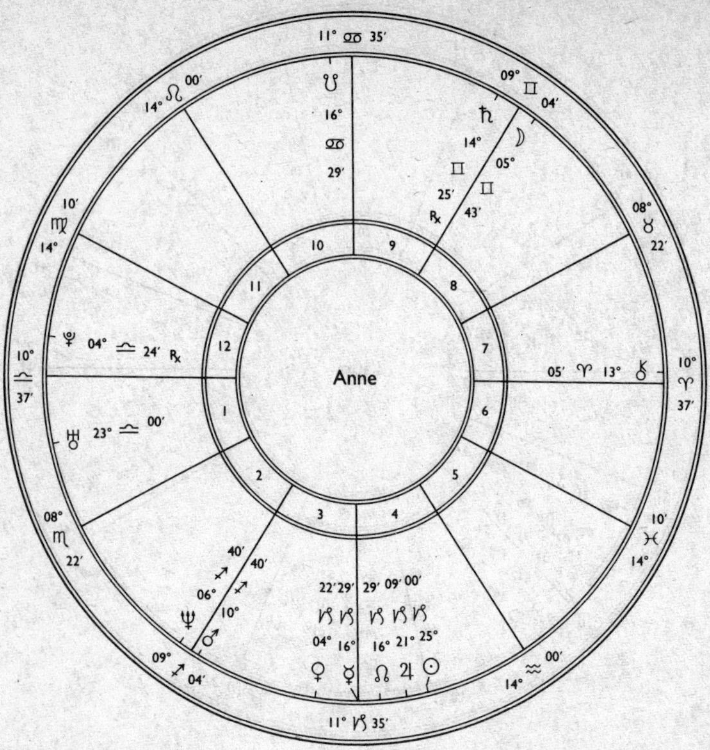

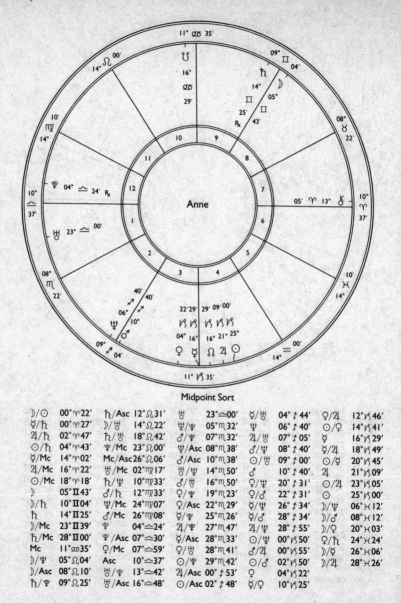

Midpoint Sort

☽/☉	00°♈22'	♄/Asc	12°♌31'	♅	23°♎00'	☿/♅	04°♐44'	♀/♃	12°♑46'
☿/♄	00°♈27'	☽/♅	14°♌22'	♆/♇	05°♏32'	♆	06°♐40'	☉/♀	14°♑41'
♃/♄	02°♈47'	♄/♅	18°♌42'	♂/♇	07°♏32'	♃/♅	07°♐05'	☿	16°♑29'
☉/♄	04°♈43'	♇/Mc	23°♌00'	♆/Asc	08°♏38'	♂/♆	08°♐40'	☿/♃	18°♑49'
☿/Mc	14°♈02'	Mc/Asc	26°♌06'	♂/Asc	10°♏38'	☉/♅	09°♐00'	☉/☿	20°♑45'
♃/Mc	16°♈22'	♅/Mc	02°♍17'	♅/♆	14°♏50'	♂	10°♐40'	♃	21°♑09'
☉/Mc	18°♈18'	♄/♆	10°♍33'	♂/♅	16°♏50'	♀/♆	20°♐31'	☉/♃	23°♑05'
☽	05°♊43'	♂/♄	12°♍33'	♀/♇	19°♏23'	♀/♂	22°♐31'	☉	25°♑00'
☽/♄	10°♊04'	♆/Mc	24°♍07'	♀/Asc	22°♏29'	☿/♆	26°♐34'	☽/♆	06°♓12'
♄	14°♊25'	♂/Mc	26°♍08'	☿/♇	25°♏26'	☿/♂	28°♐34'	☽/♂	08°♓12'
☽/Mc	23°♊39'	♇	04°♎24'	♃/♇	27°♏47'	♃/♆	28°♐55'	☽/♀	20°♓03'
♄/Mc	28°♊00'	♇/Asc	07°♎30'	☿/Asc	28°♏33'	☉/♆	00°♑50'	♀/♄	24°♓24'
Mc	11°♋35'	♀/Mc	07°♎59'	♀/♅	28°♏41'	♂/♃	00°♑55'	☽/☿	26°♓06'
☽/♇	05°♌04'	Asc	10°♎37'	☉/♇	29°♏42'	☉/♂	02°♑50'	☽/♃	28°♓26'
☽/Asc	08°♌10'	♅/♇	13°♎42'	♃/Asc	00°♐53'	♀	04°♑22'		
♄/♇	09°♌25'	♅/Asc	16°♎48'	☉/Asc	02°♐48'	☿/♀	10°♑25'		

Figure 23

life-transition. For one of the symbols of Scorpio is the Phoenix rising out of the ash of a previous existence. I have often said that Scorpios can prove reincarnation because they do it several times in a single lifetime.

With Neptune also in the fourth, Laura's ancestral legacy is to serve the ancestors by liberating them from spiritual bondage, and to enter into an endless quest for self-realization which would have the effect of purging the family of its sense of rootlessness. The fourth house is complex for Laura; it shows her need to please (Saturn/IC) and to sacrifice her own path, if only temporarily or for a specific end, as well as the bright hope of the Sun in there which lights the path towards a sense of spiritual destiny. There may have been a long line of religious or spiritual ancestors which suffered when the religion of its history degenerated or else was abandoned by someone in the family history.

When I asked her about this, and if it had any relevance at all, Laura said, 'I have a maternal "Marion" ancestral line stemming from the Wisdom roots, with strong Madonna/Magdalene links. I experienced a physical-linking at the Shrine of Our Lady of Guadalupe, Mexico City, a geographical place where Christian and Maya roots cross.' She has experienced past-life recollections of the end of the Maya civilization; end of Earth/Nature spiritually; in the British Isles; of excommunication as a nun *circa* the tenth to thirteenth century, over ethics and mysticism. There seems, indeed, to be a long line of soulful martyrdom. She felt that the spiritual decay in the family that I mentioned was relevant to her original work in the 'family of origin' as being the white, European origins which drew her to her first path in Christian work, based on a return to the early church's path of metanoia and conversion, first to fourth century. This she considered to be the personal work; the collective work was to evolve from that base.

In fact, from 1986 to 1991 she worked within the Catholic church as a lay minister. She was based in an extremely orthodox religion while acting out a most heterodox role. A new vision of Catholicism arose in the eighties, through the work of Matthew Fox. His book, *Creation Spirituality*, attracted many people who were Christian-orientated but deeply unhappy with the patriarchal focus, and many men, and women particularly, were drawn to exercise their spirituality through this reframed old religion. Matthew Fox was silenced by the Vatican on 15 December 1988, and effectively Laura was too. Thus she was rejected by the 'mother', the church, along with Fox. At that point, however, she remained with the group, working in Central America (Guatemala/Honduras) and continuing with her focus until she left in early 1991, having visualized that another path was about to resolve itself on her ever-expanding horizon.

Laura described her main influences as being through the order of the Benedictines but theologically influenced by the Jesuits. She worked within the 'radical' new order, trying to synthesize the Eastern religious world-view with Catholic precepts – a lovely example of her singleton Jupiter retrograde at the MC in opposition to her Saturn IC. The ministry eventually took her to Central America, to work there right up to February 1991. Her north node in Pisces in the ninth house would try to seek a way of finding spiritual release through the church, but her Jupiter retrograde in Aries would eventually show her that only her own way would win out. Also, the Jupiter retrograde, the 'stranger in a strange land' aspect, would take her far and wide to find her true homeland and roots; a Jupiter retrograde person is often born to a family in a location which is not the spiritual roots for him or her.

Laura's paternal links go back three generations to the native American Indians, and link her to Guatemala/Honduras, the Maya and the California deserts – but then, on the maternal side, we have the Western Highlands, Scotland, England and Christianity! (North node in Pisces in the ninth.) She eventually arrived in the British Isles, to her third 'personality' life, in September 1991!

The Jupiter/Saturn opposition from MC to IC is a bi-polar framework – Laura has vastly contrasting images for parents and, thus, for parenting herself. With this aspect, extremes of experiences are bound to occur within her own family of origins and in any family she would create for herself. The first part of life, prior to the Uranus opposition, the powerful mid-life demarcation, was lived through her Saturn, and the second half is clearly living out her Jupiter. Her parents are both strongly represented in these planets, and as Laura has said, 'My father is my Jupiter and my mother is my Saturn.'

With her Moon leading a stellium in Virgo including the south node, all in strong aspect to Mercury, it struck me that her need to 'know', to understand, to render information into intelligence would be extreme. It also struck me that her desire to know and understand everything that came within her domain was not only inherent and representative of an ancestral demand to uncover the mystery of spiritual decay in the family, but was also compounded by a childhood in which she was not included in a major decision which would affect the whole of her life – that of her father's abandonment. All children have to cope with this aspect of growing – that of having decisions made *for* them – but a young Scorpio with the Sun in sextile to the Virgo Moon and no other conventional aspects to it shows an overpowering need to control her own destiny. She would have felt disempowered and diminished each time the adults made decisions without consulting her. Long before her time of liberation would come, she was aware of her need to move beyond the confines of convention – but that would be years in the coming. In some way, she was prepared to shoulder the family burden.

That Laura's Sun lacks challenge or support from any other planet except the Moon talks about a very special purpose in life, one which would not be found in any conventional manner, where there were no clear markers for direction, and thus she would have to search for her own path. The tension of expectation with Uranus rising, and the longing for distant horizons, and feeling of religious alienation with Jupiter retrograde-singleton is profound. It is in this context that her passionate Scorpio found several avenues to express her need to be as much to as many as possible. As we shall see, her range of experience and use of that planetary array has been broad.

With Saturn conjunct IC, Laura feels the responsibility for the family fate very strongly, and was made to take on the emotional and practical aspects of family life very early, as we shall see. Laura's mother, she feels, is her Saturn – when her father left, her mother really lost herself and Laura was the one who had to look after her. When Laura was to leave her and the others at the age of eighteen, to marry, the family virtually fell apart. She *was* Saturn in the IC, caring for the family as the support-system, at the sacrifice of her own quest (Neptune). There is always something vague, mysterious and unknown about the family history or background when Neptune is in the fourth. Also, Neptune incorporates a bigger picture into the ancestral line. It is rather like the twelfth house meeting the fourth, and enfolding the collective into the personal – where the personal family-of-origin ancestors are intimately bound up with the ancestral history of the collective, the soul of the human race itself.[1]

Laura's mother's Moon is at 8° Libra, right on Laura's IC, and thus Laura's Saturn sits on her mother's Moon. (See Figure 24.) This can be viewed in myriad ways: first, her mother unconsciously regards Laura as the one who is born to sacrifice her youth to her, then goes about allowing it to happen. Even though it is circumstantial, fate operates in that way. Second, Laura is the stronger one, in fact, and here is demonstration that chronological age is meaningless in astrological symbolism. Laura is the elder of the two and the one to carry the family – in numerous ways as she matures, but in the early days as the emotional scapegoat. Third, and *very* significantly, there is a threat *in utero* when a Mars/Moon (or Pluto Moon) interaction occurs between mother's and child's horoscopes. Not least in this is the fact that Laura would eventually prove to be a 'problem' for her own mother – she would need to force her mother to come to terms with her own problems, and to face herself and her own limitations through her daughter's (Laura's) Saturn.

Laura's mother's Mars is exactly conjunct Laura's Moon (and south node), which is at best an emotional irritant and certainly places mother's rage into Laura's system, but the function of Virgo is to take emotional issues into the body and try to assimilate them in that way. Eventually this results in symptoms, but usually only long after stress, anger or repression has passed. When later we come to Anne, Laura's daughter, we shall see the Moon/Mars theme transposed in Anne's Moon opposition to Mars from Gemini to Sagittarius. (See Figure 23.)

Meanwhile Laura's father's role, magnified by her unaspected Sun and elevated Jupiter retrograde, was to pass this wanderlust on to her, and in doing so infuse her with encouragement to explore unknown and distant horizons, to move beyond the bounds of her known world – philosophically, spiritually and geographically. (See Figure 25.) He has an adventurer's horoscope: the intrepid Scorpio Sun, given directly to his daughter, with a Leo Moon. This, coupled with both Mercury and Jupiter in Sagittarius, communicates his powerful need to travel off and be on his own, seeking out challenge and adventure. His Mars/Uranus in Pisces shows an electrical energy; erratic and impulsive through with the trine to Saturn, not unkind or cruel, highly idealistic and romantic, but self-centred. His Jupiter trine to Neptune, the closest aspect in the chart, is the troubadour, the wandering minstrel, and also the likely source of Laura's theological interests and commitment to her own form of heroic quest. But, like his horoscope details, he charged off to a distant horizon, leaving Laura to hold the family-bag and ensuring that she should forever seek out her own Jupiter, which was set aside for a while.[2] His Saturn conjunct her Mercury is, frankly, depressing. It is also part of why Laura limited herself in her relationship – she had no positive fathering in a conventional sense.

Laura's father used to take her out to the California desert, on adventures which literally presented her with the unending horizon which he himself

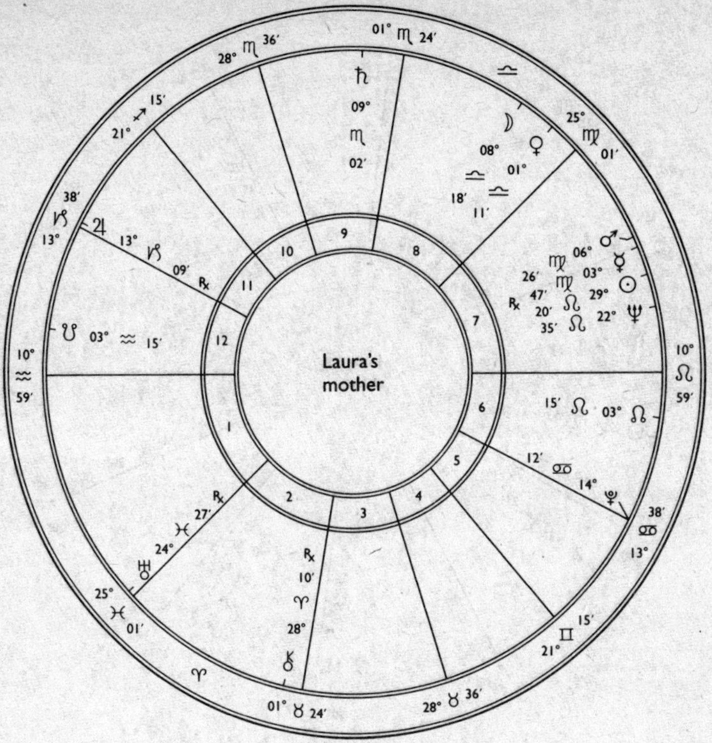

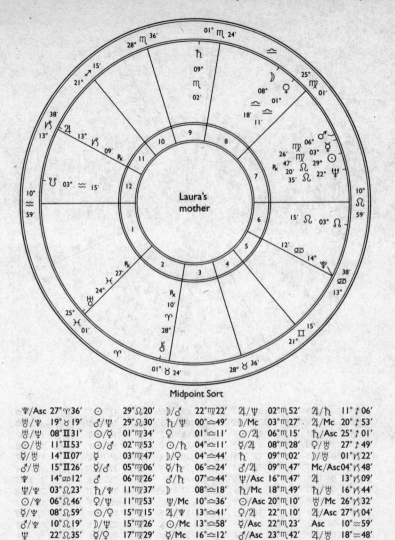

Midpoint Sort

♇/Asc	27°♈36′	☉	29°♌20′	☽/♂	22°♍22′	♃/♆	02°♏52′	♃/♄	11°♐06′
♅/♇	19°♉19′	♂/♆	29°♌30′	♄/♆	00°♎49′	☽/Mc	03°♏27′	♃/Mc	20°♐53′
♅/♆	08°♊31′	☉/☿	01°♍34′	♀	01°♎11′	☉/♃	06°♏15′	♄/Asc	25°♐01′
☉/♅	11°♊53′	☉/♂	02°♍53′	☉/♄	04°♎11′	☿/♃	08°♏28′	♀/♅	27°♐49′
☿/♅	14°♊07′	☿	03°♍47′	☽/♀	04°♎44′	♄	09°♏02′	☽/♅	01°♑22′
♂/♅	15°♊26′	☿/♂	05°♍06′	☿/♄	06°♎24′	♂/♃	09°♏47′	Mc/Asc	04°♑48′
♇	14°♋12′	♂	06°♍26′	♂/♄	07°♎44′	♆/Asc	16°♏47′	♃	13°♑09′
♆/♇	03°♌23′	♄/♇	11°♍37′	☽	08°♎18′	♄/Mc	18°♏49′	♄/♅	16°♑44′
☉/♇	06°♌46′	♀/♆	11°♍53′	♆/Mc	10°♎36′	☉/Asc	20°♏10′	♅/Mc	26°♑32′
☿/♇	08°♌59′	☉/♀	15°♍15′	♃/♇	13°♎41′	♀/♃	22°♏10′	♃/Asc	27°♑04′
♂/♇	10°♌19′	☽/♆	15°♍26′	☉/Mc	13°♎58′	☿/Asc	22°♏23′	Asc	10°♒59′
♆	22°♌35′	☿/♀	17°♍29′	☿/Mc	16°♎12′	♂/Asc	23°♏42′	♃/♅	18°♒48′
♀/♇	22°♌41′	♀/♂	18°♍48′	♂/Mc	17°♎31′	☽/♃	25°♏43′	♅/Asc	02°♓43′
☉/♆	25°♌58′	☽/☉	18°♍49′	♀/♄	20°♎06′	Mc	28°♏36′	♅	24°♓27′
☽/♇	26°♌15′	☽/☿	21°♍02′	☽/♄	23°♎40′	♀/Asc	06°♐05′		
☿/♆	28°♌11′	♇/Mc	21°♍24′	♀/Mc	29°♎54′	☽/Asc	09°♐38′		

Figure 24

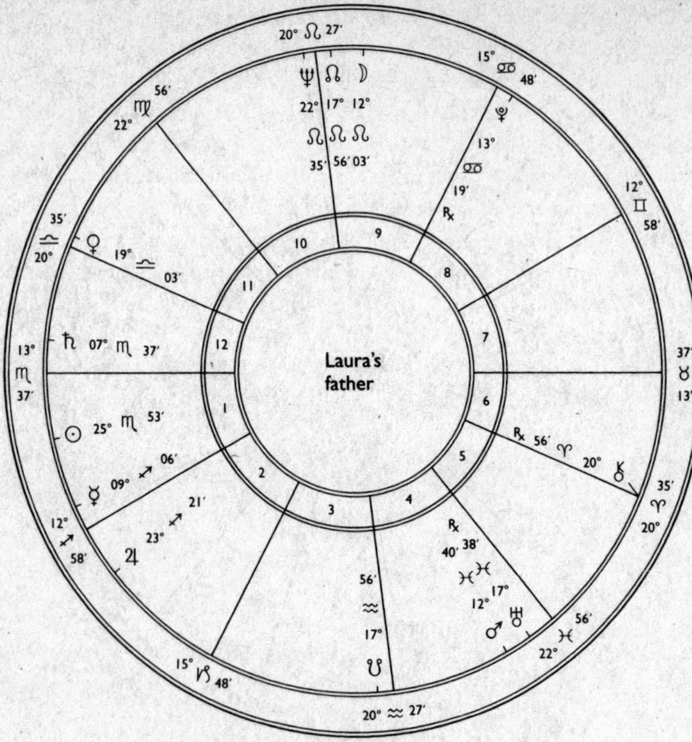

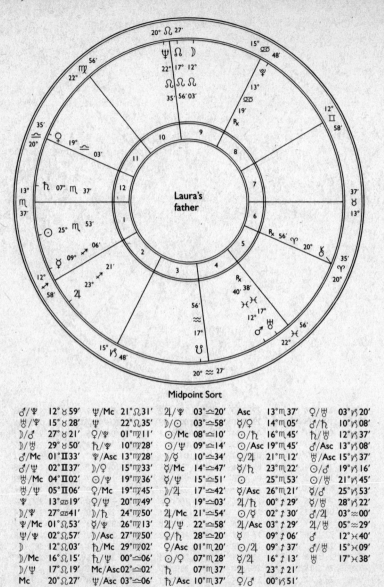

Midpoint Sort

♂/♇	12°♉59'	♆/Mc	21°♌31'	♃/♇	03°♎20'	Asc	13°♏37'	♀/♅	03°♑20'
♅/♇	15°♉28'	♆	22°♌35'	☽/☉	03°♎58'	☿/♀	14°♏05'	♂/♄	10°♑08'
☽/♂	27°♉21'	♀/♇	01°♍11'	☉/Mc	08°♎10'	☉/♄	16°♏45'	♄/♅	12°♑37'
☽/♅	29°♉50'	♄/♇	10°♍28'	☉/♆	09°♎14'	☉/Asc	19°♏45'	♂/Asc	13°♑08'
♂/Mc	01°♊33'	♇/Asc	13°♍28'	☽/☿	10°♎34'	♀/♃	21°♏12'	♅/Asc	15°♑37'
♂/♆	02°♊37'	☽/♀	15°♍33'	☿/Mc	14°♎47'	☿/♄	23°♏22'	☉/♂	19°♑16'
♅/Mc	04°♊02'	☉/♇	19°♍36'	☿/♆	15°♎51'	☉	25°♏53'	☉/♅	21°♑45'
♅/♆	05°♊06'	♀/Mc	19°♍45'	☽/♃	17°♎42'	☿/Asc	26°♏21'	☿/♂	25°♑53'
♇	13°♋19'	♀/♆	20°♍49'	♀	19°♎03'	♃/♄	00°♐29'	☿/♅	28°♑22'
☽/♇	27°♋41'	☽/♄	24°♍50'	♃/Mc	21°♎54'	☉/☿	02°♐30'	♂/♃	03°♒00'
♇/Mc	01°♌53'	☿/♇	26°♍13'	♃/♆	22°♎58'	♃/Asc	03°♐29'	♃/♅	05°♒29'
♆/♇	02°♌57'	☽/Asc	27°♍50'	♀/♄	28°♎20'	☿	09°♐06'	♂	12°♓40'
☽	12°♌03'	♄/Mc	29°♍02'	♀/Asc	01°♏20'	☉/♃	09°♐37'	♂/♅	15°♓09'
☽/Mc	16°♌15'	♄/♆	00°♎06'	☉/♀	07°♏28'	☿/♃	16°♐13'	♅	17°♓38'
☽/♆	17°♌19'	Mc/Asc	02°♎02'	♄	07°♏37'	♃	23°♐21'		
Mc	20°♌27'	♆/Asc	03°♎06'	♄/Asc	10°♏37'	♀/♂	00°♑51'		

Figure 25

would eventually head off towards. We have only a solar chart for him; however, his Moon is definitely in Leo and the aspects between his Sun and Neptune show the romantic soul. When Laura was born, her father was experiencing Pluto over his Neptune. Laura was his awakening and her spirit likely struck a chord for him – a chord which would leave him forever unable to deny his own truth, for she is the walking transit of his awakening. His presence in her life was rather like a soulmate or a friend, not as a paternal figure. Indeed, he left the family when she was really entering her solar stage, at the age of five to six, and the distant horizon became the symbol of father. He opened her mind, she says; he took her out into the desert and to gold mines, where they would explore and have adventures – both Pluto and Scorpio rule the riches hidden deep in the core of the earth and the power of the desert isolation. So no wonder that Laura knows her father to be her Jupiter.

Let us now look at the next generation, Laura's daughter – the infant who rejected her *in utero*.

ANNE – HER FAMILY OF ORIGIN

When Anne was conceived, her parents were not in a happy state. (See Figure 26 for Anne's father, Frank.) The pregnancy was hard-won – Laura had difficulties in conceiving because her mother had been given the drug DES during her pregnancy. Her mother had miscarried prior to Laura's conception, and this drug was said to have an effect on endangered pregnancies. (It has since been shown that DES administered in pregnancy produced children with a high incidence of reproductive organ abnormalities and cancer in early adolescence or early adulthood.) The Moon/Mars interchange in Laura's and her mother's charts demonstrate the *in utero* struggle for survival – with her mother's Mars right on Laura's Moon, her mother's body was a war zone in which she struggled to survive. Indeed, Laura's gestation was threatened at the second to third month, just as her daughter's was to be. A further look shows Frank's Mars in the same degree as Laura's mother – he replicated the mother-daughter legacy and passed it down the line to Anne.

They 'worked' (very Mars) to achieve her pregnancy. As Laura says, 'It was mechanical because I had to conceive through rhythm and basal thermometer-indicated cycles.' Laura was also on a hormone to stimulate

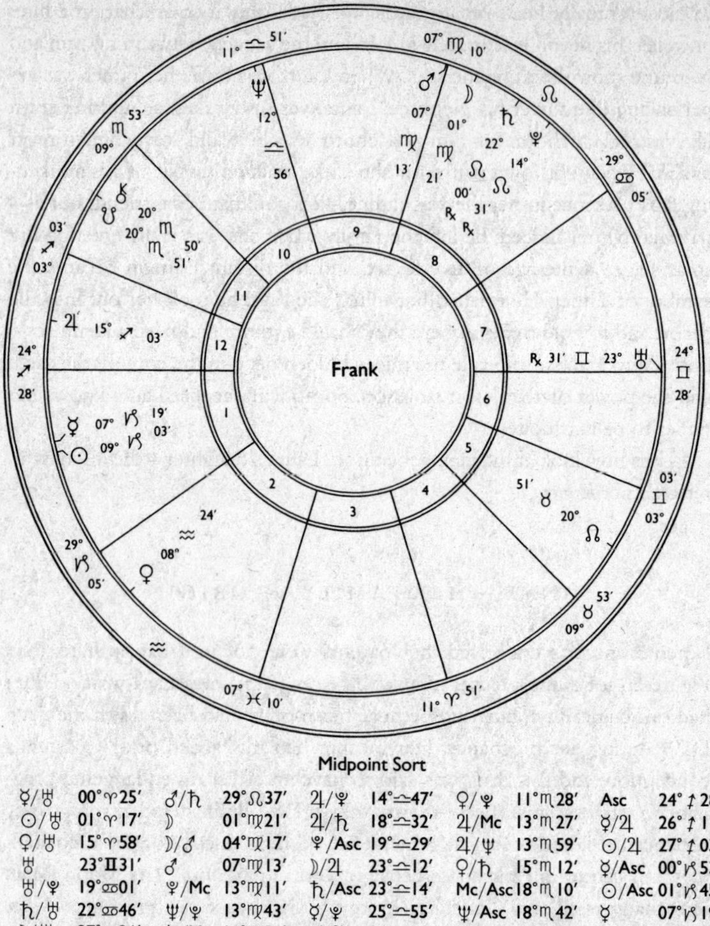

Midpoint Sort

☿/♅	00°♈25′	♂/♄	29°♌37′	♃/♇	14°♎47′	♀/♇	11°♏28′	Asc	24°♐28′
☉/♅	01°♈17′	☽	01°♍21′	♃/♄	18°♎32′	♃/Mc	13°♏27′	☿/♃	26°♐11′
♀/♅	15°♈58′	☽/♂	04°♍17′	♇/Asc	19°♎29′	♃/♆	13°♏59′	☉/♃	27°♐03′
♅	23°♊31′	♂	07°♍13′	☽/♃	23°♎12′	♀/♄	15°♏12′	☿/Asc	00°♑53′
♅/♇	19°♋01′	♇/Mc	13°♍11′	♄/Asc	23°♎14′	Mc/Asc	18°♏10′	☉/Asc	01°♑45′
♄/♅	22°♋46′	♆/♇	13°♍43′	☿/♇	25°♎55′	♆/Asc	18°♏42′	☿	07°♑19′
☽/♅	27°♋26′	♄/Mc	16°♍56′	♂/♃	26°♎08′	☽/♀	19°♏53′	☉/☿	08°♑11′
♂/♅	00°♌22′	♄/♆	17°♍28′	☉/♇	26°♎47′	♀/♂	22°♏49′	☉	09°♑03′
♇	14°♌31′	♃/♅	19°♍17′	☽/Asc	27°♎54′	☿/Mc	24°♏35′	♀/♃	11°♑44′
♅/Mc	17°♌41′	☽/Mc	21°♍36′	☿/♄	29°♎40′	☿/♆	25°♏07′	♀/Asc	16°♑26′
♅/♆	18°♌14′	☽/♆	22°♍09′	☉/♄	00°♏32′	☉/Mc	25°♏27′	☿/♀	22°♑52′
♄/♇	18°♌16′	♂/Mc	24°♍32′	♂/Asc	00°♏50′	☉/♆	26°♏00′	☉/♀	23°♑44′
♄	22°♌00′	♂/♆	25°♍04′	☽/☿	04°♏20′	♀/Mc	10°♐08′	♀	08°♒24′
☽/♇	22°♌56′	Mc	11°♎51′	☽/☉	05°♏12′	♀/♆	10°♐40′	♅/Asc	24°♓00′
♂/♇	25°♌52′	♆/Mc	12°♎24′	☿/♂	07°♏16′	♃	15°♐03′		
☽/♄	26°♌41′	♆	12°♎56′	☉/♂	08°♏08′	♃/Asc	19°♐45′		

Figure 26

the ovaries to produce an egg. So this was not a spontaneous love-conception; indeed, theirs had not been a happy sexual relationship anyway. Laura was only eighteen when she married Frank, and had done so motivated by her need to get out from under the Saturn in the home; and, though older than her, Frank never really enjoyed a sexual life. He very likely found the intimacy too cloying, with Venus in Aquarius opposite to Pluto in Leo, and there was a history of sexual conflicts and polarities in his childhood.

When Laura was carrying Anne, she was very happy to be pregnant; she loved the closeness and the intimacy. Around the second to the third month, the pregnancy was endangered – she began to spot, but it lasted only a couple of weeks. Laura simply went 'into confinement' in the classical sense; she lay down and kept her baby inside her. The first of Anne's prenatal eclipses occurred at this stage, new at 18° 37′ Cancer, and the second one followed two weeks later at full 3° 24′ Aquarius. The initial eclipse highlights Anne's natal fourth/tenth house axis, and her mother's ascendant/Uranus midpoint. Even though Laura wanted her baby very much, it was already threatening to become a major impediment to her freedom and her identity. She was also experiencing some anxiety (Uranus). The second eclipse highlights her father's Venus, if only by virtue of it being in Aquarius, but also it marked the end of the endangered gestation.

In hindsight, however, Laura recalls feeling very frightened and confused by Anne's aggressive behaviour in the womb. Even though at the time she would push it out of her mind, stuffing it away, she now says, 'It was as if she wanted to punch her way out.' (Natal Moon/Mars following on the family theme.) There was also the awareness that the baby was threatening, that the pregnancy was fraught with the lack of loving support from her husband. Indeed, Anne arrived four weeks early, hastily leaping out of her mother and into a harsh world in which she would find further difficulty lying in wait for her.

With Pluto just into the twelfth house, there is the theme of the endangered birth, and the threat in the womb is inherited, passed down the line from mother to mother. Also Anne has Mars/Neptune which is a hint of being angry at the bonding level; she raged in the womb. Her Moon/Saturn conjunction in Gemini chafes at the container, punches the mother and feels stifled, blocked, impatient to move out, and away from such a smothering condition. Some babies must hate their womb-home, and some wombs are dangerous, as Laura's mother's was when the drug was introduced into the mutual support system. Howard Sasportas used to rate wombs as one to five star – he even had a 'jaws-womb' – certainly Laura's mother's womb was an unsafe place with the experimental drug in her system! Something has passed down the line from womb to womb.

A bit about Anne's father, Frank: his own mother was burdened with six children in all, having entered into an arranged marriage, Sicilian style, at the age of sixteen. When Frank was two, however, he went to live with his paternal grandmother, who according to all accounts was a 'saint', a woman of shining valour and virtue. Frank's mother was definitely not of this order, in fact she was, at her most disturbed, a 'whore'. Frank's father was most often at sea, and his mother would go out to bars at night and pick up men, leaving the other five children at home. She would often have to be sought out and brought home. Even though Frank was spared living with her in the family unit, he was clearly not spared the inheritance of the Madonna-Magdalene complex which is bound up in his Venus/Pluto opposition.

Venus in Aquarius not only finds body-issues suspicious at the best of times, but also contains an idealized version of the feminine. The split which Frank's two primary mother-figures embodied is dramatically portrayed in this configuration. Aquarius is the sign plagued by the myth of Ouranos's castration and his divorce from and elevation beyond Gaia-earth. With the feminine Venus in Uranus's sign, Aquarius, the split between body and soul or the Real and the Ideal is vast – the inherent duality of the heavenly, divine and platonic-masculine Aphrodite Urania is in conflict with the earthy, maternal, sensual Aphrodite Pandemos. That Aphrodite/Venus was born parthenogenically from the spilt semen of Ouranos lends a power to her motherlessness, and when Venus is found in Aquarius, it resonates on the level of Urania, pure, platonic, idealistic – definitely not Pandemos, Venus of the earth.

The Venus trine to Neptune simply makes it easier for Frank to anaesthetize his pain about his mother's real nature, and elevate it or repress it. His own romanticism is divided as well, and would likely harbour in Anne's psyche, especially as she has rejected consciously her same-sex parent and opted – *at this stage* – to go towards the opposite sex parent.

His own sexuality was possibly frightening to him, and almost certainly disgusting. With his sainted grandmother and tainted mother as the two classical feminine images held within his psyche, both perfectly conforming to the archetypal Venusian split, his own terror of descending into the earthiness of sex and sensuality was very, very high. Losing control in sex would threaten him with the loss of his self and identity into the devouring abyss of the darkest side of the feminine. That Venus is in a trine to Neptune only facilitates his escape from the earthiness. Frank wanted a child in theory, but was frightened of it as well.

Frank's Chiron in Scorpio sits right on Anne's Venus/Pluto midpoint. She awakened his deep wound of being born to the 'whore', and this daughter by her birth manifested his sexual anxiety for him. All women carry within them the dual archetype of the feminine. This is the double-Venus, the polarity of celibacy/promiscuity, which is a great source of shame and anxiety for Frank. Pluto/Venus goes both ways, for the power of sex is the power of life and death.

With his Mars on Laura's Moon, his own anger at his mother and the feminine function as he had experienced it was projected on to Laura as psychological abuse through withholding love, affection and sex. Recall that Laura's mother has Mars in the same place – essentially, in Frank, Laura married her mother, someone who would emotionally upset and hurt her, love her while at the same time disapproving of her, expecting her to contain her own rage and his own, as well as carry the instinctual aspects of emotional life. He was 'brought in' to tie together the maternal lineage which settled in Anne. Frank ties in astrologically with his mother-in-law in other ways, too – Frank's Uranian Venus is on her ascendant, near her south node.

The parental marriage as we see it in Anne's chart is remarkable! Within herself she has embodied and polarized the family-circuit rage in her Moon/Mars opposition. This family aspect is further amplified by Moon conjunct Saturn opposite Mars conjunct Neptune. With her Sun/Mercury/Venus trinity – her 'identity trinity', the north node and Jupiter in her father's sign, in the house of the ancestral 'gene-pool', the psychic repository for the family lineage, the house of the womb, it rings true that she used her mother's body to get through to her father's family.

Anne's cluster of four planets and the node in the IC region, which replicate her father's Capricorn Sun/Mercury, seem to be saying the same thing – the womb is a trap, a place of confinement, and the mother is a dragon who will devour her. Whether or not this is a conscious truth is quite beside the point – Anne felt this and has enacted her rejection of her mother in various ways, all fed by her father. For her father's rejection of *his* mother was passed on to his daughter, who assumed the role of mother-rejector.

There are two significant events which occurred early in Anne's life. The first was the day she had been brought home from hospital, and was in the nursery with her mother and grandmother (Laura's mother). Laura was breast-feeding her. Laura says it was a beautiful, tender moment between her and her baby and her mother, as well . . . three generations of women, sharing a moment of intimacy together. However, Frank came into the nursery, saw her breast-feeding the baby and was horrified. He went into a hysterical, screaming rage, claiming that Anne wasn't being fed properly, and that bottles were better, and so forth. This was so shocking to both women, one wonders how it affected Anne. Certainly Laura was terrified, humiliated and deeply affected. Over the next week she continued to try to nurse little Anne, but the anxiety and fear of the father's rage was so great that she gave up after a few days, thus thwarting both of them at the breast.

Frank's Venus/Pluto split could not cope with the earthiness, the healthy eroticism and intimacy of seeing the baby at the breast. His own rejection would have arisen like a ghost from the past, and his revulsion quickened. The trinity of women is mythological – the Fates, the Furies, the Sirens, the triple lunar goddess, Cerberus with three heads, Persephone's underworld hound, and so on – all three women are a vision of the unity-in-variety of eros, emotion and body.

The second major event was when Anne was three months old, and Laura and Frank went away for a weekend. Anne was a very demanding baby. (Indeed she would be, with all that emotional energy. Neptune with the Moon/Mars 'globalizes' the infant's rage – she was later to be hyperactive.) They left Anne with Frank's family – his mother and sisters. When they returned, Laura felt they had taken her over – and, indeed, from that time on, Anne always responded more to them than to her . . . Anne had bonded with her paternal grandmother. With Saturn in her ninth house of grandparents (and Moon tied in), and it being the dispositor of her IC and four planets/node in the IC/fourth house, it makes perfect sense that she was born to the father's family, especially to his mother.

Until around the time of this writing, at twenty-one years of age, she was still totally enmeshed in her father's family, declaring herself to be Italian, not half-Italian, but fully so, and related to that side of the family exclusively. The most difficult aspect of this situation is that her father was disapproving of her, abusive to her, never accepted her shortcomings, always criticized her and was generally rejecting. Anne has multiple, if mild, learning disabilities. As mentioned before, she was hyperactive and disruptive and between the ages of three and four endured three adenoidal surgeries – she had developed severe allergies which damaged her hearing, and at one stage, between the ages of two and four, was totally deaf. She has auditory processing difficulties – when she hears something she cannot understand it fully as it is being received. She shuts out the world as it comes into her sphere, and rejects what she is hearing.

Mars at 10° Sagittarius sits exactly at her Sun/Uranus midpoint (9° Sagittarius) – the inherent, thus inherited rage is part of her individuation process. Initially the Mars = Sun/Uranus is nervous, hyperactive, susceptible to sudden ailments, bizarre perceptions – her auditory distortions – and bursts of rage; however, with time and maturation it can become the impetus to break away from stifling situations and strike out on her own. Because the Mars is the most 'occupied' degree in the family circuit, it seems that the combined family anger has settled in her and in her it will reside until she can find a way out. She had such problems, however, that by the time Anne was seven Laura had finally sought various experts' opinions and advice and her own instinctive knowledge was confirmed – she really had deep emotional scars and learning difficulties. There began a quest to help her and solve her problems; however, Anne never felt happy with her mother's support, and was more at home in herself with her father's abusive criticism.

She became a scapegoat at school, bullied and taunted for her differences, seen as being dull, and because her problems were acted out, the other children turned on her. She had two bouts of suicidal tendencies which were serious and alarming to her mother – one period was when she was between nine and ten. In that year, Jupiter was in Sagittarius all of 1993, and the transit of Uranus was back and forth her Neptune/Mars conjunction, in opposition to the Moon/Saturn conjunction. Uranus seems to be a strong planet in her chart – as mentioned, it is strongly configured with the Sun and when its transit was moving over the midpoint, on Mars/Neptune, the darkness became overwhelming. Uranus can open the doors to perception, but what one sees can be very disturbing, and at the age of nine and ten one's inner resources and ability to use the clarity of vision of Uranus is not developed well, if at all. Basically, she wanted to die – to return to the womb.

This transit resonated throughout the entire family – the Mutable degrees are those most in common. Laura had Uranus square her Moon/Node; her mother had Uranus square her Mars, as did Frank, while Laura's father was about to experience the transit conjunct his Mercury and square his Mars. That Anne was experiencing the conjunction to her Mars speaks eloquently of releasing the anger and opening up the underside of repressed anger, which is depression. She was too young to realize that the source was from a collective story; that no one person was to blame or at fault, but that a kind of ancestral conspiracy was afoot to employ her to be the one to institute changes.

Anne's second bout of suicidal fantasies occurred when she was thirteen – in January 1987, Neptune had just begun to transit her Capricorn planets and, at this writing, has not yet (1995) quite done its job. Neptune was conjunct her natal Venus in December 1986, and was back and forth through the whole of 1987. Neptune over Venus is a call back to the womb, to the unified feminine, literally to the salty sea of the oceanic consciousness. Because she was still very young, it didn't manifest as a triangulated relationship in an adult way, but the Oedipal context of Neptune and Venus brought in the triangulation of the archetypal mother and father and divine child. In her mind, her own mother, her own father and her self were confused by the imminent promise of years of Neptune (and Uranus) transits. However, by the time Anne was fifteen, and through the worst of her descent and coming into strength, Laura felt it was safe to make the break and leave her husband.

She had devoted her life first to her own mother's well-being and then to her daughter's; she now felt her daughter was at the stage where it would be OK to let go and she did. Anne chose to live with her father, and finally, after all the years of systematically rejecting her mother, she ultimately moved fully into her father's life and family, completely denying her mother.

Between December 1987 and October 1988 there was a Saturn/Uranus conjunction occurring at three points – at 26–28° Sagittarius and at 0° Capricorn. For Anne, 28° Sagittarius is marked by the meeting of Mercury/Mars midpoint and Jupiter/Neptune midpoint. Oddly, by enmeshing herself in her father's family, and fully, finally, rejecting her mother, she had begun a period of gestation. She had entered a period – a long one, right through to around the end of 1997 – of secondary gestation. The breaking out that can occur with the transit of those two midpoints for Anne required that she re-enter a kind of 'secondary womb', one of her own making, to undergo a form of long incubation or gestation and emerge later, giving birth to her own self as an adult.

The whole situation looks very much as if Anne 'used' her mother's body to move through to her father, in turn, then uses her father to fold back into herself and undergo first an enmeshment in and then a dissolution of her family attachments. This to-ing and fro-ing from the extreme poles of parental influence – the supportive but rejected mother and the abusive, rejecting father – could very well prove to find a balance in the middle; that is, without being responsible for or to either parent. Her situation has all the potential to break down a whole family theme which has rested in her soul – her fourth house – since her birth. The fact that both Uranus and Neptune have conspired to transit all her Capricorn IC and planets in the fourth simultaneously speaks of a profound fate. At the moment of her birth it was written that this transit would occur. As a result something deep inside was always in preparation for this moment of reckoning. The mystery, of course, is why. But astrology cannot always tell us why, but only how and when.

The Uranus/Neptune conjunction occurred at a time when global and individual boundaries were dissolving and shattering. Uranus represents the one out of the many, while Neptune is the many. To have them together in Capricorn created the ultimate dissolution of both personal and collective boundaries. The entire time Neptune transited Capricorn, over its fourteen-year period, Uranus moved through its orb during its seven-year period. The maximum time of the actual conjunction took place between 1991 and 1994 – and in January 1994 there were seven planets in Capricorn at the new Moon on the 11th, all of which settled in Anne's fourth house. This was a major turning-point in her secondary gestation. From this time, she has seeded herself and made some attempts at independence.

The passage of Saturn in Capricorn through the Uranus/Neptune conjunction occurred in 1993–4 and planted the seeds of a new life. Saturn is the planet of manifestation, of earthiness, and he is also the god Kronos, who swallowed his own creative issue to gestate them – he is the surrogate mother in this form. The secondary gestation of the children of Kronos eventually resulted in the new pantheon, the new mythology of Zeus/Jupiter. It has been and shall still be a lengthy self-gestation for Anne; she has to liberate herself from her Kronian father, and give birth to herself, but she is beginning to achieve that. Big transits, the outer planetary transits, do not do their work overnight. They take years, a lifetime to fully explicate their meaning.

Anne now lives in her own flat, though she works for her father's company. She has strong tendencies towards weak, abusive men – as did her paternal grandmother and as she herself experienced her own father. She still seeks ultimate approval from her father, and is still very enmeshed in her Italian family. However, inklings of change are appearing. The autumn of 1995 will see the final transit of Uranus over Anne's Sun, and its departure from Capricorn. Neptune will linger on till 1997, dragging out the birth process; however, the Uranus statement will have left its mark. Uranus will have opened the doors to self-clarity and urges for freedom from the past, but Neptune's sojourn for a bit longer will prolong her quest for self-identity. The fact that Uranus will then move quickly on to make strong, positive aspects to all the complex planets as soon as it enters Aquarius – first to Pluto, then her Moon and Neptune then, Mars and Saturn – all speak of a slow but sure individuation.

In a recent transatlantic telephone call, Anne asked Laura, 'When you left was it because there was something wrong with me?' Laura said no, that she just had to go – in fact had to go because she had done all she could, and to stay on further would damage everyone more than her leaving. By leaving, she was being truthful. Then Anne responded, 'You have to be your own person, don't you, Mom? I guess I can't base my life on being married, so I have to have my options open.' By leaving Anne's unloving and abusive father herself, and having the courage of her own convictions, knowing that when she left him she left Anne with all the resources she could give her, Laura has acted as an exemplar for her daughter. Sometimes the pay-off comes later, much later, but it seems that Anne is now looking at her mother with different eyes, perhaps seeing that having broken the chain of maternal martyrdom and rejection, her mother has given her the option of doing the same thing. By having left the 'bad father', she gives her daughter permission to do the same at some stage in her young life.

I asked Laura how she felt about all this, how she had come to terms with it, why it might have been this way and what was the point as far as she was concerned. She said that she felt she had learned compassion, and how to compartmentalize. She had also learned that there is something bigger going on out there than personal individuation, that there is a larger framework and a more cosmic order. Because Laura is a person seeking the truth, she has had to face some very sad truths, but face them as a true Scorpio can – with hope. She said she was 'Sherlock Holmes re-embodied'! Too true. Also, Laura knew deeply that there was some kind of debt being paid out to the family line and that she had a role in breaking the chain (fourth house Neptune and Scorpio influence).

She has coped by stepping out of the emotionalism of the situation and by working on her own self. Also she has benefited from looking at it from all viewpoints – mother, father and child's viewpoints. She can see this very clearly, and her own clarity is being slowly fed back to her by her daughter, the next in line to hold the family fate, in fact, the last in line.

'The tension of all this suffering has led to "Me", to a deepening of understanding. To consciousness, in fact,' Laura said. She has suffered tremendously, for she loves her daughter very much, but has been able to stand back and see that her daughter has a very difficult life. And, though she experiences a great deal of pain through that awareness, she no longer feels guilt or anger. She has moved it outside her ego and into the realm where it belongs. She says, 'My daughter has taught me patience. [*Such a Capricorn.*] Perhaps in this way I will finally hold my daughter in my spiritual womb comfortably, and she will be re-born into her Self. Surely other daughters, and sons, will take the seeds of these truths, birthing truths [*of this story*] in many ancestral lines.'

Laura transplanted herself back to her ancestral roots, having met a man from there in February 1991, and married him in July. Together they moved to the 'homeland' in that same September, both beginning new lives together. She says that the story does continue, but on a new plane. Her husband was born at six months' gestation because his mother's body rejected him and he has been rejecting her as well as carrying the natal rejection ever since! He is Laura's 'traveller' and self-realized 'father' – while she expands his horizons of consciousness, he expands her geographical horizons. She says, 'In this way, we are soul-mates, carrying the same ancestral lineage to work out between us individually and in relationship, which mirrors self-integration and relationship-integration.' And life goes on.

Epilogue

After reading her own story, Laura added some additional family information which is significant in the light of the Saturn/Jupiter theme and the Mars/Moon theme:

'My sister's daughter – my niece – endured a threatened gestation, at two to three months, as well. She was born two weeks late, on 14 January 1972, exactly one year earlier than my daughter, Anne. Her mother, my sister, left the marriage while she was a child, and my niece remained living with her father. To this day she is still living with and enmeshed in him. My sister feels rejected by our mother. My half-brother was born early and given to foster care until he was six months old, at which time Mom retrieved him and entered into marriage disaster number two.

'This family history of maternal rejection/rejecting which you have indicated traces back to both of my grandmothers. My paternal grandmother committed suicide and my paternal aunt was killed, both within the space of two years, leaving my father abandoned in early adulthood.

'My maternal grandmother spent the last twenty-five years of her life as an invalid. This would suggest that a consequence [*sic*] of lack of holding (rejection) was unconsciously played out in that my grandfather – her husband – had to tend to her as if an infant. This also reinforces the need to be "mothered" by the father. Consequently, my own mother suffers the same rejection/rejected issues with her mother. She has had major periods of physical and emotional illness in her adult life which have been a cry to be held and cared for, but by a husband or father-figure. She had little relationship with her mother, and bonded strongly with her father.'

Well!

Saturn ate his own children, and carried them in his body/womb. I have always seen the Kronian theme in the family lineage as a series of surrogate father-mothers. Though Kronos/Saturn swallowed his creative issue, his offspring, out of fear of losing power, he also inadvertently acted on their behalf by 'holding' them until Zeus/Jupiter was born to liberate them into a new mythology. Now, we see that there was a new mythology released when Laura found Creation Spirituality came close to her own personal cosmology, and she is the Jupiter to the family Saturn. Also, by letting go of her own child, giving her over to the father to re-gestate, we might just be looking at a mythological re-enactment of creation. And Anne to be the new order of things to come in the family. She is the last in line.

Summary

I. FAMILY CONNECTIONS, FAMILY THEMES

(a) The Cardinal Cross (see Figure 27) There are a total of twenty-five planets, angles and nodes in all the Cardinal signs, with the majority of them being held in Capricorn, and most of those by Anne herself. Second, Libra is strong, then Cancer, with two Plutos, a Uranus and Anne's south node; finally, we have Aries in which Chiron figures strongly in Anne's and both maternal grandparents' charts, while Laura, her mother, has Jupiter retrograde and the MC there.

Cardinality in families speaks of a genetic flaw, a physically based problem which affects all aspects of family life. Origins, ancestral roots, dynastic lineage and incarnation are the Cardinal cross. To some degree we all bear it,

CARDINAL – *Cross of Origins*

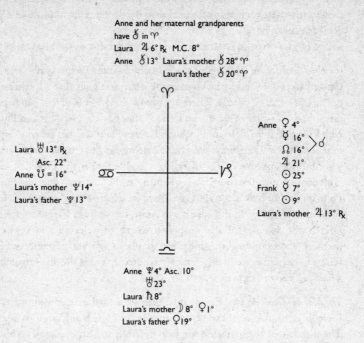

Anne and her maternal grandparents
have ♂ in ♈
Laura ♃ 6° R͓ M.C. 8°
Anne ♂ 13° Laura's mother ♂ 28° ♈
Laura's father ♂ 20° ♈

♈

Laura ♅ 13° R͓
Asc. 22°
Anne ☋ = 16°
Laura's mother ♆ 14°
Laura's father ♆ 13°

♋ ——————————|—————————— ♑

Anne ♀ 4°
☿ 16°
☊ 16° ⟩ ♂
♃ 21°
☉ 25°
Frank ☿ 7°
☉ 9°

Laura's mother ♃ 13° R͓

♎

Anne ♆ 4° Asc. 10°
♅ 23°
Laura ♄ 8°
Laura's mother ☽ 8° ♀ 1°
Laura's father ♀ 19°

Total: 25 points in Cardinal

Figure 27

but dominance speaks of a particular problem to work through, especially if all the signs are equally represented. The person who has the majority of them is frequently the one who is the manifestly obvious bearer of the family cross. The very issue of rejection in the womb is the ultimate of Cardinal crosses to bear.

ANNE IS THE MOST CARDINAL OF ALL THE MEMBERS OF THIS GROUP.

(b) The Fixed Station (see Figure 28) Fixity in a family theme symbolizes its capacity to endure and maintain its homeostasis so rigidly that it might need to crack in order to change. There are twenty fixed points in this family picture, but most of them are the nodes and outer planets, Neptune and Pluto, with Frank's Saturn right in there with Laura's Pluto and her parents' Neptune – all at 22° Leo. Frank was the Capricorn father – the Kronian father who did not approve of his offspring – and Saturn is the planet of embodiment or manifestation ... his Saturn on the maternal line Neptune/Pluto implicates him as the vessel or container which would bring the family complex into reality. In this case it was Anne, through her Capricorn fourth house, who manifested the unspoken theme of rejected and rejecting mothers, incorporating the polarized positions of her parents, seeking refuge in her father's enmeshed family syndrome. She is the 'missing link'.

ANNE HAS NO FIXED PLANETS AT ALL.

The Mutable Dilemma (see Figure 29) There are a total of eighteen points in Mutable signs, two of those being Laura's nodal axis from Virgo to Pisces. The majority of those planets are held in Virgo and Sagittarius, with all of the extended family but Laura's mother represented in Sagittarius.

Laura's father's Mercury is 9° Sagittarius, Laura's Moon is 7° Virgo (with south node). His Mars is 12° Pisces, while hers is 12° Virgo. Laura's mother has Mars at 6° Virgo. Laura marries Frank, who has Mars at 7° Virgo and Moon in Virgo, as well. They have a daughter, Anne, who has Moon at 5° Gemini and Saturn at 14° and in opposition to Neptune at 6° Sagittarius and Mars 10°.

The theme is Mutable and the common planetary link is primarily the Moon and Mars. This signature is of deep emotional rage combined with the confusion which can abound in Mutable crosses. The lack of communication across and between family lines is evident and it is displayed in the dichotomy of Anne's Moon/Saturn opposition to Mars/Neptune. It is as if she needs to find her own distinct container away from the family anger and work through a process of separation first from mother, then from father,

FIXED – *Cross of Embodiment*

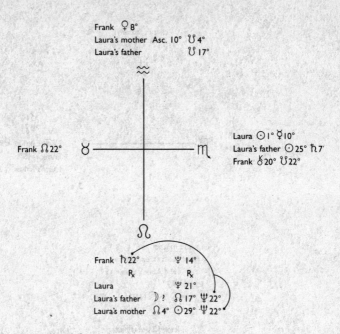

Frank ♀ 8°
Laura's mother Asc. 10° ☊ 4°
Laura's father   ☊ 17°

Frank ♌22°   ♉ ─────────── ♏

Laura ☉ 1° ♀10°
Laura's father ☉ 25° ♄ 7'
Frank ♅ 20° ☊ 22°

Frank ♄22°   ♅ 14°
         ℞   ℞
Laura   ♅ 21°
Laura's father   ☽ ?   ♌ 17° ♆ 22°
Laura's mother   ♌ 4° ☉ 29° ♆ 22°

Total: 20 fixed points Mostly ♌'s, outer planets. Laura and her father have the personal ♏ contacts while his ♄ is on her ♀ and □'s Frank's ♀ which is on Laura's mother's Asc. (☊).

Figure 28

MUTABLE – *Cross of Perception*

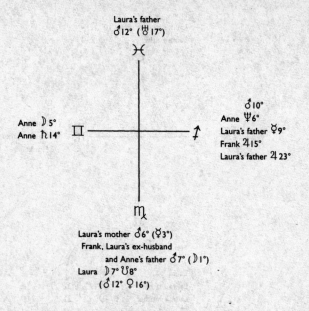

Laura's father
♂12° (♅17°)
♓

Anne ☽5°
Anne ♄14°
♊

♐

♂10°
Anne ♆6°
Laura's father ☿9°
Frank ♃15°
Laura's father ♃23°

♏

Laura's mother ♂6° (☿3°)
Frank, Laura's ex-husband
and Anne's father ♂7° (☽1°)
Laura ☽7° ☋8°
(♂12° ♀16°)

Total: 17 points mutable

Anne embodies everyone's ♂/☽/☿ into her ☽☍☍(♆17°)
AND she's the only ♄ in mutable.
AND the only ♊ planets whereas Laura's father is the only ♓ representative
AND, we are doing this family while t–♄ is in those degrees of ♓... embodying the family theme.

Figure 29

then back to herself via a balance between the parental energies embodied in her.

The Mutable theme also speaks of 'passing the buck', of not taking responsibility for one's own problems, but assuming them to belong to others. This is projection and transference at a visceral-body level. Mutable is also contagious – Mutable is miasmic; traits, characteristics, ideas, feelings, and so forth are all interchangeable and of all three modes, Mutable has the most difficulty creating and maintaining appropriate boundaries – both personally and collectively within the family itself. Characteristics cross boundaries and become infused, enmeshed in each other and in individuals themselves.

ANNE'S MUTABILITY IS SPLIT EXACTLY BETWEEN GEMINI AND SAGITTARIUS – NOT IN THE DOMINANT SIGN OF VIRGO.

2. WHAT HAVE WE SEEN IN THIS STORY?

1. This entire picture shows consistent aspect, planetary and modal themes threaded throughout an extended family which become centred in one individual who has experienced profound symptoms which are literal manifestations of all the astrological and familial themes.
2. Transits to the main family theme which have brought out observable changes in all parties. The degree links are powerful and consistent, showing that the racial and familial memory is strong. This story also shows the power of attraction – that Laura should 'choose' to marry Frank, whose story falls so cleverly into place, is the power of the memory we have in the astrology of our lives. Never doubt the story, but look for the connections.
3. A picture of one person's perspective – that is, Laura's perception of being rejected by her child in the womb might have sounded completely mad, but the planetary array, its clarity of statement, validates the story completely. The entire story portrays a lineage as profound as any Greek myth could dramatize! When an individual tells a story, especially one as dramatic as this, astrology can help them with the truth of it. Astrology never lies.
4. The Moon and fourth house as personal, family-of-origin ancestral legacy symbols. Saturn as the surrogate mother, and midwife of wisdom. Jupiter as the liberator of swallowed creative issue and the creator of a new pantheon, a new mythology, a new way of being.
5. Current time: as this story was being told and written, Laura's progressed Mars had moved to 8° 17′ Libra – conjunct the IC and her mother's Moon,

which is Anne's Pluto/ascendant and Venus/MC midpoints. By cutting through the veil of mystery lying in the fourth house, and experiencing the Mars running through this family, she synchronistically found someone – I asked her – to do this analysis. Meanwhile Saturn is retrogressing back to station-direct opposite her natal Venus in November 1995, to finally allow a proper delivery to occur.

Anne has found a new relationship which encourages her independence – he is a young Capricorn . . . and she will be moving away from the father's family towards her own life, not with anger but with more confidence, having seen this story being told.

NOTES

1. See Chapter 10, page 170.
2. See Erin Sullivan, *Retrograde Planets: Traversing the Inner Landscape*, Arkana, Contemporary Astrology Series, London, 1993, for an in-depth analysis of natal Jupiter retrograde.

16.

What's Bred in the Bone: The Circuit Breaker

When someone in a family becomes the nucleus of group anxiety, complexes or stress, whether conscious or not, he or she becomes ill. Often, an illness is a way of purging. For instance, when we have a cold or fever, we are allowed to collapse with a legitimate excuse, withdraw, contemplate, sleep, read, lie about and process the illness through its various stages to recovery. After an illness we are given a new lease on life, a small feeling of having survived – our mortality is tested and we encounter things we cannot control. It is generally accepted that periodically we do succumb to normal stress and anxiety by getting ill . . . of course, we can 'catch' a cold from others; however, there are times in which we are emotionally more vulnerable than usual to whatever bug is going around.

When a family dynamic is involved, however, there are many mysterious avenues through which illness might pass and lodge in one or more of the members. The more intricately enmeshed a family is, the more difficult it is to separate out the elements of the individuals – and there can be a crisis in one of them which radiates throughout the entire family. Often this occurs with what appears to be some kind of intent! When one individual finally succumbs to something dramatic, it is often followed by a sequence of symptoms in the rest of the family which can all point to a collective breakdown and healing!

In the following family situation we see a remarkable occurrence which ties all these factors in. Fiona came to see me as she stood on the threshold of a major breakthrough, on the edge of a complex which was about to grip her entire life and force a change to occur. This was in April 1993, when Saturn had first begun the transit of the sixth house in opposition to her twelfth house natal Moon. (See Figure 30.) She had just had her progressed lunar return four months prior to this, as well, so the close relationship of progressed Moon and transiting Saturn was just beginning to wane – the progressed Moon was moving away from its opposition from transiting

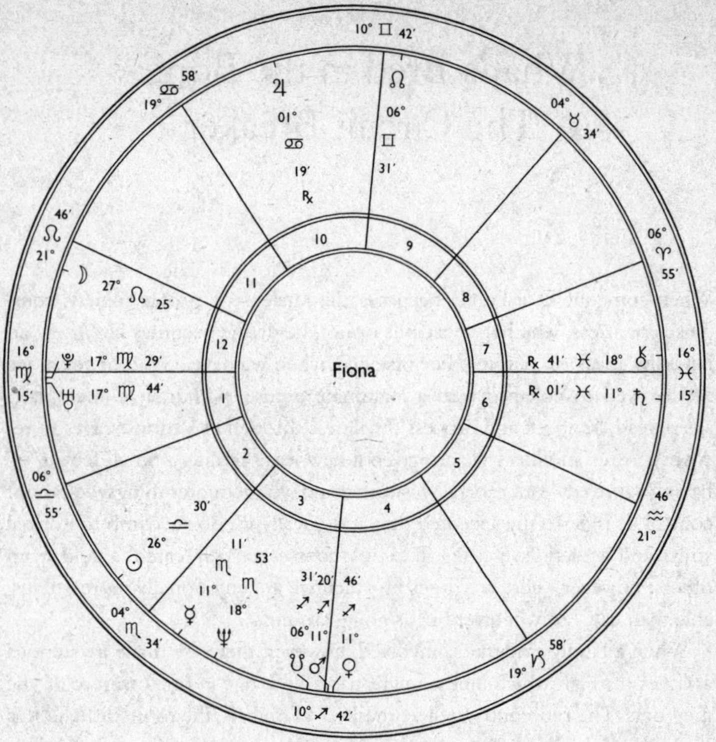

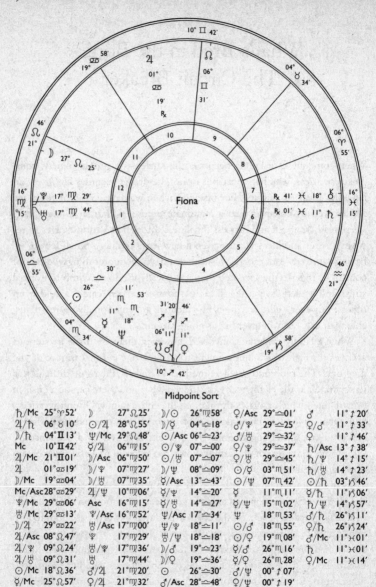

Midpoint Sort

♄/Mc	25°♈52′	☽	27°♌25′	☽/☉	26°♍58′	♀/Asc	29°♎01′	♂	11°♐20′
♃/♄	06°♉10′	☉/♃	28°♌55′	☽/☿	04°♎18′	♂/♇	29°♎25′	♀/♂	11°♐33′
☽/♄	04°♊13′	♆/Mc	29°♌48′	☉/Asc	06°♎23′	♂/♅	29°♎32′	♀	11°♐46′
Mc	10°♊42′	☿/♃	06°♍15′	☉/♇	07°♎00′	♀/♇	29°♎37′	♄/Asc	13°♐38′
♃/Mc	21°♊01′	☽/Asc	06°♍50′	☉/♅	07°♎07′	♀/♅	29°♎45′	♄/♇	14°♐15′
♃	01°♋19′	☽/♇	07°♍27′	☽/♆	08°♎09′	☉/☿	03°♏51′	♄/♅	14°♐23′
☽/Mc	19°♋04′	☽/♅	07°♍35′	☿/Asc	13°♎43′	☉/♆	07°♏42′	☉/♄	03°♑46′
Mc/Asc	28°♋29′	♃/♆	10°♍06′	☿/♇	14°♎20′	☿	11°♏11′	☿/♄	11°♑06′
♇/Mc	29°♋06′	Asc	16°♍15′	☿/♅	14°♎27′	☿/♆	15°♏02′	♄/♆	14°♑57′
♅/Mc	29°♋13′	♇/Asc	16°♍52′	♆/Asc	17°♎34′	♆	18°♏53′	♂/♄	26°♑11′
☽/♃	29°♋22′	♅/Asc	17°♍00′	♆/♇	18°♎11′	☉/♂	18°♏55′	♀/♄	26°♑24′
♃/Asc	08°♌47′	♇	17°♍29′	♅/♆	18°♎18′	☉/♀	19°♏08′	♂/Mc	11°♓01′
♃/♇	09°♌24′	♅/♇	17°♍36′	☽/♂	19°♎23′	☿/♂	26°♏16′	♄	11°♓01′
♃/♅	09°♌31′	♅	17°♍44′	☽/♀	19°♎36′	☿/♀	26°♏28′	♀/Mc	11°♓14′
☉/Mc	18°♌36′	♂/♃	21°♍20′	☉	26°♎30′	♂/♆	00°♐07′		
☿/Mc	25°♌57′	♀/♃	21°♍32′	♂/Asc	28°♎48′	♀/♆	00°♐19′		

Figure 30

Saturn. She had been working hard for several years and the cumulative exhaustion was beginning to take its toll. Although a greater part of the last ten-year period had been spent acquiring her law degree, she did find plenty of time to play, then went straight into international work abroad before entering a firm in the City for the two-and-a-half-year period prior to the consultation.

As so frequently is the case, Fiona's timing for an initial consultation was impeccable – she came the day after Saturn had moved past the opposition to the Moon by only a few minutes of arc. However, the transit would station, turn retrograde, pass back over the Moon in mid-August and then make its final, direct pass over it again in January of 1994. As a long-term process, we were uncertain of the transit's ultimate properties and thus how it would manifest in the end, after its nine-month gestation. A number of concerns arose in the course of the session, all of which related to Saturn/ Moon symbolism in general and to the sixth/twelfth house axis more specifically, which amounted to the following:

1. Generally, she was concerned about her then eighty-three-year-old grandmother's health as she is very close to her – how close, we shall discover soon. Also, there were new feelings arising within her about her own mother, and questions being asked of herself as a direct result from having entered therapy about six months previously.

2. She had also been forced to move out of her home after two and a half years, and was about to begin renting a new house.

3. She was suffering through an emotionally passionate but tumultuous relationship with a man with whom at this stage she'd been with for about a year.

4. She was experiencing a lack of ambition in her work – something very foreign to her, as she'd always had a natural wish to do whatever she did very well. This seemed to stem from a desire to please her father, to gain approval from him (Saturn on the descendant in square to Venus/Mars).

5. She was physically and mentally exhausted, and suffering from acute guilt over this condition. Basically, Fiona was at the end of her tether at the time of this first session. She was also taking roaccutane, an ingestible form of Retin-A – a powerful acne medication – (natal Saturn square Mars · Venus – skin problems) for a condition from which she had suffered on and off since adolescence.

Fiona came back to see me seven months later, in November 1993; her situation had evolved, many circumstances had transpired. Not only had she moved twice in two months, but the subsequent period was quite chaotic: a transitional kind of living situation and visiting her family and so on left her with no real sense of home as safe-place – her Saturn/Moon transit cycle – which very likely contributed to the slow running down of her system!

But, more significantly, she had been diagnosed with ME in July and had not worked since then. She'd had a severe kidney infection in the second week of June and large doses of antibiotics had probably wiped out her remaining immunity, leaving her vulnerable to the virus which triggered the ME. She was then off work for a week with flu, tried to go back, but was sent home due to her exhaustion. The diagnosis of ME was final. Her first kidney problem was in the autumn of 1973, around the age of eight (close to the Saturn cycle) – (Libra 'rules' the kidneys). She was also struggling with guilt and anxiety over the circumstantial drastic change in her work-ethic and productivity. She was working very hard on maintaining her long-distance relationship with her lover, who, although he felt deeply for her, was unable to express it as openly as she needed at that time – and, considering her depleted energy, contributed to her feelings of insecurity. And, to top it all, her once greatest ally – Granny – was finding it hard to believe she was so severely ill; she kept asking when she was going to 'be better', and so on. Things were very desperate indeed.

Let's look at Fiona's natal horoscope first, then allow the unfolding of events and circumstances to follow on.

This is the chart of a diligent, caring woman with a tremendous amount of power, much of it locked in until after her Saturn return. When the outer planets are highlighted in the natal chart, it speaks of a 'late bloomer', an individual who matures into the power that is contained in those distant-most planets until well into the mid-life. It is as if we grow into Uranus, Neptune and Pluto in stages, as we gain age, experience and inner depth. The Uranus opposition to itself which occurs between the ages of thirty-eight and forty-two, depending on what sign Uranus is in natally, begins the process of growing into the outer planets and their dynamic power. The opening of the transition into mid-life will offer the strongly outer-planetary person an opportunity to gain access to his or her unlived life, and much of what has been held in check or simply latent emerges for development. This process is fundamentally true for everyone, but dramatically so when the outer planets are distinctive in some way. As we see, Fiona has Uranus and Pluto exactly conjoined right on the ascendant.

In itself, 1965–6 was an astrologically significant year highlighted by the Uranus/Pluto conjunction opposed by Saturn, a time when the birth of global consciousness created a revolution in social order, one which still has yet to come to pass in its final stage. In a sense, Fiona's chart is tied very deeply into the collective ethos, and she will manifest many of the issues that are brought to bear upon the collective through her own personal, individual life. Her sense of responsibility for the collective is inherently great. The positioning of the global 'turning-point' configuration of Saturn opposite Uranus/Pluto brings her personal life and identity (the ascendant) in close collusion with collective trends and experiences. The precise conjunction of Uranus and Pluto in Virgo smack on the ascendant brings a sense of lonely power and strong sense of social-ethos awareness – Fiona was born during the dramatic years of the global shift in collective awareness about social justice, the 'Gaia Hypothesis', social unrest, revolution of consciousness and the turning point for the world.

The first part of one's life is often hard when major configurations such as the Saturn/Pluto conjunction, Uranus/Pluto, Neptune/Pluto, Saturn/ Uranus, Uranus/Neptune, etc. are found in prominent places in the horoscope, because growing into the power of and taking responsibility for the influence and consciousness of the outer planets takes time. Literally it takes *years*, from maturity beyond the Saturn return (around twenty-nine) and into the beginning of mid-life transition (somewhere between thirty-seven and forty-two), and indeed, a lifetime of working through the process demanded by these kinds of aspects. They are often the significators of the 'family circuit breaker'. (See Chapter 6, page 124.)

Maturing into Uranus/Pluto power takes phenomenal energy and life-experience. Configurations of such magnitude sitting in tight relation to personal points in the natal horoscope normally isolate children with these configurations starkly from others – their inner experiences are often deeper, richer and bigger than their peers. Keeping in mind that in the first twelve years of schooling and beyond, even, *all the people who are pushed together are the same age*, and therefore have the same outer-planetary configurations, thus all are involved in the collective picture. However, the individuals who have these major configurations in intimate participation with Sun, Moon and/or angles are often either victims of, or voices of the collective – or 'both/and' periodically. Certainly the awareness of a powerful destiny is not always available to a young child, and Fiona did not wander around feeling particularly threatened or abused, or special in any sense.

Indeed, it appears that she was a bright, active, outgoing child, saying that when problems arose she hid her feelings, and tended to keep her concerns to herself.

Fiona went on to say, 'I was very happy as a child, and had no worries about the family itself until Dad told us he and Mum were to separate. Until then, I had no idea that there were problems – Mum did her best to keep things hidden and she succeeded (at great personal cost, I am sure). Dad wasn't there that much, but then, he had always been away at work, or shooting, fishing, golfing or entertaining at weekends, so I didn't really notice any changes. Thus, until I was nine, I had a very happy childhood.' Her horoscope shows the mark of the wounded child; we never know when the wound will occur, and how, but when it does it creates an opportunity for the child to turn inward and deepen her contact with a more serious side of herself.

Because the nuclear family is the training ground for the individual's relationship with the world-family, a chart with such powerful aspects as Fiona's will frequently harbour difficult childhood experiences – either within herself or in the environment, or both, and we shall see that she had a particularly challenging history even before the age of fourteen. Fiona's way of coping was fairly set by her university years. Her inherent sympathy for the underdog and her experience of suffering in her surroundings and within herself, combined with the strong-willed nature of her being, prepared her for her vocation. She went to law school and eventually became a corporate lawyer working in the City – maintaining an active interest in human rights in her spare time. She was acutely aware that corporate law was not what she wanted to do, but at the time of our consultation she did not know quite why she was so disaffected by it or what to do about it.

This feeling is associated with the transit of Saturn in the sixth house when a person feels a sense of pointlessness about their occupation – a deeply unconscious awareness that they are simply marking time until the transition from the sixth house to the upper horizon occurs. In a sense, it is the preparation time for bringing something of greater value to the surface. Fiona was aware that this lack of engagement with her work contributed to her weakening health – and with Virgo rising, and the sixth house being largely Pisces, if her soul was not in her work, her body would give all the signals. She had tried for a job with EC law, which she enjoys, but the timing was wrong. While Saturn is transiting the sixth house – usually for a period of around two and even up to three or so years – people seem always simply to have to continue doing what they are doing. She said, 'I think this was probably a causal factor in the ME – I was doing the wrong thing for me – I could do it, but it wasn't me. Yet I didn't know what else to do. I felt stuck.'"

With her Moon in the twelfth house in Leo, Fiona's feelings are passionate and intense; she is very open and expressive with her friends, but with boyfriends, there is a reservation. She feels this is a hangover from the loss of closeness so early on with her father, and his abandonment of the family. She had to work hard to win back his affection and attention, and then it was more of a 'mate'-type friendship, rather than father/daughter. The sextiles from the Moon to the Sun and to Jupiter show her secret-most self being tied to a vocational purpose which would involve the characteristics of justice, humanity, mediation, and spiritual development. Children begin to manifest their vocated traits very, very early in life, but we do not often see this until there are about thirty or more years' age-perspective! A deeply private and naturally self-contained person, her Moon could easily become the repository for other people's feelings. Planets in the twelfth house are 'last to be born', and Fiona might well have held her own feelings in check in favour of keeping the peace. She would also have learned very early on how to manipulate other people's feelings. Also, the twelfth house is the house of 'confinement', and it is remarkable how many people with twelfth house Suns or Moons – indeed, other planets as well – at some point have been confined literally. But, psychologically, the confinement is innate and internal.

This duality – being a Leo Moon, which is open, generous, friendly, gregarious and expressive of feeling, being in the twelfth house, which is private, reserved and contained – is expressed in a split in the way she can express herself and to whom. Fiona says that with friends she is all the Leo part, there is no threat of loss there, no history of rejection or hurt, but with her family she is not able to be the same open person; her twelfth house 'secrecy' factor is enacted for their sake. She has a great reserve around the family context and I should think this is because she has had to be the 'balancing act' in the family, the one who was the cheerful, mature stronghold of the family feelings. Since she feels that she needs to continue to be that way – that is, not arriving at the family homes for a short visit, letting it all spill out, and leaving – she still feels that she must contain a great deal of her feeling in favour of diplomacy, tact and sincere care not to leave people all upset and confused. She does not want to rock the boat of other people's emotions.

Even though the Moon's position shows a strong link to eventually achieving a 'purpose in life' (sextiles to Sun and Jupiter), her bond with her mother was initially weak – as if she might have to look after her mother, rather than the other way around. Also, her Moon is void-of-course, and did not progress into the next sign, Virgo, until her fourth month of life. Undoubtedly this aided in weakening her constitution, resulting in her mother's suffering becoming her own in a vicarious or transferred fashion, as it does with infants. Because the birth was traumatic – and she would have felt rejected and unwanted as an infant – this theme would repeat itself whenever she would stand on the threshold of change (birth) in the future. In order to achieve change, she would need to re-enter a symbolic womb and form a chrysalis around herself (Moon in twelfth) on a fairly regular basis in the course of her life. Being able to deconstruct old, ineffective boundaries while simultaneously erecting new, more appropriate ones for the future is a challenge unique to Fiona.

The third house is the area traditionally known to represent 'siblings' – Mercury in Scorpio trine Saturn shows a remarkably tenacious mind – one which will not let go of a mystery until it is solved, a kind of mental relentlessness with a purpose. It also talks about her need for privacy and for supremacy in intellectual areas, showing a sense of responsibility for her own mind and the capacity to endure pressure. Scorpio feels responsible, and with Neptune there too, the responsibility seems almost a spiritual or a karmic duty towards brothers and sisters. There can be a confusion of roles and it is difficult to discern who she is in relation to the siblings – is she meant to be exemplar, parent or friend?

Other family signatures lie in the fourth house.[2] She has a T-square pattern pointing to the IC which says she carries the propensity for breaking the chain of the family fate. Fiona has Mars and Venus exactly conjunct the IC in square to Saturn. Saturn there is one of the significators of being the eldest or only child and, more importantly, feeling the responsibility of that position (other classic placements for eldest/only are Saturn rising, Saturn in the third, Capricorn rising and Sun/Saturn squares or oppositions – in that order).

(Her brother, whose horoscope we are not seeing because of confidentiality, has Saturn in the third house with a Capricorn Moon rising. He is *not* the only or the eldest, but *is* the only son. Also, Father has Saturn rising and he *is* the eldest in his sibling-set.) First, the Mars/Venus conjunction alone speaks of Fiona being deeply sensitive to undercurrents in the family, especially the erotic or the angry tones. Second, it is the position of the mediator, the one who is inherently aware that others will cause problems, so she had better not. The fourth house is a key to the family inheritance which Fiona seems to bear in the form of responsibility and awareness. Her sister, shown also, has Neptune in the fourth, which actually is more difficult to work through because it shows a lack of strong identity within the family system, and the umbilical attachment to the mother which might never be fully severed.

The same challenge located at the IC is also her hidden strength – by digging deeply into her unconscious, she can draw on resources handed down through the family line, those of industry, power, strength, will, charisma, passion and control.

Fiona is distinct; this is in her favour because she has strength, charisma and power in the family, but that can also work against her. She did become the one whom everyone could count on to be cheerful, useful, helpful, reliable, successful and so on. Her fourth house suggests also that the only way of breaking out of this mould would be to rebel, to challenge (Mars) the balance (Venus) and declare war on the status quo (Saturn square to those and in opposition to Uranus-Pluto on the ascendant).

Fiona's relationship with her father played a powerful role in her desire to please and to perform – to show her value and worth through masculine success routines. If we were to balance mother and father in Fiona's life, we would see the father as the shaper of her assertiveness, goal-orientation and outreach (Sun) while her mother's influence facilitated her compassionate nature, her sensitivity to suffering and sorrow (Moon). However, Saturn squaring the IC/Venus/Mars conjunction spells out a feeling of distance, separation and rejection by the father, which ultimately would influence her adult relationships. Fiona's way of dealing with her father would be to strive towards a goal, whereas her lunar placements indicate a much less aggressive need to achieve and one more inclined to mediate, meditate and live a rich inner life.

Fiona says, 'I feel having had ME has enabled me to do this. At the start of having the ME I was in a terrible state, being used to being very busy and occupied, then to suddenly find myself unable to do anything but sit around and think. It was terrifying. However, over the years of enduring the illness, I "learned" to be on my own, which I always avoided before, and I now really enjoy it. To have enjoyment of time with myself, I feel is a real achievement.' Too true. With such a dynamic T-cross, relaxation and simply 'being' rather than 'doing' or 'being something' *is* a real achievement. And it is not unusual for a body-crisis or a symptom (Virgo rising, Saturn strong) to alert such an active, mental person to the need for quiet, contemplative and relaxing time.

The family legacy indicated that Fiona would need at least the first Saturn cycle (about twenty-nine to thirty years) to move outside the family bond to further her own self-understanding, after which she might re-enter the family in a new way, to reclaim any of her natal characteristics left in the matrix of the family-dynamic. This is a cyclic process for everyone, and it gets done in various ways – regardless of how benign or malignant a family system is, each individual must, at crucial points in his or her life, go back into the family to re-establish renewed identity as he or she matures. Fiona's ongoing job of self-identity requires many departures from and re-entries into the family system – for the process of individuation for Fiona occurs in clear, successive cycles, all in coincidence with the transit of Saturn.

When Fiona was born, her mother contracted a severe pelvic infection and also suffered from post-natal depression – so she was both morally and physically depleted. Therefore, at Fiona's birth, her mother had to withdraw and rest because of her own illness and internal problems for the few weeks afterwards, but did deeply enjoy her as a baby and child. This is the Uranus/Pluto on the ascendant, the 'endangered birth' spoken of earlier. Very often mothers who are ill at childbirth feel very guilty and anxious for their infant because they know the bond is threatened, and Fiona's mother was, as we shall see, very happy to have her to shower love and affection upon. (See Figure 31.) The Uranus/Pluto conjunction on her ascendant speaks of Fiona's first glimpse of the world, and it is a world in which she would have to 'fend for herself', so to speak, which is an infantile response to maternal rejection which would mould her adult behaviour until some new crisis would mark a change-point. Because of her mother's circumstances, both she and Fiona went to live with the paternal grandmother immediately after the birth and stayed for a month or so, during which time Granny became Fiona's virtual mother, establishing a bond that runs deep to this day. (See Figure 32.)

Granny's Moon is exactly conjunct Fiona's Neptune, and she *is* her spiritual mother, having a deep psychic connection to her. Also, Granny's Sun is exactly square Fiona's Uranus/Pluto and ascendant, implicating a paternal-type energy to their relationship. Indeed, Granny is her *paternal*

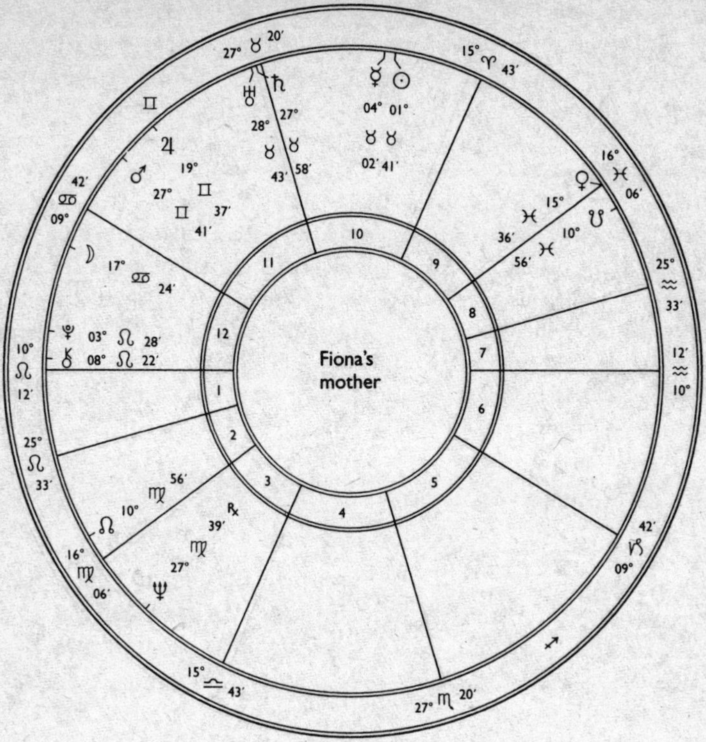

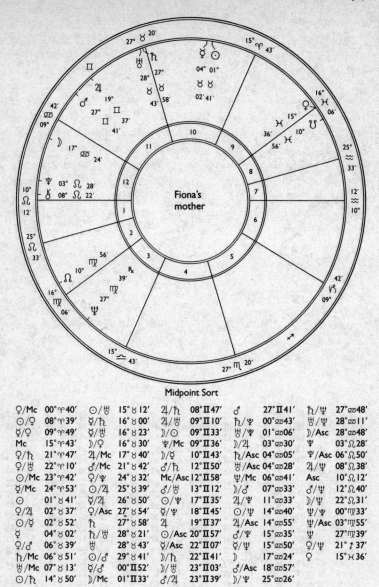

Midpoint Sort

♀/Mc	00°♈40′	☉/♅	15°♉12′	♃/♄	08°♊47′	♂	27°♊41′	♄/♆	27°♋48′
☉/♀	08°♈39′	☿/♄	16°♉00′	♃/♅	09°♊10′	♄/♇	00°♋43′	♅/♆	28°♋11′
☿/♀	09°♈49′	☿/♅	16°♉23′	☽/☉	09°♊33′	♅/♇	01°♋06′	☽/Asc	28°♋48′
Mc	15°♈43′	☽/♀	16°♉30′	♇/Mc	09°♊36′	☽/♃	03°♋30′	♇	03°♌28′
♀/♄	21°♈47′	♃/Mc	17°♉40′	☽/☿	10°♊43′	♄/Asc	04°♋05′	♇/Asc	06°♌50′
♀/♅	22°♈10′	♂/Mc	21°♉42′	♂/♄	12°♊50′	♅/Asc	04°♋28′	♃/♆	08°♌38′
☉/Mc	23°♈42′	♀/♇	24°♉32′	Mc/Asc	12°♊58′	♆/Mc	06°♋41′	Asc	10°♌12′
☿/Mc	24°♈53′	☉/♃	25°♉39′	♂/♅	13°♊12′	☽/♂	07°♋33′	♂/♆	12°♌40′
☉	01°♉41′	☿/♃	26°♉50′	☉/♇	17°♊35′	♃/♇	11°♋33′	☽/♆	22°♌31′
♀/♃	02°♉37′	♀/Asc	27°♉54′	☿/♇	18°♊45′	☉/♆	14°♋40′	♆/♇	00°♍33′
☉/☿	02°♉52′	♄	27°♉58′	♃	19°♊37′	♃/Asc	14°♋55′	♆/Asc	03°♍55′
☿	04°♉02′	♄/♅	28°♉21′	☉/Asc	20°♊57′	♂/♇	15°♋35′	♆	27°♍39′
♀/♂	06°♉39′	♅	28°♉43′	☿/Asc	22°♊07′	☿/♆	15°♋50′	♀/♆	21°♐37′
♄/Mc	06°♉51′	☉/♂	29°♉41′	☽/♄	22°♊41′	☽	17°♋24′	♀	15°♓36′
♅/Mc	07°♉13′	☿/♂	00°♊52′	☽/♅	23°♊03′	♂/Asc	18°♋57′		
☉/♄	14°♉50′	☽/Mc	01°♊33′	♂/♃	23°♊39′	☽/♇	25°♋26′		

Figure 31

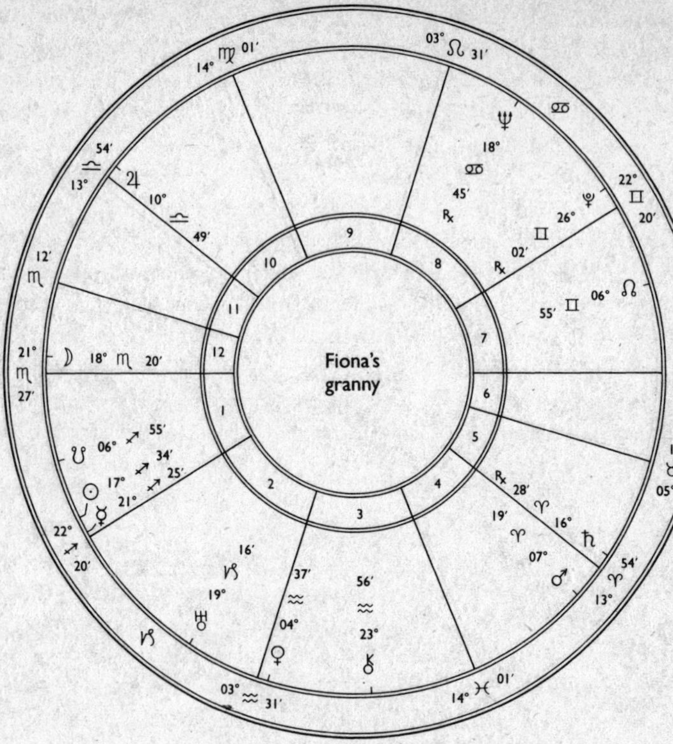

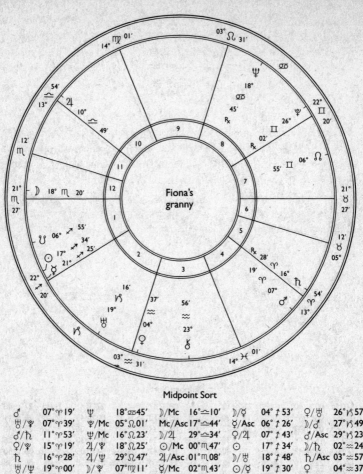

Midpoint Sort

♂	07°♈19′	♆	18°♋45′	☽/Mc	16°♎10′	☽/☿	04°♐53′	♀/♅	26°♑57′
♅/♇	07°♈39′	♇/Mc	05°♌01′	Mc/Asc	17°♎44′	☿/Asc	06°♐26′	☽/♂	27°♑49′
♂/♄	11°♈53′	♆/Mc	16°♌23′	☽/♃	29°♎34′	♀/♃	07°♐43′	♂/Asc	29°♑23′
♀/♇	15°♈19′	♃/♇	18°♌25′	☉/Mc	00°♏47′	☉	17°♐34′	☽/♄	02°♒24′
♄	16°♈28′	♃/♆	29°♌47′	♃/Asc	01°♏08′	☽/♅	18°♐48′	♄/Asc	03°♒57′
♅/♆	19°♈00′	☽/♇	07°♍11′	☿/Mc	02°♏43′	☉/☿	19°♐30′	♀	04°♒37′
♀/♆	26°♈41′	♇/Asc	08°♍44′	☉/♃	14°♏11′	♅/Asc	20°♐22′	☉/♂	12°♒26′
♂/♇	16°♉41′	Mc	14°♍01′	☿/♃	16°♏07′	☿	21°♐25′	☿/♂	14°♒22′
♄/♇	21°♉15′	☽/♆	18°♍32′	♅/Mc	16°♏39′	☽/♀	26°♐28′	☉/♄	17°♒01′
♂/♆	28°♉02′	♆/Asc	20°♍06′	☽	18°♏20′	♀/Asc	28°♐02′	☿/♄	18°♒57′
♄/♆	02°♊36′	☉/♇	21°♍48′	☽/Asc	19°♏53′	☉/♅	03°♑25′	♂/♅	28°♒18′
♂/Mc	25°♊40′	☿/♇	23°♍44′	Asc	21°♏27′	☿/♅	05°♑21′	♄/♅	02°♓52′
♇	26°♊02′	♃/Mc	27°♍25′	♀/Mc	24°♏19′	♂/♃	09°♑04′	♀/♂	05°♓58′
♄/Mc	00°♋14′	☉/♆	03°♎09′	♃/♅	00°♐02′	☉/♀	11°♑05′	♀/♄	10°♓32′
♆/♇	07°♋23′	☿/♆	05°♎05′	☽/☉	02°♐57′	☿/♀	13°♑01′		
♃/♄	13°♋38′	♃	10°♎49′	☉/Asc	04°♐30′	♅	19°♑16′		

Figure 32

grandmother, and thus through her she passes down some of Fiona's father's fate. Fiona might 'replace' her son (Fiona's father) for her in some oblique fashion – but more importantly, that aspect shows the degree to which Granny helped foster Fiona's self-direction and purpose in life. Their north/south lunar nodes are also conjoined at 5–7° of Gemini/Sagittarius. With Fiona's north node in Gemini in the ninth house, it speaks of a grandparent being of singular importance in the development of her life and formulation of her ideas (ninth house rules grandparents), but because it is precisely *the same* as Granny, it suggests that her grandmother will eventually, through act and thought, lead her to independence.

Granny's Pluto is on her son's Moon, and Fiona's father has probably felt the pressure of his mother's over-ministering and may have rejected his mother in a meaningful way to 'save' his own sense of masculinity, and also set the pattern for his subsequent inability to display feelings or give and receive nurturing. Father's Mercury square to Saturn on the nodal axis makes it virtually impossible to express himself openly, or at all, especially with his children. This aspect can mean that he relates better to the children when they are older (Saturn) than when they are very young or adolescent. In fact, Fiona says that their relationship improved dramatically when they could work together, which they did for a time on some speculation properties, go to lunch, to pubs and be friends. Her brother has also discovered this facet of his relationship with his father, much improving it. Their sister, however, 'calls him to account as a father more, which he finds difficult to say the least!' says Fiona. (See Figure 33.)

Also, Fiona's father himself had had a 'hard father' who was fundamentally absent, who in turn had been harshly raised by *his* own father. It seems that the men in the family were all of the 'strong, silent type', not lacking in loving feelings or affection, but not inclined or perhaps even capable of demonstrating them openly. Fiona's father appeared to be an emotionally distant man, and this shows in Fiona's chart by the Saturn squares to her Venus and Mars. Because of his own training and his nature, he could not express his feelings, thus he inadvertently suppressed the creativity of his own young children as Kronos/Saturn did with his offspring in the myth by swallowing them and not giving them birth. However, Fiona has an elevated and illuminated Jupiter (main aspects are to the trine to the Sun and sextile to the Moon) – and, like Zeus/Jupiter who liberated his swallowed offspring, she will be required to give birth to her own creativity rather than have it fostered by another.

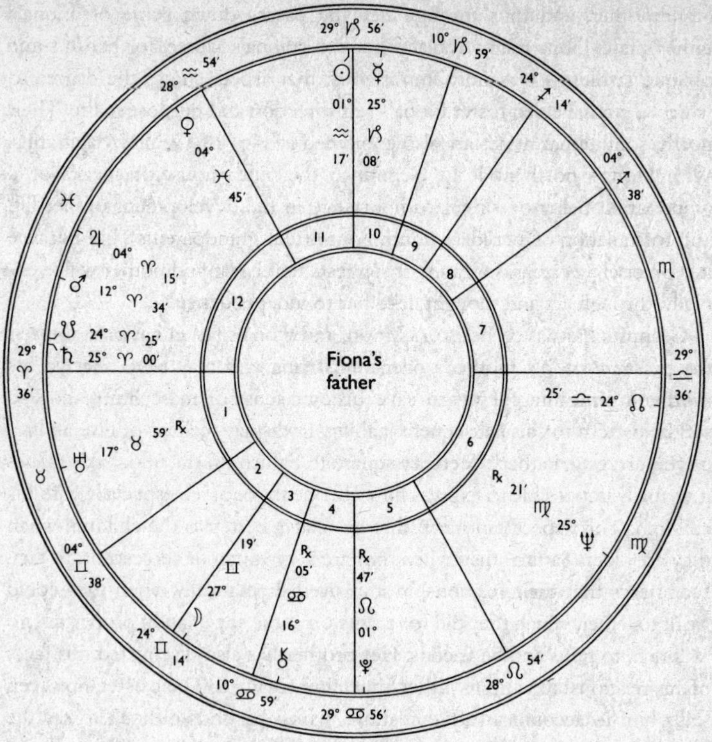

Midpoint Sort

♀/Asc	02°♈11′	♂/♅	00°♉17′	☽	27°♊19′	☉/♆	28°♏19′	☿/♂	03°♓51′
☽/Mc	04°♈09′	☽/♀	01°♉02′	♃/♆	29°♊48′	♀/♆	15°♐03′	♀	04°♓45′
♃	04°♈15′	♄/♅	06°♉30′	♂/♆	03°♋57′	Mc	10°♑59′	Mc/Asc	05°♓18′
♂/♃	08°♈25′	♅/Asc	08°♉48′	♄/♆	10°♋11′	☿/Mc	18°♑03′	☉/♂	06°♓55′
☽/☿	11°♈13′	☽/♃	15°♉47′	♆/Asc	12°♋29′	☉/Mc	21°♑08′	☿/♄	10°♓04′
♀/♅	11°♈22′	♅	17°♉59′	☽/♇	14°♋33′	☿	25°♑08′	☿/Asc	12°♓22′
♂	12°♈34′	♀/♇	18°♉16′	♅/♆	21°♋40′	☉/☿	28°♑12′	☉/♄	13°♓09′
☽/☉	14°♈18′	☽/♂	19°♉56′	♇	01°♌47′	☉	01°♒17′	♅/Mc	14°♓29′
♃/♄	14°♈38′	☽/♄	26°♉10′	☽/♆	11°♌20′	♀/Mc	07°♒52′	☉/Asc	15°♓27′
♃/Asc	16°♈56′	☽/Asc	28°♉28′	♆/♇	28°♌34′	☿/♀	14°♒56′	♀/♃	19°♓30′
♂/♄	18°♈47′	♃/♇	03°♊01′	♆	25°♍21′	☉/♀	18°♒01′	☿/♅	21°♓33′
♂/Asc	21°♈05′	♂/♇	07°♊11′	♇/Mc	21°♎23′	♃/Mc	22°♒37′	♀/♂	23°♓40′
♄	25°♈00′	☽/♅	07°♊39′	☿/♇	28°♎27′	♂/Mc	26°♒46′	☉/♅	24°♓38′
♃/♅	26°♈07′	♄/♇	13°♊24′	☉/♇	01°♏32′	☿/♃	29°♒41′	♀/♄	29°♓53′
♄/Asc	27°♈18′	♇/Asc	15°♊42′	♆/Mc	18°♏10′	☉/♃	02°♓46′		
Asc	29°♈36′	♅/♇	24°♊53′	☿/♆	25°♏14′	♄/Mc	03°♓00′		

Figure 33

The Kronian father is one who swallows his creative issue. For Fiona, she would have to liberate herself from a feeling of being oppressed and undervalued as a person. Her Saturn placement indicates that about every seven years she would have to make great leaps forward towards her own authenticity – and this would always involve a struggle, a specific obstacle and a threshold crossing.

Fiona and Granny *have* always been close, and it was her health that Fiona was worried about when we first met. It is rather interesting how things have evolved, for I was confident at the original session that Fiona needed to stay out of her mother's domain while she processed her new feelings about her – her mother seemed to have deeply influenced Fiona's illness, and while the transit of Saturn was in opposition to her Moon, it seemed time to take a break from her. There is always an abandonment theme when a mother is ill at birth, and the infant psyche/body experiences rejection; this birth-pattern was about to repeat itself (Saturn return coming up) and it was time for Fiona to stand apart from her mother in a positive way. Uranus and Pluto rising opposed by Saturn on the descendant and square to her Mars/Venus conjunction at the IC speak directly of the hardship of 'loss' of mother at birth, replacement factor or not.

Now Granny herself is a woman who, with no malignant intent, busies herself with everyone else's life, causing a great deal of commotion at times, interfering with and interpreting others' actions and motives and setting family relationships on end. She has a strong 'masculine replacement' factor in her nature, also – Sun in Sagittarius with Mercury trine Saturn in Aries retrograde. Granny just might be a patriarch! Even at eighty-five, her amusing concern on the subject of death was that 'she'd not know what everyone is up to', and she told Fiona (when they were talking about death) that she'd like to be a 'fly on the wall'! Fiona herself was not subject to the more difficult aspect of this characteristic until she reached her precise Saturn return – but more on that later.

In Fiona's story her sense of isolation and differentness was both inherent *and* circumstantial. She grew up in Scotland, and in her class at school she was the only child whose parents were divorced! Death of a parent was one thing, but divorce was considered to be a stigma at that time and for many years after, though this attitude has relaxed somewhat since the mid-seventies. As a single-parent, however, Fiona's mother turned her daughter into her 'partner', which Fiona rather enjoyed when she was young because, being inherently more mature than her age, it gave her a feeling of equality in her adult world.

The entire family moved to the country in 1973, and shortly after that there was a financial crisis which took mother back to work, and father was gone most of the time. Unbeknown to any of the children, Fiona's father had an affair about two years after her sister was born. Her mother did not like country life and was very lonely there; however, she and her husband never let the children know the state of their affairs – they knew nothing consciously of their family crisis until it was time for the separation and the move back to the city in the summer of 1975. Father later married (and remains married to) the woman he was seeing at that time. Fiona's mother had a lot to be angry about in her life, but rather than demonstrate that anger in an overt and directed fashion, her body became the focus and battleground and she suffered a number of illnesses and symptoms – thus her body became the scapegoat for her own natural rage at her unhappy circumstances.

Fiona has a sense of spiritual and moral obligation towards her siblings, and possibly even had to experience the sacrifice of her own childhood for her sister and brother: in her brother's case, his ascendant is the same as Fiona's IC – 10° Sagittarius! As if his persona is formed by Fiona's position in the family fate – she was selected to be the successful one. Her brother has always felt overshadowed by her accomplishments (her Jupiter is conjunct his natal Sun at 1° Libra – she appears larger than life, and this, sadly, has been reinforced by their father's criticism of him, carrying on the male legacy of being 'hard on the sons'). But, in the case of her sister, Fiona was indeed a kind of replacement mother, which was part of her being her mother's 'partner' from the separation, in the summer of 1975, onward.

Fiona's sister has the Sun and Moon in Pisces in the eighth house, disposited by Neptune in the fourth house. (See Figure 34.) Her family legacy is a bit less clear than Fiona's Mars/Venus message. Neptune in the fourth house brings a sense of uncertainty and insecurity to the individual's perception of his or her place in the family – in fact, Sister would have virtually no concept of who she is in the family picture. She would be highly susceptible to the 'moods', the undercurrents, and the general ethos of the family system, likely carrying much of the sadness of her mother (fourth house Neptune). Sister's responsiveness to her mother is amplified by her 12° Pisces Moon conjunct her mother's south node and Venus – she feels her mother's pain and suffering and absorbs it. They have no boundaries between their feminine selves; in some sense, Sister never really left the womb,

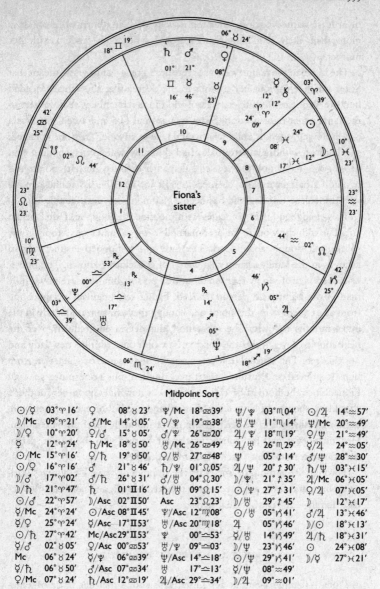

Midpoint Sort

☉/☿	03°♈16'	♀	08°♉23'	♆/Mc	18°♋39'	♆/♀	03°♏04'	☉/♃	14°♒57'
☽/Mc	09°♈21'	♂/Mc	14°♉05'	♀/♆	19°♋38'	♅/♆	11°♏14'	♆/Mc	20°♒49'
☽/♀	10°♈20'	♀/♂	15°♉05'	♂/♆	26°♋20'	♃/♅	18°♏19'	♀/♆	21°♒49'
☿	12°♈24'	♄/Mc	18°♉50'	♅/Mc	26°♋49'	♃/♅	26°♏29'	♀/♃	24°♒05'
☉/Mc	15°♈16'	♀/♄	19°♉50'	♀/♅	27°♋48'	♆	05°↑14'	♂/♆	28°♒30'
☉/♀	16°♈16'	♂	21°♉46'	♄/♆	01°♌05'	♃/♆	20°↑30'	♄/♆	03°♓15'
☽/♂	17°♈02'	♂/♄	26°♉31'	♂/♅	04°♌30'	☽/♆	21°↑35'	♃/Mc	06°♓05'
☽/♄	21°♈47'	♄	01°♊16'	♄/♅	09°♌15'	☉/♆	27°↑31'	♀/♃	07°♓05'
☉/♂	22°♈57'	♀/Asc	02°♊50'	Asc	23°♌23'	♃	29°↑45'	☽	12°♓17'
☿/Mc	24°♈24'	☉/Asc	08°♊45'	♆/Asc	12°♍08'	☉/♅	05°♋41'	♂/♃	13°♓46'
☿/♀	25°♈24'	☿/Asc	17°♊53'	♅/Asc	20°♍18'	☿/♅	14°♋49'	☽/☉	18°♓13'
☉/♄	27°♈42'	Mc/Asc	29°♊53'	♆	00°♎53'	☽/♆	23°♋46'	♃/♄	18°♓31'
☿/♂	02°♉05'	♀/Asc	00°♋53'	♅/♆	09°♎03'	☉/♆	29°♋41'	☉	24°♓08'
Mc	06°♉24'	☿/♆	06°♋39'	♆/Asc	14°♎18'	☿/♆	08°♒49'	☽/☿	27°♓21'
☿/♄	06°♉50'	♂/Asc	07°♋34'	♅	17°♎13'				
♀/Mc	07°♉24'	♄/Asc	12°♋19'	♃/Asc	29°♎34'	☽/♃	09°♒01'		

Figure 34

or at least wanted back in after the novelty of being born wore off. It is more than likely that baby Sister's troubles began in tandem with her mother's.

The move to the country, and her mother's going out to work, meant that Sister was left without her mother to the degree that she actually needed her; she went early to nursery school and Fiona remembers, as do others in the family, that right up until Sister was around two and a half she was a cuddly, loving, friendly child who would take to anyone. Then she changed; she became withdrawn, troubled, had difficulty with other children and hated going to school (Fiona used to take her each day herself). So around two and a half everything seemed to shift for her; she has found her life very difficult to this day, and has been a victim in ways uncountable.

This change in Sister coincides with the time we know her father began an affair with the woman he later married in 1979. Father was simply gone, so she felt doubly abandoned. The little girl responded instinctually to changes in the family system that were not consciously known. The power of secrets is profoundly registered in every person, but no more powerfully than in the Neptunian person. Indeed, Father was gradually disappearing from all of them from this point on. Though they saw him frequently in the initial months following the separation, this decreased gradually over the next couple of years and the children saw him only with his new lady and her children. This created jealousy, naturally, and a sense of alienation from him. It grieved and insulted the three children, but none more so than Fiona. Since the burden of child-rearing was now fully upon her mother's shoulders, she would have felt pressured and needful of time of her own, quite naturally, but these feelings are never rationally received by children. Her initial grief and her subsequent anger worked into the family system and was transmitted into each of them by degrees.

Through the autumn of 1974 into the summer of 1975, Uranus was transiting back and forth a degree which threads through and connects the nuclear family – 26–27° Cardinal signs.

THE TRANSIT OF URANUS

1. Fiona – Conjunct Sun at 26° Libra. This shows that her sense of equilibrium is deeply shaken and it is the foreshadowing of the ME, which has been in tandem with the square of Uranus in Capricorn (with Neptune by

1995) to her Sun. (Also, her first kidney trouble had been in the autumn of 1973, just after Saturn transiting her fourth house opposed her natal Jupiter and was squared by transiting Pluto at 2–3° Libra!)

2. Father – Opposing Saturn at 25° Aries – needs to break out of past, make new patterns, oppose the status quo and break structures. Also, his need for adventure is highlighted, but feelings of anxiety accompany Saturn/Uranus contacts, and his behaviour would have appeared to be erratic.

3. Sister – Conjunct Sun/Saturn midpoint (father) 27° Aries – creates havoc with her 'father' principle in herself, her sense of containment, security, identity. Could have triggered her first depression, which creates a habit for future reactions to separations, changes, trauma.

4. Brother – Conjunct Moon/Venus midpoint 27° Libra – his feeling nature and relationship within himself of his own self-worth and self-nurture shaken, it also shows his mother and sisters implicated in the upset.

5. Mother – No transit of Uranus at all. However, in September 1974 Saturn was conjunct her 17° Cancer Moon, while the Uranus transit began to move over the above points for everyone else! This is a classic indicator of depression and serious concerns about family, home, children, security and relationships.

What is truly significant about this transit list is that everyone is receiving strong Uranus 'hits' but the mother. All their realities are being shattered, split and scattered about, while only the mother is receiving the leaden, cold, depressing and finalizing transit of Saturn. This seems to say that she is the one who receives the burden of depression and conclusion, while everyone else is in a state of chaos. Ultimately, a Uranus transit leaves more potential for rearranging one's circumstances or perspectives than does a Saturn transit, which simply seems to terminate situations. Mother would have felt the full weight of the emotional situation without feeling any real hope for several years after that. She might have found herself at the end of her limit – their relationship had likely been unsatisfactory for her for some time already, but she would not have instigated a breakdown herself. Her loyal Cancer Moon would be likely to have stood up under the pressures, at her own emotional risk.

When the children were told that their father was leaving, and their mother moved back to the city with Fiona and the other children in August 1975, Saturn had moved to 26° Cancer – the degree that Uranus had broken up all through the previous year-and-a-half. All that had gone on under the transit of Uranus in the form of upset, chaos, forced change was finalized and solidified under the transit of Saturn to the break-up degree. Saturn picked up the memory which lay in the collective psyche of the family at 26° Cardinal and completed the work done. Only Mother knew consciously that Father was having an affair, but the children were registering the collapsing family structure deep down inside, and it was showing in each of the members in individual ways. Every single member of the collective had the same anxious, changing Uranus transit, except the mother – she had the depressing Saturn transit to her Moon, showing that for all conscious efforts, the family as she knew it was at its limit. She did work hard, but felt 'beaten' by the other woman, lost, and took it as a personal failure. Her feelings were not only for herself but for her children, to whom she felt a great responsibility . . . her role as a 'good mother' was challenged in her own eyes.

Their brother, who was receiving the Uranus transit to his Moon/Venus midpoint, began to have temper tantrums and became withdrawn. His emotions were volatile and his sense of balance clearly thrown off. This was compounded by the insensitivity of his teacher at school. who handled him very badly. The headmistress had told their mother that there was no point telling the teachers about their home problems, the divorce, that is, and implied that the whole thing was terribly sordid. There was no consideration of the effect that the home situation was having on the children and how it might be alleviated by care from teachers in the school system. So society was not to help out either.

Sister's work, her relationships and her inner life have caused her grief and sadness and she has suffered off and on from depression. In 1993 she broke up a relationship and became needy, hysterical and depressed. The family doctor was deeply concerned and voiced these concerns to Fiona. So Sister has overtly experienced the sadness and sacrifice of happiness in the family, while Fiona has soldiered on, being the strong one, the successful one – the son her father wanted and didn't have first.

Fiona's Mars/Venus/IC in square to Saturn shows her ability to contain and control the undercurrents of the family system. It is also the signature of her own impoverished sense of self-value. This, coupled with her formal training as an advocate and mediator in her legal career, primed her for becoming a super-active organizer – both at work and at play. There is also a hint of her taking on the entire family situation as something she herself is responsible for. To some degree, the horoscope is a picture of our fate, but then there are the circumstances in which this fate is enacted. Fiona was the balancing act between her parents after their separation. Just before Father finally married his lover in December 1979, Mother had a dangerous asthma attack – rather than a tantrum or overt expression of rage (natal Mars in Gemini (lungs) square Neptune in the third (breath/lungs)), her body took the brunt of her stress.

About her childhood Fiona says, 'I was a sociable child and had lots of friends – I was pretty outgoing; however, I went through a withdrawn phase which started around the time Dad and his (now) wife moved in together, which was April 1979 and continued until the New Year of 1980.' So, all through this time, Fiona was finding it difficult to maintain her own equilibrium, and her own stress levels were rising. I believe this was the first hint that her own Virgo rising system had a sympathetic reaction to family problems. In fact, by October 1979, Uranus had moved for the second and last time to 18° Scorpio, conjunct Fiona's Neptune – that is a transit which I have equated with the shutting off of the anaesthetic. There is no escape from pain under that transit, and anything lurking under the surface, anything hidden, covert, suggested, hinted at and so on erupts to the surface.

Fiona says that although she was unaware of it at the time, in retrospect she sees that she was very close to a complete breakdown. She had been going back and forth to her grandmother's at weekends, feeling all the anger at her father but particularly at his girlfriend, whom she would naturally envision as being the source of so much pain for her and the family. She was so unwell that her grandmother became alarmed, really the only one to see just how close Fiona was to collapse, and sent her to stay with an aunt in France for a few weeks over Christmas to 'get away' from the family stresses. Then Fiona's natal Mars/Venus to Saturn square erupted on the surface of her skin as virulent acne – as she said, fourteen was a bad year! Her father, with the Mercury square to Saturn, had also struggled with acne as a young man and this, too, he had passed on to Fiona; however, it took Saturn, the events and the circumstances to bring the inner condition to the surface.

Saturn rules the skin as a container of the body, and Venus is the cosmetic factor of the skin's appearance; and the blemished skin was a perfect physical metaphor for the 'ugliness' she felt within herself, the virulence (Mars) in the family and her own despair at the adolescent transit of Saturn opposite itself – all of which began in September 1979. While transiting her ascendant, it replicated her natal Mars/Venus to Saturn square, but from the first house of 'appearance' to the fourth house of the deep, unconscious family fate, as well as inherited physical traits from her father. Just prior to, and during, her Saturn return, Fiona had to be treated for a serious bout of acne again – with the Retin-A substance, roaccutane, that she was on when we first met. She had first had the roaccutane treatment in 1991, at the expense of her father, who expresses great concern over her skin in a rather heavy-handed way. There is always a sad feeling of guilt in a parent when a trait which has hindered them is present in one of their children – as if they could have done something about it. With Saturn running around his and Fiona's charts, he undoubtedly feels very badly about her skin problems, but, given his nature, he cannot show this tenderly! Rather, it compounds her feelings of being marked or ugly. Clearly, his financing the treatment helps her, but he cannot be diplomatic about it.

Twenty-six to twenty-seven degrees of Cardinal shows up again in 1982–3 . . . in June 1983 Fiona had meningitis when Pluto and Saturn were stationing at 26° and 27° of Libra respectively, right on her natal Sun! (And Uranus was conjunct her south node.) One wonders what everyone else had, since her Virgo rising body seemed to be the thermometer of the family's emotional temperature! Pluto and Saturn at 26–27° of Libra was a deadly threat to her life, and it also would have triggered all the points mentioned above in the family charts.

Now we arrive at the present time when I am writing this case (January 1996), and Fiona has not been able to work for two and a half years. However, the mysteries of ME have uncovered some significant family dynamics and might just be the illness that cures. For Fiona has become the alembic of transformation in her family. The hard-working girl became the over-achieving woman – the Saturn transit through her sixth house brought to the fore both work and health concerns. As Saturn worked its way through the sixth house, all the troubles, hardships, suppressed feelings and experiences held deep in the subjective self (lower hemisphere of the horoscope) were being embodied. If one is going to flag at work or in body/spirit, it is when Saturn is in transit, especially in the sixth house – even at its most benign, Saturn in the sixth brings an attitude of ennui to whatever one has been doing for the last seven or so years.

At first, no one in the family could accept the fact that Fiona was ill, most especially herself. It is clear that really we can change no one but ourselves; however, in doing so, we can perform some fundamental changes in the family system itself. At our first consultation, I was concerned that Fiona's level of exhaustion was so deep and cumulative, and that considering the future of aspects to come – which would include Saturn return, cresting the descendant and opposed to Uranus/Pluto, followed by the transits Uranus and Neptune conjunction square her Sun to that critical degree of 26° Cardinal in Capricorn – it could lead to a breakdown in her immune system and she could fall ill with 'something like ME', I said.

She agreed with me, and was herself concerned about such a possibility. She had entered therapy six months prior to the first consultation to understand more about herself in the context of her relationships, both personally but primarily within the family. ME is a strange disease; it has no sound symptoms upon which to focus. They shift, they are chimerical and whimsical. Fiona, particularly, would have a hard time with ME because it's not like having a broken leg, one can't 'see' it, or 'fix' it with plaster or an operation. It was very eerie for me to hear the tape of the first consultation and actually hear myself say those words, and then, several months later, have them validated. ME was in her system as we spoke that first time.

So she suffered not only the illness but also the attendant guilt – because of her mother's reflection on her own symptoms, and her sister's victim-status, Fiona was a harsh judge of herself. Her desire to please and achieve ran deep in her viscera – her body had to give up because her mind could not. She always worked 'another half-hour, or hour' longer than she needed to or should. She played equally hard – it is a good ethic, really, the work hard, play hard lifestyle. However, there was an underlying unconscious motive feeding into her dynamic life – that being that Fiona did not know what it was like to simply 'be'. She was rarely alone except to sleep – her work days long, and her social evenings fun and equally long! She says she did not want to be alone, perhaps fearing the engulfing loneliness that might ensue, but also she simply loved to party. She was not consciously miserable at all! However, it is people whose time is fully occupied, and who find it difficult to do nothing at all, who are most at risk from warnings from their bodies.

By April 1994, as I suspected initially, it was clear that Fiona was indeed, the 'circuit breaker' – she came in for another session, and was in very bad shape from the illness. Meanwhile good things were also afoot – Fiona's love-relationship had begun to stabilize, and become more intimate and reliable, and she was travelling back and forth from the UK to the continent to be with her partner, who himself had changed considerably and was continuing to do so. However, in this spring of 1994, she went back home to the family bosom to visit – her mother had become caring, a nurturer and protector to her now, truly understanding her condition and situation, offering the support that Fiona needed. She had always been Fiona's champion, but Fiona had been born with the strong desire not to place a burden on others – this might well have interfered with her own mother's desire to be more supportive than Fiona would let her! But, significantly, her mother shared feelings with Fiona which she had not been able to express before, about herself, and also spoke of the past, which has healed many small wounds and cleared things for both of them – it is likely that their work will have its effect on her sister, too. Sister remained 'histrionic', a victim, and showed some signs of jealousy of the renewed relationship that Fiona and her mother were creating. And Granny was beginning to show signs of feeling left out, it seems. She now began to meddle in Fiona's affairs and, rather than treating her as her repository for the family's 'secrets and conspiracies', began to actively create some problems for her with her father.

Poor Granny – now that the whole system was shaking, she was feeling vulnerable and very likely angry with Fiona for being the catalyst! At one point she told Fiona that her father had said that 'if she was gadding about Europe, she couldn't be all that ill'. Upon confronting her father with this, he replied, 'No, I don't *not* believe you, I just don't *understand*.' Fair enough, no one understands ME, and people around it often are very unsympathetic; it has been called the hypochondriacs' disease. The 'me' disease. The problem is, it is totally incapacitating and lasts for years and usually befalls those who most hate to be idle! And thus they are literally forced to sit for hours, days, years, contemplating their inner lives, while the world revolves on around them.

Fiona's Saturn return was beginning at this time; it would go up to 12°, station-retrograde, and make its final return in February 1995 – at the same time Uranus would be at the square to her Sun at 26° Capricorn (that familiar/familial 26° Cardinal). I had felt it would be after that time that she would be on the mend. I was keeping in mind that following its transit to the descendant and opposition to Uranus · Pluto, there would be a long transit of Neptune to finally distil the material which had come to the surface while she underwent her incubation in the form of illness. After that, she would need to give birth to herself slowly.

If birth was hard, so all subsequent births will be a challenge. Our natal charts are the blueprint for all change that occurs in our lives. Giving birth to one's own self is not easy, but is especially difficult if the origins have hard aspects – and Fiona's chart illustrates how a return to the womb in order to incubate a 'new' self can be life-threatening, but also life-giving. Her illness is a metaphor for this act of self-delivery. Because inherently she is the family mediator, she holds a special charge – that of freeing up the other members of the family to experience themselves in a new way, also.

The Saturn return in itself is a time of re-meeting the family in a new way. A time of integrating all of life's opportunities and blows, as well as a time to address one's own authority, authenticity and to make all attempts to become the true author of one's own destiny. The Saturn return is usually a time when we look very closely at who is shouting the orders, and how we are responding to those orders. It seems that Fiona just wanted out for a few years in order to restructure the existing status quo and to re-visit her family in a way which would allow her to free herself in ways which were very subtle. She needed to fall ill to see how they would respond to this 'new her' – she was no longer the cheery one, the encouraging one, the support-ive one, the one who would be the rock under all storms! She needed the support and backbone of her family. Slowly they changed; slowly she began to recover. However, recovery of the 'identified one' means that the homeostasis of the family system has to kick in, and indeed, we find that everyone has begun to experience their own symptoms.

Considering that at birth Fiona was temporarily 'rejected' by her mother and enveloped by her grandmother, it stands to reason that at her 'second-birth', the Saturn return to its original statement, she might have to reverse this and reclaim her actual mother and give Granny her place as the elder, but not the mother. Fiona's relationship with her mother has undergone a terrific transformation and they now relate much more equally; Fiona feels that she is now protected by, supported by and nourished through her own mother. On a very deep level, Fiona needed to 'reject' Granny in favour of Mother to complete her own rebirthing ritual. The need for rejection is symbolic rather than actual; rather, she would need to distinguish herself from her grandmother's needs and attend to her own needs first. In the end, it all comes around again.

The mystery of the family is unending – as Fiona recovers from her long illness, other family members are having symptoms, perhaps being allowed to let their repressions surface and emerge. Everyone is changing. Father is more available, Mother is more supportive, Granny is being kept more in her place, Sister has consented to treatment and hopefully will begin her process of individuation in earnest as Saturn continues to transit her eighth and ninth houses, heading to the 'Call to Adventure' at the MC!

Oh, in January 1995 her father had a hip replacement and in May 1995 her mother had a serious neck operation in which bone growths were scraped from the third to sixth vertebrae and two discs were removed! The mother and father, so long separated but so tightly bound, have managed to experience something so close to the bone as their daughter has given permission for everyone to change. Also, Uranus was at that critical family degree in January, while Neptune was there in May – 26° Cardinal! Recollection and healing of a time so long passed. So the family skeleton was rattled to its very backbone!

As for Fiona, her ongoing relationship throughout this whole period had undergone various developments and level-shifts. It did reach a critical point in the autumn of 1995, but blossomed to fruition in the last days of 1995 – her marriage in the summer of 1996 is the happy note of the new beginning for her own life.

NOTES

1. Erin Sullivan, *Saturn in Transit: Boundaries of Mind, Body and Soul*, Arkana, Contemporary Astrology Series, London, 1990.
2. See Chapter 10 (page 170) and Chapter 3 (page 61).

17.

The Procession of
the Ancestors

There are times in the life of certain individuals when it is necessary for them to purge a line of characteristics which has become so concentrated and fully ripe in a family that these traits or energies begin to deteriorate or decay. This is not necessarily indicated by particular aspects in the natal chart, nor is it typical of every person. As we have already discovered, there are mysterious forces afoot in the human experience which we may not measure.

It is not out of evil intent that families hold their shapes too long for their long-term good, but usually out of unconscious habit. Although by now it is clear that the dynamic family is a moving machine, one which is in constant motion and flux, there is still the holding-pattern, the structure and the homeostasis to contend with. Families all have their common links, either through patterns in planetary contact, sign or elemental or modal dominance – all this is clearly part of an accepted status quo. What is more significant, perhaps, though I cannot prove this, is how long a dynasty can maintain the same shape or astrological theme or pattern and survive without dying out or fragmenting or worse, turning rotten in the process. As Dr Hyman observed in Arthur Miller's play *Broken Glass*, people do not behave singularly, but operate in groups in deeply unconscious collusion. What the intent underlying the collective participation is seems completely mysterious and I cannot hope to penetrate that veil. However, astrology can offer us a window through which to view the agencies that signs and planets and houses symbolize. For instance, when we see a collection of themes or tones threaded through a natal chart, we can arrive at some sound conclusions about what an individual's purpose in life is, and how he or she might best enact that. Looking at a dynastic pattern or theme is no less effective, just more complex.

Families always have a thread; we have seen that in the stories told in this book. From the classical understanding of certain signs, we know that there is a linking factor between generations which periodically and apparently randomly select one of their individuals to carry out a major task of re-ordering the system. The leitmotifs in family themes are very clear indicators of what the underlying intent is in the family line.

The necessity for cleansing or catharsis is marked by an over-concentration of energy in the psyche of the person, and he or she falls victim to a form of possession. The possession by ancestral spirits takes the form of symptoms – physical or psychological. Our received information, thus our collective perception – primarily a Western one – leads us to believe that these symptoms are curable by medical or psychological techniques. This is most often not the case. Indeed, it is clear that treating the symptom, not the cause, results in a deadening or flattening of the tone of the individual who has had the fate to carry this phenomenon.

Individuals who find themselves in the unenviable position of being the alembic for the alchemical transformation or clearing of the family fate have the dubious gift of being the testing ground for the entire human experience. Their own personal lives take on the tone of something much grander. Essentially, their soul becomes the meeting place of past and future; their 'now' is obscured by the confrontation of the ancestors at a meeting point in time. This can be further complicated by the involvement of the individual within the collective ethos, not only that he or she might be very connected to the family-group, but that they might also be tied very closely to what their cultural ethos is. Many times recently I have seen the horoscopes of eastern European people since the 'liberation' of the eastern bloc, and from other fraught cultures, and these people's charts have reflected precisely the revolution in their country. Where once kings and leaders reflected the psyche of the land, and its people, we now have individuals living in accord with a much bigger picture.

Since the Uranus/Neptune conjunction, this phenomenon has increased. Now, granted, as an astrologer, I am going to see only select people, and perhaps part of this experience is the metalogue, wherein 'that which is being discussed is also arising' (Gregory Bateson). Perhaps, as an astrologer, I *am* only going to see individuals whose charts do reflect the bigger picture, because they are the ones who are walking moments in time which are representative of their cultural ethos. They are the people who are deeply in tune with the collective. I have not been into war-torn zones doing the horoscopes of the masses, I have only seen the horoscopes of those who have managed to leave, to escape and find the complicated 'peace' outside their homeland; however, they are ambulatory, feeling, thinking individuals who have the war-zone inside, they carry it with them in their essence, in their being. They, then, *are* their culture, they lose their individuality in the sense that their planetary array is wholly descriptive of the status in their motherland. These people's horoscopes are the horoscopes of the kings, the leaders – they are a mundane event.

In Chapter 1 I talked about the impact of the times and the context in which a person lives. It is here, at the end of the book, that I hope to demonstrate just how this works. Though there are many people whose personal story ties in with the change or degeneration of their society, I will use one person whose consciousness of this phenomenon has quickened her own process and who has worked with this individual/collective enmeshment. There have been some rather profound attempts to understand this experience in the realm of psychology, but I think in astrology we have taken it for granted. Again, the individual is part of the collective and is now increasingly reflecting collective experiences. That we as individuals develop in parallel to cultures is fairly clear, but that one might participate in the whole of it to such a dramatic degree is the magical part of that.

The encounter in the early part of the twentieth century between the two progenitors of modern psychoanalytic theory and practice, Sigmund Freud and Carl Jung, enacted a collision of heaven and hell. Freud unlocked the door to the personal unconscious, allowing that there was a personal unconscious realm in the psyche of an individual in which lay dormant or hidden needs and characteristics. These lay apparently unknown, except as underlying motives for neurotic behaviour. The unconscious was the repository of all unwanted, unpleasant or asocial characteristics and remained dormant either through necessity or through repression. However, Jung went further to open the gates – and introduce us – to his idea of the collective unconscious, a realm which he claimed housed the primary archetypes of the human condition.

Both men were products of their times, and their innovative contributions to psycho-philosophy are invaluable. However, we have come to yet another threshold in the realms of the human experience. The astrology of the times shows that we are at the portal of a new realm of vision and circumstance. That some things remain unchanged is true – elements, components or archetypes. However, those elemental components' arrangement can alter in subtle ways which change drastically their function and intent.

The outcome of this threshold is the rise in personal contact with the ancestral domain. There are times in epochal history when individuals are sacrificed to the collective vision, and times when the collective is sacrificed to the individual. We are moving in a time which requires a degree of personal involvement with collective and ancestral numina. There are cultures which have never abandoned this ancestral link, such as the Africans, Maoris, Aborigines, certain South American tribes and myriad indigenous peoples, but it was necessary for a sector of the global collective to undergo a form of individuation which led it away from the mysterious places of immortality. The need to understand, explain and rationalize was and remains a significant method of civilizing the primordial material of consciousness.

The Western world has rapidly moved to the extreme end of reason, whereby it has denied its contact with the mystery-regions, which is precisely why a man like Jung was needed at the turn of the twentieth century – to reconnect the reasonable, rational mind to the non-rational underworld of the psyche.

However, the concepts and terms of psychology are constrained and modular; they do not move outside the realm of formula. Jung's terms 'archetypes' and 'collective unconscious' are scientific and rational terms. Jung's idea of the collective unconscious is still a psychological rationalization which is experienced only in its own context. This other-dimensional experience is encountered in another order of reality, one which is extended beyond or rather outside psychology. The idea of the collective unconscious is still buried in the matrix of what that kind of psychology is all about. Jung knew about these other realms because he hinted at them and used words like 'pleroma' (full void) 'numina' (shining beings) and so on, but he was a rational man, working with the limits of his own personal experience and within the *Zeitgeist*.

Other-dimensional aspects of the ancestral experience simply cannot be confined to the realm of psychology. The domain of the spirit, for instance, or the realms of the soul, are not psychological, but are outside psychology. Psychological terminology has desacralized *participation mystique*, wherein a person is one with his or her total experience, not separated as an object from its subject. In spite of our long love affair with the rational, we have not subordinated the gods and spirits – they are in their place. And they can enter our soul because our soul is in their place as well.

In the classical period in Greece, as in all other archaic cultures as well, the 'mad person' was considered to be god-filled – *enthousiasmos*, to be precise. To be filled with the god was a sacred state. People who were in touch with the spirit world or the ancestral realm were cared for by the community and treated with the utmost respect. This respect continues today in certain *participation mystique* cultures. Shaman always have to throw off the cloak of time and space to move beyond the rigours of the temporal zone in order to become channels for pure energy. This is all considered to be quite mad in our society. And, in our society, it *is* dangerous to go about in this state, for the necessity of a bounded reality is extremely high. However, some individuals have been selected to undergo the rituals of cleansing and purging and some of them have been very successful. Not only have they liberated themselves from personal neurosis and miasma, but have inadvertently released their families and, thus, the collective by that much.

Therefore it seems it was absolutely necessary for us to become in contact with the primordial psyche. As the world became closer knit, more connected and truly an *unus mundus* it became imperative that the conscious mind be aware of an unconscious. At the same time as the world becomes one, the gulf between the sacred and the profane, the rational and the non-rational, nature and culture grows more vast. By reconnecting with the mysteries, with the sacred or the non-rational, and becoming consciously aware that such a realm existed, we allowed that place, the unconscious, to contact our conscious minds. As the numbers of people multiplied, so did the contents of the collective unconscious become more demonstratively restless. Jung was an agency for the irruption of the daemonic; however, it does not stop there. The release of the daemonic into the open consciousness has occurred, is now present in the collective consciousness.

The theory of the psychological development of the self holds in part the idea that if we 'get in touch' with our dark side, with our primal self, the instinctual nature or whatever one wants to call it, and bring it forth into the light of day, we then can civilize it. This is quite true. The forced and continued repression of the primitive self results in a sickness of soul. And this ailing soul experiences gripping psychological complexes, depressions, blind rages, unhappy relationships and various other rather normal, but dis-eased human experiences. We have seen so far in the book that in the stories of each individual it is the secrets that made them sick – the truths were the healing factors. When the feared thing is brought forth, it either begins to humanize or it withers and dies.

Implicit at some stage in this process is the necessity to release the darkness, not to cling to it or to spend unnecessary time wading around in the primordial mire without purpose. The point is to bring the dark forces, shadow or demons to the surface, to the light and let them go. To spend inordinate periods of time lurking in the shadows of Hades is not only perilous, it is also not possible to retain one's rational grip in doing so. The astrological Uranus brings clarity and liberation to anything repressed, whether that is whole cultures, people, unconscious contents, information or volcanic material in the mundane sense.

Daemonic beings, gods, forces or entities are undifferentiated while remaining in the nether regions, but once brought forth, begin to take shape and form. The condensed, unrealized, undifferentiated forms of the darkest part of the psyche are far more dangerous in hiding than they are in the clear light of day. Even demons individuate. They can become personified and embodied in collective characters such as political figures, religious leaders, social trend-setters, media pundits and so forth. They can further condense in the psyches of 'ordinary' individuals whose fate it is to transform the collective figures through their own personal individuation process.

In this spirit form, the ancestors who have been unable to access their developmental process will assert themselves into the psyche of an individual. An encounter with the spirit world is harrowing and potentially lethal, as I have understood it myself and as I have experienced it through friends and colleagues intrepid enough to foray into that landscape. That the collective can be assisted in its organic individuation process through the agency of a selected person is evident. When the time is ready for this to occur in a family depends on the degree to which that family line has a connection to the ongoing process of the continuum of the greater whole, the global family. An urge arises in the family-soul, creating a rift of *frisson* which opens the door for a new opportunity for growth. When this urge settles in the soul of one person, he or she can become personally imperilled in every way. The individual's personal system begins to dissolve in the precise fashion in which the family system is rigidly entrenched.

Astrology exists outside chronological time. But it is also a chronocrator, a demarcator of sequential time. Add to this its marked periodicity and its both vast and minute depictions of cyclic time, and we have a tiny glimmer of the power of the astrological matrix. That individuals exist in a finite period, but are connected by signs and planets in other individuals' charts who also existed finitely but in other periods of time, crosses temporal boundaries which dissolve the idea of conventional relationships. For example, a person can be so astrologically linked to a dead relative that she embodies some of that relative's timeless personality. On some level she *is* that relative. Thus, she can continue developing that other person congruent with her own development. We are all made up of and make up our families.

In their search for roots, people discover fascinating tales of adventure, tragedy, romance and unlived lives. To some degree we must all make this journey, for the fourth house, the family soul, of the horoscope can remain dark for only so long through so many generations before someone in a family is born who will dig deeply into that most mysterious part of the chart and find the source of his or her very origins, the origins of being. What we discover there can only heal, what we continue to repress there can only sicken and lie in wait, for it is deathless.

To each of us is left a legacy from our parents, which in turn is one that they have been bequeathed by their parents, and so on back to the origins of our time. Our family of origin is the foundation of our personal psychic fortune, but that family is the small picture. As we read in Chapter 1, our nuclear families are cells in the organic whole of the collective family, just as each of us are cells in the grouping of our nuclear families.

Certain people are not only the purifiers of their family line, but also mediums for the collective. Their own process is directly linked to a cultural transformation. I have seen this time and time again, in ways both ordinary and dramatic. Some individuals are required to become voices of the collective at the risk of being its victims. Cultural *Angst, Weltschmertz,* social revolution and global transformation are all registered in the horoscopes of individuals. However, in particular individuals, there is a clear connection to the events and conditions of their cultural roots.

It is interesting to note that Jung was fascinated by the symbolic heart of darkness in Joseph Conrad's world. Jung found Africa to be a source of origin for him; he felt it took him to a place of lost magic and numinosity in his own nature. I believe that if Jung had not been constrained by his innate racism and the morality of his era, and was living and writing today, he might have developed his thinking in synchrony with the spirit of our times. Jung's work (which is not the work of 'Jungians', I must emphasize) on the archetypes appears to be an open-ended inquiry, one which if followed through in the vein in which it was flowing would have led straight to the heart of the situation which befalls us now. If we can perceive a culture, country or continent as a state of mind, and the world as an entity, then the release of black Africa and its individuation process marks a pivotal point in global consciousness. As long as the white European culture continued to oppress the blacks in Africa, wholeness could not be achieved. This is also the origin of the idea of blacks equalling or being symbolic of the primitive in the unconscious of the white, European race – an idea that resulted in Jung being called a racist. Though black people are not primitive at all, the indigenous peoples are by nature more connected to their cultures and to the rituals of their ancestors.

Mundane aspects mark such global turnings – and the long conjunction of Uranus and Neptune in Capricorn created a mass of confusion. That Neptune rules the collective and Uranus the individual speaks of how conflicting that 171-year cyclic conjunction is to both individuals and the world-at-large. On the one hand, the rise of the individual in Western society has reached astounding power, but the oppression of whole cultural groups into formless, homeless, boundaryless masses has also occurred. The thing hidden has surfaced, and that which is enslaved and repressed is manumitted. The repression of the instinctual, of the feminine and of nature has been released. The mid-nineties brought a perfect image of the movement of Uranus's passage out of the fog of Neptune's orb – on television screens world-wide, long queues of black South Africans stood patiently awaiting their moment to be named individually and vote in the first democratic election ever in their history. One by one, each person stepped out of the amorphous crowd, named him or herself, and moved away, now an individual out of the body of one people. Prior to that precise moment, the blacks as a collective lacked individual identity in white-dominated southern Africa, but from that point on they stepped out of the unintegrated, undifferentiated mass of them as a 'people' and individuated. This is the Uranus/Neptune conjunction – the one out of the many. The power of naming lies in its capacity to bridge the Ideal and the Real, to bring the heavens and the earth together. To say 'I am' at the *right time* is to give voice to the power of the individual.

Uranus plays such a strong role in the freeing up of individual needs that it is frequently the planet of both personal and collective revolution. For a true revolution to occur, there has to be a *volte face* which brings the unknown into the place of power. The unknown or the hidden has to replace the old known standards. In a sense, Uranus brings liberation at all costs, which invokes *his* own father, Chaos. But chaos, in all myth, is the genesis of all things.

In the Greek origin myth Chaos was the beginning and it brought forth Gaia, our earth. Gaia, in turn, created Ouranos, the god of the sky. His

Titan son, Kronos, our Saturn, castrated him because he refused to allow Gaia to give full birth to the monstrous offspring which he had fathered on her, keeping them repressed, deep inside her, until she could bear it no longer. This angered the goddesses of the *chthon*, the earth. Ultimately Gaia employed Kronos to the purpose of freeing her; to this day Saturn stands on the horizon between heaven and earth, creating time, rules, limitation and mortality, as the guardian of the threshold of past and future, ancestors and progeny. Saturn is incarnation.

It is interesting that it was Ouranos, Gaia's consort, who repressed the Hekatonchires, the monsters of the Greek origin myth, causing a mythological rift between the heavens (mind) and earth (body). And it is now Uranus who is doing the liberating. Perhaps we can live in the heavens only so long, and now must return to earth for the sake of the entire human race. The repression of the instincts, the damming of the feelings, the elimination of nature, will simply not sustain life. Imprisonment in the mind, in dogma and in old, tired hierarchies has taken its toll on both the one and the many. Individuals are feeling this, and it is reflected in the collective. Or is it the other way around?

Ideally, individuation is the process by which we do compartmentalize our various parts and then integrate them as best we can. This is a deeply unconscious experience, but there are times when the process is quickened. A Uranus transit forces us to witness ourselves, and anything that has lain sleeping, dormant or uncivilized in our unconscious, as it were, will rise to consciousness for development. It is always a bit harrowing, for although it is part of us, we might not recognize it and might think it is coming from some disorganized place and that the integrity of the ego is threatened. One can stuff these parts of the self back 'down' into unconsciousness, but it is not a particularly good idea if one is interested in becoming as fully as possible whom one is to become. For Uranus acts on behalf of the future.

Just like cultures which live out their purpose and end finally, there are also families whose line dies out and finally terminates. It has to end somewhere with someone. When this is the situation, that person is the gene-pool, the astrological cosmic terminus of the entire ancestral line. This situation places the onus on that person to spend a lifetime weaving the threads of the past into a tapestry of now. They are required by natural law to complete the individuation process for their family, and very possibly their culture. This individual feels a sense of urgency and often will experience periods of deep anxiety which act as a trigger to explore their inner world deeply. In that exploration, they often find themselves face-to-face with what seems an insurmountable task – that of purifying their family legacy.

SKELETONS IN THE CLOSET

The ancient Athenian lawmaker Solon decreed that the sins of the father shall fall upon the head of the sons: '. . . And those who themselves flee and escape the pursuing destiny of Heaven, to them vengeance cometh always again, for the price of their deeds is paid by their innocent children or else by their seed after them.'¹ Sometimes we wonder what it is that we have done to make things the way they are. The concept of dynastic pollution reaches far back into the history of mankind; rituals of clearing and purifying the ancestors are age-old, older than the laws of Athens. It may well be that a 'cursed' person has done nothing, but that there is a thread that runs down through the family line which has settled in that person for a reason unknown to anyone. In these days of psychology they are called various types of family complexes, but in the old days it was family fate. Now, can fate be bargained with, can one call upon the ancestors for absolution? Is it possible to come to terms with a fate or a complex which has chosen to nest within the soul of a modern person?

Poor old Oedipus Rex. A king among men, who was the unfortunate repository for the sins of his father. This is how it went: Laius, King of Thebes, was in exile in Elis. While in Elis, he was made at home and comfortable in the home of the king, Pelops. The guest-host relationship in ancient Greece was the most sacred of human relationships, and if ever violated, the wrath of Zeus Xeinios (Zeus of the Strangers) would come down upon the head of the fool who did so. Fool that Laius was, he fell in love with Chrysippus, Pelops's son, and abducted him, causing Pelops to lay a curse upon Laius's descendants.²

Long before his exile, Laius had been forewarned by Apollo at Delphi that if he had a son by Jocasta 'he would be destined to die at his hand'. When, therefore, a son was born, Laius attempted to thwart the Fates by having the child exposed – the ancient tradition of driving a spike through the ankles of the infant and leaving it on a mountain top. The child was left to die, never to be seen again as far as he knew. The old shepherd who was ordered to do this had pity on the baby and took him to the home of the King of Corinth, Polybus, to be raised by him. He and his wife named him Oedipus (which means 'swollen foot') because of his wounded feet.

Time passed. Years later, Oedipus was mocked at a dinner party that he was not Polybus's natural son. He was shamed and frightened, so he sought the advice of the Oracle at Delphi – the Pythia's cryptic response was a warning. He was told to avoid his homeland at all costs, as it was ordained that he must murder his father and marry his mother. Oedipus, determined to avoid this fate, left his 'homeland', Corinth, and hit the road. At the famous crossroads, he met with a chariot that drove him off the road. In anger he killed the driver, and the whole lot.

More time passed. Oedipus arrived at Thebes. The city was in distress. Not only was the king dead, but it was also afflicted by a monster sent by Zeus's wife, Hera, called the Sphinx (which means 'strangler'), in retribution for the terrible crime of the murder of the king. This creature with the face of a woman, the body of a lion and an eagle's wings had a riddle learned from the Muses. It was said that the person answering the riddle would solve the problems of Thebes, and become king. The riddle: 'What is it that has one name that is four-footed, two-footed and three-footed?' And Oedipus answered correctly: 'Man, for as an infant he goes upon four feet; in his prime upon two; and in old age he takes a stick as a third foot.'

So Apollo's prophecy is fulfilled, and so will all the others be. The rest of the story is commonly known. The man whom Oedipus killed at the crossroads was his actual father. The king's widow, then, whom he married, was his mother, Jocasta. They had four children. A pestilence fell upon the city. It was said a miasma affected everyone because a terrible sin was being committed. Apollo said it was because a pollution was in their state, that the murderer of King Laius was in their midst. Oedipus set about finding this killer. And, to make a long story short, found the enemy in himself. The horror of Oedipus's predicament, to find himself the inadvertent recipient of a long line of cursedness, is the same fate as an individual who has had the dubious luck to be the resolution to a family problem.

The line of Jocasta's when she is trying to smooth the way for Oedipus's self-discovery, 'Many men have in dreams lain with their mothers',[3] is the Freudian gold-mine. An apocryphal story has Freud leap out of his seat in a Viennese theatre during a Greek production of *Oedipus Tyrannus*, and race off to begin work on his seduction theory, the famous Oedipus complex. However, Oedipus was not soothed by dreams or the unconscious being non-rational, nor did he feel that curses from generations past meant nothing; he was filled with horror. Jocasta killed herself, and Oedipus blinded himself with her brooches; then he went out into the desert and embarked on a purgation ritual. He was assisted by his daughters and, finally, by Zeus himself, in his guise as 'Zeus Chthonius', a rare connection of Zeus to the powers beneath the earth. In paying homage to the right gods, in propitiation of the powers of the *chthon*, the earth, Oedipus cleanses himself of the blood-curse, appeals to the feminine goddesses of the underworld and is finally assisted by the highest of the gods to his end. He passes out of mortal sight and becomes a hero, to perform miracles for those who worship him.

The cosmology of the Shona, a tribe of Zimbabwe, has a long history of complex rituals for the ancestors depending on their stature in the clan. There are several which are enacted in accord with the death anniversary. Nothing of the person's belongings or legacy is touched for a year. In the course of the year, much interdimensional interchange takes place so to clear the inheritance of all debts, spiritual or material. This is all observed religiously, so that resolution can take place on all levels. The underlying purpose of this rigorous practice is: they believe that right relationship with the ancestors is a priority for a healthy, happy life. The ancestors form a protective membrane which surrounds the family, and they construct an important strata-hierarchy within the family circle. As mentioned in the eighth house section (page 187), these strata become increasingly rarefied as one reaches higher levels, eventually incorporating tribal ancestors, protectors of the entire race. For them, reconnecting to the ancestors is to protect, resolve and create anew. Their concept of the individual is not existing as an isolated unit separate from the family matrix or from the tribal society – or from the ancestral realm, for that matter.

The profound assistance of dreams in reconnecting to one's ancestral roots and furthering the development of one's whole self is part of the cultural cosmogony of so many peoples, ancient and modern, that we need to take the function of dreaming and ancestral connection seriously. In *Creation Myths*, Marie Louise Von Franz speaks often of the importance of dreaming and the ancestral league: 'Again, whenever people have to make a very important decision, a tremendous step on which one could say their whole future depended, they get such dreams as the assembly of the ancestors or the assembly of the dead.'[4] I have used this quote before, in reference to Saturn descending over the ascendant, because that is a time in which our twelfth house spills over into the first house, bringing the collective and personal unconscious to the same horizon.

These dreams, which deal with aspects of our daily life in exalted ways, are supremely helpful because they let us know that we are acting out a very small part in a very large experience. I have seen this many times, where dreams of primitive or animal things are deeply connected to a fear of moving forward, and once the dream has happened, the fear is dissipated. But, more, if one works actively in both mind and imagination, the 'primitive' can become civilized through exposure to the conscious mind and become integrated into the whole of a person's psyche. Furthermore, Von Franz writes: 'They [dreams] generally occur when the individual really has to concentrate all his potential personality in order to take the next step, a decisive step upon which the whole individuation process depends. Such steps are so terrifying that the weak ego cannot make them; this is why such concentrating processes occur and show in the dreams, because the ego cannot concentrate its powers.'[5]

From what we have seen in the stories told so far in the book, the ethereal inter-dimensional aspects of family matters are very real. There is nothing about them that rings false, they are as archetypal as the myth of Oedipus and they demonstrate that proper action, taken at the right times, brings resolution and health, not just to the 'chosen one' but to the entire family line. The stories in the book might be mysterious and demonstrate themselves in symbolic form through astrological patterns, but they are as palpable as the kitchen table. No Platonic forms, here, but real, active and effective beings, very much a part of our psyche and of our family dynamic.

In our last story, we shall see how very significant dreams are for Rosemary, and the many parallels that exist between our daily, waking life and the nightly, sleeping life, and how the planets are so very eloquent in speaking the connection between the Self, the ego and the transcendant. For, even though it is rarely convenient for everything to happen all at once, it does.

NOTES

1. Solon, *Elegy and Iambus*, Loeb, page 129.
2. Pelops, son of Tantalus, was a man to be avoided at all costs. It was at his dinner table that the curse of the House of Atreus occurred . . . dogging Atreus, Agamemnon, Iphigenia and finally Orestes. This most famous of Mycenean sagas was the epitome of the 'sins of the fathers' on down the line, generation after generation, to settle in Orestes, and only be resolved at the courts of Areopagus, presided over by Athena. This is where Athena casts her vote for the 'male' line, demoting the Furies, the Erinyes, to mere household minions, the Eumenides.
3. Sophocles, *Oedipus Tyrannus*, line 981.
4. Marie Louise Von Franz, *Creation Myths*, Spring Publications, 1972, page 209.
5. ibid., page 210.

18

The Last in the Line:
The Many in the One

The story I am about to relate is true, and belongs to a woman of courage and integrity, one which – like all the stories in this book – is unending. Rosemary is an individual who has had both the good sense to recognize her fate as a transformer of her ancestral line, and the courage to take the steps towards that end. But hers is a bigger story than just her own – for her personal story is not only of herself, her family and her ancestral line, but is also the story of South Africa, the darkest, most divided self of Africa. (See Figure 35.)

The signals for individuals who are custodians of the family fate, or are marked to do deep family-work, lie primarily in the angular zones of the horoscope, in particular the ascendant and the IC and in the Watery houses of the twelfth, fourth and eighth. Marked emphasis in those areas in the horoscope is a signal to pay special attention to their origins and roots. I am going to look at Rosemary's horoscope, reflecting this emphasis, and speak only of her experience in the realm of the ancestors. Later I shall draw in some significant astrological patterns that have been powerfully at work in the greater family and cultural dynamics related to her horoscope.

Mercury and Venus are in conjunction in zodiacal longitude, but they are, in fact, in opposition to each other heliocentrically. With Mercury retrograde by just five days, and Venus direct, this means that Mercury is positioned in its orbit between earth and the Sun, and Venus is on the other side of the Sun. This implies that there is a Janus-faced effect going on, where Mercury sits in the threshold looking both forward into the future, and backward into the past. The Janus-faced god was a symbol for being able to look in both the realms of the living and the dead, the past and the future, simultaneously. This gives not only the capacity to discern where the boundaries are that can be crossed safely but also the discrimination when to do so. Her received values, Venus, are in diametric opposition to her understanding of her own personal values, and since Mercury is retrograde,

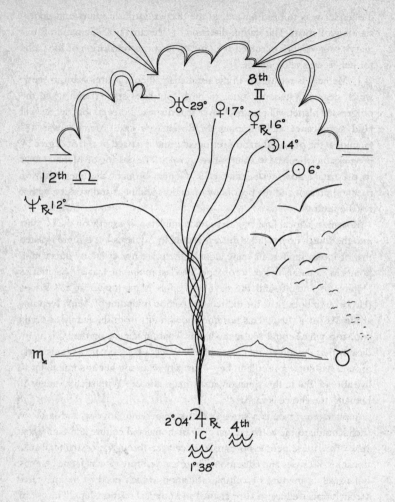

Figure 35. Rosemary

the tendency is to head inward, to the deeper, intrinsic values and understanding of them. The station-direction of Mercury at 8° Gemini in Rosemary's progressions occurred at a time of major reconciliation of life paths
for her, as we shall soon see.

If Mercury is retrograde in the natal chart, then it is important to see at
which degree it stationed prior to birth (pre-natal station) and when the
progressed planet will pass back over that degree.[1] Forever, that degree will
hold significance and meaning. In Rosemary's case, Mercury was 18°
Gemini at the pre-natal station-retrograde, and it passed over that degree by
progression when she was thirty-five, in 1984. The passing of Mercury over
its pre-natal station-retrograde at 18° Gemini brought the integration of
past and present and the possibility of understanding it and working with it
for the future.

Rosemary's focal Jupiter, a retrograde singleton, is exactly on the IC, just
into the fourth house and is the *only* feature in Aquarius – it is more isolated
than it looks. Jupiter sits quite alone – there are not even any direct midpoints in Aquarius in her horoscope. The last midpoint is at 22° Sagittarius
(Jupiter/ascendant) and the next one on is Mars/Jupiter at 26° Pisces.
(However, it does sit at the indirect opposition midpoint of Mars/Neptune
at the MC at 1° Leo.) This position shows a gift from the family-of-origin
ancestors which could take many forms. That Jupiter sits on the IC is an indicator that the inter- and cross-cultural aspect of Rosemary's family background has come to settle in her – virtually requiring her at some point to
live abroad. But in this situation, just what is abroad? With such a variety of
heritage, the choice is vast!

Jupiter retrograde is a stranger in a strange land, anyway, and it allows
such latitude to the conventional view of home and culture and family that
very often these people do transfer allegiance through cross-cultural relationships, lifestyles and education. There is no culture to which one belongs,
but usually a mixture of cultural affiliations which need to be integrated
through travel, education or personal and political relationships. The gift of
the family line was for Rosemary to have the freedom to move and collect
about her the various root systems which had woven themselves into her IC
and Jupiter. There is some religious and spiritual legacy as well.

Neptune in the twelfth house connects Rosemary to the collective of
humanity. She is musically gifted, and when very young showed remarkable
ability, understanding both theory and practice. As a result her parents –
both of whom were musicians themselves – offered her the best of training

and made every natural attempt to put this ability in a box. Indeed, Rosemary did do a music degree at university, but has never been a professional musician. Part of her adult development has been to un-train herself and be more in tune with the harmonies of a universal sound. She has found that her 'voice' is not for songs, nor scores nor classical nor even indigenous music, but for sound, pure sound. I felt that it was a literal translation from Neptune retrograde in the twelfth house, trined by the stellium in Gemini – an ability in mid-life to find harmony and resonance with the universal sound, a song of ancestral origin so vast as to be uncontainable in conventional music.

Rosemary's horoscope has the majority of Air planets and points in the Water houses – placing emphasis on all realms of family dynamics, from the personal family of origin and its home (fourth house), to the cultural/family split (eighth house), and finally to the ancestral realm of both personal and collective ancestry (twelfth house). All her Air planets triangulate the Water houses. There is a closed circuit of communication between the three primary levels of ancestral relationship. She has no planets in Water signs, but only Scorpio rising with Pluto in the tenth house. She is required to take coded information from her point of origin (ascendant) and bring it to super-consciousness by the position of Pluto. Indeed, there is evidence that the secrets of the family became a professional impetus for her.

Air in the Watery houses speaks of the natural connection of feelings to thoughts. No feeling would go unconsidered in this case, whereas loaded Water charts tend not to think about feelings. Considering that water represents our deepest values and the capacity to value our feelings and earth is the most fundamental value we have, there is clearly a struggle to come to terms with the body, the work, the world and its people. Those are the most basic values we have. On cursory glance, we might think this chart shows someone very disconnected from her body and from the body of the earth itself; however, there were times in her life, as we shall see, that she embodied ancestral and collective grief and pain. Because Rosemary has had to intellectually embody so much of the feelings, emotions, practical issues and earthiness of her personal, historical and ancestral background, it is likely that only a horoscope as extreme as this would withstand the onslaught of experiences and events which have been a part of her process of individuation.

Frequently people with great stellia in their eighth house have near-death experiences or endangered lives where a wound or illness forces them to repair to isolation and think. It also puts them in a psychological and spiritual place which gives the ancestors greater access to their unconscious mind, with which, if then accepted, they will become constant companions. When our bodies are not terribly attached to the world, the protective membrane between habitats and realms is thinned or even broken, and there is an opportunity to move between those worlds. If this wound, or illness, occurs when a child is very young, he or she won't always be able to use that experience until much later, or until an awakening episode triggers recollection of that 'other' place.

Peculiar to Gemini is the capacity to witness one's own behaviour and perceive it in a manner which allows windows to open on many sides. But when Scorpio is rising, there is the power to look both broadly and deeply and to understand things both in the symbolic realm and on the intellectual level. This potential is one which Rosemary has spent a lifetime developing. Disregarding the chatter of the mind, the 'Gemini jive', is a major achievement while spending time in deep contemplation of the mysteries of the eighth house, and working with the messages sent forth from the unconscious is part of a life-path. Gemini is random, multi-levelled and the gatherer of masses of data, while Scorpio is discriminating and highly selective – the combination is rich with perception. Rosemary both thinks and feels, having the combination of Gemini which is broad in its scope and Scorpio which is deep in its probing.

It is only in conversation with a person that their horoscope truly becomes alive, when the symbols speak through the individual themselves. The story of Rosemary is a living symbol, and she has tried to take personally the metaphor of her origins and work with the divided self of the Gemini.

Rosemary was born in Rhodesia, of an Irish mother and a second-generation white South African father. She is the last in her line, and when she was thirteen she knew this, and felt very strongly that she would have the task of breaking the patterns in her family. Every individual to whom I have had the courage to suggest that they were, or might be, the harbourer of the family fate, or the transformer for the family system, has always been relieved, for it is in the recognition and acceptance of this situation that real healing occurs. People tend to think themselves either mad or wildly inflated to assume such a thing; however, they always know, and usually at a very early age.

In 1965, Rhodesia declared UDI – Unilateral Declaration of Independence – which effectively ostracized the country from the international community through its refusal to accept the 'One Man One Vote' stance. The old order, headed by Ian Smith, refused to surrender. This collective paralysis of staving off the inevitable was also reflected personally in Rosemary's life, as she became paralysed with rheumatoid arthritis just as this act was being undertaken by the cultural milieu in which she was born. In the few years prior to this, the white collective mood was dominated by denial and fear, and Rosemary's uncle, also a multiple Gemini (all around 7–9°), sickened gradually and died in the same year. Her body told this story, and as her progressed Mercury stationed-direct, she regained her full mobility.

Rosemary left southern Africa in 1971 and made her home in London. In 1980 Rhodesia became Zimbabwe, and, as her divided culture of origin dissolved, she began to experience a powerful chain of inner and outer events which linked England and Africa together over the next few years. Her father died on 8 June 1983, and she went back to independent Zimbabwe for the first time for his funeral in the first week of July. He was the last remaining family member of three generations who had lived in Rhodesia, thus spanning most of its brief history. She felt lost, as if 'my entire root system had dissolved into historical oblivion'.

The night after the funeral, Rosemary related a dream: 'I saw the planet Uranus ploughing through a crowd of screaming people, and marching relentlessly towards me on its prong, casting behind itself a vast shadow of *brilliant light.* It electrified and swallowed up a girl in its huge mouth, red-lipped and revealing a set of enormous teeth. I grabbed this girl, trying unsuccessfully to prevent her falling backwards into the void; she screamed and screamed and finally fell. I was so preoccupied with the futile struggle to hold on to her that I only dimly noticed that I had also been "zapped", or electrified by this "thing". As she was wrenched from my grasp, I helplessly witnessed her vanish backwards, into an increasingly large pool of black light. I was told by the "thing" that I would be receiving a "voltage-change", like it or not.'[2] (Italics mine.)

The brilliant light shadow cast by Uranus is the image of knowledge and enlightenment in hindsight, after the scourge, the revolution or the uprising. Dreams of this archetypal nature almost always presage a very long-term change. They are literally turning-point dreams, and are recollected by the individual over and over during the course of their lives. This dream was prophetic, not simply a foreshadowing of things to come. Her dream of the glyph for Uranus, in July 1983, was a portent of experiences which would not develop fully for years; in particular, the movement of Uranus into Aquarius, over her IC, and Jupiter retrograde in 1995–6.

The night of her father's death, the Sun and Mars had been at 16° Gemini, right on Rosemary's Mercury/Venus, and transiting Mercury was at 22° Taurus, right on Rosemary's natal Mars, while Jupiter and Uranus within a degree of each other were conjunct her natal Chiron at 5° Sagittarius. Pluto and Saturn – both stationary-direct conjunct her twelfth house north node – were close in the heavens, a degree apart around 26–27° Libra, and in trine to her natal Uranus in the eighth house. This is like a call from history via the ancestors to her eighth house planets – the house in which we individuate the personal ancestors through our own personal experience. This time began the six-year trek of transiting Uranus in opposition to all her Gemini stellium. It also began the long transit of Chiron in Gemini over those same planets, to oppose itself. The year following the death of her father, Uranus would go over and back and over again her Sun, dredging up the suppressed instincts, the primal unconscious, and bringing her 'inside' to the outside. Uranus plays a very large role in the individuation process, and for Rosemary it is a literal interpretation. She was split off from her father, as Ouranos was from Gaia; she was in a foreign country; her own culture of origin had ceased to exist. Parts of her became so separated from other parts that she could witness them with the clarity of Ouranos, the god of heaven.

If we now look at the horoscope of UDI (see Figure 36), we see the Moon at 16° Gemini, which is where the Sun and Mars were when her father died, and we see the south node at 4° Sagittarius, conjunct Rosemary's Chiron and where Jupiter/Uranus were at her father's death. The UDI horoscope has Saturn retrograde in Pisces at 10° and Chiron in exact opposition to the Uranus/Pluto conjunction of revolution at 18° Pisces/Virgo. UDI Mars is 27° Sagittarius, opposite to Rosemary's natal Uranus at 29° Gemini, the last planet in the eighth house stellium and at the last degree of the sign. Rosemary's father's Pluto is 27° Gemini. The father and the fatherland are intermingled in the symbolism. There is no 'time', no quantitative duration with planetary degrees, only association, memory and relative experiences which bind multi-dimensional experiences together. In this way the degrees of the zodiac, when seen experientially and qualitatively, are pan-temporal.

Indeed, the next afternoon, after the funeral, Rosemary was to begin in earnest her personal resolution of a collective conflict. 'I began to feel an

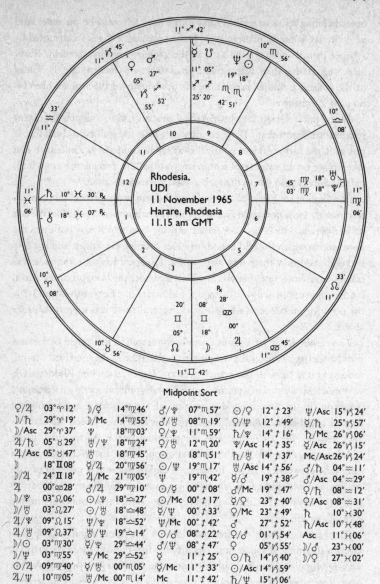

Midpoint Sort

♀/♃	03°♈12'	☽/☿	14°♍46'	♂/♆	07°♏57'	☉/♀	12°♐23'	♆/Asc	15°♑24'
☽/♄	29°♈19'	☽/Mc	14°♍55'	♂/♅	08°♏19'	♀/♆	12°♐49'	☿/♄	25°♑57'
☽/Asc	29°♈37'	♀	18°♍03'	♀/♀	11°♏59'	♄/♀	14°♐16'	♄/Mc	26°♑06'
♃/♄	05°♉29'	♃/♀	18°♍24'	♀/♆	12°♏20'	♀/Asc	14°♐35'	♀/Asc	26°♑15'
♃/Asc	05°♉47'	♅	18°♍45'	☉	18°♏51'	♄/♅	14°♐37'	Mc/Asc	26°♑24'
☽	18°♊08'	☿/♃	20°♍56'	☉/♆	19°♏17'	♅/Asc	14°♐56'	♂/♄	04°≈11'
☽/♃	24°♊18'	♃/Mc	21°♍05'	♆	19°♏42'	☿/♂	19°♐38'	♂/Asc	04°≈29'
♃	00°♋28'	♂/♃	29°♍10'	☉/♀	00°♐08'	♂/Mc	19°♐47'	♀/♄	08°≈12'
☽/♆	03°♌06'	☉/♀	18°≏27'	☉/Mc	00°♐17'	♀/♂	23°♐40'	♀/Asc	08°≈31'
☽/♅	03°♌27'	☉/♅	18°≏48'	☿/♀	00°♐33'	♀/Mc	23°♐49'	♄	10°♓30'
♃/♆	09°♌15'	♆/♀	18°≏52'	♆/Mc	00°♐42'	♂	27°♐52'	♄/Asc	10°♓48'
♃/♅	09°♌37'	♅/♀	19°≏14'	☉/♂	08°♐22'	♀/♂	01°♑54'	Asc	11°♓06'
☽/☉	03°♍30'	♀/♀	29°≏44'	☉/♃	08°♐47'	♀	05°♑55'	☽/♂	23°♓00'
☽/♆	03°♍55'	♀/Mc	29°≏52'	♀/♅	11°♐25'	☉/♄	14°♑40'	☽/♀	27°♓02'
☉/♃	09°♍40'	☿/♅	00°♏05'	☿/Mc	11°♐33'	☉/Asc	14°♑59'		
♃/♆	10°♍05'	♅/Mc	00°♏14'	Mc	11°♐42'	♄/♆	15°♑06'		

Figure 36

overwhelming sense of guilt. I sank into what I felt must be the quicksand of collective white Rhodesian guilt, feeling my personal grief consumed by a larger pain; I disintegrated as it pushed for expression.' Actually, Rosemary's ego, rather than disintegrating, had to grow to incorporate the forces of the collective cultural revolution: the newly merging black and white cultures of Zimbabwe.

As she put it herself: '. . . my personal process had to a significant extent synchronized with that of the country in which I was fated to be born. It was as if the historical and political shift from Rhodesia to Zimbabwe had taken place on an inner level within my own psyche, forcing me as an individual white person, to go through a similar transformation.'[3]

Her Gemini soul was split in two, and the rent was now becoming manifest in both the outer world and in her inner environment as she lost the last of her personal threads – her father and the land which was not even the same one in which she had been born. Her country, her father, and her self had died, and now there was work to do. The focal Jupiter retrograde was calling out to integrate that vision which lay under the horizon, at the nadir, hidden and suppressed – in Aquarius, to liberate it. The fourth house IC is the point of recollection of cosmic order, and there was a great disorder about.

The earlier dream of Uranus is eerily connected to the transit of Uranus over Rosemary's Chiron at 5° Sagittarius at that time . . . her personal wound, though bound up with her actual, personal father as a white Rhodesian, is very much implicated in a cultural, moral, philosophical split (in Sagittarius), based on élitism (Uranus) and repression of the instinctual and primordial nature. That her own father died as this transit occurred sealed the connection between the archetypal and the personal father. As we read in the eighth house, the symbol is the meeting of opposites, and in that meeting, a luminous experience occurs. Rosemary's eighth house is a meeting of opposites, and with Uranus to transit it by opposition for the next six years as it slowly treks to her IC by 1996 is a preparation for the reconnection to the root of her life-force.

The next night, after the dream of Uranus (the planet signifying the individual) storming through and electrifying the crowds, Rosemary had a waking visitation from her father's spirit; she felt he was trying to take her over. Rosemary was well schooled in symbolism, as well as being inherently devotional – she coped with the fear by opening her journal and allowing her pen to flow automatically. In the communication, her father instructed her to complete a certain task which involved travelling to a sacred site in the Matopos range, Malindri Nzema, whose name means 'worship of the Departed Spirit'. It is also the burial place of Cecil Rhodes. Personal, family and historical threads were again interweaving. She was forewarned of illness if she did not obey this. Although Rosemary took this warning seriously, aware that messages from the ancestors are to be taken gravely, so to speak, she was unable to fulfil the request literally but fervently hoped to be able to work it through on the imaginal level.

In the course of the following day, she and her sister sorted through the family possessions, the belongings and material things left by her parents. She said, 'I felt already "possessed" with a burdensome collective and family inheritance . . .'

Rosemary, with all her eighth house Gemini, is instinctively in tune with images, metaphor, signs, symbols, ciphers and all means of indirect and other-dimensional methods of communication. The eighth house is the house of the ancestral inheritance, and when there is an inheritance which is not received, or is badly dealt with, there is a repercussion. Rosemary instinctively knew that the 'debt' which her father had left her was a debt far beyond the personal, but incorporated the resources and the spirits of a divided culture. By 'chance' she discovered a cosmology which synchronistically wove itself into her already well-developed instincts about what needed to be done and how to go about doing it.

The Shona world-view appealed to Rosemary – her own perceptions were validated as she discovered that the dead are very much integrated with the living. As mentioned before, it is largely the modern cultures that have become fearful and antiseptic about death and the ancestors, but that does not make it go away. If we are beckoned or called towards ancestral healing, it must be done. It is essential that we find a way to work with this in a fashion which has integrity. We might otherwise think ourselves mad, or become ill and neurotic. Once we see that this is healthy, natural and, indeed, necessary, then it is not morbid and weird. The eighth house is a clean house, if it is kept so.

Also, we need to have our inner world validated by the outer world. It was with this knowledge that Rosemary began to arm herself for the inevitable meeting with the ancestral spirits. She recognized herself in their teachings: 'The family medium is usually female, and her initiation process is often signalled by the onset of a strange illness that does not respond to normal treatment, that frequently occurs after the death of a male elder in the family.' At the age of five, Rosemary was ill with malaria after her grand-father died; when Rosemary was sixteen her close uncle died (the one with the Gemini stellium, with Pluto conjunct her natal Uranus), after which she contracted rheumatoid arthritis, synchronous with the death of the father-land, Rhodesia. And she would become ill again, '. . . a strange illness that does not respond to normal treatment . . .' It was beginning to become very clear that Rosemary was 'the family medium'.

She began to work with healing plants – her father had been a nursery-man, and Rosemary, with only one planet in earth in her horoscope, was finding an earth connection both to herself and to the culture. She says, 'Al-though I had refused to follow [in my grandfather and father's] footsteps by taking over the family business growing and selling plants, and I have very little conscious botanical knowledge, I had been experiencing a *participation mystique* with the plant world which could be understood within this para-digm as the connection with my paternal ancestral spirits.'[4] The plant-world was a medium for relating to the earth and its natural laws. As above, so below.

In breaking a family pattern, we are also in harmony with global pattern breaking. And as Rosemary became increasingly in participation with the spiritual teachings of her own interior process, the ancestors continued ac-tively to engage in her waking and sleeping life. And Zimbabwe continued to undergo its processes of transformation, while Uranus continued in op-position to her Gemini planets. By the first anniversary of her father's death, however – that important releasing time for the dead relative – Saturn had moved to transit her ascendant. And the procession of the an-cestors began in earnest.

The first anniversary of the death of a family or tribal member is most important – as we have read, the necessity for communing with the spirit of the person and with all attendant spirits facilitates their well-being and ob-serves laws of nature which sift through various dimensions, affecting our own, that is the living world. Rosemary had gone back to England, aware of things left undone, but still drawn along in the inevitable healing process of the split both in herself and in the multi-layered cultural/familial composite. She had become increasingly aware of the entwined destinies of herself and her family-of-origin's ancestral realm and the shadow of that in southern black Africa.

Just before the first anniversary of her father's death, Rosemary became ill with bronchial pneumonia (Gemini 'rules' the lungs and respiratory system). And she had a dream: 'I dreamed of my father's head gardener, an old Matabele man called Zephyr. I peered down into a dark abyss, and his face loomed up. I was very pleased to see him and greeted him; he likewise seemed pleased to see me.' The next day she had a dream-vision of death. Her father had died of pneumonia – and Zephyr (wind/*pneuma*) had come to her in her sleep! The transits of this anniversary are very revealing: the death of her father, when the Sun was at 16° Gemini, would always recall the message sent to her via her natal Mercury at the same degree – so each year, the Sun's contact renews the communing between them. Mercury as psychopompos, guide of souls, has been to-ing and fro-ing the boundary, at this time, only one year old, between Rosemary and her father, alerting Rosemary to the necessity for clearing the way for the family.

I mentioned that Rosemary was the last in line of her family; thus she is the psychic and genetic pool of the entire ancestral line in the family as far back as it might reach. Jupiter retrograde in Aquarius at the IC dramatizes this so well, and the concentration of planets in the Airy sign of Gemini symbolizes her direct line of communication with the ancestors, and their ease in making themselves known to her. The collective becoming individuated through eighth house down into her IC Jupiter – as an individual, she would give birth to the collective dream.

Remarkably on the first anniversary, Venus was at 16° Gemini, the solar return degree and right on Rosemary's natal Mercury/Venus. Ultimately, this links the body (Venus/viscera) to the soul of the departed; Venus brings a relationship to consciousness. Venus was born out of the split between the heavens and earth, and her presence is often as a mediator. The realm of Aphrodite spans the heavens and earth – she is also sister to the Erinyes, the Furies, who are the underworld goddesses of unavenged souls. Certain aspects of Venus are chilling – she has the power of the earth but is her father's daughter, being born out of the semen of Ouranos's castration. Venus has the power to give life, to bring *eros*, to sleeping or 'dead' things.

Also, transiting Mars was ten days from its station-direct, when the cumulative rage of times past begins to surface. Mars and Saturn were both retrograde in the twelfth degree of Scorpio – Rosemary's ascendant! So the wars of the culture were meeting on the horizon of Rosemary's personal experience. Uranus was trine Neptune, clearly indicating that the big collective, the ancestry of humanity, was also being contacted. Hence the imperilled body, the illness that presages a cleansing. It is not surprising that she might think herself bewitched, and in need of returning to Zimbabwe for instruction on how to proceed with the journey of purgation and liberation. About this Rosemary said: '. . . a part of me sensed that it was not exactly that I *personally* had been bewitched, but that this was an enactment and release in consciousness of a monstrous collective projection which was centuries old and seemed to be the very basis of racism.'

It would not be far-fetched to assume that there was something dark afoot, that the veil between the living and the dead was thin at best. It is important that we keep our connection with the ancestral elements because it is the only way by which we can reach direct knowledge of the collective unconscious. But Western culture has suppressed this, and Rosemary would be by nature in very close contact with the past, but by training fearful of it. She had the requisite illness, the body purge, and almost died herself. However, respect for the process took hold, and Rosemary began a series of ritualistic activities.

She said, 'On a transpersonal level, the structure of the Rhodesian collective psyche consisted of a thin and short-lived veneer of European influences resting uneasily on the black African psyche. As part of me had already retreated into the collective unconscious, so to speak, and identified with the plight of the black people, my bitter renunciation of white Rhodesian society had paradoxically brought the possibility of a journey into the inner terrain of black African cosmology in order to retrieve her.'[6]

Quite. If something is wrong on the top, then we must look underneath. If the tree withers at its leaves, we must examine its root. Rosemary's 'root' is split off, segregated and divorced from the upper *Gestalt* of her horoscope, but exactly conjunct the IC – her family of origin and the cultural origins are intertwined. Jupiter depicts a segregated culture, but it is in Aquarius, the sign of integrated individuals. Therefore it is cut off not from the ancestral line, but from her consciousness of it – that is, until she began to accept and make contact. That it is retrograde indicates that she needs to go back – back into the ancestral root, to both the division between the cultures and the split that occurs in the family. Now Rosemary's mother was not born in South Africa, but was transplanted, also separated from her family of origin, like both of Rosemary's paternal grandparents. So part of Rosemary's personal yearning for a 'home' is linked to this, but the greater split is reflected in the black/white dilemma in southern Africa at that time. Much later than this in our story, the grandfather came to her in a vision and said, 'Don't make the same mistake that I made' – in other words, do not cut yourself off from your roots. But where are Rosemary's roots?

This existential question leads to the possibility that some of us are already global citizens but well ahead of our time. Rosemary is not the first or the only person I have talked with whom I have become convinced is without culture as we know it to exist. She is an individual and she is tribal but she has no 'country'. And in these times tribes are not territorial, they are ideological. We must travel the world, finding our familiars. The tribal life today consists of people from all cultures who have found themselves on the same spiritual or ideological path. That Rosemary is a tribal person is partly symbolized by the segregated Jupiter, and fully portrayed by the tree I have depicted as her horoscope. There is a single focus of a big philosophy and idea (Jupiter in Aquarius at the root, alone and retrograde), and the branches reach to the sky, searching through ideas (Gemini) which will connect her to the universal soul (all trine Neptune in the twelfth house).

This is a blissful condition, if not constrained within conventional mores and rigid structures about families, cultures, religions and so forth. Measured against a static 'norm', she definitely stands outside that fence. Always, a young person with this future to come is lonely, isolated, gifted, precocious and trouble for its parents. By instinct her 'small self' knew what her 'big self' would become. It is not easy, but it is fated. It is a chart like this, a person like this who has found that she has to be part of the new wave of global citizens. Rosemary has found two important tribal connections in her life, and though all respect and consciousness is paid to the family of origin, to the ancestors and to the cultural split she embodies, she has woven together with other global citizens. Rosemary has always had the blessing of fellow spiritual travellers, as true to the Jupiter at the IC. She has sought out, and found, her tribal companions and her communities of familiars.

Back to her story. After having almost died at the first anniversary of her father's death, the year passed, and at the approach of the second anniversary came a sign. She had prayed earnestly to the Spirit of Zimbabwe for help, and heard about a group of Shona spirit mediums coming from Zimbabwe to take part in a presentation called 'Ancestral Voices'. This is the kind of synchronicity that arises when one is on the right track, miserable and sick-at-heart or not. Astrologically, the second anniversary brought Uranus to the Moon – its opposition to the Moon was exact, and it was fast heading towards her Mercury retrograde and Venus! The Shona were due in the week of her father's death – 8 June 1985.

The transit of Jupiter had returned in Rosemary's chart and was stationary – it had stopped in the heavens just four days before, and was turning in its path at 16° 55' Aquarius. Time to go back into the deepest roots, to the cultural origins, and re-examine the foundation of the spirit. This brings the collective and the personal ancestors together. And so it did. Prior to the visit from the Shona, Rosemary had dreamed again about fulfilling her father's request. After consulting with two of the Shona women, she was reaffirmed in her belief that all was not right in the veil of the ancestors and that she must do the right things. They offered her advice which she accepted with alacrity.

Transiting Jupiter retrograde in the fourth house – in station-retrograde in exact trine to the already-loaded-with-history Mercury: something in Rosemary told her to bring the Shona a gift in gratitude from her ancestors to theirs. She bought several tins of snuff for sacramental use. (This is interesting in the light of the bronchial problems of both Rosemary and her father, also the 'snuffing' out of the instinctual self.) She presented the elders with the snuff. They were thrilled; she was invited to the Zimbabwe High Commission for dinner. At first she was uncomfortable and fearful of being the token white, but the elder of the Shona group recognized her, they saw the person who she was, and said, 'So, she's here looking for peace and unity' – and indeed, the symbolic overtones of the meeting were not lost.

It provoked a deep consideration of her own limits and social-cultural boundaries – for transiting Saturn was active in the chart at this time, too. And after much soul-searching Rosemary said, 'I realized how hard I'd had to hang on to valuing the non-rational side of life, to avoid being snuffed out by this inner shadow-sister. I had fought her instead, refusing to own this part of myself, which thus remained outside, projected, and inside as rheumatoid arthritis . . . Now a parade of collective shadow figures presented themselves inside me, from my white colonial background. Here were the very qualities to which I had said, on some level, "I'd rather die than be like that." I did nearly die, and the "not wanting to be like that" was the very thing which nearly caused it . . . not wanting anything to do with my white roots.'[7] The meeting of opposites. The symbol arises.

By the third anniversary of her father's death, there had been many visitations, demands, dreams and inter-dimensional experiences all surrounding the integration of these many opposites. Rosemary had a dream of resolution with her father, in which they exchanged a commentary of modern Jungian interpretations, and he seemed to enjoy and understand this! She realized that wherever he had been, he had become fairly familiar with some of these concepts with which 'we mortals try and approach the workings of the soul. [She] woke up feeling a sense of resolution and relief.'

Now the third anniversary brought transiting Saturn to natal Chiron at 5° Sagittarius; where Uranus had broken the archetype of the wounded culture-father to light at the death, now Saturn was asking for a solid, embodied reality-frame. Revolution always becomes the status quo at some point. For good or worse, the revolutionary eventually becomes the ruling class. Rosemary would need to find 'reason' and meaning for the break-up (analysis and subsequent individuation) of her consciousness and the irruption of the contents of her own unconscious and the entire duality of the southern African experience into her waking daily life. Also, at this anniversary, we don't find Mercury or Venus in the familial/familiar degrees of 16° Gemini (though the Sun, obviously, is there). To me the solar revolution or solar return chart of an event is a re-statement of original intent, but with new options, perspectives and goals based on that unchanging purpose. That is, the Sun is fixed in the anniversary degree, thus the purpose is constant; however, the movement of the other planets, especially the satellites of the geocentrically viewed Sun, Mercury and Venus *is entirely different* in this array! The possibility of an entirely new perspective on the same old event is very high.

This opportunity for renewed perspective was coupled with transiting Chiron at 14° Gemini, conjunct Rosemary's natal eighth house Moon. She was getting closer to the emotional plane, now being able to connect on a personal, emotional, visceral level with what had been veiled by the ancestral lament. The gulf between the personal and the ancestral was getting smaller, it was bridgeable, there was to be a meeting and a conversation between the feelings and the thinking process. She'd had a dream '. . . of reconnection with Africa, of flying around a room, not able to get down from the ceiling. There was a beautiful black person down below whom I wanted to meet, but I was stuck in the air. I wept with shame, fear and frustration.'[8] This dream prompted her to go back and reconnect with her plants and create a ritual, to which the ancestors were treated. She endured a flare-up of rheumatoid arthritis, and while in physical and psychic agony she painted a portrait of her split psyche, a face one half white, one half black. 'Each side leered at the other with contempt and suspicion, but with longing to relate.'[9]

By giving life to a symbol, we reduce its darkness and release it from its angry prison. Like the release of Ouranos's monsters, we allow the dread thing to come up and become civilized, to individuate, as it were. So the process is well in motion, and by the time this part of the journey was done, she was well towards a re-membering of a dismembered inner cosmos.

In autumn 1987, Rosemary was invited to an evening reception in London to meet Dr Ian Player, director of the Wilderness Leadership School, and Qumbu Magqubu Ntombela, his game scout and mentor, a powerful figure, whose great-great-great-grandfather was an induna of one of the earliest Zulu kings. He is an exemplar of the ancestral link in his culture. And he is both a holy man and a pragmatist. For Rosemary the transit of Saturn had reached 14° Sagittarius where it had stationed-direct, having passed over Rosemary's Moon in December 1986 the first time, and was now sitting in its station right opposite the Moon. To me, this image has always meant birth – that Saturn, as a surrogate-mother, swallows his off-spring, to liberate them at some future point (thanks to Jupiter/Zeus) and from that secondary gestation to create a new mythology or new pantheon. A new set of beliefs and symbols always arises from a Saturn retrograde cycle, and the station in precise opposition speaks of a literal birth of renewed feeling and meaning. Her Moon, in the eighth, is the feminine contact with the spirits of nature and the repressed feminine and instinctual side of the ancestors. Saturn and the Moon are archetypal parent figures, and the meeting was ostensibly between Rosemary and the African wilderness-guide, Magqubu, but really, it was between their ancestors.

Rosemary had finally learned to trust. Another visitation from Rosemary's father occurred, this time instructing her to take a gift for Magqubu's father's spirit on his behalf. On the way to the reception, she stopped to buy some snuff to give to Magqubu. When she gave it to him he was deeply pleased, and later told her that her father's spirit would be accompanying them to the World Wilderness Congress . . . It transpired that the real reason for the stopover visit in England of Magqubu was to heal an ancestral rift that dated back to 1879, and to the battle of Isandlwana, during which his father had killed four redcoats of the famous Welsh Borderers regiment. He had come to make restitution. He had been anxious about this journey and the appropriateness of it, and had asked his father's spirit to send him a sign confirming its appropriateness. Rosemary's giving of the snuff from her father's (white) spirit to *his* father's (black) spirit was the sign he needed.

Uranus was stationary-direct within a couple of days of the reception, releasing the energy pent-up. Station-directions of Uranus let the civilized 'monsters' rise from the primordial level and don the clothes of civilized beings. The transit of Jupiter, the focal planet of Rosemary's roots, was in an exact trine to her natal Uranus in the eighth house. I think this is what is called civilizing the ancestors. As Rosemary said, she had finally learned to trust – the long process of being in the limen of a personal, cultural and ideological split had resulted in a more natural relationship with all the participants. As she said, 'Even my own intransigent, stubborn, white Rhodesian shadow was convinced beyond doubt of the spiritual reality of what had been happening.'[10] Rosemary was to go on a wilderness journey in Zululand with a group under Magqubu's guidance the following year, her Uranus opposition bringing the unlived life – the wilderness – to her. Her Uranus opposition brought the ancestral to the personal realms, and she was well on the way to integrating the opposites, the *mysterium coniunctio* of the inner and outer worlds.

Uranus over the IC and coming to Jupiter should bring the resolution to a long conflict over 'place'. Earlier we asked, 'Where is Rosemary's root?' And, still, the answer is not clear. However, there is an inner resolution which occurs in the interior region of the soul in split cultures, split families, which lack 'religious' context. Rosemary says of her journey, 'Ritual needs to be approached through the intuitive mind, and responded to with the emotions. For example, imagine a learned anthropological observer watching me performing the rituals [that I exercised]. He or she might understandably have thought I was completely mad, or childishly superstitious, at the very least. When the true inner context is not seen for what it is, we all too easily apply clinical labels, try to exorcise it with reductive analysis, or make entirely inappropriate interpretations based on the wrong cultural framework, or an inadequate set of symbols or ideas.'

So much is lost in the translation – from one culture to another, from one context to another, from one member of a family to another. Such a chart as Rosemary has embodies the mutable dilemma of communing on as many levels as possible, while retaining the rational ability to understand and articulate, yet still to hear the music of the cosmos and dig deeply for the root of being.

Today (1995), as Uranus is moving over her IC, the whole release of South Africa and the repeal of apartheid has taken place. The long process of organizing this still lies in our future. And so does Rosemary's process of the next phase of her root search. Because Jupiter in Aquarius is benign and its elemental ties to her majority planets create a circuit of clear understanding, the transit will unfold a new world. Not just a new world for Rosemary herself, but in tandem with her own inner world opening up so will the cultures to which she has been attached. The re-connection with Africa and her inner self is already in motion; slowly the symbols emerge. Surprising new vistas will open with this transit, the horizons of which will be not unlike the original dream, the dream of Uranus ploughing through the crowd, casting the bright shadow of knowledge and wisdom behind it. Uranus moves towards the liberation of Jupiter in the fourth house – the ancestors will be freed, and Rosemary's global root will find new soil for its nourishment.

Summary

o This story has shown multi-levelled and traverse connections between actual events and inner experiences. It has crossed cultures, family lines, and borders. It has shown the web of connectedness that exists in the psyche regardless of what continent the story has been played out on.

o It has brought us to the end of our book, and back to the beginning, to 'The Big Picture'. Rosemary's story has shown that we are not alone, that we are deeply, irrevocably connected to our personal and collective families and our ancestral heritage.

o The transits have been explicit in meaning – simplistically interpreted, they have classical overtones. There has been no need to over-psychologize this story; it speaks for itself.

o The interconnections between the sacred, observational days, the death anniversary, and events in the world and in Rosemary's personal life have also been explicit. This demonstrates the timelessness of astrological symbolism and the capacity for it to cross temporal boundaries and exist in its own space.

o We have seen a perfect demonstration of the Water houses and the ancestral relationships that are found in them.

o We have seen that there is within us all an Africa, an apartheid, waiting to be freed.

NOTES

1. With respect to this technique, it will only happen for certain with Mercury, can happen with Venus but with less chance, and can only then happen with the other planets if they are close to station-direct in the natal chart.

2. Graham Saayman (ed.), *Modern South Africa in Search of a Soul*, Sigo Press, Boston, 1990, page 176.
3. ibid., page 182.
4. ibid.
5. ibid., page 185.
6. ibid., page 186.
7. ibid., page 192.
8. ibid., page 196.
9. ibid.
10. ibid.

Appendix

The graphs of the Kennedy family are included here – they are in the software program *JigSaw*, for researching groups and family systems, developed by Bernadette Brady and Graham Dawson. In the process of finishing *Dynasty*, I wrote to Bernadette Brady asking for these graphs as well as the ones seen in 'Tobias: Touched by God' on pages 264–9. As *Dynasty* was in production, an article appeared in the *Mountain Astrologer* (Vol. 9, No. 1, December 1995) in which Ms Brady delineates the Kennedy family and these very graphs which follow (she also shows the Beatles-grouping in the same piece). I recommend this article for supplementary reading.

With such a program the depth-research potential for groups of people has only just begun. Throughout *Dynasty* I have shown various ways to approach family patterns in astrology, most of them practical and feasible to the practising astrologer working without aid of a vast computer program. With the advent of a program that not only can seek and find patterns, collect and connect the most fundamental astrological signatures (Suns, Moons, ascendants, house placements, and so forth) but also locate those more powerful complexes that lurk in the intradimensional and midpoint zones of collective planetary groupings, we are going to be able to discover some hidden factors in relationships that have remained obscure. Astrology has already revealed hidden dynamics in individuals which they were unaware of until brought to light by the astrologer – not through the power of suggestion, but through bringing to awareness – and when this is done, the healing power is tremendous.

The use of a seek-and-find program such as *JigSaw* is going to abet the further understanding of how groups function – it will show us that even if we consciously think a group is together for a reason (or the group *itself* thinks it is together for a specific function), we might find another purpose underlying that conscious intent. It is still very early on in the new phase of this type of work, so to apply hard-and-fast rules is a bit presumptuous, but if we stick to the tried-and-true principles, the astrology of the configurations – whether it is a deeply buried ninth-harmonic Venus/Saturn, or a simple emphasis of group-housing falling into the fifth sector – we cannot go far wrong.

When we explore deeply the dynamics in a family we always find startling patterns which follow the lines of classical astrology – the most fundamental interpretations work. We can read more deeply into them, and develop complex interpretations for them, but the basics say a lot. For instance, in the article referred to above, Ms Brady writes, very briefly, on types and purposes of groups, their *raison d'être*, and deals briefly on house emphases, sign emphases and midpoint patterns. We can take the core of a sign, a planet, a house or a midpoint energy-blend and apply it to the dynamic of a group – in this case, a family-system and its core *modus operandi*, and uncover some very interesting hidden facets.

In the Sun-sign emphasis and house-placement delineations which follow this, I mention that Virgo family themes are centred around body-concerns and that the physical is a thermometer of the health and well-being of the dynasty. Indeed, the Kennedy family has had much trauma in the organic realm – deaths through cancer, assassination, alcoholism/drug-use and so forth – all experienced in public and in very dramatic ways. The Virgo Sun is highlighted in the Kennedy family and in the tenth house venue, which naturally brings their situation to high prominence; their troubles and traumas will become public issues. Not only was their focus a public one, but their fate as well. (See Chapter 8, 'The Modal Family', page 151, and Chapter 9, 'The Elemental Family, page 158, for more in-depth interpretations of the modes and the elements as dominant features in families. See also page 56, 'The enmeshed family'.)

We have much research to do, and in the doing of it will find new truths which can be applied to our own families but most interestingly to natal astrology itself. For if individuals make up the collective, then the collective will show how individuals in themselves develop and become more whole. New understanding of group dynamics will inevitably lead to some surprising new ways of viewing the individual.

THE KENNEDY FAMILY

FIGURE 37 AND FIGURE 38: FIFTH-HARMONIC SATURN/PLUTO Both the wheel-graph and the harmonic pattern with Pluto and Saturn in bold type (Joan and Jackie have Venus in the SA/PL contacts) show an esoteric pattern with the two planets which, in strong configuration, imply a magician; a dark sorcerer's type of power. There definitely was 'magic' afoot in the Kennedy family, a kind of daemonic power which is deeply unconscious and fated. There is no doubt that the power and the force of the Kennedy dynasty has had its trials. This is also very male – and to see Jackie and Joan's Venus (and Caroline, for that matter) in that pattern is rather sad. Both these beautiful and powerful women suffered tremendously in their personal and emotional lives, and their Venus did not thrive well under the Saturn/Pluto contacts. Jackie Kennedy lived her 'own life' after her divorce from Aristotle Onassis and once her children grew up, but in the thrall of the Kennedy enchantment she endured much pain.

Also, I am reminded that John F. Kennedy was the first non-Masonic, Catholic (redundant because Catholics cannot be Masons) president of the United States. The Masons were based on a 'magic' circle and have been involved in arcane rituals. Mind you, Masonic affiliation appears no more esoteric these days than having good, solid political and business connections, but do remember that the one-dollar bill has the pyramid and eye of horus on it.

FIGURE 39 Here we have the house emphasis from all the entered data depicted in a clear line-graph around the wheel. The strongest point is the group first house, very closely followed by the tenth and weakly accenting the eighth house. The persona of the family was overwhelming – the family had an image, a very powerful self-presentation as a collective. They were a genuine dynasty with a powerful personality and a public destiny. There was very little influence upon them from the outside world except that which came through forces of politics, money, powerful economic standards or violence. They were self-contained, personally – collectively, that is – motivated and very, very secure in their self-confidence. In the face of disaster, they banded together. They were highly competitive in their own spheres but with the dynastic attitude.

JigSaw 1.0 –Family/Group Search Report

Project Title:	Kennedy Family (In part)
SubTitle:	Enabled Records

Tropical Zodiac – Geocentric Coordinates – True Node

Search Pts:	♄ ♇ ♄/♇
Harmonics:	5 to 5 – 1st Harmonic Orb = ±10°00'
Position:	Any
Matches:	3+ To Any Combination of Search Points

Selected Match
5th Hm – 7 Hits – 6 Charts – 23°09' ±2°00' – 5 13 6 13 7 12 3

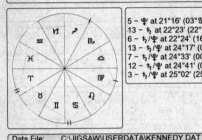

Charts in Match

5 – ♇ at 21°16' (03°♋16') John F Kennedy
13 – ♄ at 22°23' (22°♈23') Robert's assassination
6 – ♄/♇ at 22°24' (16°♍24') Robert Kennedy – Brother
13 – ♄/♇ at 24°17' (06°♋17') Robert's assassination
7 – ♄/♇ at 24°33' (00°♐33') Patrick Kennedy – Son JFK
12 – ♄/♇ at 24°41' (00°♐41') JFK Assassination
3 – ♄/♇ at 25°02' (25°♈02') Edward Kennedy – Brother

Data File:	C:\JIGSAW\USERDATA\KENNEDY.DAT
Saved:	Jan 31 1994 1:52 pm

List of Enabled Records

1. Joseph Kennedy Sr. – Father   6 Sep 1888   EST +5:00
    7:06 am, 42N22 074W04 Boston, Mass

2. Rose Kennedy – Mother   22 Jul 1890   EST +5:00
    10:00 am, 42N22 074W04 Boston, Mass

3. Edward Kennedy – Brother   22 Feb 1932   EST +5:00
    3:58 am, 42N17 071W04 Dorchester, MA

4. John F Kennedy Jr. – Son JFK   25 Nov 1960   EST +5:00
    0:22 am, 38N53 077W01 Washington, DC

5. John F Kennedy   29 May 1917   EST +5:00
    3:00 pm, 42N20 071W07 Brookline, Mass

6. Robert Kennedy – Brother   20 Nov 1925   EST +5:00
    3:11 pm, 42N20 071W07 Brookline, Mass

7. Patrick Kennedy – Son JFK   7 Aug 1963   EDT +4:00
    12:52 pm, 41N39 070W33 Otis AFB, MA

8. Ethel Kennedy– In Law   11 Apr 1928   CST +6:00
    3:30 am, 41N52 087W39 Chicago, IL

9. Caroline Kennedy – Daughter JFK   27 Nov 1957   EST +5:00
    8:15 am, 40N45 073W57 New York NY

10. Joan Kennedy – In Law   5 Sep 1935   EDT +4:00
    6:10 am, 40N45 073W57 New York NY

11. Jackie Onassis – Wife   28 Jul 1929   EDT +4:00
    2:30 pm, 40N53 072W23 Southampton, NY

12. JFK Assassination   22 Nov 1963   CST +6:00
    12:30 pm, 32N47 096W49 Dallas, TX

Figure 37

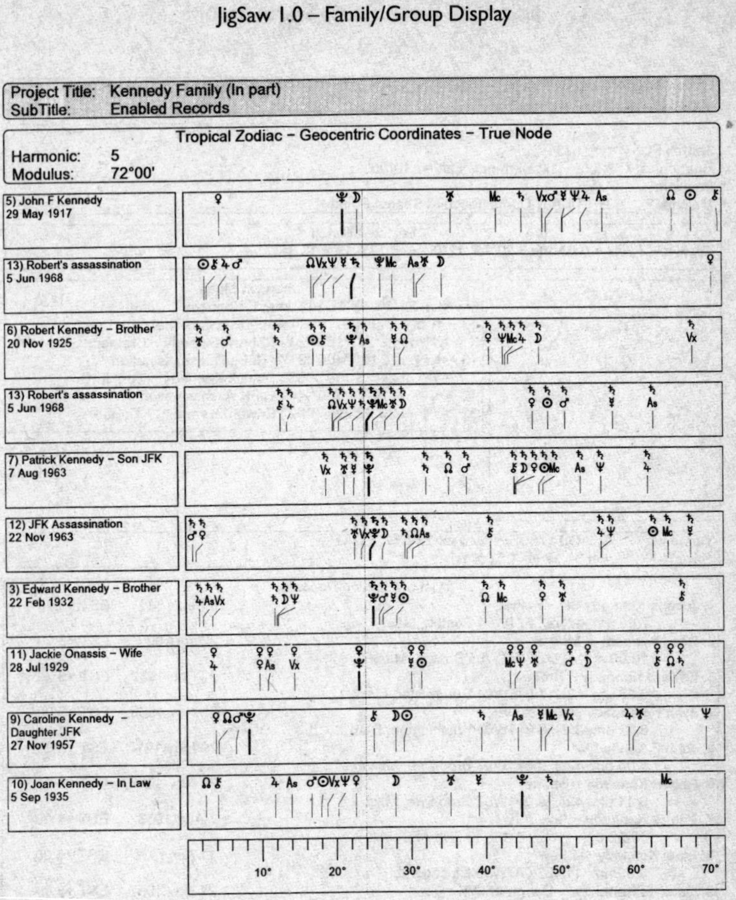
JigSaw 1.0 – Family/Group Display
Project Title: Kennedy Family (In part)
SubTitle: Enabled Records
Tropical Zodiac - Geocentric Coordinates - True Node
Harmonic: 5
Modulus: 72°00'
5) John F Kennedy 29 May 1917
13) Robert's assassination 5 Jun 1968
6) Robert Kennedy - Brother 20 Nov 1925
13) Robert's assassination 5 Jun 1968
7) Patrick Kennedy - Son JFK 7 Aug 1963
12) JFK Assassination 22 Nov 1963
3) Edward Kennedy - Brother 22 Feb 1932
11) Jackie Onassis - Wife 28 Jul 1929
9) Caroline Kennedy - Daughter JFK 27 Nov 1957
10) Joan Kennedy - In Law 5 Sep 1935
10° 20° 30° 40° 50° 60° 70°

Figure 38

FIGURE 40 All planet points of all entered data were used and sorted according to zodiacal longitude in a 72° sort. The strong point is at twenty-four. Five times twenty-four is 120° which is 0° Leo. The second strongest point is 5° Sagittarius (found at the number 49 on the circle). *Homo ludens* – the playing men – should have been their motto; it is well known that vicious football games were played by the Kennedy men, and their life-style was play hard, work hard. The greatest leaning is on the Leo to Sagittarius side of the zodiac, and this is the sector of the signs which deal primarily with others, with dependency issues and relationships highlighted. The Kennedys were (and still are, but the new generation has not been used in this study) intradependent to the point of being symbiotic within their own group and, though highly influential in society, were also very dependent on society for their power. The paradox of independence is that it is only measured against a collective body – the group mind determines the degree of independence that one might achieve.

FIGURE 41 This is the elemental sort in which all points of the group data are used and it produces a balance with the emphasis (slight) in the element of Fire. (See the Fire family in Chapter 9, 'The Elemental Family', page 161.) Inspired and inspiring, inflamed, extraverted in appearance and goals, devil-may-care in appearance, original, hot, exciting, flamboyant – all are keywords for Fire and for the Kennedy group. Also, their energy burned out. They were stopped by this very force. However, I have found when a profound kind of balance is achieved, either in a typology test (Myers-Briggs or Grey-Wheelwright, MMPI, etc.) or in any astrological synthesis, that the dinosaur stage has been reached. The entity is about to die out. This balanced elemental pattern speaks of a complacency and a sense of well-being and security – there are no blanks that need to be filled. The group has achieved its purpose and has come to a stasis.

FIGURE 42 Here we have the modal sort which shows a Mutable dominance in the group dynamic. (See Chapter 8, 'The Modal Family', page 156.) This is an enmeshed group, a 'Neptunian' family type. There is very little in the way of personal boundaries between individual members and any events that occur to a single individual. For instance, if something happens to one person, the entire group as an organic entity is deeply and markedly affected; the collective psyche and persona are notably shifted. Similarly, if something happens to the 'group' not one individual will remain unscathed by it. This kind of symbiosis is both supportive and protective while simultaneously being adverse to individuality.

JigSaw 1.0 – Research Polar Graph

Project Title:	Kennedy Family (In part)				
SubTitle:	Enabled Records				

Zodiac:	Tropical	Divisions of:	Houses	Harmonic:	1
Coords:	Geocentric	Division Type:	House	Modulus:	360°00'
Houses:	Placidus	No. Divisions:	12	Total Charts	13
Node Type:	True	Anchor Point:	n/a	Points Used:	660

Avg Count = 55.00
Division = 10th House
Count = 91
Chi Sq (11) = 23.6
Prob. = 1 in 70

ALL POINTS

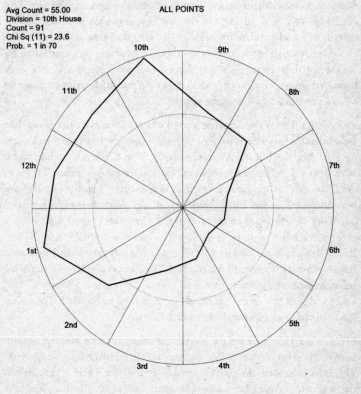

Figure 39

JigSaw 1.0 – Research Polar Graph

Project Title:	Kennedy Family (In part)				
SubTitle:	Enabled Records				

Zodiac:	Tropical	Divisions of:	Longitude	Harmonic:	1
Coords:	Geocentric	Division Type:	User Defined	Modulus:	360°00'
Houses:	Placidus	No. Divisions:	72	Total Charts	13
Node Type:	True	Anchor Point:	0°00'	Points Used:	660

Avg Count = 9.17
Division = 115°00'–120°00'
Count = 18
Chi Sq (71) = 8.5
Prob. = 1 in 2

ALL POINTS

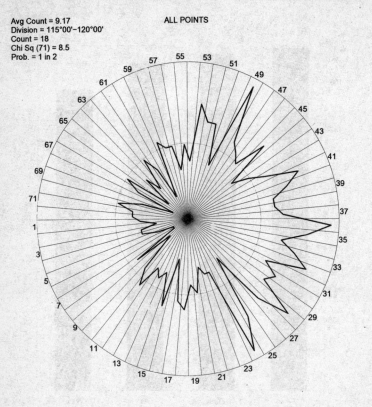

Figure 40

JigSaw 1.0 – Research Bar Graph

Project Title:	Kennedy Family (In part)				
SubTitle:	Enabled Records				

Zodiac:	Tropical	Divisions of:	Longitude	Harmonic:	1
Coords:	Geocentric	Division Type:	Element	Modulus:	360°00'
Houses:	Placidus	No. Divisions:	4	Total Charts	13
Node Type:	True	Anchor Point:	0°00'	Points Used:	660

ALL POINTS

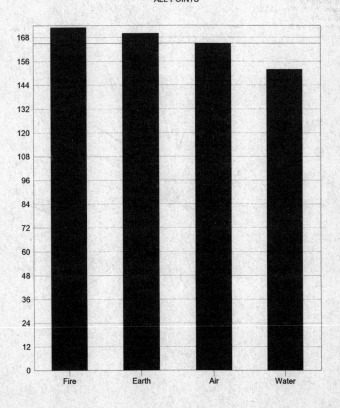

Figure 41

JigSaw 1.0 – Research Bar Graph

Project Title:	Kennedy Family (In part)		
SubTitle:	Enabled Records		

Zodiac:	Tropical	Divisions of:	Longitude	Harmonic:	1
Coords:	Geocentric	Division Type:	Mode	Modulus:	360°00'
Houses:	Placidus	No. Divisions:	3	Total Charts	13
Node Type:	True	Anchor Point:	0°00'	Points Used:	660

ALL POINTS

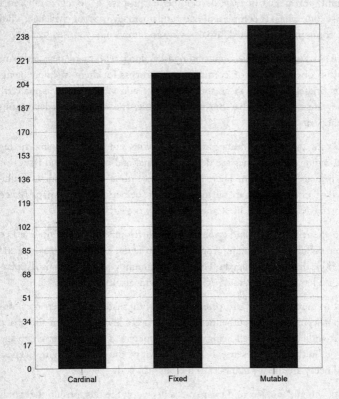

Figure 42

OVER-DEVELOPMENT IN A SIGN

ARIES has all its fighting/survival instincts intact and charges about creating new orders and collecting new people, themes and energies, battling its way through the forces of life. They can be chaotic, hierarchical, authoritative, exhausting, open and active.

TAURUS theme families are content and indulgent, physical and sensual, not terribly threatened in their developmental process, a 'young family', in a sense, one which is complacent and fundamentally without challenge. They are community-orientated, tribal, loving and imposing.

GEMINI families are disconnected and far flung, with many new additions and no obvious sense of continuity; the process for them is simply being, thus finding difficulty in creating substance and vitality which is material. They are communicative, but mobile, tactile, friendly, nervy, adventurous and open.

CANCER families are dealing with swallowing and devouring, smothering and hiding; their themes are deeply maternal and centre around issues of nurture and possession. There are deep fears about being invaded, annihilated or violated. They are nurturers, healers, helpers and clannish, tribal and protective. Altogether, the Cancerian family is a large mother.

LEO themes are regal and imperious; the development of the ego in a Leo theme family is paramount, lending itself to feuds, hostilities, great love and passion, drama and tragedy. They are community-minded, sponsors, players, leaders, renegades, mavericks and individualistic.

VIRGO family themes are often riddled with anxiety and deep concerns about legitimacy and authenticity. Their bodies are vehicles for the group soul, and health and well-being are thermometers of the family strength and vigour in the dynastic sense. It being the last of the personal signs, sickness and decay are usually manifest in the physical body.

LIBRA theme families find their soul reflected in the relationship the family has within its larger context, the community. As a group, the family theme largely revolves around the deception of appearances, social graces and romanticism often resulting in star-crossed love tales and Romeo and Juliet scenarios where love must cross social bars.

SCORPIO: By the time we reach Scorpio, the themes become more difficult to disentangle; the Scorpio theme is centred around death, loss, abandonment, thence to resurrection, redemption and purification. Deep, dark secrets can nestle in the corners, and serpents insinuate themselves into the souls of the individuals. A fear of evil can result in puritan-evangelism. Monks, revivalists, healers, law-makers and law-breakers.

SAGITTARIUS family themes have high moral tones, strongly religious motifs which go back generations; often there is a renegade who has either exalted or defiled a religious tenet or crossed a cultural bar for moral or political beliefs. They are, like their Gemini opposite, far-flung, adventurous, iconoclastic and individualistic.

CAPRICORN family themes always gather around authority, authenticity and autonomy. The struggle to survive and survive with dignity under duress will permeate all aspects of the individuals' lives. They are faithful, steadfast, reliable and constant. The past can hold a long line of guilt, fear and oppression which can result in either ascetics and/or materialists.

AQUARIAN themes produce family motifs in which the struggle for individual identity confronts unity in the family; the members are anxious to individuate beyond the actual capacity to do so in the context of their collective circumstances. Disconnected from each other, the family extends itself beyond its boundaries. Idealism is frequently the alibi for absenteeism.

PISCES family themes have to do with scapegoating and sacrifice, where a family has run its final course and an individual is born into it who must distil or purify the contents for the family line before moving on – if it is intended to move on at all. Often a Pisces family theme is constantly in danger of dissolving and disappearing, needing to be resurrected in more earthy ways.

Bibliography

* Highly recommended

RECOMMENDED READINGS FOR FATHERS AND DAUGHTERS

Sylvia Fraser, *My Father's House: A Memoir of Incest and of Healing*, Virago, London, 1989.

Germaine Greer, *Daddy We Hardly Knew You*, Hamish Hamilton, London, 1989.

Linda Leonard, *The Wounded Woman*, Shambala, London and Boston, 1983.

Ernest Thompson, *On Golden Pond*, 1981, a novel of reconciliation – popular movie.

RECOMMENDED READINGS ABOUT MOTHERS AND DAUGHTERS

Lyndall P. Hopkinson, *Nothing to Forgive*, Chatto & Windus, Sceptre, London, 1990. About the author's mother, Antonia White, author of *A Frost in May*.

Susan Chitty, *Now to My Mother*, Weidenfeld & Nicolson, London, 1987. About Antonia White, by the sister of the above author, Lyndall Hopkinson.

Antonia White, *A Frost in May*, Virago, London, 1993. A Catholic-girl's-school horror-tale of rejection by both parents but ultimately by her father – written by the mother of the two previous authors, who have become enemies because of the difference in relationship between each of them and their mother and some ensuing publishing contracts regarding Antonia White's *Diaries*.

Rachel Billington, *The Great Umbilical*, Random House, Hutchinson, London, 1994.

*Carrie Fisher, *Delusions of Grandma*, Simon & Schuster, New York, 1994. A woman's letters to her unborn daughter.

Nancy Friday, *My Mother, My Self*, Dell, 1987.

Esther Freud, *Peerless Flats*, Penguin, Harmondsworth, 1993.

*Janet Hobhouse, *The Furies*, Doubleday, London, 1993.

*Jan Waldron, *Giving Away Simone*, Random House, Times Books, 1995. A memoir of daughters, mothers, adoption, and reunion.

RECOMMENDED READINGS ABOUT FATHERS AND SONS

*Robert Bly, *Iron John*, Addison Wesley, USA, 1990. A poet's view of male-bonding and role-modelling; also general for and about men – really excellent reading. (See Sam Keene, *Fire in the Belly*.)

Homer, *The Odyssey*, trans. E. V. Rieu, Penguin, Harmondsworth, 1946, revised translation 1991. Concentrate on Telemachus' adolescent search for his wayward mid-lifing father, Odysseus.

Samuel Oscherson, *Finding Our Fathers*, Fawcett Columbine, Valentine Books, 1986.

*Howard Sasportas with L. Greene, *The Luminaries*, Weiser Publications, New York, 1993, pages 117–64.

Gregory Max Vogt, *Return to Father: Archetypal Dimensions of the Patriarch*, Spring Publications, Dallas, 1991.

RECOMMENDED READINGS FOR MOTHERS AND SONS

Michael Gurian, *Mothers, Sons and Lovers: How a Man's Relationship with His Mother Affects the Rest of His Life*, Shambala, London and Boston, 1994. Kind of watery, Jungian view.

RECOMMENDED READINGS ABOUT FAMILIES/ PARENTS/SIBLINGS IN GENERAL PSYCHOLOGY

*Patricia Berry (ed.), *Fathers and Mothers*, Spring Publications, Dallas, 1991. Many excellent contributors on being a mother and/or a father.

John Bradshaw, *Family Secrets*, Piatkus, UK; Bantam, USA, 1995.

John Cleese and Robin Skynner, *Families and How to Survive Them*, Methuen, 1983.

Annette Kuhn, *Family Secrets*, Verso, London, 1995. An extremely biased attempt at a scholarly rant about the author's mother. In fact, the book is terrible, and has no real content or thesis – worth reading!

*R. D. Laing, *The Politics of the Family*, Tavistock, London, 1970.

R. D. Laing, *Sanity, Madness and the Family*, Tavistock, London, 1964; Penguin, Harmondsworth, 1990, 2nd edition. Case histories of families of 'schizophrenic' patients with theory interspersed.

Luthman and Kirchenbaum, *The Dynamic Family*, Science and Behavior Books, USA, 1989.

*Alice Miller, *The Drama of the Gifted Child*, Basic Books, New York, 1981.

*Alice Miller, *Thou Shalt Not be Aware*, Meridian, New York, 1984.

Salvadore Minuchin, *Families and Family Therapy*, Tavistock, London, 1974.

Desmond Morris, *Babywatching*, Jonathan Cape, 1991.

*Virginia Satir, *Conjoint Family Therapy*, Souvenir Press, 1978.

Virginia Satir, *People Making*, Science and Behavior Books, USA, 1972.

Maggie Scarf, *Intimate Partners*, Random House, USA, 1987. Genograms.

ASTROLOGY

Barry D. Cowger with Martha Christy, *Reconstructing the Real You: Applying Astrology to Family Psychology*, Mercurius, Arizona, 1993.

Samantha Davis, *Understanding Children through Astrology*, Top of the Mountain Publishing, Largo, Florida, 1993.

Debbie Frank, *Baby Signs*, Arrow, London, 1993. A sun-sign book for babies.

Michel Gauquelin, *Planetary Heredity*, ACS Publications, San Diego, 1988.

Liz Greene, *The Astrology of Fate*, Weiser, New York, 1985.

Richard Idemon, *Through the Looking Glass* (pages 33–73 especially, regarding the Moon and parent/child relations), Weiser, New York, 1992. Transcribed from taped seminars and edited by Howard Sasportas in 1991/2). Richard Idemon died in February 1987, and Howard Sasportas did not live to see the publication of this volume which he did for Richard . . . both died of AIDS.

Alexander Ruperti, *Cycles of Becoming*, CRCS Publications, 1978. Excellent classic on age-periods and planetary philosophy from the humanistic viewpoint.

*Howard Sasportas and Liz Greene, *The Luminaries*, Weiser, New York, 1992.

RECOMMENDED READINGS ABOUT WOMEN/DAUGHTERS/MOTHERS GENERALLY

Robert E. Bell, *Women of Classical Mythology: A Dictionary*, Oxford University Press, 1991.

Jean Shinoda Bolen, *Goddesses in Everywoman*, Harper & Row, 1984. A 'psychology–mythology' book.

Euripides, *Medea*, in Donald Davie, trans., *Alcestis and Other Plays*, Penguin, Harmondsworth, 1996.

Demetra George, *The Asteroid Goddesses*, ACS Publications, San Diego, 1986. Astrology/mythology.

Germaine Greer, *The Change*, Penguin, Harmondsworth, 1992. About post-menopausal women, though oddly leaves out the function of grandmotherhood!

*Janet McCrickard, *Eclipse of the Sun: A new look at the Sun and Moon in myth and history*, Gothic Image Publications, 1990.

Erich Neumann, *The Great Mother: Mythology of the Feminine*, Bollingen Series, Princeton University Press, 1963.

Marie Louise Von Franz, *The Feminine in Fairytales*, Shambala, London and Boston, 1993.

RECOMMENDED READINGS ABOUT MEN/SONS/FATHERS GENERALLY

Ken Fergradoe, *The Quantum Man*, Bloomsbury, London, 1992.

Homer, *The Iliad*, trans. Martin Hammond, Penguin, Harmondsworth, 1987.

*Sam Keene, *Fire in the Belly*, Bantam Books, New York, 1991. A thinking-man's *Iron John*.

Peter A. O'Connor, *The Inner Man*, Pan Macmillan, Sun, Australia, 1993.

Peter A. O'Connor, *Understanding the Mid-Life Crisis*, Pan Macmillan, Sun, Australia, 1981.

Jean Shinoda Bolen, *Gods in Everyman*, HarperCollins, USA, 1990. A 'psychology–mythology' book.

Murray Stein, *In Mid Life*. Spring Publications, USA, 1993. For men.

ABOUT PEOPLE IN GENERAL

Robert Calasso, *The Marriage of Cadmus and Harmony*, Jonathan Cape, London, 1993.

Oliver Sacks, *An Anthropologist on Mars*, Picador, London, 1995.

Theodore Zeldin, *An Intimate History of Humanity*, Minerva, London, 1995.

AUTISM

Uta Frith, *Autism and Asperger Syndrome*, Cambridge University Press, 1991.

Uta Frith, *Explaining the Enigma*, Blackwells, Oxford, 1989.

Temple Grandin with Margaret Scariano, *Emergence: Labelled Autistic*, Costello, Tunbridge Wells, 1986. An autobiography of an autistic woman who has become an expert in anthrozoology. (Oliver Sacks deals with this case in depth.)

Donna Williams, *Nobody Nowhere*, Avon, New York, 1992. An autobiography of an autistic woman.

*COMPUTER PROGRAM FOR WINDOWS/PC

(Advisedly for experts in PC use and astrology *only* – otherwise have an expert use and explain results of data.)

Research and Family Patterns

JigSaw. Bernadette Brady and Graham Dawson. Program purchase available through several outlets:

- North America: Astrolabe, Inc., 350 Underpass Road, Box 1750, Brewster, MA 02631, USA.
- Australia: Astrolabe Australia, 94 Blaxland Road, Wentworth Falls, NSW 2782, Australia.
- Europe: Astrolabe (Europe) Ltd, 24 chemin des Daillettes, CH-1009 Pully (Lausanne), Switzerland.
- England: Astrolabe Britain, 32 Glynswood, Camberley, Surrey GU15 1 HU.

Index